Charles E. Ives
Memos

Charles E. Ives

— Memos —

Edited by JOHN KIRKPATRICK

NEW YORK

W · W · NORTON & COMPANY · INC ·

COPYRIGHT © 1972 BY W. W. NORTON & COMPANY, INC.

First Edition

Library of Congress Catalog Card No. 76–77407

SBN 393 02153 X

ALL RIGHTS RESERVED
Published simultaneously in Canada
by George J. McLeod Limited, Toronto

PRINTED IN THE UNITED STATES OF AMERICA

1 2 3 4 5 6 7 8 9 0

Ives wrote and dictated the *Memos*
to answer questions
from people curious about his music.
In his mind and heart
it was dedicated to them all.

Contents

PART THREE   Memories

Appendices

Illustrations

(between pages 160 and 161)

Preface

Born in Danbury, 20 October 1874, with extraordinary talents (musical, athletic, generally original)—educated by his father, the Danbury Schools (1881–91), Danbury Academy (1891–93), Hopkins Grammar School (1893–94), Yale University (1894–98)—Ives for twenty years led a double life of insurance man by day and composer by night, weekends, and vacations. When the United States entered the First World War, he worked hard for the Red Cross and Liberty Loan drives, and in September 1918 he was confident that another physical test would remove any doubt about his fitness to drive an ambulance in France. Less than a month later his first heart attack, a severe one, called a halt and imposed a quiet assessment.

The piece he most liked to play, usually in snatches, each time with new variants, was still a mass of hasty sketches, so among the first acts of his convalescence were making the clear ink copy of *Concord* and finishing the *Essays*. Privately printed in 1920, these were sent to many people who Ives hoped would be interested. Though much of his earlier music had been played or sung in public, particularly by choirs and church soloists, there is not a single Ives performance on record between 1902 (when he resigned from his last church job) and 1920 that was not of his own instigation. But now, at the first sight of these printings, Henry Bellamann immediately recognized a significant new voice, and started a new breed of Ives enthusiasts.

No sooner were *Concord* and the *Essays* in print than Ives set about putting his songs and potential songs in order, adding many new ones. These were also privately printed as *114 Songs* in 1922, and again sent to many prominent musicians. Apparently the first singer to include them in public recitals was George Madden.

In the fall of 1923, the French pianist, E. Robert Schmitz, met Ives while in search of insurance. Friend of Debussy, founder and president of Pro Musica, Schmitz engineered performances in 1925 of Ives's quarter-tone music, and in 1927 of the first two movements of the *Fourth Symphony*, conducted by Eugene Goossens, Schmitz playing the solo piano part, Bellamann supplying program notes.

From this year dates the friendship with Ives of Henry Cowell, whose *New Music* issued the second movement of the *Fourth Symphony* in 1929, and who urged Nicolas Slonimsky to do something of Ives with his Boston Chamber Orchestra. As a result, in 1931, Slonimsky conducted the *Three Places in New England* in New York, Boston, New York again, and Havana—and also in Paris in a series of two Pan-American concerts, the programs of which must be given in full. On Saturday 6 June: Weiss *American Life,* Ives *Three Places in New England,* Ruggles *Men and Mountains,* Cowell *Synchrony,* Roldan *La Rebambaramba.* And on Thursday 11 June: Sanjuan *Sones de Castilla,* Chavez *Energia,* Salzedo *Préambule et Jeux* (Lily Laskine, harpist), Caturla *Bembé,* Riegger *Three Canons,* Varèse *Integrales.*

André Cœuroy, writing in *Gringoire,* spoke for many in calling Slonimsky a Christopher Columbus thanks to whom they had just discovered America—"an astonishingly gifted young musician . . . not only a gifted leader . . . but he has a finesse of ear that renowned conductors might envy. . . . What seemed most striking . . . was the contrast between North and South. . . . Ives, with his *Three Places in New England,* composed over twenty years ago, strong and original in rhythm . . . seems the most interesting. . . ."

Emile Vuillermoz in *Excelsior:* "A dozen extremely interesting scores were revealed to us . . . so new and original as to deserve long study. . . . In the *Three Places in New England* . . . one meets an astonishing prescience . . . this is a painter's orchestration . . . and it is a real find, to have imagined two village bands . . . in different tempi. . . ."

Paul le Flem in *Comœdia:* "One of them, Charles Ives, seems, before *Le Sacre du Printemps,* to have forged himself a style which, by its boldness, puts him among the precursors. Beside his compatriots, he appears the most spontaneously gifted. . . ."

Others suspected a modern academicism. Florent Schmitt in *Le Temps:* "It is improbable that, if Stravinsky had not invented *Le Sacre du Printemps* or Schoenberg *Pierrot Lunaire,* most of these works would ever have seen daylight." But he acknowledges Ives as "a very erudite musician-philosopher."

Boris de Schloezer in *Les Beaux-Arts* (Brussels): "Even if one admits . . . that these innovators only follow, more or less ably, Schoenberg, Hindemith, and Stravinsky . . . we owe a debt of gratitude to Slonimsky. . . ." But de Schloezer seems to contradict himself in the case of Ives, "a true precursor, a bold talent . . . who, going straight ahead on his own path . . . has discovered many of the procedures in vogue today. With him, in spite of or because of his awkwardness, this modernism acquires a wholly individual flavor."

Back in the States, these critiques were seen not only by Ives, and some of the words quoted above may have been the basis of an editorial by Philip Hale in *The Boston Herald* of Tuesday 7 July: "Nicolas Slonimsky of Boston, indefatigable in furthering the cause of the extreme radical composers, has brought out in Paris orchestral compositions by Americans who are looked on by our conservatives as wild-eyed anarchists. He thus purposed to acquaint Parisians with contemporaneous American music. But the composers represented were not those who are regarded by their fellow-countrymen as leaders in the art, nor have they all been so considered by the conductors of our great orchestras. If Mr. Slonimsky had chosen a composition by Loeffler, Hill, one of Deems Taylor's suites, Foote's suite, or music by some who, working along traditional lines, have nevertheless shown taste, technical skill and a suggestion at least of individuality, his audience in Paris would now have a fairer idea of what Americans are doing in the art.

"Are these Parisians to be blamed if they say that the American composers thus made known to them are restless experimenters, or followers of Europeans whose position in the musical world is not yet determined, men who show ingenuity chiefly by their rhythmic inventions and orchestral tricks; men who apparently have no melodic gift, or, having it, disdain it for the tiresome repetition and transformation of an insignificant pattern; who neglect the sensuous charm of stringed instruments and put their trust for startling effects in combinations of wind and percussion choirs; followers, but with unequal footsteps, of Stravinsky, Prokofieff and certain continental composers of whom Hindemith is a prominent example?

"It may be true that old musical forms are passing. No one demands that a composer today should make a fetish of the sonata form, provided he show skill and eloquence, and sends forth music that charms or impresses outside that cast-iron form. How many of those now throwing overboard sane rules, traditions of proved worth—the adventurous and daring souls—have contributed to the glory of the art?

"They may say that they are writing for posterity. It is a proud boast, but posterity is an uncertain audience. The great composers did not say, 'Hang the age; I'm writing for the years to come.' They wrote because there was something in them that must out. They enlarged or modified the forms accepted in their own day, still preserving harmonic lines, striving for a personal expression along these lines, in harmonic and orchestral invention that would bring strength and beauty. That great innovator Claude Debussy, trained in the severe school of the Paris Conservatory, did not turn his back on what he had learned; he utilized it as an indispensable aid to the outward revelation of his own thoughts and visions."

The day Hale's editorial appeared, A. H. Handley (Slonimsky's Boston manager) wrote Ives: "Thank you very much indeed for your check of the 6th which I really appreciate. I likewise appreciate the copy of the cable Mr. Slonimsky sent you. . . . We have, however, received two packages of programs like the enclosed and, following out our usual methods, sent copies of this program to all of the newspapers here in Boston. The enclosed editorial headed 'Mr. Slonimsky in Paris' written by Philip Hale himself will undoubtedly be of interest to you. What we have got to do is really believe what we so often know to be true, 'that every knock is a boost'."

Ives's sketch of a reply to Handley survives: "Thank you for [your] note and the enclosed pretty lines from a nice old lady. Mr. Hale has quite the philosophy of Aunt Maria—'When you don't understand some'm, scold some'n.' Where does he get all the facts underneath his 'ultimatum'—where does he find the authority for all his sweeping statements? All the Paris papers which I've seen give rather the opposite impression [from the one] that Mr. Hale hands out to Boston. One of the easiest things for some men and most ladies to do, is to make predilection, prejudgment and feebly examined premises resemble statement of facts. Does Mr. Hale actually know all this music he knows so much about?—and do the conductors of orchestras, in whose mouths Hale puts his 'opinions,' know it? I can say for one— they do not.

"Hale gives an opinion in such a way that it sounds (at least to me) as a 'pronunciato'—he is willing to have his readers think that it's the only opinion and the only right opinion. The casual reader (and 90 percent of the people are casual readers) will take it as such. Every human being is more or less a partialist, but partialism itself is always a 'half-truth.' What Mr. Hale [says] is partially true—in every movement in art, in politics, in every kind of evolution, there is a struggle for a changing bad, good, and towards perfection. But it sounds to me that he wants everybody to think that there is only one kind of good music and he knows exactly what it is—which is what he has been brought up on—what he has been told—what he has limited his mind and ears to—habit forming thoughts and sounds—which go on in the cosmic process of degeneration, whether in art, business, religion, or any part of humanity.

"If men like that were the only influence in music or any art—it would die out of the world—it would first fall into a static, adding-

machine state—and finally into a pretty 'lily pad' over its own tombstone.

"Just to show the other side of things, I'm sending a few translations
of some criticisms in Slonimsky's letter—also a few sentences in which
he gives, not his own impression, but what he has heard from others,
and the reactions of the public in general (a conductor, at all sensitive,
can quite readily feel the general trends of any audience)." [Unfortu-
nately there are lacunae in the letters from Slonimsky that Ives kept,
that make one suspect that Ives sent parts of the letters themselves to
Handley, which cannot have survived the dissolution of Handley's
managerial office.]

Then, on Sunday 12 July 1931, the *New York Times* printed a long
review of the past season, dated 1 July, by their Paris correspondent,
Henry Prunières, including detailed critiques of a few recent concerts:
". . . The presentation of American music has been the object of two
symphony concerts directed by Nicolas Slonimsky, leader of the Boston
Chamber Orchestra. They revealed to Paris the works of the advance
guard of the young American and Antillean schools, which are wholly
unknown here and, with the exception of the compositions of Edgar
Varèse, a naturalized Franco-American, little known, I believe, even
in the United States.

"I cannot say that these concerts had a very great success. The first
left a terrible impression of emptiness, which the second succeeded in
effacing only in part. If it be true that Charles Ives composed his *Three
New England Scenes* before acquaintance with Stravinsky's *Le Sacre
du Printemps,* he ought to be recognized as an originator. There is no
doubt that he knows his Schoenberg, yet gives the impression that he
has not always assimilated the lessons of the Viennese master as well
as he might have. The second part, with its truculent parody of an
American march in the Sousa vein and the unloosing of its percussion
achieves a picturesque effect. The third part presents a typical American theme with pretty orchestral effects. The composer is manifestly a
musician. . . .

"The only thing that caught my attention was the paroxysmal tendency of the writers, which was curious to note. It corresponds pretty
well to the intensity of living and the precipitate rhythm in the great
American cities. We are no doubt in the presence of a school still in
the embryonic stage in which the influences of Europe are all too easily
discernible. In it, however, are undeniably some germs of originality.
Credit is due these explorers. . . ."

Some discussion among members of the Pan-American Association of
Composers (including Ives) may have preceded the reply to Prunières
by the secretary, Adolph Weiss, which was dated 18 July 1931, **and**

printed in the *Times* on Sunday the twenty-sixth: "Mr. Prunières's article on 'American Music in Paris,' printed in the *New York Times* of July 12, does not do justice to the importance of this event. Americans, reading this article, will hardly feel that the compositions performed are at all significant. But permit me to cite what a few of the principal critics of Parisian papers have said in some of the long first-page reviews of the two Pan-American concerts given in Paris on the 6th and 11th of June.

"Paul Le Flem, critic of *Comœdia:* 'Nicolas Slonimsky presented compositions of the composers who are representative of the avant-guard of the contemporary American school, Weiss, Ives, Ruggles and Cowell. These four composers lay claim to the most recent and disquieting acquisitions of the music of today. They live in this atmosphere, their natural element. Synthetic chordal structures, intertwining counterpoints, harsh orchestral sonorities that despise mezzotints; these are their common traits. One feels a daring craftsmanship among these courageous pioneers, more volitional, more cerebral than emotional.'

"Emile Vuillermoz, *Excelsior:* 'There is in these works a benevolence [*une générosité*], a faith, and a glowing life which makes them all extremely sympathetic in spite of their crude form, their polytonality, or their aggressive atonality.'

"Paul Dambly: 'At the moment of its close the musical season experienced a sudden shock through two concerts conducted by Slonimsky, which enabled us to discover the New World a second time.'

"And so I might continue to cite from the eight columns of newspaper clippings before me, in which the compositions are reviewed collectively and individually."

All these thoughts went on rankling in Ives's mind, coloring a letter to Schmitz on 10 August (in §3), and were unburdened in the first drafts (no longer extant) of the letter to "Dear Sirs and Nice Ladies" which starts these *Memos*—the earlier drafts being implied by the double dating at the end of §4: "Aug. 1931—Mch. 1932." But this imaginary open letter turned out to be only the introduction to an autobiographical scrapbook of reminiscence designed not only to show that Hale, Prunières, and others didn't know what they were talking about, but also to supply information to a fast-growing nucleus of Ives enthusiasts.

Throughout this editing of the *Memos*, the different sources are indicated on the left-hand margins by the following symbols:

M = the earliest extant manuscript, pp. 1–16 and [18]—(p. 17 and the rest missing—see Appendix 1). The brilliant performance of seven Ives songs by Hubert Linscott and Aaron Copland at Yaddo, on Sunday

1 May 1932, was a revelation to all present—as expressed in Wallingford Riegger's letter of 4 May: "Your beautiful songs that were given at
Yaddo aroused not only enthusiasm . . . but keen appreciation in the
numerous composers present. . . . There was much curiosity about the
facts of your life—musical and otherwise. . . . Will you not consider
seriously the recording of rather copious biographical matter concerning yourself, that you could dictate from time to time to a stenographer?"

By this time, Ives was doing just that—dictating from M to Miss
Florence Martin, who had been doing part-time secretarial work for
him. (Unfortunately the Ives family lost contact with Miss Martin—
her most recent known address in 1947 offers no forwarding address,
and in view of her devotion to the Iveses it may be presumed that she
passed on shortly thereafter.)

As Ives's dictating became more concerned with particular works,
he merely listed the titles in the order he wanted to follow. As a result,
the first and third parts of the *Memos* are largely written out in M, but
the second part is mostly a table of contents (pp. 11–12 of M) with a
few key words as reminders. Whether he read from what he had
already written (changing and interpolating as he went along), or made
it up out of his head, Miss Martin took his words down faithfully in
shorthand. Apparently Ives, who could be very reticent with his manuscripts, did not suggest that she take the pages of M home with her to
check from, in typing.

T = Miss Martin's first set of typed pages from her shorthand (pp. 1–73,
both originals and carbons, skipping p. 35, perhaps to leave room
for a projected insertion never filled in). Many details reveal that her
shorthand reproduced consonants better than vowels (for instance, in
§13, first sentence, M9: "suppressed"—T11: "surprised"), and that
she was not entirely at ease with musical terms. There are no clues
showing when Ives dictated from which pages of M, but at the top of
p. 12, over "Orches Sets Ist" he wrote in pencil "Start Sat."—then
crossed out "Sat" adding "Thurs." Half way down, at "Holidays," he
wrote "begin Sat"—but there is no telling if what was planned above
for Saturday was put ahead to the preceding Thursday or had to be
put off till the next Thursday. Nor is it known if Miss Martin came
every day—maybe only on Ives's "good days." In any case, the material
between "Thurs" (above) and "Sat" (half way down) comprises pp.
30–39 of T, and if this represents two sessions, it suggests a rough
equivalent of four or five pages of T per session.

An undated letter from Edith (as her father's amanuensis) to John
J. Becker, possibly of Wednesday 6 April 1932, says that they plan to

sail for Europe on Wednesday 4 May. But actually they sailed Thursday 12 May (on the S.S. New York, for Southampton). The postponement may have been to give an extra week to reach the end of the *Memos*. The indication in §2—"(a good deal was dictated offhand and not looked over)"—suggests that Ives saw by no means all of T before they left, and that Miss Martin probably sent it or the last part of it after them, perhaps keeping the carbons. Ives certainly had the originals of T with him in Europe, both in 1932–33 and in 1934.

m = Ives's corrections of T and revisions or additions—either recto or verso, mostly in pencil, rarely in ink. Many of the corrections are simply to restore forms like "didn't" where Miss Martin had dutifully preferred "did not." The additions range from single words to whole pages or sequences of pages, some spilling over onto extra sheets. Few are datable, but they must have started with the first pages Miss Martin brought back. The latest definite date is Sir Henry Wood's conducting Sibelius in Queen's Hall on Tuesday 4 September 1934 (m50v). Back in the States, Ives read some of the longer of these additions to Miss Martin, revising and interpolating as before.

t = Miss Martin's typed pages (both originals and carbons) from her shorthand of Ives's readings from m, again apparently without checking back with the text of m (for instance, in §13, end of third paragraph—m12: "German"—t12: "general"). All the pages of t are headed by reference to m: "Bottom of Page 11"—or "Back of Page 39" —or even "Back of Pages 31, 34 and 36" (a three-page sequence of t, which Ives numbered "34a-34b-34c"). But many of these long interpolations are not for the pages whose backs they fill—for instance: "Back of Page 16—(But not for Page 16—look up connection)"—or "Back of Pages 32 and 33" (to which Ives added: "but not related here—should go elsewhere?"). So, even though the headings of t appear to maintain the page continuity of T, the material of t keeps jumping back and forth. It is surprising how many pages of m are not found in t. Maybe the later dictating was interrupted either by one of Ives's "slumps" (as he called them), or perhaps by the sudden trip to England in August 1934, and was never resumed.

m = Ives's corrections of t and further revisions or additions, which again range from single words to sequences of pages, some spilling over onto extra sheets. Almost none of these are datable.

Ives's later use of all these leaves must have been just as fantastic as the vagaries of the balloons within balloons. His remark about Emerson's thoughts—that he "seldom arranges them along the ground first"

—shows his disdain of orderly sequence (the *New Music* issue of *34 Songs* was in reverse chronological order according to the dates Ives was using). His mind could easily embrace a multiplicity of data all at once, with no need of clarifying the relations among various groups. Probably every time any biographical data were called for, different pages of the *Memos* would be pulled out, rearranged, even possibly lent out, according to need. There was also his habit of tucking things into books, so much sometimes that the binding would be sprung out of shape.

So it is not surprising that, when Henry and Sidney Cowell embarked on their book in the late 1940s, and Ives wanted to lend them the *Memos*, he could lay his hands on only about three-fifths of the leaves. As it worked out, the Cowells' book included less than one-sixth of the text here given.

After Ives died, on Wednesday 19 May 1954, his papers were gradually put in order, and in time almost all the remaining leaves came to light, mostly interlarded between leaves of various sketches, scores, copies, in the music storeroom of the barn at West Redding. Once the two "halves" of the *Memos* were dovetailed, the three-part form could be better appreciated. It is tragic to find no trace of page 31 of T (neither original nor carbon—except that m31v exists in t)—but it is even more of a wonder that so much did survive (see Appendix 1).

The present editing, aiming primarily at a readable continuity, makes no pretense of giving variants, but does give the available sources on the left-hand margin of each page (each set of symbols remaining in force until the next set takes over at some point in the apposite line). These symbols are the only clues to the longer interpolations—as when a paragraph from m49 intrudes between two from T49. Many shorter interpolations are within italic parentheses *(especially if they should be shown to be later than the context)*. Normal parentheses are used in the normal way (Ives used them very freely). Brackets enclose words [added by the editor].

T and t are taken as the central text wherever possible, as being Ives's own words in dictation, and corrections by him or from his manuscript are not mentioned. Wherever his manuscript is the only source, the supplying of articles and the trueing up of numbers, tenses, etc., are not mentioned (he usually thought, talked, and wrote fast, and often changed syntax in mid-sentence without going back to rectify)— in such cases, the way he filled in details in dictating from M or m is taken as guide (for instance, in the last paragraph of §20, m16v: "in same position to sounding body"—t16v: "in the same position to the sounding body"). Anyone acquainted with his writing knows his habit of qualifying (even counter-qualifying) what he was saying, but in his talking these clauses were apt to be fast enough to hardly interrupt the sense. Mrs. Ives recalled that "mostly he talked rather fast and vehemently." Apparently he often tried to write as fast as he could talk, omitting articles, suffixes, auxiliaries, or connectives wherever the sense seemed to him to be self-evident.

Dictating the *Memos* as a partly improvised reminiscence, Ives rarely repeated himself. He often came back to something mentioned before, but gave it a new slant or brought in other details. Only at the very end (just to be sure he got it in, and forgetting he already had), he dictated a less complete duplication of the next to last paragraph of §20, which is omitted.

Sometimes his first thought is the best, as in the beginning of §4, where T and m include some redundant detail, spoiling the directness of M. But in §31, after note 6, his reiterated "No" shows a characteristic resilience in changing his mind. Through editorial freedom in all such choices, the text here given has become a composite, from all the sources, of whichever words best serve the thought or sound most like him.

One detail of spelling is intentionally inconsistent—Charlie or Charley—depending on the usage of the person who is quoted, or through whom the event at hand is remembered.

Given the spontaneous informality of the *Memos*, it is not surprising that they raise all kinds of unresolved questions. Wherever possible, these are answered in footnotes. But some of the answers and some of the related data have grown into a sequence of appendices with footnotes of their own. The first four are lists. The next eight are other writings of Ives that round out the *Memos* (as the *Essays Before a Sonata* are rounded out with other finished writings in the volume edited by Howard Boatwright). The next seven aim to clarify Ives's relations to various people whose influence he felt. Next are a play and a story that he had thought of as operatic possibilities. Last are three indices: chronology of dates, music of Ives, and index of names.

In some of the footnotes, pages of Ives's music manuscripts are identified by the numbers of the photostat negatives in the Ives Collection at Yale University, as listed in the editor's *A Temporary Mimeographed Catalogue of the Music Manuscripts . . . of Charles Edward Ives* (1960, now out of print). "Q" numbers refer to negatives made for Ives at the Quality Photoprint Studio, New York, about 1927–50 (small q indicating a page to which Ives added something after the negative had been made, capital Q a page to which Ives added nothing further)—

"n" refers to a general photostating of the manuscripts in Ives's own hand, carried out in the spring of 1955 at the New York Public Library under Mrs. Cowell's direction—and "Y" to those made later at or for Yale University.

Four helpful sources are referred to enough times to warrant short titles explained here in the preface. A copy of Trow's New York Directory for 1902–03 is called simply "Trow." In November 1907 Ives and Miss Twichell started listing their most memorable times together in a notebook, but gradually it became more prosaic, including moving days, and broke off in 1924—they called it *Our Book.* Henry and Sidney Cowell's biography of Ives (Oxford University Press, 1954, revised paperback 1969), invaluable in many ways, is referred to as "Cowell." Howard Boatwright's editing of Ives's *Essays Before a Sonata and Other Writings* (Norton 1961, paperback of only the musical writings 1964, complete paperback 1970) is called simply "Boatwright."

In reading these *Memos,* one must constantly remember that Ives was not dictating them for publication, but only as a fund of data to be drawn on when needed—also to get things off his chest in a private way. Many rather personal observations he would certainly have deleted, and it is hoped that their inclusion (for the sake of completeness) will not be offensive.

To acknowledge all the different kinds of help from all the generous helpers would require a volume in itself. Some are mentioned in footnotes or appendices. Precedence of seniority is held by the Danbury architect, Philip Sunderland, now a buoyant-spirited centenarian. Those who have lent their Ives letters include Sol Babitz, Mrs. John J. Becker, Mary Bell, Mrs. Henry Cowell, Jean Leduc (Schmitz's son-in-law), George Roberts, Carl Ruggles, Nicolas Slonimsky, and Edgard Varèse. Aaron Copland, Lehman Engel, and Radiana Pazmor have sent Xerox copies or had them sent. Anne Timoney Collins and Lou Harrison have given theirs to the Ives Collection.

To the Music Librarians of Cornell and Yale, and to the staffs of various other libraries large debts are due, also to Cornell University for a sabbatic leave in 1966–67, during which the basic text of the *Memos* was again trued up. The generous help of Professor Norman Pearson shows what a privilege it was for Ralph Moore '54 to have him as American Studies Adviser for his excellent Yale senior essay, *The Background and the Symbol: Charles E. Ives.* Many graduate students have contributed fresh insights: Donald Wilson and Jon Barlow at Cornell, Garry Clarke and John Mauceri at Yale, Dennis Marshall (1942–67, University of Pennsylvania), Frank Rossiter (Princeton), and many others. A uniquely valuable source is the collection of tapes of Vivian Perlis interviewing many people who knew Ives (first sponsored by Yale Music Library and Columbia Records, later by the National Endowment for the Humanities).

The editor will ever be indebted to Mina Hager, Hope Kirkpatrick, and Helen Boatwright for enlightening collaboration in the songs, and to Mrs. James H. Perkins (later Mrs. William Arthur) for her steadfast faith in his earliest Ives performances.

Members of the Ives family have been both helpful and encouraging —Mrs. Henry Van Wyck (née Amelia Merritt Ives), Mr. Bigelow Ives, Chester Ives, Mrs. Moss Ives (1878–1963), Edith Ives Tyler (1914–56), and others—above all Mrs. Ives (1876–1969), whose far-sighted generosity has also helped publish these *Memos*. But the greatest debt is to Ives himself in ways that can't be adequately described. As in all Ives performance, he bestows the privilege of a great unfolding, demanding a steady growth toward the horizon of the unknown.

John Kirkpatrick.

The Ives Room, Yale University, January 1972.

Charles E. Ives

Memos

PART ONE

Pretext

1

[Introduction as of November 1931]

M1

After a nice fat Thanksgiving Dinner—
Mamma, Red, Mac! Edeeth! Nov. 28, 1931.[1]

[1] Ives added these few words on the upper right hand corner of p. 1 of M, as if recalling the occasion when it occurred to him to make something bigger out of the letter to "Dear Sirs and Nice Ladies." But the wrong Thanksgiving date (it was the twenty-sixth) and Ives's first writing 1831 (corrected to 1931) both suggest that he was adding these words much later.

"Mamma" is Mrs. Ives, "Edeeth" is Edith (possibly recalling the accent of Nicolas Slonimsky, who came to the States in 1923 and was already a close friend of the Ives family). "Mac" is Prof. T. Findlay MacKenzie, from Australia, A.B. 1918 Sydney University, M.A. 1921 Columbia, Ph.D. 1933 New York University, Professor of Economics at Brooklyn College. From February 1921 for about a year, MacKenzie tutored Ives's nephew, Moss White Ives, both in New York and West Redding, and he continued to see the Iveses from time to time as at this Thanksgiving ten years later.

MacKenzie recalls no "Red." The only "Red" Mrs. Ives could think of is the now well known writer, James Thomas Flexner, who then had chestnut hair, and later was a friend of Edith—"I never heard Charlie call him 'Red,' but it would have been like him to." But Flexner first met the Iveses in April 1933 at the Villa Annalena in Florence, and he retains "many agreeable memories of the courtesies of the elder Iveses to their daughter's friend." If Ives was adding these words say around 1936, he may have confused this 1931 dinner party with another later one at which Flexner was present. (His book *The Traitor and the Spy* has been helpful in editing App. 20.)

2

[Introduction as of May 1932]

m47v

The principal thing that started this collection of "hawks" was a letter from Wallingford Riegger, May 1932 (see file).[1] This is now a desultory scrapbook (= "memos"—not memoirs—no one but the President of a nice Bank or a Golf Club, or a dead Prime Minister, can write

[1] For part of Riegger's letter of 4 May 1932 see Preface, at "M."

"memoirs"). Many of these things are of no interest to anyone but a stray and distant cousin or so—or to me—sometimes. When you get started putting things down (a good deal was dictated offhand and not looked over), one thing would come up from another thing—incidents that I or Mrs. Ives or someone of the family, or old friends, might remember or refer to—various family scrapbooks, old letters, programs, clippings, margins in old books, music and manuscripts, even a quotation over the wood house door.[2] Some of the remarks may be rough, but they're the way I feel about things, right or wrong, and I don't apologize for them as such—only for the bad spelling, punctuation, et al.

This introduction is just put in, now and later, to be more polite—(the "memos" originally started with the letter on page 1)[3]—that is, when I got W. R.'s letter, I naturally started to look around to collect things and found, over a letter to E. R. Schmitz, these remarks to an "old lady", a typical type. This and other similar remarks have a right to be—for the same reason it is right to throw a bottle at the umpire who closes his eyes and yells "foul!" And then they all [have] a double use, in getting something off the chest and over the garden wall, where it may disturb a pansy.

[2] From 1885, Ives and his brother Moss used to play grocery store in the wood house back of their grandmother's house, then 172 Main Street, Danbury (changed to 210 Main St. in 1887). There are letters of 1886 about changing the sign over the wood house door from "Abbott Bros." (chosen because it would be first in any directory) to "Ives Bros." (see App. 13). Ives may have meant to mention all this in one of the interpolated balloons.
[3] That is, the letter of 10 August 1931 to Schmitz, on p. 1 of T—see §3.

3

M1
T1m

Dear Sirs and Nice Ladies:—

(This is not for publication, but anybody who can read can read it.) The following statement is made, not because it's important to anything or anybody, but because there are "lilies" taking money from newspapers and other things, whose ears and brains are somewhat emasculated from dis-use. They have ears, because you can see them—they may have brains, but you can't see them (in anything they write). Every so often, an article or a clipping or a "verbal massage" is sent to a man (see name on dotted line), which shows that Rollo[1] has a job,

[1] Rollo was a creation of the Rev. Jacob Abbott (b. Hallowell, Maine, 1803, Bowdoin '20, teacher or principal of various colleges or schools, d. Farmington, Maine, 1879—see Abbott's "Young Christian", memorial edition, 1882). The Rollo Books (1834-58) were only one of his many didactic series, and became a staple in American homes. Rollo is a good little boy with an inquiring nature, and the more he has to have everything explained to him in great detail, the more information could be packed into each Rollo

writing his opinion about things the facts of which he doesn't know and doesn't try to know—or about music he doesn't hear or try to know. If he can't hear and doesn't know it, he's a mental-musico-defective (from his neck up)—if he doesn't try to hear and knows he doesn't know, then he is getting money under false pretenses! In other words, these commercial pansies are either stupid or they are liars (mean word, but put there after careful consideration). For instance, see the following letter written to E. R. Schmitz by C. E. Ives:

"West Redding, Conn., August 10th, 1931.

letter
T1m

"My dear Mr. Schmitz:

"In writing you yesterday, I meant to have put in the enclosed. The Paris concerts given by Slonimsky were better received than I expected they would be; the only unfavorable comment which I saw was by a Prof. Prunières—it wasn't so unfavorable as unfair or weak-eared.[2] He says that I know my Schoenberg—interesting information to me, as I have never heard nor seen a note of Schoenberg's music. Then he says that I haven't 'applied the lessons as well as I might.' This statement shows almost human intelligence. It's funny how many men, when they see another man put the 'breechin'' under a horse's tail, wrong or right, think that he must be influenced by someone in Siberia or Neurasthenia.[3] No one man invented the barber's itch.

letter
T2m
tm

"But one thing about the concerts that everyone felt was that Slonimsky was a great conductor.[4] I will now say good-by. You have more to do than listen to a poem like this.

Sincerely,   Chas. E. Ives"

Book. For Ives he became a symbol of the literal mind unable to imagine anything beyond what he'd been taught.

2 Henry Prunières (1886–1942), French music historian, founded *La Revue Musicale* in 1919. Schmitz wrote Ives from Los Angeles on Monday 7 September 1931: ". . . Those two programs you sent me of the Slonimsky concerts in Paris are indeed very interesting, and as to the criticism of Prunières, let me say that he 'used to be' alive—now we all consider him as defunct mentally. It is just too bad. . . ."

About Schmitz himself, Ives wrote Slonimsky in 1935: "Milhaud told me that Debussy said that Schmitz had more music sagacity than most young men he knew."

3 Ives elaborated this image on both sides of T2 and in t*m*, in a way that suggests the beginning of a six-line stanza (to be rhymed aabccb?) but lapses into prose: "It's funny how many men there are / (who ride in their or fortune's car, / over or under fifty), / when they see another man / put the breechin' under a horse's tail, right or wrong, but not the nice way they always done it—or like Uncle showed 'em—think that the other feller must be influenced by some hostler in Siberia—etc. etc. But no one man invented the barber's itch—etc."

4 Nicolas Slonimsky, born St. Petersburg 1894, studied at St. P. Conservatory, came to Eastman School, Rochester in 1923, secretary to Koussevitsky at Boston 1925–27, founder and conductor, Boston Chamber Orchestra 1927–34, conducted many concerts for Pan-American Association, later compiled many musicological reference works.

4

M2
T2m

Another instance:—a nice and dear old lady in Boston (with pants on, often) who sells his nice opinions about music and things to the newspaper and the paper to the public (see editorial entitled "Mr. Slonimsky in Paris"). In this editorial, there are two principal subjects or statements that need attention:

1) Hale is speaking of the modern American composers represented in the two Paris concerts. Eleven names were on these two programs. He says they are influenced by —————— (naming European composers etc.—see above article). I don't believe his statement is wholly true of any of the other ten composers, any more than it is of me or my music. But I'm speaking here of what I actually know of the facts, and what they have to do with his implied opinion (an opinion implying that he knows the facts underlying his opinion), and as far as I am concerned the facts are as follows. All of the music that I have written, with the exception of about a dozen or fifteen songs,[1] was completed before I had seen or heard any of the music of the European composers he cites as influencing all of the above American composers.

M3
T2m
M3
T3m

And besides this, it is interesting (and perhaps funny) to know that I (as I am included in his sweeping statement) have been influenced by one Hindemith (a nice German boy) who didn't really start to compose until about 1920 (according to an article [in] *Modern Music*, March–April 1928, page 18)[2] and several years after I had completed all of my (good or bad) music, which Aunt Hale says is influenced by Hindemith. It happens that the music of mine on this particular program, *Three New England Places*, was completed and scored (for large orchestra) almost a decade before Hindemith started to become active as a composer.

m3v
tm

In other words, the gist of Aunt Hale's remarks is that the music of one man was influenced by the music composed by another man ten years after the music so influenced was composed by the man who was influenced by the other man (or see Mark Twain's story about his nice funeral,[3] or any other funny story). Now all this may have been quite all right if Rollo was paid as a humorist by the weak but snappy management of a nice magazine, which hires grave decorators to sell uninteresting premises made interesting to the disinterested.

---

[1] Ives would be referring to the songs composed in 1921 and later—if it was in February 1921 that he heard Stravinsky's *Firebird* suite (see §55, note 2).
[2] In Aaron Copland's article, *Music since 1920* (*Modern Music*, Vol. 5/3, Mar.–Apr. 1928, pp. 16–20), he discusses Hindemith on p. 18.
[3] In *Tom Sawyer*, Chap. 17, Tom, Huck, and Joe Harper sneak in to their own funeral.

M3
T3m

Again, up to the present writing [August 1931], I have not seen or heard any of Hindemith's music.

2) Another inference given in this more or less sweeping statement (see same clipping) is that conductors of American orchestras do not like the music of modern American composers. To have this statement taken as even comparatively true would have to have for its basic

M4
T3m

premise that all these conductors agreeing with this statement had examined (and carefully enough to be able to play) the greater part of these eleven composers' music, or a large enough part of it, covering the different periods of their life and the varying types and forms of their music—enough to be fairly representative of their general

m3
cm

ability as composers. (To this, I can only say, from my experience, that not enough conductors have seen enough of my music to be able to get even a good impression of how bad it is.)

M4
T3m

I imagine that what I give as my actual experience is, to a great or some extent, true of some of the other composers. During the twenty years ending in 1919, only one conductor had seen any of my music. One (in 1910) did try over a part of a *First Symphony*, which was completed in college (1898).[4] In the ten years ending [in] 1929, two other

M5
4

conductors saw one score (and the same score) of mine—Mr. Schmitz asked me to send the *Three Places in New England* to Monteux, when he was with the Boston Symphony—and Mr. Eugene Goossens played one movement of the *Fourth Symphony* in 1927. In January 1929, *New Music* (Henry Cowell, Editor, San Francisco) published the score that Goossens played. In other words, in this thirty-year period, only four conductors, as far as I know, have seen any score of mine—and, with the exception of this one movement published in 1929, it is safe to say that at least 90 percent of my orchestral music has been seen by no conductor. Nicolas Slonimsky in 1929 saw the score *Three Places in New England*, and he is the only conductor (at present writing, August 1931) that has made any adequate and comprehensive study of my music for orchestra.

Take these above facts in detail, and then take the statement that the old lady makes—and all a man can say is that she, Philip Nathan Hale, is either musically unintelligent or deliberately unfair. To say it quickly, he is either a fool or a crook.

Chas. E. Ives   August 1931, March 1932.[5]

4 For this reading by Damrosch on Saturday 19 March 1910, see §14 and §31.
5 In M4, Ives's writing of these two dates is obviously coeval, suggesting that, in March 1932, he was finishing a clear copy from first drafts that have not survived from August 1931. Such painstaking revision was typical—for many of his letters there are two different sketches, for some, three or even four (see App. 8).

5

m1v
tm
Another Rollo who has taken a good deal of money for many years for telling people what he knows and hears (whatever that means) now says or insinuates that there has been no great music in America. He is quite right this time—but Rollo made a little slip and got a nice word off—for "America" he should of course have written "the world". For ladies, let any man stand up and *prove* that there ever has been any great music composed in the world since it started off—and why?

m1b
p. 1
(Rollos—resting all their nice lives on, and now hiding behind, their silk skirts—too soft-eared and minded to find anything out for themselves. Their old aunt (for her old aunt had told her) told Nattie when he was youthful: "This is a masterpiece—this is a great artist"—it has the same effect on their heads that customs stamps have on their trunks.[1] Every thing *that* man did is "great" because they were *told* so when young and grew up with it hanging around their nice necks, and every thing *this* man did is "no good"—whether or not they have ever seen any of his pictures has nothing to do with it—Aunt put the bangle on his vest and it sticks there as a cobweb sticks to the pigsty window.

It has never entered their pretty heads—or even to sit down near the bangle for twenty, thirty, or fifty years or so, and hear anything out themselves, or think anything hard and long—it has never occurred to them—and how cross they would get, and scold and caper around peevish-like in their columns, if anyone should happen to say that music has always been an emasculated art—at least too much—say 88⅔%.

Even those considered the greatest (Bach, Beethoven, Brahms, etc.) have too much of it, though less [than] the other rubber-stamp great
m1b
p. 2
men. They couldn't exactly help it—life with them was such that they had to live at least part of the time by the ladies' smiles—they had to please the ladies or die. And that is the reason—through their influence —that no one can prove (not even the ladies) that there has been [any] great music ever composed—that is, in this world. And this is not [so much] criticising or running down or under-appreciating Beethoven, Bach, et al, as it [is] a respect and wonder that they didn't do worse under the circumstances. Music is a nice little art just born, and they ask "Is it a boy or a girl?"—and one voice in the back row says "It's going to be a boy—some time!")

[1] Ives has developed this image as if it were derived either from Nathaniel Hawthorne's experience as customs official (Boston 1839–41, Salem 1845–48, consul at Liverpool 1853–57) or from the customs scenes in *Rollo on the Atlantic* (Rollo's little brother is called Nathan)—apparently from neither but from his own imagination.

m1v
tm

But to get down to Rollo Henderson,[2] he has for over sixty years heard, and now knows, several nice chords (the three fundamental triads and a few more that have been made into a nice bouquet around them for 150 years or so). He also knows the *Fifth Symphony,* whether it is played or not, and also when it is played, and he has heard it probably somewhere between 365 and 721 times. He has been able for many years to detect a fantasia masquerading as an overture, or a suite disguised as a symphony—nay more, he can now tell when the composer drops the elementary rhythm of the valse to take up that of the polonaise. He does not lift his brows at Brahms, and he does not convict Wagner of lunacy (see Rollo's own book, pages 3 and 4).[3] His ears, for fifty years or so, have been massaged over and over and over again so nice by the same sweet, consonant, evenly repeated sequences and rhythms, and all the soft processes in an art 85 percent emasculated, that when he says "There is no great music in America", one begins to have a conviction that that is the best indication that there *is* some great music in America.

t1a
p. 1m

But to put the matter to some nice people (including R. W. J. H.) so that it may more clearly be seen that Rollo Henderson is taking money for telling the public about something he knows not enough about to warrant his taking a nice "Cremo"—it is apparent (probably certain—in fact I will bet him up to 100 boxes) that he does not know clearly enough to know (or has not heard clearly enough to hear), to pass a fairly intelligent opinion on the music of [those who] in a general way [are] called the modern American composers. Furthermore, and to make the matter more concrete and definite, I am sure it can be proven to be a fact, that he has not seen (to say nothing of studied—probably listened to, but not heard) but a small part, probably much less than fifty percent, of the music of these composers, say since 1900. And how does he know whether most (or at least a great deal) of this music which has not been heard is better than some that has been heard?

If he should sometime be compelled to listen, or try to hear, and then try to tell others what is going on in this music, first from a technical

2 Wm. James Henderson (1855–1937) was music critic from 1883 on the *New York Times,* from 1902 on the *New York Sun.*
3 In Henderson's *What Is Good Music?* (New York, 1898—Ives had the third edition of 1905), pp. 3–4: "No one presumed to pronounce an opinion on the merit of a picture or a statue who had not at least learned the difference between a pen-and-ink drawing and a water-color, and few persons would have ventured to write down Shakespeare an ass before having acquired a sufficient knowledge of poetry to tell a sonnet from a five-act tragedy. But it was deemed altogether fitting and, indeed, intellectually satisfying that Beethoven should be smugly patted on the back, Brahms viewed with lifted brows, and Wagner convicted of lunacy by persons who could not, while in the concert-room, detect a fantasia masquerading as an overture, nor a suite disguised as a symphony—nay, more, who could not tell when the composer dropped the elementary rhythm of the valse to take up that of the polonaise. For music was, if you please, not matter to be reasoned about, but just to be listened to and to be enjoyed."

standpoint (enough to know that he has sensed what the technical substance implies), not in too much or every detail (he must be fairly
dealt with), but in the fundamental problems that have to do with
all music in general—(such, for instance, as absolute pitch, so called—
but near enough to keep a fairly true tone-relation in his ear, and so
mind—that is, if a tone-center is pivoted on A, he should know it's
not F♯)—what would he say? Of course here we are referring to a
kind of music that he is not much accustomed to, and which he has
not trained himself to listen to and hear. What would he tell the public
about what is taking place, as to its form, as to its tone-associations, as
to its rhythms, as to its tonalities (poly-, a-, or others), its division of
tones, as to the recurrence or sequences of the musical thought, its
sound-centers, the relation of the different groups of tones and intensities, etc. etc.? In the premises, what would he do? And if he did anything, should he be justified in taking money for selling his opinion to
the public? Answer, Raven—"Nevermore."[4]

Before writing an article as he did (or similar articles that others
have written), is it not his duty (or [that of] others, or of any man),
and is it not a point of honor that a man or a lady should examine,
study, and learn to understand, even moderately well, all (or enough to
be fair) the music of all the composers of his own country before
making or selling [such] a definite opinion to the public? (It is assumed
that Rollo received more than $19.95 for writing this article.)

[4] For Ives's feelings about Poe generally, see *Essays Before a Sonata*, section 3 of the
Epilogue (Boatwright, p. 76).

6

Many American composers, I believe, have been interested in working things out for themselves to a great extent, but it seems to be the
general opinion that, unless a man has studied most of his life in a
European conservatory, he has no right (and does not know how) to
throw anything at an audience, good or bad. I saw some time ago an
article in the paper about this matter saying that only quite recently
(or within the last half a dozen years or so, and after they had gone
abroad and studied with some of the modern masters) were any unusual harmonies, rhythms, or original ideas started to be found in
American music.

In this connection, the issue of the *Musical Courier* of April 22, 1902,
published in New York, in speaking of my music (as it appeared to their
critic, who attended a concert April 18, 1902, in which a Cantata of
mine was presented), says that in this music there are some unusual
harmonies, original ideas, complicated rhythms, and effective part-

writing.[1] As I look back on those times (and also on the music written at that time), the music which is the subject of this criticism is, comparatively speaking, not [so] experimental or very different from the accepted way of writing at the time—(though, in this concert at the Central Presbyterian Church, I played a short organ Prelude, with eight notes (C E G Bb, Db F Ab Cb) *pp* in swell organ, pedal playing the main theme *f* under these eight notes, etc.).[2]

When I look at this score, it is hard for me to realize that anybody could have found anything very unusual or original in it (except the eight-note chords over the main theme). The *First Symphony* and *Second Symphony*, written (fully completed and copied) just before this cantata,[3] some of the songs and other music (Chorales, Psalms, piano), some of the organ pieces (one in 1892, *Variations on America*, has off-rhythms and two keys), and an *Adagio* from a *First Violin Sonata* (1900—which was never completed as such)[4] seem to me to come closer to this criticism. That probably goes to show how very little was the interest, at the time, in anything but the German and usual European conventions and traditions—because this critic must have heard, and been adequately conversant with, the music that was considered at all new in those days.

But, come to think, in recent playing and looking over the sketches [and choir] parts of this music (since writing the foregoing, I got out some of it), and to be fair to Mr. Musical Courier (I forget his name—nice old German—I met him in church about a year after that—in this connection I have something to say about the business methods of the

[1] This review of *The Celestial Country* says: ". . . The work shows undoubted earnestness in study, and talent for composition. . . . Beginning with a prelude, trio and chorus, with soft, long-drawn chords of mysterious meaning . . . the music swells to a fine climax . . . throughout the work there is homogeneity, coming from the interweaving of appropriate themes. Following the opening chorus there is a bass solo, sung on this occasion by the alto. . . . There follows a quartet in D minor, difficult, with chromatic harmonies, and in the trio with alternating 3/4 and 4/4 time measures. . . . The intermezzo for strings alone . . . the Kaltenborn Quartet will find useful for their concerts. It is full of unusual harmonies and pleasing throughout. The a capella octet . . . [is] followed by the tenor solo. . . . The finale is composed of a . . chorale and fugue. This shows some original ideas, many complex rhythms and effective part writing. . . ." (App. 3, #13.)

[2] This is the same chord-type that Ives used in the hymn interludes (see §47, note 12). In *The Celestial Country*, there are four different versions of the introduction to #1, a prelude before #2, interludes before and after #4, and two versions of an introduction to #7, all in the same style (other versions of these or other interludes must have been in the lost organ part).

[3] These comparative datings are interesting (see §14–15, and App. 3, #13, 16 and 17).

[4] If Ives means the original slow movement of the *Pre-First Violin Sonata* (later arranged as a *Largo* for violin, clarinet and piano), it was indeed finished and bound in buckram. According to a memo on the ink copy, Wm. Edward Haesche played the *Adagio* with Ives at the organ, "at Organ recital Central Presb. Church, 57th St., New York, Dec. 16, 1901" [a Monday—?].

Haesche (1867–1929, born at New Haven) was an old friend. He took part in a concert in Danbury, 20 February 1889, and studied at the Yale School of Music 1894–99. He was Acting Battell Professor of Music in Parker's absence 1902–03, continuing at Yale until 1922, when he went to teach at Hollins College, Virginia.

Musical Courier—I can call as a witness the Hon. Keyes Winter,[5] U. S. District Attorney at New York and Republican Leader and Congressman)—but in re music, I often played not exactly as written in the nice copied copies (see ⊡, bottom [of] back [of] page 4).[6] I do remember that, in playing the first and last choruses of [the cantata, I] would throw in 7ths on top of triads in right hand, and a sharp 4th [f♯] against a Doh-Soh-Doh in left hand (see 5th page where organ comes up in this chord-fashion).[7] This would give a dissonant tinge to the whole, that the Musical Courier man was not quite used to, and so to him it seemed unusual.

Also at the end of the Intermezzo [for] string quartet [in the] same cantata, though distinctly in B♭ major, the last chord is a minor 6th, unresolved—in other words it doesn't end in the key (tonic). Gustave Bach, who [played] viola at this concert, insisted he couldn't stand it not to resolve [and] slide to the tonic [chord] (G♭ to F, [at the] end). At the concert he looked at me and winked but didn't resolve. He is a nice man!

m6v   In re, old Gustave Bach, who wanted not to hold on to G♭ against F, I made a little practice piece called *Holding your own* as a joke (partly serious), and dedicated [it] to Gustave in memory of his old forebear.[8] One man plays the chromatic scale and another a diatonic [scale] in different time etc.—we played it over and had a laugh. But the last time I found it, it seemed quite (or partially) musical, and worth playing—and [I] put it, as a slow bit, into a fast Scherzo[9] (see the Set of *Three Short Pieces* for string quartet and basso and piano—photo [as] copied nicely by Hanke).[10]

---

5 The *Musical Courier* offices are unable to identify the "nice old German" critic.
    For Keyes Winter see Appendix 17. Ives is probably referring to the review of the *114 Songs* in the *Musical Courier* of 21 September 1922, which strung along, out of context, whatever would make a funny effect. Ives's sketch of a reply says: "I don't remember sending a copy of the book to you. Though I'm glad of any criticism that's frank, thoughtful, and constructive, I'm *not* looking for publicity. . . . I ask you not to publish this letter. Most of your readers have forgotten the article and me, I hope, by this time, and I prefer to be unnoticed, if you don't mind." Ives probably discussed this with Winter, who must have agreed on the impropriety of the review. Compare also the letter to the *New York Sun* (Boatwright, p. 132) and App. 3, #2.
6 This probably refers to the back of the original of T4, which is missing.
7 These added-7th effects are found, in the first chorus in m. 128–30, 4th beat, and in the last chorus in m. 46–58 (added by Ives to the copy in Price's hand), but the left-hand tritones nowhere at all. They must have been in the lost organ part. But this tritone effect does show up in a piano-drum texture (see §11) in the *Trio*, 2nd movement, m. 43–44.
8 Ives is probably being facetious—Gustave must have known that he wasn't descended from J. S. Bach, whose last descendant with the Bach name died in 1845.
9 See the different dates in App. 17, p. 264, and in App. 3, #31.
10 Emil Hanke, Ives's most expert copyist, whose scores look like engraving, abandoned this kind of work to join Jehovah's Witnesses. He introduced George Roberts to Ives— "When I told him that Madge Roberts was my aunt, I was *in*." [Margaret Roberts, contralto soloist at Center Church, New Haven, in the 1890s, was one of the few who encouraged Ives to follow his own musical ideas.] "Hanke had a kind of a palsy—his hand would shake on the way down, but he never missed."

PART TWO

Scrapbook

7

M5
T5m

More for my own records (and also as a kind of family scrapbook—putting down the foregoing page has started me again on memos etc.)[1] and as a reference for any who may ask me for data (and as I have now got sort of started on the job), the following facts (a kind of general resumé of my music) are put down.

m5

It [may] seem somewhat forward, on my part, for a man to make "memoirs"—unless he is a President of a Bank or a U.S. or a R.R., but I've just jotted down and collected old notes. But I am asked for data etc. which I have not in shape to send. At the present time there [are] five unanswered letters[2] on my desk asking for various things which this note partly covers in a way.

M5
T5m

All the facts given, I and Mrs. Ives, and others both of the family and friends, know to be correct—([they] have helped me in bringing [them] to mind), and there is much documentary evidence (as also from old letters [in the] safe,[3] beside reference to) programs, clippings, etc. etc. The facts that I do not know to be correct (or am not certain) are not (yet) put down.

[1] Since these words are added in pencil to T5, the "foregoing page" must be the original of T4, which is missing.

[2] The "five unanswered letters" [perhaps partly unanswered] might have included those from Amadeo Roldan, Havana, 1 October 1931: "Please send me as soon as possible some information about you and about your work *Decoration Day*."—from Henry Cowell, New York, 5 January 1932 (enclosing his Ives article for *American Composers on American Music*): "Here it is . . . We can talk of corrections when I see you Thursday . . . I hope there are no serious errors of fact."—from Lehman Engel, New York, 21 January 1932 (planning some lectures): "My friend, Bernard Herrmann, told me that you might be able to supply me with either material or information or both."—and from Wallingford Riegger, New York, 4 May 1932 (see Preface, p. 0, and §2).

[3] The words "also", "from", and "safe" are uncertain guesses, but seem the most likely solutions of Ives's hasty writing.

8

To start with, see Bellamann's article of July 1931,[1] pages 11 and 12 (*Musical Quarterly*), given below:

T5
MQ

"The book of *114 Songs* was published in 1922. As was said, there are a few of those songs that are conventional lyric expressions—mostly dating from 1895 to 1901. Among these is an exquisite and touching setting of *Songs My Mother Taught Me*,[2] that envelopes the familiar text with a gentle, nostalgic atmosphere of singular appropriateness. But right in with these are songs of the same period which contain some of the germs and beginnings of the harmonic, rhythmic, and general texture that were developed from that time on. In this connection it may be of interest to give a few details:

T6m
MQ

"In *A March Song*,[3] 1894 (p. 128), some not strictly consonant chords used in a percussive way, and a shift of main beats to weaker beats—now called 'rag'.

"*The Children's Hour*[4] (Longfellow), 1901 (p. 163). Melody in C major with accompaniment blending between A minor and A major, also a chord suggesting later tone clusters, the voice ends on the second of the scale while the piano has a dominant 9th chord.

"*Walking Song*,[5] 1902 (p. 149). Dissonant chords, others of consecutive 4ths and 5ths with major 3rds between, a B♭ major 7th chord held over a general G major, cross-rhythm phrasing and an uneven measure in middle of song, throwing the following even measures on the off-beats.

"A little song, 'Dost Thou',[6] 1894 (p. 210), ends on the dominant 7th. *A Song to Rossetti*,[7] 1900, ends on the chord of the 9th.

m6

"*Tarrant Moss*, 1902 (p. 160). A rough song, some chords of bare 5ths, ending in keys of C major and F♯ major together." (Giles sang it [at the] Waldorf around 1901. Mr. Modeln[?] cut out the last measure of discords, as he called [them], and ended on C. Some copies by Tams show this compromise.)[8]

1 July 1931 must be the date either of Bellamann's writing the article, or of his giving Ives a typed copy (no longer among Ives's papers) from which he would have dictated to Miss Martin, probably in March 1932. The article appeared in *The Musical Quarterly* in Vol. 19/1, pp. 45–58, January 1933. Ives was then at Taormina.
2 App. 4, #108.
3 Some of Bellamann's paragraphs about the songs are so sketchy that they seem more like reminders of points to discuss than like the intended discussions, with titles put down from memory without checking—this is *The Circus Band*—App. 4, #56.
4 App. 4, #74.
5 *Walking*—App. 4, #67.
6 *Kären*—"Do'st remember . . ."—App. 4, #91.
7 *Mirage* (Christina Rossetti)—App. 4, #70.
8 App. 4, #72. Ellis Ellsworth Giles was the tenor soloist at Central Presbyterian Church, and sang in *The Celestial Country* in 1902. The name of his accompanist is a hand-

T6
MQ

"*Harpalus*,[9] 1902 (p. 161). Chords of the 4th in treble, 5th in bass, off-rhythms with voice ending on 6th of scale, and piano with a chord of the 4th on the 3rd.

"*Rough Wind* (Shelley), 1898[10] (p. 155). Taken from a theme in an early symphony, a melody going through eight different keys in twelve measures and ending in two keys.

"Even the earliest song in the book, 1888 (p. 259), although a very simple one, shows an interest in putting melodies together. The *Dead March* in *Saul* as a cantus firmus with an original melody starting over it in the treble.[11]

T7m
MQ

"*A Song to German Words*,[12] 1899 (p. 190), shows a few vicious dissonances.

"*The Old Mother*,[13] 1900 (p. 183). Some elided beats and off-groups of three, beginning on a second beat of a 3/4 measure.

"*The Cage*, 1906 (p. 144). A song taken from a Chamber-Orchestra Set; chords of 4ths and 5ths throw the melody and general harmonic scheme into an atonality, the rhythm changes in each measure, there are no measures consecutively of the same time duration.[14]

"*To Moore's 'Evening Bells'*,[15] 1907 (p. 142). Song in E♭ until last few measures, going through E major and ending in C♯ major with a 6th. There are two rhythms throughout, 3/4 and 6/8, though that was not so unusual at that time.

"A study of other music of that period shows similar trends and tendencies."

---

writing puzzle: Madeln?—Modehn?—Trow lists an "Adam Mader, musician"[?]. No Tams copy with "this compromise" was among Ives's papers. But these do contain a program of the Apollo Club (Wm. R. Chapman, conductor; Emile Levy, accompanist) in the ballroom of the Waldorf-Astoria Hotel on Wednesday 15 May 1901, in which Giles sang *When Dreams Enfold Me* [*An Old Flame*, App. 4, #87]—might he have sung *Tarrant Moss* as an encore? The program does not specify whether Levy accompanied only the Club or the solos too.

9 App. 4, #73.

10 App. 4, #69. 1898 is probably the date of the ink copy of *Judges' Walk* (prototype of *Rough Wind*), whose composition may span several years, since the poem appeared in the *Danbury Evening News* on Monday 12 September 1892. The opening theme of the *First Symphony* is more probably derived from early sketches of this song. Bellamann's typed copy of the article may have said "eight different keys"—in *The Musical Quarterly* it says "a half a dozen".

11 This is not true. The Handel tune serves only as introduction and coda, the voice part being accompanied by non-thematic chords in both versions (the sketch in George Ives's copybook and the revision in *114 Songs*). App. 4, #114.

12 *Ich grolle nicht*—see App. 4, #83, and App. 6, which disproves the 1899 date.

13 App. 4, #81.

14 See App. 3, #62a, and App. 4, #64, also §17. In *114 Songs, The Cage* is unbarred. But in the orchestra score, Ives perpetrated an unnecessary metrical difficulty, putting the barlines with the string chords, which are mostly syncopated against the more stable meter of the melody.

15 Possibly Ives's own title, since it was to Moore's poem that he adapted the music of *The Sea of Sleep*, in which the surprise modulations at the end are expressively functional. App. 4, #63.

9

M6
T7m

The above has more to do with the songs and shorter pieces etc. About the first of the large and serious pieces, as I remember, were a Communion Service (St. James' Episcopal Church, Danbury, 1889 and '90),[1] and an organ sonata à la Mendelssohn[2] (but with a movement, *Chorale*, of three old hymns—in the coda ending with the three going together)—an organ fantasia (*Variations on America*), played in 1891–92 in organ recitals in Danbury and Brewster, N.Y. One variation was the theme in canon, put in three keys together, Bb-Eb-Ab, and backwards Ab-Eb-Bb[3] (but this was not played in church concerts, as it made the boys laugh and [be] noisy).

m7v

In the manuscript at the bottom of p. 8, there are two rhythms made by off-accents:[4]

In some of these passages, the lower pedal rhythm keeping the regular 3/4 is omitted—this is done often in jazz today. Also [there are] short Interludes between variations (right hand starting Hymn in F, left hand Hymn in Gb, as a kind of canon together).[5] These lasted only five or six measures, and Father would not let me play them in the Brewster concert, as they made the boys laugh out loud.

M6
T7m

The first serious pieces quite away from the German rule book were a Fugue for strings, or organ and violins, [in] four keys (1896),[6] (though this was suggested by a *Fugal Song* [*for Harvest Season* for] tuba, trombone, cornet, voice—in C, F, Bb, Eb—see Father's copy book),[7]— (several attempts at Psalms—see middle [of] Father's old copy book),[8] —and an organ *Prelude and Postlude for a Thanksgiving Service* played in Center Church, New Haven, Conn., in November 1897, the

[1] This must be the Communion Service of short movements sketched in George Ives's copybook, pp. [62–77]. The sketch is headed "1890 Jan 8"—but the writing suggests 1891 (Ives often continued writing the date of the previous year)—and his final copy is headed "Mch. & Apr. 1892"—so "1889 and 90" should read "1891 and 92".
[2] Ives destroyed the organ sonata.
[3] This can refer only to an interlude that has not survived.
[4] Measures 183–86 (9–12 from the end).
[5] Ives certainly means the interlude after Var. II, right hand in F, left hand and pedal in Db.
[6] This must be the fugue on *The Shining Shore* (neg. Q1889–90, Q2359).
[7] This *Song for Harvest Season* was sketched in the copybook, pp. [77–79], probably in 1893. App. 4, #118.
[8] There are no psalm-sketches now in the copybook, but they might have been on pp. [75–76] or [93–96], now missing.

first piece that seems to me to be much or any good now. Parker made some fairly funny cracks about it, but Dr. Griggs said it had something of the Puritan character, a stern but outdoors strength, and something of the pioneering feeling. He liked it as such, and told Parker so. Parker just smiled and took him over to Heublein's for [a beer].[9]

M6
T8m

These pieces were an organ *Prelude, (Offertory)* and *Postlude.*[10] The *Postlude* started with a C minor chord with a D minor chord over it, together, and later major and minor chords together, a tone apart. This was to represent the sternness and strength and austerity of the Puritan character, and it seemed to me that any of the major, minor, or diminished chords used alone gave too much a feeling of bodily ease, which the Puritan did not give in to. There is also in this some free counterpoint in different keys, and two rhythms going together. There is a scythe or reaping Harvest Theme, which is a kind of off-beat, off-key counterpoint.[11] Six or eight years later, some time before we left 65 Central Park West, which was in the fall of 1906[12]—(a date on the score gives November 1904)—these two pieces were arranged as a single movement for orchestra in the shape now found (never fully copied out in ink on separate staves).[13]

[9] Heublein's Café (Gilbert F. and Louis F. Heublein) was listed in New Haven directories of 1893–1901 at 151 Church Street (local pronunciation "Heiblein's" or just "Heib's"—see App. 6). The word "for" is only in M6 followed by a circle with a dot in the middle—to represent a beermug?—or the coaster?—or the ring on the table?
[10] This seems to be Ives's only mention of a Thanksgiving Offertory—or did he insert "Offertory" absent-mindedly, thinking of the titles of the *First String Quartet*? (see App. 3, #15). Of the *Postlude* only the first page survives (Q0904), and possibly a sketch combining *Federal Street* with *The Shining Shore* that might be for its end. Otherwise it and the *Prelude* are known only through memos referring to them in Ives's ink score of *Thanksgiving*, which make one suspect that the *Prelude* was the prototype for the whole middle section, m. 130–209.
[11] This theme is most prominent in m. 88–95.
[12] This move was in September 1907 (probably Saturday the 21st).
[13] See §34, third paragraph.

10

While in college, some things were written and played by the Hyperion Theater Orchestra, New Haven, some short overtures and marches, some brass band pieces, and short orchestra pieces. Some had old tunes, college songs, hymns, etc.—sometimes putting these themes or songs together in two or three differently keyed counterpoints (not exactly planned so but just played so)—and sometimes two or three different kinds of time and key and off-tunes, played sometimes impromptu. For instance, a kind of shuffle-dance-march (last century rag)[1] was played on the piano—the violin, cornet, and clarinet taking

M7
T8m

[1] Though the term "rag" seems to have been first used in the 1890s, there must have been an unbroken development of this syncopated style all the way from the folk sources

turns in playing sometimes old songs, sometimes the popular tunes of the day, as *After the Ball,* football songs, *Ta-ra-ra-boom-de-ay*—something in the way of the second movement [of the] *Theater Orchestra Set* (published in *New Music,* January 1932).[2] The pianist (who was I, sometimes) played his part regardless of the off-keys and the off-counterpoints, but giving the cue for the impromptu counterpoint parts, etc.

m8v   In house cleaning preparatory to being away for a year or so,[3] I found some sketches and manuscripts of pieces for orchestra written several years ago somewhat as while in college—among them were two called *Calcium Light Night* and *A Yale-Princeton Football Game* in tones as such. The [second][4] one, I remember, was fully scored and copied out in ink and sent to Hunt Mason, sometime in 1899—but so far [I] can't find [it]. The other is practically all there in the sketch, but not fully scored—that is, not all on separate staves. There are some indistinct measures, but I'm going to have them copied out soon. These are good evidences of how, when once one [is] using "tones" to take off or picture a football game for instance, [how] natural it is to use sound and rhythm combinations that are quite apart from those that would be a "regular music." For instance, in picturing the excitement, sounds and songs across the field and grandstand, you could not do it with a nice fugue in C.

M7
T8   Some similar things were tried in the D. K. E. shows, but not very successfully, as I remember. Marches with college tunes in the trio[5] against the original themes went better,—though Prof. Fichtl,[6] in the

---

of Gottschalk (1829–69) to the supremely refined rags of Scott Joplin (1868–1917). See for instance the song Ives quotes in §17.

2 *After the Ball was Over* appears in *In the Inn* (in the *Theater Orchestra Set* but not in the piano version), *Ta-ra-ra-boom-de-ay* in the second movement of the *Trio.*

3 Ives's second trip to Europe lasted over a year, from 12 May 1932 to 6 July 1933.

4 Ives by a slip of the pen wrote "first," but it was the *Yale-Princeton Game* that he sent in 1899 to Mason, who died in 1914. In June 1933 Ives wrote from Exeter, England, to Julian Mason, asking if this score might still be among Hunt's papers. Julian wrote Ives on 5 July 1933: "My brother, Huntington, lived away from home many years before he died. Furthermore, just after his graduation we broke up our old home and dumped out about half of everything in the way of papers and letters that any of us had. We completed the job two years later while Huntington still was at home when we moved from the south side to the north side in Chicago. He lived a rather lonely life in hotels and clubs, and was laden with no luggage beyond his clothes and a few cherished books. I am afraid, therefore, that there's nothing to be done as to the finding of the music mss. which you want. I am awfully sorry." (See also §19, second paragraph.)

5 Among college tunes quoted in Ives's extant marches are *Here's to Good Old Yale, Omega Lambda Chi,* and *A Son of a Gambolier*—also the popular tunes *My Old Kentucky Home* (Foster), *Annie Lisle* (H. S. Thompson), and *That Old Cabin Home Upon the Hill* (Frank Dumont).

6 Frank A. Fichtl was a versatile musician, principally a violinist, but also played cornet, piano, etc. For years he led the Second Connecticut Regiment Band and the orchestras of various New Haven theaters, the Grand Opera House, the Hyperion, and the Shubert. He died in 1926, age 67. A memo on a sketch of Ives's *Ragtime Pieces* says: "piano arrangements from 1st & 2nd Rag Time Pieces (Fiddles, 2 Clar., Piano, Trombone) played by Fichtl, New Haven, May 21, 1904 [Saturday]."

M7
T9m

m9

theater orchestra, would get students in the audience whistling and beating time (sometimes) to the off-key and off-time tunes.

When other similar things (half in fun, half serious) were tried, as I remember, there were usually one or two, either among the players or the listening students, who would be sort of interested and ask to have it played again. And in playing the songs in D. K. E., I used to play off-beats on black keys, etc., and often men would ask to have those "stunts" put in. Some said—one was Sid Kennedy[7]—that it made the music stronger and better, after he had got used to it. Now this may not be good evidence, but it shows what the ears can handle, when they have to, and [with] practice—not that the things then were worth much —but the ears have to be on their own.

M7
T9m

If more of this and other kinds of ear stretching had gone on, if the ears and minds had been used more and harder, there might have been less "arrested development" among nice Yale graduates—less soft-headed ears running the opera and symphony societies in this country —and less emasculated art making money for the commercialists controlling the movies, tabloids, and most of the radio programs.

m9v
tm

Also and similarly, a stronger use of the mind and ear would mean less people (usually ladies) whose greatest interest and pleasure in art, in music, and in all nice things, is to get their names down among the Directors and Patrons of Rollo's friends, and in giving dinners to European artists, conductors, etc., with more reputation than anything else (that is, artists and conductors, not dinners)—letting themselves become dumb tools of a monopoly, kowtowing to everything the monopolists tell them about America being an unmusical country, and creating a kind of American Music inferiority complex. These commercial monopolists, whether prima donna conductors, pianists, violinists or singers, have so long fostered and held their monopolies (for just about a hundred years in this country) that as a result too much of the American ear has become a Soft-Static Co. (Limited), and the Gabrilowitsches et al. have got the money and coll[ected] the ladies' smiles.

I personally (this is a personal remark) think that many or most of the celebrities of world fame are the greatest enemies of music—unless the art is going to lie forever as an emasculated art, degenerating down to one function and purpose only—that is, to massage the mind and ear, bring bodily ease to the soft, and please the ladies and get their money. For example, note the expression that speaks louder in their

---

7 Sidney Robinson Kennedy (1875–1962), Yale '98, was President of the Buffalo Insurance Co., 1925–45, then retired to Litchfield, Connecticut. The DKE show, *Hells Bells* (28 May 1897) "was written by Hinsdale, Kennedy, Wadsworth. . . . Mr. C. E. Ives has furnished much original music for this play; his latest masterpiece will be sung at the close of the 3rd Act. The words were written by F. G. Hinsdale. You are all requested to join in the chorus, but kindly wait until it sounds familiar."

faces than in their music, when big business men like Kreisler, Mischa Elman, Josef Hofman, etc. exhibit their wares.

M7
T9m

There may be an analogy between (or at least similar results from similar processes of) the ear, mind, and arm muscles. They don't get stronger with disuse. Any art or any habit of life, if it is limited chronically to a few processes that are the easiest to acquire (and for that

M8
T9m

reason are said to be some natural laws), must at some time, quite probably, become so weakened that it is neither a part of art nor a part of life. Nature has bigger things than even-vibration-ratios for man to learn how to use. Consonance is a relative thing (just a nice name for a nice habit). It is a natural enough part of music, but not the whole, or the only one. The simplest ratios, often called perfect consonances, have been used so long and so constantly that not only music, but musicians and audiences, have become more or less soft. If they hear anything but doh-me-soh or a near-cousin, they have to be carried out on a stretcher. (Rhythm is too often a thing of comparative precision and repetition, and ear and mind stretching has opened up the way.)

11

M8
T10m

When I was a boy, I played in my father's brass band, usually one of the drums. Except when counting rests, the practising was done on a rubber-top cheese box or on the piano. The snare and bass drum parts were written on the same staff, and there were plenty of dittos.[1] In practising the drum parts on the piano (not on the drum—neighbours' requests), I remember getting tired of using the tonic and dominant and subdominant triads, and Doh and Soh etc. in the bass. So [I] got to trying out sets of notes to go with or take-off the drums—for the snare drum, right-hand notes usually closer together—and for the bass drum, wider chords. They had little to do with the harmony of the piece, and were used only as sound-combinations as such. For the explosive notes or heavy accents in either drum, the fist or flat of the hand was sometimes used, usually longer groups in the right hand than left hand.[2]

Father didn't object to all of this, if it was done with some musical sense—that is, if I would make some effort to find out what was going

---

1 In M8, Ives wrote: "plenty of •/ ."
2 This kind of piano-drum writing, and chords derived from it, may be found in: "1776" (measures 10–38, 63–76), Country Band March (mm. 45–63, 69–72, 87–112, 126–36), In the Inn (mm. 1–7, 38–39, 78–80), Calcium Light Night (m. 1, etc.), Over the Pavements (mm. 46–48, 94–95), Second Violin Sonata, 2nd mvt. (mm. 50–56), Trio, 2nd mvt. (mm. 43–67, 93–126), Hawthorne (the roll-off ending the march), The Fourth of July (mm. 66–74, 84–86, 93–113), Putnam's Camp (mm. 47–58, 68–84, 113, 126–33, 157–62), General Booth (introduction and coda), Fourth Symphony, 2nd mvt. (Nos. 4–6, 10, 15, 20, 28–29, 44).

on, with some reason. For instance, I found that often I kept a different set of notes going in each hand, and that the right-hand chords would move up and down more, and change more, than those of the left hand. And then for accents the hands would go usually in opposite directions, the right hand up, the left hand down—also that triads and chords without bites were quite out of place, or any combinations that suggested fixed tonalities. And sometimes, when practising with others or in the school orchestra, I would play drum parts on the piano, and I noticed that it didn't seem to bother the other players—*if* I would keep away from triads etc., that suggested a key. A popular chord in the right hand was Doh♯-Me-Soh-Doh♮, sometimes a Ray♯ on top, or Doh-Me-Soh-Ti, and one with two white notes with thumb, having the little finger run into a 7th or octave-and-semitone over the lower thumb note. The left hand often would take two black notes on top with thumb, and run down the rest on white or mixed.[3]

In re piano playing drum rhythms etc.—Fred Sanford (a boy friend of mine fifty years ago in Danbury, now dead) was playing his drum in the yard just by the parlor windows—his sisters, Gracie and Mattie, were playing the piano. They called out to Fred, "You put us all out, you're out of time"—Freddy said, "*You* put me all out, you're all out of time." Father used to like to tell this, as showing Freddy's independence —witness: "They're all out of step but Jim."

I just mention the above, not that in itself it is much, but to show how the human ear (not one but all) will learn to digest and handle sounds, the more they are heard and then understood. In this example, what started as boy's play and in fun, gradually worked into something that had a serious side to it that opened up possibilities—and in ways sometimes valuable, as the ears got used to and acquainted with these various and many dissonant sound combinations. I remember distinctly, after this habit became a matter of years, that going back to the usual consonant triads, chords, etc., something strong seemed more or less missing (at least quite often, if not always)—(a feeling one has now, only worse, after the usual hotel-, boat-, and summer-garden, and most nice concerts).

While we were living in East 40th Street (1915–16), Clara Clemens (Mrs. Ossssssipy Gabrilowitsch) invited us to go with her to an all-Beethoven recital in Aeolian Hall, New York, played by Osssssssip.[4]

---

3 Of these first three chord-types, the first is approximated in *Calcium Light Night,* m.1, the second in *General Booth,* m. 1, and the third in *The Fourth of July* at letter Q. A typical passage with both thumbs playing seconds is in *The Fourth of July* at letter L.
4 This was the second in a series of Six Historical Recitals given by Gabrilowitsch (with program notes by Huneker) at Aeolian Hall on six afternoons in the season of 1915–16: Tue.   2 Nov. (16th–18th centuries),   (*continued overleaf*)

After two and a half hours of the (perhaps) best music in the world (around 1829), there is something in substance (not spirit altogether) that is gradually missed—that is, it was with me. I remember feeling towards Beethoven [that he's] a great man—but Oh for just one big strong chord not tied to any key. I made some remark to that effect— that even two hours of Beethoven is quite enough—or something to that effect—but I was glad she misunderstood me and said, "Yes, an audience like this—an all-Beethoven program is a little too much for their musicianship." I meant just the opposite. The more the ears have learned to hear, use, and love sounds that Beethoven didn't have, the more the lack of them is sensed naturally.

m44v

In some of the piano pieces, *The Fourth of July, The Masses* (score), some of the take-offs, etc., [there] are wide jumps in the counterpoint and lines.[5] The ears got gradually used to these, as they, like the piano-drumming, started in fun—in this case by playing the chromatic scale in different octaves, and seeing how fast you could do it—for example, starting say on low C, then C♯ middle, D top, or D♯ low, etc., and then back again in different ways—as:

And gradually, as the ears got used to the intervals, I found that I was beginning to use them more and more seriously, that these wide-interval lines could make musical sense (see some of the old short piano studies, in photos [of] pencil [sketches], not all copied out).

Sat.   13 Nov. (Beethoven *Sonata in A*, Op 2/2, *32 Variations in c, Rondo in G,* Op.
              51/2, *Sonata in f,* Op. 57, *Sonata in A flat,* Op. 110),
Sat.   11 Dec. (Schubert, Weber, Mendelssohn, Schumann),
Tue. 28 Dec. (Chopin),
Thu. 24 Feb. (Brahms, Liszt),
Sat.   11 Mar. (modern composers, starting from Franck, including Schoenberg Op. 19).
[5] This wide-interval writing appears most clearly in the first variation midway in *Emerson*—also in the *Varied Air and Variations* (Merion, 1971), in *The Fourth of July* (in the explosion after letter M), in *Majority* (or *The Masses*), verses 5–6 (which Ives omitted from the arrangement in *114 Songs*), and in most of the studies.
Ives told George Roberts that his father had him do chromatic scales with each interval a minor 9th—"If you must play a chromatic scale, play it like a man."

12

M9
T11m

Also as a boy I had heard and become somewhat familiar with tone-divisions other than the half-tone (see article of mine, *Some Quarter-*

Tone Impressions,[1] in the *Franco-American Musical Society Bulletin,* March 1925 [pp. 24–33]—this gives Father's experiences in some detail with quarter and other tone-divisions).

In testing or experimenting in the divisions of tone, father tried:

1) the slide cornet,
2) glasses for very small intervals,
3) tuned piano in actual partials (as well as he could by ear—no acousticon),
4) new scales without octaves (glasses),
5) also violin strings stretched over a clothes press and let down with weights.

Father had a kind of natural interest in sounds of every kind, everywhere, known or unknown, measured "as such" or not, and this led him into positions or situations (some described elsewhere or above) that made some of the townspeople call him a crank whenever he appeared in public with some of his contraptions. But as I and (better) my aunts and some of the older people remember, this was not often. The "Humanophone"[2] and Glass Orchestra were some of these contraptions. This interest in this side of music took all his extra time. He did but little composing—a few things or arrangements[3] for bands—in fact he had little interest in it for himself, and it was too bad he didn't, for it would have shown these interests, and they would have been in some keepable form. He didn't write text books (though I have some copies of some of his class talks[4] etc.) and he didn't write many letters. He left little behind except memories of him in others.

Father also had a gift for playing. He'd take a familiar piece and play it to make it mean more than something just usual (see *Danbury Evening Times,* August 2, 1932: *Colonel Wildman Reminisces*[5]—about

1 See the reprint in Boatwright, pp. 105–119.
2 For more about the Humanophone see §56.
3 There seems to be no trace of any of the music used by George Ives's band, except, among Ives's papers, a cornet part for his *Rale Ould Irish Medley.*
4 This must refer to an article or syllabus on music theory, of which two incomplete copies were among Ives's papers (now in the Ives Collection).
5 Ives wrote and dictated the headline of this article from memory as "General Wildman's Reminiscences." It recounts the funeral at Waterbury of James R. Young, a Civil War veteran prominent in the Connecticut G.A.R. Col. Ira Wildman, who headed the delegation from Danbury, was recalling that Young was a great story teller.
"One of Mr. Young's favorite stories, Col. Wildman said, was that concerning the conversation in which General Grant made his historic remark. While Mr. Young was an orderly at General Grant's headquarters in the siege of Richmond, President Abraham Lincoln was visiting with General Grant after a review of the army. They were discussing the relative merits of the various sections of the army.
" 'That's a good band,' President Lincoln remarked, indicating the First Connecticut Heavy Artillery band under Mr. Ives' leadership. Mr. Ives was then but a boy of 16 years [by then 19].
" 'It's the best band in the army, they tell me,' General Grant replied. 'But you couldn't prove it by me. I know only two tunes. One is *Yankee Doodle* and the other isn't.'
(*continued overleaf*)

what Lincoln and Grant said about Father's band—and Rosie Mulligan's story). The things he played then (during the war) were mostly the things that most bands played, but he put something in them that most band leaders didn't—ask Mr. Lincoln or Mr. Grant!

m13
t

[There was] something about the way Father played hymns. Even if some of the choir could read music readily at the rehearsals, he always liked to play each part over with his horn, and have them get it entirely through listening,[6] through the ear, through his phrasing, tone, and general style of playing. He had the gift of putting something in the music which meant more sometimes than when some people sang the words. He once gave a concert in Danbury on the basset horn, playing songs of Schubert and Franz. He had the words printed on a sheet and passed them through the audience, who were expected to read the words and sing silently with him. Somebody heard him play the *Erlking* (Schubert) and felt that he sang it (through the basset horn or trombone, I forget which it was) and carried him away with it, without the words, as Bispham[7] did singing it. Hearing him play these songs got me, to a certain extent, writing songs for the horn or some instrument, with the words underneath, which should be sung. Some of the songs in the book of *114 Songs* were first written in this way, partly because singers of the time made such a fuss about the unfamiliar "awkward intervals" they called them.

m11v

As said above, Father was not against a reasonable amount of "boy's fooling", if it were done with some sense behind it (maybe not very much or too good a sense, but something more than just thoughtless fooling)—as playing left-hand accompaniment in one key and tune in right hand in another (probably started with singing in two keys—see above).[8] He made us stick to the end, and not stop when it got hard. This led into trying to write duets and pieces in more than one, or two keys together—some of those in the old copy-book—also a fugue going up in 4ths in four keys, or up in 5ths in four keys, etc. Also I remember there was a kind of game—a way of playing off-beats *pp* on the nearest

---

"Several cabinet officers and other notables were in the group and General Grant's witticism made an impression that lasted. The young leader of the band, of couse, never heard the praise which the president gave his organization . . ." [This must be the review at City Point, Virginia, on Sunday 26 March 1865.]

The article goes on to extol George Ives's part in Danbury's musical life and the way it was reflected in his son's music, which was then becoming known internationally.

So far Rosie Mulligan's story has eluded search.

6 t13 has "system" (impossible), George Ives used "listening" in just this way in the syllabus mentioned above in note 4.

7 David Bispham (1857–1921) was one of America's greatest singers, both vocally and dramatically. The editor still remembers a recital he sang at Lawrenceville School around 1918, and the gooseflesh he raised with *Danny Deever* (Kipling, set by Walter Damrosch).

8 Adding this long balloon later, Ives forgot that he had mentioned this kind of "singing in two keys" not "above" but below (in §43).

black notes (as the *Arkansas Traveller*), singing the air, right-hand chords in G, left-hand bass in G, and off-beats *pp* in G♭, etc.

Father used to say, "If you know how to write a fugue the right way *well*, then I'm willing to have you try the wrong way—*well*. But you've got to know what [you're doing] and why you're doing it." It was his willingness to have boys think for themselves—within reason—that I looked back on later as quite remarkable, but it didn't seem [so] to me then as a boy. I had to practise right and know my lesson first, then he was willing to let us roam a little for fun. He somehow kept us in a good balance. It was good for our minds and our ears.

m37v   As for example (as in making chords a boy's way), if two major or minor 3rds can make up a chord, why not more? And also, if you can play a tune in one key, why can't a feller, if he feels like [it], play one in two keys? For instance (some measures copied in father's old music scrapbook)—tune: soh la [soh] fah mih fah soh—re mih fah—etc. in F, and accompaniment in E♭—then repeat: tune same, but accompaniment in G♭⁹—then, in the tune, throwing off the last ♪ of a phrase, and beginning the tune (on repeat) on that off-beat, thus making it a main beat! Beat that, Jamey boy! Even in some of the old Psalms for choir or quartet and sometimes instruments (if around the corner), two or even three keys were tried out, or at least thrown in together. Father let me do it, if I knew what I was doing and could play and sing them —even knew them well enough to play them without looking at the notes on paper.

m11   This reminds me also of some pieces, some to church anthems and to psalms, that Father let me work over—and some he tried in the choirs but had a hard time. The 150th Psalm was one—part of the 90th—and the 67th. This he thought the best for singing for church (see memo, copied)[10]—(also 54th, and 24th also?).

m28v   I have a letter of Father's written to Orrin Barnum[11] (when [he was] studying at the New England Conservatory). He says, "The older I get (he was about 42 [at] this [time]), [and] the more I play music and think about it, the more certain I am that many teachers (mostly Germans) are gradually circumscribing a great art by these rules, rules,

---

9 Ives is using "movable do" in F. In George Ives's Copybook there are other polytonal harmonizations of *London Bridge*, G/F# on p. [71], and F/G♭ on p. [102]. But this pair (F/E♭ and F/G♭) is on a separate sheet of music paper (n1762).
10 See App. 5.
11 Orrin S. Barnum was born about 1866, the son of William H. Barnum. He studied violin with George Ives, and the story goes that at Boston they told him he'd had excellent instruction (though he does not appear in the archives of the New England Conservatory, which unfortunately are incomplete for that period). He played cornet in the Christmas 1888 performance of Ives's *Holiday Quickstep*. At the time of his marriage in New York to Josephine Patten on 16 October 1889, he was a salesman in the New York office of C. H. Merritt, the Danbury hatter. He is listed in the Danbury Directory of 1907. Further information about him would be gratefully appreciated.

rules, with which they wrap up the students' ears and minds as a lady does her hair—habit and custom all underneath. They (the Professors) take these rules for granted, because some Prof[essors] taught them to them, and[12] [before that some other] Prof[essors] taught them to them, etc., ad lib. And when you begin to really consider it, you ask, 'Why? Why do you say this should never be used—this is [the] right way—this [is] wrong?' They['d be] surprised, sometimes dazed, and babble something that some old Prof. has told them fifty years ago. What they teach is partly true, but is it all true? See what Helmholtz[13] says about natural laws—the danger of restricting music to habits and customs, and [giving] these natural laws as an excuse." I am fully convinced [that], if music be not allowed to grow, if it's denied the privilege of evolution that all other arts and life have, if [in the] natural processes of ear and mind it is not allowed [to] grow bigger by finding possibilities that nature has for music, more and wider scales, new combinations of tone, new keys and more keys and beats, and phrases together—if it just sticks (as it does today) to one key, one single and easy rhythm, and the rules made to boss them—then music, before many years, cannot be composed—everything will be used up—endless repetitions of static melodies, harmonies, resolutions, and metres—and music as a creative art will die—for to compose will be but to manufacture conventionalized MUSH—and that's about what student composers are being taught to do.

[12] In *m*28v, after this "&," Ives (copying from his father's letter) wrote "(can't make out)." Unfortunately the letter is missing, and Ives indicated no close-quote. Its placement after "excuse" is an editorial guess—the following long sentence sounds more like Ives than like his father.
[13] No family copy of Helmholtz was among Ives's papers. See §13, note 6.

13

M9
T11m

In the music courses at Yale (four years with Parker)[1] in connection with the regular college courses, things or ideas of this nature, or approaching them, were not so much suppressed as ignored. Parker, at the beginning of Freshman year, asked me not to bring any more things like these into the classroom,[2] and I kept pretty steadily to the regular classroom work, occasionally trying things on the side, some-

[1] See the intimately perceptive book on Parker (1863–1919) by his daughter, Isabel Parker Semler (Putnam, 1942), including many letters and other writings of Parker, a reminiscence by William Lyon Phelps, and a memorial sermon by Winfred Douglas. See also §44.
[2] If the memo in App. 5 is correct, Ives would have recently composed *Psalm 67*, and one can't help feeling sympathetic to Parker's complete unpreparedness for such a prophetic masterpiece. See also App. 6.

M10
T11

M10
T11m
tm

M10
T12m

m12
tm

M10
T12m
tm

m12v
tm

times with the Hyperion Theater Orchestra, and in organ works, and sometimes in church services, as for instance the *Thanksgiving Prelude and Postlude*.

Father had kept me on Bach and taught me harmony and counterpoint from [when I was] a child until I went to college. And there with Parker I went over the same things, even the same harmony and counterpoint textbooks (Jadassohn),[3] and I think I got a little fed up on too much counterpoint and classroom exercises (maybe because, somehow, counterpoint gradually became so much associated in my mind as a kind of exercise on paper, instead of on the mountains).

And I did sometimes do things that got me in wrong. For instance, a couple of fugues with the theme in four different keys, C-G-D-A— and in another, C-F-Bb-Eb.[4] It resulted, when all got going, in the most dissonant sounding counterpoint. Parker took it as a joke (he was seldom mean), and I didn't bother him but occasionally after the first few months. He would just look at a measure or so, and hand it back with a smile, or joke about "hogging all the keys at one meal" and then talk about something else. I had and have great respect and admiration for Parker and most of his music.[5] (It was seldom trivial—his choral works have a dignity and depth that many of [his] contemporaries, especially in the [field of] religious and choral composition, did not have. Parker had ideals that carried him higher than the popular) but he was governed too much by the German rule, and in some ways was somewhat hard-boiled.

For instance, to show how reasonable an unreasonable thing in music can be—look at a fugue. It is, to a great extent, a rule-made thing. So, if the first statement of the theme is in a certain key, and the second statement is in a key a 5th higher, why can't (musically speaking) the third entrance sometimes go another 5th higher, and the fourth statement another 5th higher? And if it must hold to the same nice key

3 The only copy of Jadassohn among Ives's papers is a later printing of 1904. Even though his theory work at Yale involved some repetitive review, the surviving counterpoint exercises show clearly that those for Parker maintain a more exigent level than those for his father.

4 There are also two tiny fugues in George Ives's copybook, on p. [92] (4/4, incomplete, in Cowell p. 28) and on p. [99] (12/8, complete), both in C-G-D-A, but Ives seems not to have had the copybook at New Haven. The fugue on *The Shining Shore* is in C-G-D-A. The *Song for Harvest Season* is in C-F-Bb-Eb. Ives must have shown these to Parker.

5 While at Yale, Ives would certainly have heard Parker conduct the New Haven Symphony in the bass aria from *Hora Novissima* in March 1897, the overture *Count Robert of Paris* in January 1898, and the *Ode for Commencement Day* in March 1898. And Ives might have gone in to New York to hear the first performance of *St. Christopher* in April 1898. That he was familiar with *Hora Novissima* is shown by a copy among his papers with tempo reminders in #2 and organ registrations in #9 (the alto aria—might Madge Roberts have sung it at Center Church?—see §6, note 9).

system, why can't these themes come back in the same way? "Because Bach didn't do it," Rollo says, "and that's the best reason I know." The reasons of the others are not as good as Rollo's. One Mus. Doc. says, "Because it destroys tonality." Having four nice different men playing tennis together doesn't always destroy personality—tonality is more of a man-made thing than personality. Then the Musdock says, "It violates the true, fundamental, natural laws of tone."[6] Does it? What are the true, fundamental, natural laws of tone? The people who talk and tell you exactly what they are, who teach them explicitly, who write treatises about them—ipso facto,—know less about them than the deaf man who wonders! They measure a vibrating string and want to tie your ears to it. When it's easy to catch the vibration, then it's "natural", and they smile. When it's hard, then they scold or get mad, or go to sleep.

m12a
tm

They talk about some fundamental laws [of] sound—for instance, an obvious physical phenomenon, or rather a material arrangement of things, is 2:1 (that is, an octave). It happens to be self-evident, easy to hear and understand—but when you think of it, for that reason it is no more a fundamental law than 1:99. (Yet, if Rollo [should] hear this "just horrid" interval, he would raise an eye or say "not nice" [with] a falling smile (from a corner of [his] mouth—west?) to the girls in his class.) 1:99 is just as fundamental and natural as 2:1. The physical movement of a string vibrating or dividing into segments is but a thing the eye and ear can know and see easily. Does that make it, or not make it, a fundamental law?

m15v
tm

The obvious movements in the mechanico-physico world of nature are too often by men taken for the whole, to a great extent, because it is easy to take them as such. Yet the overtones that a string may give are just as natural—more so—than some of the triads used by the partialists as evidence of their fundamental laws. But their 5ths are flat, and their 3rds off, and when it comes to using the [11th] partial, F♯ in C (which has been found to be nearer [to] a quarter-tone than to the written [F♯]), they would call you unnatural and violating a fundamental law. How about that, Mama Nature? Professors, Doctors of Music, and some Germans call you somewhat unnatural and a tough man, when you play a few quarter-tones!

[6] In regard to pedantic ideas on "natural laws of tone," Ives clearly took great comfort from his copy of William Pole's lectures of 1877, *The Philosophy of Music* (6th edition, 1924, with introduction by Edward J. Dent), in which he marked many passages, particularly where Pole was quoting Helmholtz. Ives treats all this more fully in *Some Quarter-Tone Impressions* (see Boatwright, pp. 105–19).

14

M10
T12m

The *First Symphony* was written while [I was] in college. The first movement[1] was changed. It (that is, the symphony) was supposed to be in D minor, but the first subject went through six or eight different keys, so Parker made me write another first movement. But it seemed no good to me, and I told him that I would much prefer to use the first draft. He smiled and let me do it, saying "But you must promise to end in D minor." (And also he didn't like the original slow movement, as it started on Gb[2]—he said it should start in F. Near the end, "the boys got going"—so at the request of Parker and Kaltenborn[3] I wrote a nice formal one—but the first is better!)

T12m

The last three movements of this symphony I showed to Mr. Walter Damrosch over twenty years ago (after yanking back the first page [of the] *Black March* together with a page of something else—see elsewhere), and he tried them over at a rehearsal.[4] "Tried" is a good word. He started with the second movement (adagio), an English horn tune over chords in the strings. (When he heard the pretty little theme and the nice chords) he called out "Charming!" When the second themes

T13m

got going together, and the music got a little more involved (but not very involved), he acted somewhat put out, got mad, and said it coul[dn't] be played without a great deal of rehearsing.[5] When I showed this score to a modern orchestral conductor[6] a few years ago and told him this story, he fell into a swoon.

1 See §8, note 10. (App. 3, #16.)
2 This seems to prove that the original slow movement of the *First Symphony* is now in the *Second Symphony*. The first sketch did start with a Gb chord (n2323), and "the boys got going" in the second page (n2322).
3 Existing documents seem to suggest that Ives wouldn't have met Kaltenborn until later—so his "request" may have concerned the movement as transferred to the *Second Symphony*.
4 This reading session was at a Saturday morning rehearsal, 19 March 1910. See also §31.
5 See Cowell, pp. 67–68.
6 Nicolas Slonimsky suggests that this conductor was probably Eugene Goossens (1893–1962)—see page 12.

15

The *Second Symphony*, written partly in college and finished in 1901 or 1902, was the result of the overture habit, common about two generations ago. The Largo[1] was a part from a Revival Service for string

1 Here Ives seems to be telling us that the same slow movement mentioned above (in §14, note 2) had done duty also in the Revival Service that was the source of the *First String Quartet*.

quartet, and played in Center Church, [New Haven]—but this was revised (à la Brahms, at Parker's suggestion), and scored in 1909 or 1910, when the symphony was copied out in ink by Mr. Price, who came from Wales. (But the first version was the best, "when the boys got going"—but Parker [said it was] not dignified [enough] for a real symphony[2] (from margin, page 4, Symphony #2)[3]—[and] the original scoring is better, but [it's] not copied out in ink.) Some of the themes in this symphony suggest Gospel Hymns and Steve Foster. (The last movement was a kind of overture[4]—played partly as a shorter piece by Father's Orchestra [in] 1889, [and by] the Danbury Band—[with the tune] *The Red White and Blue* and old barn-dance fiddles on top.)[5]

m13v
t

Some[6] nice people, whenever they hear the words "Gospel Hymns" or "Stephen Foster", say "Mercy Me!", and a little high-brow smile creeps over their brow—"Can't you get something better than that in a symphony?" The same nice people, when they go to a properly dressed symphony concert under proper auspices, led by a name with foreign hair, and hear Dvorak's *New World Symphony*, in which they are told this famous passage was from a negro spiritual, then think that it must be quite proper, even artistic, and say "How delightful!" But when someone proves to them that the Gospel Hymns are fundamentally responsible for the negro spirituals, they say, "Ain't it awful!"—"You don't really mean that!"—"Why, only to think!"—"Do tell!"—"I tell you, you don't ever hear Gospel Hymns even mentioned up there to the New England Conservatory."[7]

In the middle and last half of the last century, in the churches throughout the north, negro choirs (usually male choruses) called "Jubilee Singers," would often come north to give concerts, or sometimes sing in the church services. Grandma Parmelee[8] went to hear one of these choruses in Danbury in the '80s, and said, "Why, they do sing

2 These comments of Parker probably refer to the movement as in the *First Symphony* (see above).
3 This "page 4" must be lost.
4 Ives has written of his father's conducting *The American Woods Overture* at Danbury in 1889 (see App. 3, #17), but there is no mention of this in the Danbury newspapers.
5 One of Ives's boyhood heroes was the country fiddler, John Starr, of Brookfield, and the fiddler style reflected in this fifth movement is probably a memory of him. The obituary notice in the *Danbury Evening News*, Tuesday 23 September 1890, says: "Mr. Starr was as familiar a person to Danbury people as to citizens of his own town. He was a well-known musician, being a skillful violinist, and was from his youth up identified with orchestral music at sociables and other entertainments in Danbury and neighboring towns. . . . Mr. Starr was a native of Brookfield and was born in the house in which he died. He was forty-eight years old . . ."
6 On the back of T13, this paragraph is headed "Zermatt." The Iveses were at Interlaken from 22 September to 22 November 1932, and there is no evidence of an excursion to Zermatt, but they may have gone there just to see the Matterhorn.
7 Might this be Orrin Barnum speaking? See §12, note 11.
8 See App. 13, p. 247.

nice, but they're a good deal the same tunes we used to sing in our old church down in Weston, but they don't sing 'em quite right always." It struck many the same way. Recently some study has been made of this matter, and there is now a general realization that the negroes drew on these old hymns more than most people realize. As I remember, there was an article in the *Musical Quarterly*[9] some years ago by Carl Engel about this influence.

t13

When Father was in the Civil War, a negro boy, whose mother did the washing for the band, would stay around the tent while the band was practising, and Father said that the boy would stand by him whistling and humming the airs and tunes the band would play. And [Father] found quite often that he would change the melody by leaving out the 7th of the scale and sometimes the 4th,—for instance, if the tune ended lah-te-doh upward, he would sing either lah-lah-doh or lah-doh-

t13m

doh. Incidentally, Father taught this boy how to read and write (both English and music) [and] brought him home with him. (Grandmother took him in, brought him up) and sent him to school in Danbury. (She and Grandfather would take anybody and everybody in, and give them their last cookie or last cent, if their sense of injustice was stirred.) This negro boy later became a (revered and respected) teacher[10] in Hampton College, Virginia. His name was Anderson Brooks.

In some of the churches, and in the camp meetings, I remember hearing hymns written in rather even time sung with the off-accent.

m13v
tm

One Grandma Parmelee used to sing [and] hum around some:

There's no hope with-out Je-sus, The sin-ner's on-ly friend.   (This isn't quite right)

The negroes took many of the phrases, cadences (especially plagal— they liked the fah chord), and general make-up, and the verse and refrain form, and the uneven way many of these hymns were sung rhythmically, especially the choruses. The congregation would get excited and start a strong phrase by a shortening of the phrase before. The negroes took and exaggerated some of these things in their own way and especially a melodic phrase like this:

9 Ives must be referring to the *Views and Reviews* section of *The Musical Quarterly*, vol. 12/2, April 1926, pp. 299–314, a long ramble in which Engel discusses among other things Gershwin's *Concerto* and jazz, and negro spirituals in James Weldon Johnson's *The Book of American Negro Spirituals* and in R. Emmet Kennedy's *Mellows*. Engel points to the extravagance of Johnson's claims ("America's only folk music"), and to the spirituals' debt to older American music, but does not mention the Gospel Hymns.
10 This cannot be true, but is a product of Ives's transferring his filial enthusiasm to Brooks. See App. 14.

lah doh__ lah soh me ray [me] *etc.*

The Gospels used the 4th and 7th sometimes, but the negroes were still too near Africa and the oriental five-tone scale to get these. But it was not, to my mind, these physical techniques as much as the fervor, conviction, and a real human something underneath, that the negroes heard in these Gospel Hymns and reproduced in a little more drawling way, their own way.

m14v
tm

Some thirty years ago, in a downtown corner saloon in New York, I picked up a *Puck* or *Judge* magazine and saw a set of verses. The writer had apparently heard some negro workers singing in a stone quarry in Georgia while breaking and chipping stone. I don't remember the words, except a kind of doggerel about "breakin' de debbil on de haid"—but the tune was *Nettleton,* with a blow on the third beat:

Here I raise my E - be - nee - zer *etc.*

Nettleton was one of the Gospel and Camp Meeting Hymns, and down in the Redding Camp Meetings I heard it sung with exactly those accents, almost shouted. I used it, or partly suggested it, in a string quartet (which I played with two violins, using reed stops in the organ for the viola and cello parts, while in Center Church, New Haven), and also later in a violin sonata.[12]

But the darkies used these things in their own native way, and made them somewhat different—"more beautiful and more artistic" says Rollo. Yes, and so did some of the Yankees. I'm not trying to say that many of the spirituals, jubilees, etc. aren't in their own way natural, spontaneous, beautiful, and artistic—but some white Congregationalists or Methodists (drunk or sober) already had somepin' also natural, spontaneous, beautiful, and artistic—and that somepin' was to start the negro spirituals.

[11] This fragment sounds like a germ of the theme in the *Concord Sonata* which Ives called "that human faith melody"—but without the three-note upbeat.
[12] Ives must have used all the movements of the *First String Quartet* as church music, with or without cooperating strings. The slow movement is on *Nettleton.* The third movement of the *Second Violin Sonata (The Revival)* is also on *Nettleton.*

Ives's "blow on the third beat" is actually on the second beat of the hymn-rhythm, but on the third beat of some of Ives's adaptations.

16

T13m   The *Third Symphony* was finished and copied out in full in 1911.
(It was mostly scored between 1901–1904—good ink copy made by
Tams 1911.) The middle movement was the *Children's Day Parade* (for
string quartet and organ), and was played in Central Presbyterian
Church, New York, [on] organ alone in 1902. (The first and third
movements were played [in] Central Presbyterian Church 1901 [by a]
string quartet—as strings (in score) and organ (wood and brass).) The
first and last movements were fully scored a few years later, (mostly
about 1901 to 1904, and from organ pieces played [in] Central Presbyterian Church in May 1901.) The themes are mostly based around
hymns. (The lead pencil score was finished in August 1901—but the
final score, now lost, had (I think) a few of the off shadow parts in, and
also church bells, crossed out in the old score.)[1]

1 This tantalizing paragraph (with contradictory balloons) may be supplemented from
memos on various manuscripts of the *Third Symphony*. The three organ pieces are lost,
but Ives wrote that he played the *Prelude* (prototype of the first mvt.) on 12 December
1901 [Thursday—organ recital?] and on 2 February 1902 [Sunday],—the *Postlude*
(prototype of the 2nd mvt.) on 12 May 1901 [Sunday],—and the *Piece for Communion* (prototype of the 3rd mvt.) in December 1901. Unfortunately no file of service
programs of the Central Presbyterian Church has come to light, by which one might
check these dates.
    The cover for the three score-sketches is entitled: "Symphony #3 (The Camp Meet-
ing) . . . 1. Old Folks Gatherin' . . . 2. Children's Day . . . 3. Communion . . . fully
scored in 1904, rescored copy 1909 . . . Ink copy 1910 . . ." On the score-sketch of the
first mvt., Ives wrote: "ended 1909 at Elk Lake." Mrs. Ives in *Our Book* described their
stay at Elk Lake (20 August–12 September 1909) as "a perfect vacation. Charlie working on the Symphony" [probably both on this one and also on the fugue for the *Fourth
Symphony*].
    The Tams score of 1911 is clearly "the final score, now lost"—which Gustav Mahler
(conductor of the New York Philharmonic 1909–11) took back to Germany in 1911,
shortly before he died. (Trow lists "Wm. Tams, music, 109 W. 28th"—also "Arthur W.
Tams, pres." at the same address.)
    See also §51. For Ives's statement that he showed Max Smith some of the orchestra-
tion "in 1901 or 2" see §47, after note 14. (App. 3, #53—see also App. 4, #47.)

17

         The *Theater or Chamber Orchestra Set* is a combination of separate
things. The first [*In the Cage*] is a result of taking a walk one hot
summer afternoon in Central Park with Bart Yung (one-half Oriental)
and George Lewis (non Oriental), when we were all living together at
65 Central Park West in 1906 (or before).[1] Sitting on a bench near the
T14m   menagerie, watching the leopard's cage and a little boy (who had
apparently been a long time watching the leopard)—this aroused Bart's
Oriental fatalism—hence the text in the score and in the song. Tech-

1 See App. 17. The full score of *In the Cage* is dated "Bart & Geo. 65 Central P. W.
July 28[?] 1906" [Saturday].

nically this piece is but a study of how chords of 4ths and 5ths may throw melodies away from a set tonality. The main line in 4ths had two lines of inverted counterpoint going with it (see old manuscript).[2] Whether this was meant to increase the fatalism or reduce it, I don't know. It was left out of the printed score and the song copy (I can't remember exactly why, except [that] it's hard to play, and for some lady-boys to listen to)—(see lead-pencil score in safe, 46 Cedar Street). A drum is supposed to be the leopard's feet going pro and con. Technically the principal thing in this movement is to show that a song does not necessarily have to be in any one key to make musical sense. To make music in no particular key has a nice name nowadays— "atonality."

The second movement [*In the Inn*] is one of the several ragtime dances[3] which have been used in whole or in part in several things (and some of the same strains are used in part in several). Some of them started as far back as George Felsberg's reign in "Poli's". George could read a newspaper and play the piano better than some pianists could play the piano without any newspaper at all.[4] When I was in college, I used to go down there and "spell him" a little if he wanted to go out for five minutes and get a glass of beer, or a dozen glasses. There were black-faced comedians then, ragging their songs. I had even heard the same thing at the Danbury Fair before coming to New Haven, which must have been before 1892.[5] One song I remember hearing while I was at the Hopkins Grammar School in 1893 and 94, and this is the song:

T15m

```
"I'm      a-liv - in'   ea  -   sy
On        pork chops    grea - sy"    etc.
("I'm     al - ways a- pick -  in'
On        a  spring    chick - in'")
```

---

2 These "lines of inverted counterpoint" are perfectly clear, though not quite complete, in the pencil score (Q2849). See also §8, note 14.
3 See App. 3, #20 and #62.
4 According to the dean of New Haven musicians, Edward Wittstein, George Felsburg later accompanied silent films at Poli's Bijou Theater, which was across Church Street from Poli's larger theater where there was an orchestra of seven, whereas Felsburg was alone. The Bijou was small (a kind of "poor man's theater") and a terrible firetrap, but Poli was influential and sidetracked efforts to get it condemned.
    As in Felsburg's earlier accompanying of vaudeville shows, reading a newspaper never interfered with his following the gist of things and keeping the music in time and in character. This is corroborated in *Stover at Yale* by Owen Johnson, Yale '00, Chapter 7—"the sleepy pianist pounding out the accompaniments while accomplishing the marvelous feat of reading a newspaper." Felsburg died in 1909 or 1910.
5 In October 1892, Ives was playing right halfback on the Danbury Academy football team and could perfectly well have taken in the Danbury Fair of that year. He didn't go to Hopkins Grammar School at New Haven until the spring term of 1893.

throwing the accent on the off-beat and holding over—a thing that so many people nowadays think was not done until jazz came along. I remember playing this at Poli's.

If one gets the feeling, or shall I say the bad habit, of these shifts and lilting accents, it seems to offer other basic things not used now (or used very little) in music of even beats and accents—(it will naturally start other rhythmic habits, perhaps leading into something of value)—at least it seems so to me. Even in the old brass-band days, there was a swinging into off-beats, shifted accents, etc.—and these ragtime pieces, written from about that time until ten or fifteen years ago, were but working out different combinations or rhythms that these began to suggest. For instance, if, in a few measures in a 2/4 time, the second beat is not struck and the 16th-note before the second beat is accented, other combinations of after-beats and beats and minus-beats etc. suggest themselves.

In one of the scherzo movements of the *First Piano Sonata,* ragging combinations of fives, twos, and sevens are tried out.[6] There are also measures of twos and threes, grouping or phrasing the various parts in different-length phrases—that is, all threes may be grouped in fours accenting the fourth, and the fours may be grouped in fives accenting the fifth. All of these things suggest themselves naturally after playing the preceding combinations, etc. I might add that a good many of these dances ended with the same chorus, but changed rhythmically each time.

T16m

The last part of the third movement [*In the Night*], where the cello starts *Abide With Me,* was played in an evening service (and at an organ recital) at the Central Presbyterian Church, New York, some time before May 1902 (when I resigned as a nice organist and gave up music). When a man has played at church services for ten or fifteen years steadily,[7] he gets slightly used to the three fundamental triads, in the hymns and anthems as well as in the plain chants. In this little piece I tried to find three chords that might be used in a similar or parallel sense to the usual tonic, dominant, and subdominant—a combination of chords that would not be undignified, that would have some musical sense and relation, and about which melodies or counterpoints could be used as a natural outcome from these combinations. In this movement, Db was taken as the main chord (or the tonic), and Bb (in this case a tone above the dominant Ab) was used as the dominant,

6 This must be the later movement of 1909, "4a" (p. 28 through the first line of p. 31 of the Peer edition), in which most of mm. 8–35 is in 5 against 2, with 7 against 2 in mm. 18 and 21, and in which the Chorus is disguised (mm. 48–51, the 2nd chord in m. 49 being c2–g2 in Ives's manuscript, not c2–b2).
7 Steadily, it was over thirteen years (10 February 1889 through 1 June 1902), but there were "supply" Sundays both before and after.

and the chord of E major (a tone below the subdominant G♭) was used as the subdominant. These chords have a note in common with the tonic, and B♭ used as the dominant seems to have a stronger resolving value than the subdominant, E major. Then the tune, *Abide With Me,* as a kind of cantus firmus, was sung by the male voices, with a [higher][8] counterpoint as a second melody played on one of the lighter manual [stops], and in this case in B♭ (the dominant chord). And a piano in the Sunday-school room played another distinct counterpoint, but, as I remember, this attempt in the church service was not successful—it went better in an organ recital—in fact, Dr. Merle Smith[9] turned around and glowered at the choir.

About two years later (to be exact, some time before June 1904), this movement (and a part of the ragtime movement) was arranged for a small orchestra and played in part in the Hyperion [Theater], New Haven, at our Sexennial Reunion. In 1906, before we left 65 Central Park West, the first and last movements were completed and scored as they stand now. In doing so, the last movement (which had begun with the *Abide With Me*) was extended frontwards. In other words, a suggestion of the old minstrel tune, "I hear the owl ahootin'," was put as a horn melody over the same set of chords, but in the key of E major with the flat 7th. As this ends, the *Abide With Me* with (as a secondary counterpoint) the "Down in the cornfield" tune start. Rhythmically, a three and a four go together throughout, and, in the off-time and off-key counterpoint part, the four 16ths going with the four-rhythm are phrased in threes.

The above may seem to indicate that the plan of this movement is a complicated one (chaotic, ugly, and unmusical—but it is, as a matter of fact, quite simple). Everybody told me, when the music was written, that it was not only complicated but involved, though today the opinions pro and con are about 50–50 (or perhaps 33⅓% against, instead of 100% against). But when you consider what the plan is, it appears not only *not* complicated but so simple and reasonable that it might be called a close relation to stupidity (or arestology). All there is to it is this:—three chords used over and over again, two rhythms (a three and a four) used over and over again in each two measures, and a melody in each of the three keys (the last two being used together), and in the accompaniment the first two measures are repeated practically the same throughout.

Of course what I had in mind was a general sounding tonal effect,

[8] T16 has "greater" (hardly possible) for which "higher" seems a plausible solution. This "second melody" is the "Down in the cornfield" phrase from Foster's *Massa's in de Cold Ground.*
[9] Wilton Merle-Smith (1856–1923) was pastor of the Central Presbyterian Church from 1889 to 1920.

and the technical plan (above) as but a ways and means. Behind the music is a simpler picture—the heart of an old man, dying alone in the night, sad, low in heart—then God comes to help him—bring him to his own loved ones.[10] This is the main line, the substance. All around, the rest of the music is but the silence and sounds of the night—bells tolling in the far distance, etc.

Franz Kaltenborn came down to the flat, 65 Central Park West, when I was scoring it, and played over some of the violin parts of the first and last movements. I suggested that he play it at one of his St. Nicholas Rink concerts.[11] He said that he didn't want to lose all of his musical backing in New York, otherwise he would have been very glad to play it. The second, a ragtime movement, was not completed as it stands now until we were in the little house at Hartsdale in 1911.[12]

10 Compare Ives's letter to Becker, October 1931: "It is a quiet piece—a sort of Reverie of an old man who has lost everything but his faith—and memories."
11 Trow lists the St. Nicholas Ice Skating Rink at 69 West 66th Street. The summer concerts there were an ancestor of the later Stadium concerts.
12 At Hartsdale, the Iveses lived in E. H. Whitman's smaller house from 2 May to 20 November 1911, and in the larger house from 15 April 1912 to early June 1914.

18

A set of pieces for cornet solo (with or without voices) and small orchestra was made in 1906[1] with some of the college event things [from] long before that (1900 [or] 1901)[2]—(see song, *Toleration*,[3] #59, p. 135 in book, arranged [from] *A Lecture by President Arthur Hadley*). Some of these were lost or made into other scores later—(see song, *The See'r*, [#29], p. 69 in book—and song, *Religion*, [#16], p. 36 in book, written before Sept. [1901], played in Central Presbyterian Church, New York). There was also a piece for triple-tonguing cornet on a Buck and wing tune, *Katy Darling*[4] (can't find all of it here). Had

1 To a hasty glance at m, "1906" looks like "1900" and Ives read it that way to Miss Martin, but 1900 seems too early. This set Ives once called "Set #1." In the pencil ms. (lacking pp. 1–2 and 8–[9?]) the titles are: [I. *The See'r*], II. *A Lecture*, III. *The Ruined River*, IV. Keats "*Like a Sick Eagle*", V. *Calcium Light Night*, VI. Byron's "*When the moon is on the wave*" . . . (and this memo seems to imply that *Religion* was No. VII). The dating, "made in 1906," is valuable, because Ives eventually forgot it and dated some of these pieces later.
2 In m18, there was only one date here, apparently "1900" changed to "1901", but the words "long before that" may quite possibly refer to the years evoked by *A Lecture* and *Calcium Light Night* rather than the year of composition.
3 In m18, Ives first wrote "Kipling" but obliterated it with a stronger "Toleration" (see App. 4, #59, and #62).
4 A book of miscellaneous songs of the 1950s that belonged to Mrs. Joseph Moss Ives, née Amelia White Merritt (see App. 13, 4th paragraph), contains *Katy Darling* (1851, anonymous) and *Katy Darling's Farewell to Dermot* by H. Kleber (1852), both routine elegies—neither recognized yet in Ives's music. "Buck and wing" was a type of step in the soft-shoe style of tap dancing, not fast—with which old tunes could go well at a neat allegretto.

T18m

m18
tm

piano pieces while in college. Before this, *Calcium Light Night* (DKE—
Ψ U)[5] and *Yale-Princeton Football Game* (for Hunt Mason OK).

Also a set for trumpet (or cornet [or] voices) called first *Songs Without Voices: The New River* (a rag), *The Indians* (1912), *Gyp the Blood
or Hearst* (topical piece)—all these are scored for trumpet (con voce
ad lib), flute, two violins, and piano ([or] for small orchestra, trumpets
or English horn solos) and were written before the spring of 1913, at
least before we were in Brattleboro in January 1913[6]—(a personal story)
—(as I remember receiving the copies from Tams while we were in
Brattleboro, and by mistake one of them was opened by a patient, who
looked quite troubled). Later in 1921, *Ann Street* was put in this set[7] in
place of the rag, which was arranged for larger orchestra—part of it is
in the second movement [of] the *Second Orchestral Set* (and part of it
is in the piece called *The See'r*)—it didn't go well on cornet.

Ann Street was put in (for violins [and] piano) also in place of *Gyp
the Blood or Hearst—Which is Worst?*, [which] was to be the fourth
[in this] set of these take-offs, but was never finished. Only the first
part of this apparently was kept, which was on the back of *The Indians*
score.[8] I can make out the reason for this piece politically, [or] socialis-
tically, better than musically. Written over the music was: "Gyp, a
prominent criminal, (legally) gets the gallows—Hearst, another prominent criminal, (not legally) gets the money. Hearst's newspapers make
Gyps. He sells sensational bunk to the soft-eared [and] soft-headed,
and headlines and pictures that excite interest in criminal life among
the weak-brained and defectives. An old-fashioned western horse thief
is a respectable man compared to Hearst. When the American people
put Hearst with the horse thief, "on the rope," American history will
have another landmark to go with Bunker Hill, and perhaps a new
song to go with *The Battle Cry of Freedom*."

---

[5] For *Calcium Light Night* (App. 3, in #52) Ives copied a memo of three of the songs,
two of DKE, and one of Psi U. Henry Cowell's score (Q2816–2825) is accompanied
by a letter of 28 April 1936 about it (Q2815). [The piece printed in *New Music*, Vol.
24/4, July 1953, as *Calcium Light* is *The Gong on the Hook and Ladder*.]
[6] See end of App. 16.
[7] With *Ann Street*, this might be the set called "[Set #6?]" in the catalogue of Ives's
mss., the "ms." consisting of three leaves out of *114 Songs*—pp. 13–14 (*The New
River*), 29–30 (*The Indians*), and 59–60 (*Ann Street*)—with indications of intended
scoring, which appear differently in the three titles as: Set for (1) trumpet, saxophone,
and piano; (2) trumpet, oboe, strings, and piano; (3) trumpet, flute, trombone (or
baritone saxophone), and piano.
   But any identification is clouded by the way the "rag" means *The New River* in the
earlier part of this paragraph, and later it means the ragtime piece that went into the
Second Orchestral Set—also by the way *Ann Street* is first substituted for the "rag,"
later for *Gyp the Blood*.
[8] Harry Horowitz (alias Gyp the Blood, b. about 1887) took part in the murder of
Hermann Rosenthal on 13 July 1912, was tried in October 1912, and electrocuted on
13 April 1914. Ives may have sketched this piece at the time of the trial. Ives once
designated *The Indians—Gyp the Blood—The Last Reader* as "Set #2."

19

m17v   *Calcium Light Night* was started as, or at least had something like, the "piano stunts" of and around college days. With these there were others—*A Full Game at the Spot*.[1] I had Hunt Mason's encouragement, even enthusiasm, when all the shysters had gone down—and the sun was beginning to show over East Rock. At least we amused ourselves. Hunt would declaim in blank verse. He quite agreed with me that music could "proclaim" any part of the human experience.

I found, with some others, in cleaning house last summer in Redding and in New York this spring, parts of old scores, sketches, etc. One was Hunt's favorite, "Elihu hears (but sees not)"—*A Yale-Princeton Game*.[2] It is "Two Minutes in Sounds for Two Halfs within Bounds." It was short, only four or five pages for full orchestra. The last two pages are quite clear and fully scored—the first part [I] have only in sketch. But to try to reflect a football game in sounds would cause anybody to try many combinations etc.—for instance, picturing the old wedge play (close formation)—what is more natural than starting with all hugging together in the whole chromatic scale, and gradually pushing together down to one note at the end. The suspense and excitement of spectators —strings going up and down, off and on open-string tremolos. Cheers ("Brek e Koax" etc.)—running plays (trumpets going all over, dodging, etc. etc.)—natural and fun to do and listen to—hard to play. But doing things like this (half horsing) would suggest and get one used to technical processes that could be developed in something more serious later, and quite naturally.

m18v   Around this time, running say from 1906 (from the time of Poverty Flat days)[3] up to about 1912–14 or so, things like *All the Way Around and Back, The Gong on the Hook and Ladder, Over the Pavements, Tone Roads, The Unanswered Question*, etc. were made. Some of them were played—or better tried out—usually ending in a fight or hiss (as in Tams later on). I must say that many of those things were started as kinds [of] studies, or rather trying out sounds, beats, etc., usually by what is called politely "improvisation on the keyboard"—what classmates in the flat called "resident disturbances." For instance, *All the*

---

1 No piece with any such title has showed up. "The Spot" was the roof garden on top of the large dry-goods store of F. M. Brown & Co., 886–900 Chapel Street, New Haven. It was apparently a convivial meeting place and the scene of minstrel shows and student-society shows.
2 This is already mentioned at §10, note 3. It exists in a sketch of the first part (Q2873–75) and full score of the last part (Q2876–77), and a memo of the songs and cheers quoted (n2871–72).
3 For Poverty Flat see App. 17.

Way Around and Back[4] is but a trying to take off, in sounds and rhythms, a very common thing in a back lot—a foul ball—and the base runner on 3rd has to go all the way back to 1st.

The Gong on the Hook and Ladder[5] is another nice joke, which most everybody can see except a nice, routine conductor (near-musician), who plays the notes "right" and beats time serious and nice, but doesn't place the music at all—he misses it (as the old lady misses, [whom] Mark Twain told about)[6] but keeps a good job beating time for the ladies and lecturing some young people, who pay tuition bills in a large and fashionable school of—music?—no, ladies—pretty sounds! But he beats time nice and regular, and knows every note in *Elijah*. The Annual Parade of the neighborhood Volunteer Fire Company was a slow marching affair—for the Hook and Ladder was heavy, and the Gong on the hind wheel "must ring steady-like"—and coming downhill and holding backward fast, and going uphill out of step, fast and slow, the Gong seemed sometimes out of step with the Band, and sometimes the Band out of step with the Gong—but the Gong usually got the best of it. Nobody always seemed to "keep step," but they got there just the same—but not with the nice conductors.

Over the Pavements[7] was started one morning, when George Lewis and I had the front bedroom in Poverty Flat, 65 Central Park West. In the early morning, the sounds of people going to and fro, all different steps, and sometimes all the same—the horses, fast trot, canter, sometimes slowing up into a walk (few if any autos in those days)—an occasional trolley throwing all rhythm out (footsteps, horse and man)—then back again. I was struck with how many different and changing kinds of beats, time, rhythms, etc. went on together—but quite naturally, or at least not unnaturally when you got used to it— and it struck me often [how] limited, static, and unnatural, almost weak-headed (at least in the one-syllable mental state), the time and rhythm (so called) in music had been:—1 - 2 -, or 1 - 2 - 3 -, and if a 5 or 7 is played, the old ladies (Walter Damrosch is one, I've seen him do it) divide it up nice into a 2 and 3, or 3 and 4, missing the whole point of a 5 or 7.[8]

m18a p. 1

m18a p. 2

[4] App. 3, #27.

[5] App. 3, #38.

[6] The editor's Cornell colleague, Donald Grout, a well-read Mark Twain fan, suggests that here Ives may be injecting the image of an aging singer into Twain's essay *Fenimore Cooper's Literary Offenses* "When a person has a poor ear for music he will flat and sharp right along without knowing it. He keeps near the tune, but it is *not* the tune. When a person has a poor ear for words, the result is a literary flatting and sharping; you perceive what he is intending to say, but you also perceive that he doesn't *say* it."

[7] App. 3, #42. The opening of *Over the Pavements* incorporates a sketch of 1906, *Rube trying to walk 2 to 3*.

[8] Might Ives be forgetting how the beauty of the 7-rhythm in the 3rd movement of *The Celestial Country* is the clarity of its 4 plus 3?—and how well it illustrates what

This piece, *Over the Pavements,* is also a kind of take-off of street dancing, and a cadenza, and some parts of piano pieces thrown in. The cadenza is principally a "little practice" that I did with Father, of playing the nice chromatic scale not in one octave but in all octaves— that is, 7ths, 9ths, etc.—good practice for the fingers and ears, especially as each time (up and down) was counted differently: 8 - 7 - 6 - 4 - 5 - 3 - 2 - 3 - 4 - 5 - etc., and accented sometimes on the beginnings of the different phrases.

m43v

About or after this time, a race on the water (from an explosion) and a race to Town Meetin' called *Tone Roads* [were made], half serious, half in fun, but carefully worked out. I'll have to admit that some of these shorter pieces like these (for a few players, and called chamber music pieces) were in part made to strengthen the ear muscles, the mind muscles, and perhaps the Soul muscles too (but we won't talk about that now, Arthur!)—not so much in *Tone Roads,* but for instance *All the Way Around and Back,* one of the *Largo Risoluto* [pieces], parts of the *In Re Con Moto Et Al.* They all had a reasonable plan to build on, from a technical standpoint.

m18a
p. 2

The *Tone Roads*[9] are roads leading right and left—"F. E. Hartwell & Co., Gents' Furnishings"—just starting an afternoon's sport. If horses and wagons can go sometimes on different roads (hill road, muddy road, rocky, straight, crooked, hilly hard road) at the same time, and get to Main Street eventually—why can't different instruments on

m18a
p. 3

different staffs? The wagons and people and roads are all in the same township—same mud, breathing the same air, same temperature, going to the same place, speaking the same language (sometimes)—but not all going on the same road, all going their own way, each trip different to each driver, different people, different cuds, not all chewing in the key of C—that is, not all in the same key—or same number of steps per mile.

m28v

> "E. C. T." is the man for us!
> He certainly is a nice old Cuss.
> He's steppin' fleet an' neat
> Right down old Center Street
> A-makin' for the Danbury Bus.[10]

---

his father was saying in the last paragraph of §55? It also illustrates a possible indebtedness to Parker, whose *Hora Novissima* (1891–92) explores the same rhythm in #3, the bass aria (see §13, note 5).

9 App. 3, #48a. Hartwell's (mentioned in the ms. of *Tone Roads #1*) was a large store in Danbury, now Hartwell & Brady. Mrs. Hartwell was the sister of Herbert Wildman, who played baseball with Ives in "The Alerts" in 1889–90.

10 Edward Carrington Twichell (1867–1934), Mrs. Ives's oldest brother (called "Deac" for Deacon), was something of a "character"—had a rare charm but could seldom earn a living. He spent some time in the little cottage at West Redding, and he and Ives were kindred spirits. This limerick has no indication of where it belongs, but running for a bus could be one kind of tone road.

So! Arthur! Why can't each one, if he feels like trying to, go along the staff-highways of music, each hearing the other's "trip" making its own sound-way, in the same township of fundamental sounds—yet different, when you think of where George is just now, down in the swamp, while you are on Tallcot Mountain[11]—then the sun sets and all are on Main Street.

Then about the same time is a sketch [for] piano, woods, and strings. Over the top is "Rondo Rapid Transit."[12] This was about the time the Subway was started, and "blocks" were regular things—getting out of the block and back into it again. So—half-tone chords opening up [into] wider and wider chords, and back again:

This may not be a nice way to write music, but it's one way!—and who knows the only real nice way?

Right or wrong, things like these—some hardly more than memos in notes—show how one's mind works. The only value probably of some of these things was that, in working these sound-pictures out (or trying to), it gave the ears plenty of new sound experiences—it strengthened the ear muscles, and opened up things naturally that later were used naturally and spontaneously—that is, without thinking of it as "this chord" or "this way"—good bad, or nice! But some of these things I did take more seriously when they were written, and so copied [them] out and had [them] played—for instance *The Cage, In the Night,* the "old man sittin'" (study in song, *Soliloquy*), the "General Slocum" explosion, later *The 4th of July,* and some of the ragtime things, etc., etc.

11 Talcott Mountain is about 10 miles NW by N of Hartford—one of Joe Twichell's and Mark Twain's favorite hikes.
12 This is a kind of subtitle of *Tone Roads #3.* App. 3, #48c.

20

Fourth Symphony.[1] This was started, with some of the Hawthorne movement of the *Second Piano Sonata,* around 1910–11[2] (though partly

1 App. 3, # 83.
2 Ives dictated "1910–11" but wrote above in pencil "1909–10." However "1910–11" is corroborated by memos in the score-sketch of the first movement: "started at Pell's Sep. 1910 with at same time Hawthorne"—and "Pell's—Sep. 1910 & 11." [Pell Jones's, on Elk Lake, 18 miles west of Port Henry, New York, was a favorite vacation haunt of the Twichell family.]
    The balloon which follows is on the top left corner of T19. Another, between the first two lines of type, reads: "though Alcotts middle part was April 1902." Might the *Orchard House Overture* (prototype of *The Alcotts*) have been started in April 1902, but shaped up in 1904?

from themes in the unfinished Alcott overture, 1904). It was all finished around the end of 1916.

Greinert had the score to copy, the day before this country went into the war.[3] He copied the prelude and part of the last movement from my lead-pencil score, and some of the pages were mislaid, and I had to re-score them from the sketch. (I called at Greinert's a few days afterwards, and he was all discouraged and cast down, almost in tears— that his fathers' country and his [had] come to make war. As a result, he copied some, mislaid some, and sent the rest back wrong. Everything [had] seemed to go well until the war [was] starting. Greinert was so troubled and discouraged [that] he couldn't seem to work at all, made mistakes by the mile, and finally gave up. In his office, they said he had not been that way before. I mention this as it brings up an interesting commentary [on] human frailty. This is just another sad but unnecessary result of the old mediaeval idea of nationalism. The only thing it does today is to make war. It is fostered and encouraged by the few—the government politicians and not the people—and it's about time we (the people) stop it.)

n19v
:m
And [I] gave the copy to Price at Tams.[4] (I mention this about Mr. Price, copyist, as Price was an ultimate type of the "perfect man" (in Mr. Price's picture). He was the opposite of Greinert. If Wales and the United States should both wipe each other out, that wouldn't bother Price—but tell him that he wasn't perfect and had made a mistake, and he would be mortally insulted. A man completely conceited has the best and the easiest time in this world. Price never made a mistake! What mistakes he made were yours. If he thought you had put down the wrong note, he would put it *right* (right or wrong), and blame you when you had the audacity to say that, not every time there's a C natural, all C sharps that happen on the same beat in the chord should be scrapped. Then he would get mad and want to charge you for correcting your right notes into mistakes. In business and in politics, and in almost every department of life, I know many Prices. But his penmanship was as beautiful as a Michelangelo—to look at a page of those "statuettes" made it hard to jump on him. And once I showed a page (I think it was one of the violin sonatas that Price had copied for me) to a well known musician. He said it was a beautiful, artistic masterpiece of penmanship—"Oh, but such awful music!"[5]

3 The United States declared war against Germany on Friday 6 April 1917. But one may imagine that Greinert had been worrying ever since the invasion of Belgium in August 1914.
4 No score of any of the *Fourth Symphony* in Price's hand was among Ives's papers.
5 Is this Milcke speaking? (see §24).
   Price may have been from Wales, but his mother tongue was German [Preis?]. His hand is identified in a copy of *At Parting* on the cover of which Ives wrote: "copied by Price in Tams—1899." When he was making a score of the finale of *The Celestial Country*, he wrote, under measure 79 of Ives's score: "up to hier finished."

T19m   The first and second movements were copied later by Mr. Reis.[6] Some things in them were from other things that I had been working on before or at that time. The theme and general make-up of the Prelude had been a part of the *First Violin Sonata* in 1908, and put into a song in 1913. The second movement, as said above, is in some places an orchestration of the "Celestial Railroad" idea from the second movement of the *Concord Sonata,* which I was working on at the same time. The last movement (which seems to me the best, compared with the other movements, or for that matter with any other thing that I've done) was finished in the summer of 1914.[7] The fugue was written just before the entire thing was finished in 1916, but the last movement covers a good many years.[8]

       In a way, as stated in Mr. Bellamann's program notes: "The last movement is an apotheosis of the preceding content, in terms that have something to do with the reality of existence and its religious experience."[9] And I always think of it somehow in connection with a Com-
T20m   munion Service, especially the memory of one, years ago, in the old Redding Camp Meetings. About the middle of this movement, there is something suggesting a slow, out-of-doors march, which has for its theme, in part, the remembrance of the way the hymn, *Nearer My God To Thee,* sounded in some old Camp Meeting services. It was put into a short organ piece[10] and played in Central Presbyterian Church, New York, in 1901. The rest of the movement gradually grew out of this.

       An incident also that had something to do with this, perhaps more than I think, was in connection with a scene one evening at Café Boulevard, New York, after McKinley's assassination in 1901.[11] Everybody stood up and sang this hymn. It brought back an incident in my father's life showing one of the finest sides of his character. I don't feel like describing it here, but Mrs. Ives remembers what it was.[12] It was a fine and deep personal experience which is better to remember than to put into words.

[6] The scores by Reis (or Reiss?) of the first two movements are in the Ives Collection.
[7] T19: 1915—m19: 1914.
[8] This dating of the fugue (some twenty years after its first version) represents an extreme of New England privacy. Since it had been transferred from the *First String Quartet* to the *Fourth Symphony,* its past history was nobody's business but his own. See App. 3, #15.
[9] This sentence is not in the program note of 1927, nor in Bellamann's *Musical Quarterly* article as it appeared in January 1933—perhaps in a first draft of either? Ives put it in the conductor's note of 1929 (see note 13 below).
[10] On the title page of the second full score: "last movement 1911–16, main part of Memorial Slow March on p. 15–18, from Organ piece 1901."
[11] McKinley was shot Friday 6 September 1901, and died on the 14th. Wednesday the 18th was a day of mourning and prayer. Trow lists the Café Boulevard at 156 Second Avenue.
[12] This is a good example of old-fashioned reticence about family matters. Unfortunately Mrs. Ives had no recollection of what the incident might have been.

Technically, an important matter that has to do with the playing of this symphony, especially the second and fourth movements, is that of varying degrees of the intensities of various parts or groups. (And the same thing, to a certain [extent], was in mind in some of the shorter pieces for smaller groups of players—some in Chamber Music Sets.) If the players are put as usual, grouped together on the same stage, the effect of the sound will not give the full meaning of the music. These movements should not be played all in the foreground, with the sounds coming practically the same distance from the sounding bodies to the listeners' ears. (See conductor's note published and distributed in the issue of *New Music,* San Francisco, California, of April 1929.)[13]

(In that connection) is a sound which is constant (and heard by an ear remaining in the same position to the sounding body) cancelled, when another louder sound (heard by the same [ear in the] same position) comes, so that the hearer does not seem to hear the first sound? I have never yet seen any theory describing (both aurally and scientifically) the nature and processes etc. of sound-waves, together with their relation to the physiology of the ear, that seemed to me absolute proof that sounds (as above) are cancelled. The Professors and musicians say—"If you don't hear this sound (and a graph does not show the waves of this sound), isn't that proof that they are cancelled?"— NO—How does the listener know that he doesn't hear? (And graphs don't prove everything—some of them may mean that nature is doing little more than being easy and obvious to some know-it-all scientist after a nice dinner!) Can he be any surer about that than an architect can be sure that a certain grain of sand is not in his dam—because he doesn't see it there?[14]

[13] This conductor's note is given complete in the published score of the *Fourth Symphony.*
[14] Compare Cowell, p. 180.

21

The *First Violin Sonata* [called by Cowell the *Pre-First*] was started when I was in college, and finished the first year or so in New York about 1901.[1] The second movement I have kept[2] (and another was worked into the *Second Sonata*).[3] The others I didn't think were much good and didn't keep them.[4]

[1] T21 has "1901"—m has "1900"—but 1901 seems more correct (App. 3, #23).
[2] The old second movement was arranged as the *Largo* for violin, clarinet, and piano (App. 3, #26).
[3] The new second movement, on *The Old Oaken Bucket,* was revised for the *First Violin Sonata* (see §22), which Ives is here calling the "Second."
[4] The rejected scherzo and the end of the first movement went into the second movement (*In the Barn*) of the *Second Violin Sonata,* and the last movement (on *Autumn*) was revised as its first movement.

m21v   I can't remember exactly, but there was another Violin Sonata started
about that time, which I have a vague feeling went with a Cello Sonata
never finished as such.[5] Some of it landed in some of the Sets or songs
later, but don't know what. It had something to do with old hymns—
was something like the string quartet in *Hymn*[6] (see photo)—at any
rate it was torn up or lost.

[5] This "another Violin Sonata" is called in Cowell the pre-Pre-First—a sketch page
(n3224) may belong to it. Ives destroyed the cello sonata.
[6] The *Hymn* had been part of the *Pre-Second String Quartet*—see §26.

22

T21m   The *Second Sonata* (called the *First*) was written in 1903 and 1908,[1]
and is a kind of mixture between the older way of writing and the
newer way. (I remember starting the first theme,[2] just the first Sunday
after [I] gave up playing in church, June 8, 1902, 65 Central Park
West.)[3] In some places it is a kind of retrogression, but on the other
hand there are things in it, rhythmically, harmonically, and struc-
turally, which Mr. E. Robert Schmitz told me last year (1931) he didn't
remember (even up to the present time) seeing in other music.

This reminds me that after a part of the *Fourth Symphony* was
played in 1927, Darius Milhaud, who was at the concert, and whose
music was also played,[4] told Mr. Schmitz that he noticed in my score

[1] Pasted into the photostat copy of the score in Emil Hanke's hand in the library of the
American Composers Alliance, New York, is a mimeographed note:

> Program Notes. First Violin and Piano Sonata by Charles Ives. This Sonata is
> in part a general impression, a kind of reflection and remembrance, of the peoples'
> outdoor gatherings in which men got up and said what they thought, regardless
> of consequences—of holiday celebrations and camp meetings in the '80s and '90s
> —suggesting some of the songs, tunes and hymns, together with some of the sounds
> of nature joining in from the mountains in some of the old Connecticut farm towns.
>   The first movement may, in a way, suggest something that nature and human
> nature would sing out to each other—sometimes. The second movement, a mood
> when *The Old Oaken Bucket* and *Tramp, Tramp, Tramp, the Boys are Marching*
> would come over the hills, trying to relive the sadness of the old Civil War days.
> And the third movement, the hymns and actions at the farmers' camp meeting,
> inciting them to "work for the night is coming."
>   This sonata was composed mostly in 1903 and completed in detail in 1908. (The
> above was mostly taken from footnotes on the back of the old manuscript.)

[There are no such "footnotes" on the backs of any of the extant sketches of this
sonata, but these are by no means complete, so they may have been on some of the
missing leaves or parts of leaves.] (App. 3, #54.)
[2] This "first theme" is a major theme of the first two violin sonatas and also colors the
"conslugarocko" part of the fourth—as pointed out in Laurence Perkins's excellent
M. M. thesis (Eastman School, 1961).
[3] Ives's resignation as organist of the Central Presbyterian Church was announced in the
Danbury Evening News of Saturday April 26, 1902, but he apparently continued another
month, to Sunday, June 1.
[4] The program of the Pro Musica international referendum concert at Town Hall,
Saturday, January 29, 1927, was: Ives *Prelude & 2nd mvt. from Fourth Symphony*,
Debussy *Musiques pour "Le Roi Lear"* (both conducted by Goossens), Milhaud *Les
Malheurs d'Orphée* (conducted by Milhaud).

many things that he'd never seen before in any other music. What they were or what he had in mind, except in a general way, I don't know. (I would not refer to these two concerts[5] if it weren't for the tiresome, easy, blab way so many (mostly Americans) say that all American modern music is just taken after the modern Europeans, of whom Milhaud is often mentioned.)

[5] One of the "two concerts" is the above program. Might the other have been a private performance of the *First Violin Sonata*—by David Talmadge (see §46)?—and heard by Schmitz?—for which the above program note was mimeographed?

23

The *Third Violin Sonata* (called the *Second)* has a second movement based, to a great extent, on the old ragtime stuff, [which] was written about the time that I started and wrote so many of these ragtime dances, all of them a great deal the same, around 1902 and 1904. But the other movements were finished after the *First Sonata,* and copied out in 1909 and 1910.[1]

[1] See Ap. 3, #65.

24

T22m

The *Fourth Violin Sonata* (called the *Third*) was finished in the fall of 1914.[1] The middle movement is from an early ragtime piece (date

[1] Pasted onto p. 39 of *Our Book* is the following note (on paper of Ives & Myrick, 38 Nassau Street, New York):

> Mr. David Talmadge . . . Violin   Mr. Stuart Ross . . . Piano
> Sonata #3 for Violin and Piano (1915)
>   1. First verse and refrain . . . Adagio
>   Second   ”   ”   ”   . . . Andante Moderato
>   Third   ”   ”   ”   . . . Allegretto
>   Last   ”   ”   ”   . . . Largo
>   2. Allegro
>   3. Adagio (Cantabile)

The Sonata is an attempt to express the feeling and fervor—a fervor that was often more vociferous than religious—with which the hymns and revival tunes were sung at the Camp Meetings held extensively in New England in the 70's and 80's. The tunes used or suggested are: *Beulah Land, There'll Be No More Sorrow,* and *Every Hour I Need Thee.* Common themes are used with or against the hymn tunes.

The first movement is a kind of a magnified hymn of four different verses, all ending with the same refrain. The second movement may represent a meeting where the feet and body, as well as the voice, add to the excitement. The last movement is an experiment: The free fantasia is first. The working-out develops into the themes, rather than from them. The coda consists of the themes for the first time in their entirety and in conjunction.

As the tonality throughout is supposed to take care of itself, there are no key signatures. (Carnegie Hall, Chamber Mus. Hall)

This performance is described in §46 as "a small invited concert," and its date is given in *Our Book* as follows:

> 1917—Charlie's violin Sonata played May 22nd, Mr. Talmadge and Mr. Stuart Ross, Carnegie Chamber Music Hall.
>   Apr. 28. To Redding.   (*continued overleaf*)

on back of sketch Aug. 1905).[2] The first movement was written a few
years before 1914 (but is really from old Camp Meeting pieces—but
first was an organ Prelude, 1901), and it started out all right. It was
finished at the time the third movement was made (also from an organ
Prelude, played in Central Presbyterian Church, 1901), and the older it
got, the worse it got.

Generally speaking, this sonata was a slump back, due, I am certain,
to a visit in Redding in August 1914[3] from a typical hard-boiled, narrow-
minded, conceited, prima donna solo violinist with a reputation gained
because he came to this country from Germany with Anton Seidl as his
concertmaster. He has given concerts in Carnegie Hall (forty years
ago), where he played the usual kind of program and everybody ap-
plauded, etc. etc. Mrs. Ives knew him in Hartford, and as I'd had so
much trouble with musicians playing my music, we thought it would be
a good plan to get one of the supposedly great players. Before finishing
the *Third Sonata*, I wanted to have the *First* and *Second* played over.

The "Professor" came in and, after a lot of big talk, started to play
the first movement of the *First Sonata*. He didn't even get through the
first page. He was all bothered with the rhythms and the notes, and
got mad. He said "This cannot be played. It is awful. It is not music,
it makes no sense." He couldn't get it even after I'd played it over for
him several times. I remember he came out of the little back music
room with his hands over his ears, and said, "When you get awfully
indigestible food in your stomach that distresses you, you can get rid of
it, but I cannot get those horrible sounds out of my ears (by a dose of
oil)."

I remember Milcke (the Professor), in looking over some of the
other music, came across a part of the *In Re Con Moto Et Al* for cham-

T23m

m22v

These events appear to be in the wrong order, and it seems unlikely that Ives should
arrange such a private invitation concert after they had moved to the country. It looks
as if Mrs. Ives had entered both items into *Our Book* not at the time but in May, and
absent-mindedly written May instead of April, and that Sunday 22 April 1917 is the
right date, especially since Ives misdated it "April 1916" in App. 11 (at note 7).
Unfortunately Carnegie Hall has kept no records of rentals from that period.

In July 1944 Ives wrote, sketching a letter to Sol Babitz and Ingolf Dahl: "At the
beginning of the 1st verse . . . was a suggestion of a two-key plan (occasionally played
in church services . . . the harmony usually a minor 3rd lower than the melody) . . .
the key of D♭ under the melody in E . . . this was from a kind of chant for organ and
voices . . . some of the singers, after getting accustomed to this, said that, going back
to one key only, they missed something—that it didn't have the strength of the two-key
plan."

[2] No 1905 date is on the back of any extant sketch page, but on p. 1 of the ink copy of
the 1st movement: "2nd movement from Theater Orchestra score played 14th Nov.
1905"—and on the title page of the ink copy of the 2nd movement: "some of this . . .
played in Globe Theater 14th in 1905."

[3] On the ink copy of *Tom Sails Away*, Ives dates Milcke's visit to Redding as "Oct. 4[?],
1914" [a Sunday], but the "4" is a combination of 1, 2, 4, and 11 written on top of
each other. Mrs. Ives recalled his periodic impulses to "get things right!"

Edward Wittstein studied violin with Franz Milcke, and says that he was a good
teacher but not a good concertmaster.

ber group (which I didn't intend to show him), and also the church bell
piece called *From the Steeples* for bells, and a Chamber [Music] Set,
etc. He jumped back, mad. Then I thought I shouldn't treat him so rude
and gave him a copy of the second movement of the *First Symphony.*
He looked [at it] and felt better and smiled—"Now that's something
like"—etc. etc. But then came a joke on both of us, for in it were
some pages of the *Tone Roads* and some part of the *Trio* (the college
days Scherzo, I think, or the first movement).[4] He stared at [it], then
threw it [down] and went out of the room—and went home that
afternoon.

T23m   After he went, I had a kind of a feeling which I've had off and on
when other more or less celebrated (or well known) musicians have
seen or played (or tried to play) some of my music. I felt (but only
temporarily) that perhaps there must be something wrong with me.
Said I to myself, "I'm the only one, with the exception of Mrs. Ives
(and one or two others perhaps, Mr. Ryder, Dr. Griggs),[5] who likes
any of my music, except perhaps some of the older and more or less
conventional things. (Why do I like these things?) Why do I like to
work in this way and get all set up by it, while (others only get upset
by it) and it just makes everybody else mad, especially well known
musicians and critics—for instance Dave Smith and Max Smith[6]—nice
boys! (Are my ears on wrong? No one else seems to hear it the same
way. Perhaps I'd better go back to Mr. Jadassohn.)"

This *Third Sonata* (the *Fourth* called the *Third*) is a good sample of
an occasional result of the above kind of experience. The last movement
especially shows a kind of reversion. The themes are well enough, but
there is an attempt to please the soft-ears and be good. The sonata on
the whole is a weak sister.[7] But these depressions didn't last long, I'm
glad to say. I began to feel more and more, after seances with nice
musicians, that, if I wanted to write music that, to me, seemed worth
while, I must keep away from musicians.

4 All this is typical of the way Ives was apt to tuck things away.
5 A too hasty reading by the Cowells of this small balloon resulted in the occasionally
quoted misnomer, "Ralph D. Griggs." It was part of Francis Ryder's farm in West
Redding that Ives bought (not directly from him) in 1912. For John Cornelius Griggs
see App. 15.
    Ives always felt that Francis Ryder had much bigger potentialities than were apparent
in his farmer's life—that he would have made a good scientist. His inquiring mind was
intrigued by Ives's music and playing, which he enjoyed listening to, sometimes for too
long, as implied at the end of *Study #4:* "Thus played at Redding Concert! July 3—
1914 . . . before F. Ryder! The audience then goes out and breaks or rocks—by Sky
Rocket—for Danbury!" (might the "Sky Rocket" be Ives's horse, "Rocket"?)
6 For Dave Smith see §47, note 3—for Max Smith see §47, note 12.
7 However, playing it with Daniel Stepner, Yale '72, has shown the editor that Ives's
genius made this triadic idiom just as fresh and strong as any experiment. His dissatis-
faction might have been partly with his own metrics in the first two movements (see §30,
note 5). For instance, on page 9 it's hard to make *Beulah Land* "slower and swinging"
(as he wrote) if the barlines contradict the rhythm.

25

The *Fifth Sonata* (called the *Fourth*) is but an attempt to write a sonata which Moss White (then about twelve years old) could play.[1] The first movement kept to this idea fairly well, but the second got way away from it, and the third got about in between. Moss White couldn't play the last two, and neither could his teacher.[2] It is called "Children's Day" because it is based principally on the church hymns sung at the children's services.

At the summer Camp Meetings in the Brookside Park, the children (more so the boys) would get marching and shouting the hymns—as *Work while the day is . . .* , *Bringing in the sheaves* (not in this sonata), *Gather at the River,* etc. And the slow movement [recalls] a serious time for children, *Yes, Jesus loves me*—except when old Stone Mason Bell and Farmer John[3] would get up and shout or sing—and some of the boys would rush out and throw stones down on the rocks in the river. At the end of the slow movement, sometimes a distant Amen would be heard—the violin holding the last E, and the piano playing the high A and middle C$\sharp$ again *pppp*, then letting the upper A come down to G$\sharp$ and the lower C$\sharp$ to B. But this Amen is a very much ad libitum matter, and may not be wanted except on a few occasions (or when the spirit moves!)—seldom if ever by the Methodists or the Baptists, (Yes, by the Congregationalists and Episcopalians)—when they were leading the meeting!

It was all composed quickly within two or three weeks in the fall of 1916.[4] The last movement in some ways is the best, and part of it was put into a song in 1921. (Since writing this, I have found a manuscript which makes me remember Dave Twichell and Saranac Lake in the summer of 1905[5]—after a prayer meeting—and making a little tune for trumpet and piano, *Shall We Gather at the River,* a tune Dave was very fond of—and they happened to sing it at the meeting that night. This was later worked into the *Fourth Violin Sonata.*)

[1] Moss White Ives (born 1905) would have been twelve in 1917, but see below.
[2] Perhaps not David Talmadge (see §46) but Clarence Nowlan (1872–1961), a Danbury violinist and teacher, with whom Moss White studied later on. Nowlan had played baseball with Ives in "The Alerts" in 1889–90, and violin under George Ives, for whose conducting he retained a deep admiration.
[3] This may be the "Alfred Bell, mason" who appears in Danbury directories of the 1880s. "Farmer John" can hardly be identified, there being no such surname in the directories.
[4] This is another example of how reluctant Ives could be to divulge how his music had evolved. See App. 3, #86.
[5] This memo (on a sketch for mm. 19–30 of the 3rd mvt.) reads: "started as cornet & Violins Qu piece 1905 (with Dave C T at Saranac) finished later as violin Sonata."

26

T24m   The *Second String Quartet* [called by the Cowells the *Pre-Second*]
was written around 1904–1906 (this was not copied and not kept, much
of it)—and in some ways it's not as good as the string quartet music
[the *First String Quartet*] written for some of the revival services while
m24   in Center Church, New Haven, in 1896–97. It is a series of short movements, each movement having its own theme. They were supposed to
be related only by contrasts—that is, related only by not being related.
Some of these had a piano part, some a bass, some a flute. Some of
these were used later or turned into other things, as songs, *Hymn,* etc.—
Hallowe'en, Hook and Ladder.[1] In short, this string quartet was not
t24m   a string quartet at all—perhaps maybe because of the fact that the
Kneisel Quartet played so exquisitely "nice" that I lost some respect
for those four instruments. A whole evening of mellifluous sounds, perfect cadences, perfect ladies, perfect programs, and not a dissonant
cuss word to stop the anemia and beauty during the whole evening.
It was probably my fault, but it somehow got me in wrong with the
string quartet. And when some properly dressed musician would say,
"That would make a good theme for a string quartet"—then, whatever
the theme was, I'd begin to lose interest right off. "You're prejudiced"
n24   they'd say—and I'd say "You betcha, and glad of it!" I got to feel, at a
Kneisel Quartet concert, finally that I was resting my ears on a par-
fumed sofa-cushion—so got out!
24   Some of this had a piano part, making it a quintet. I can find only
two movements[2] of this *Second String Quartet,* though parts of the
other movements were put into some of the songs published in the Song
Book in 1921,—for instance: #9[b], p. 18, *Vita;* #12, p. 27, [*Remembrance*]; #14, p. 29, *The Indians;* #20, p. 47, *Hymn* (a high cello taking
the tune). The song, *Like a Sick Eagle,* #26, p. 61, is not, as I remember,
a part of this quartet, but was for strings, piano, and an English horn
taking the air.

1 For *Halloween* see §32. For *The Gong on the Hook and Ladder* see §19.
2 Might these "two movements" be *Hymn* and *Halloween* (mentioned above)?—and
might the two in App. 3, #60, be different ones? For the *114 Songs* see App. 4. There
are marginal memos indicating that mm. 11–15 (piano) of *Aeschylus and Sophocles*
and some of *Sunrise* (song for voice, and instrument, and piano) were derived from this
Pre-Second String Quartet—also some of *Thoreau* (see §30, at note 12).

27

24   A better *Second String Quartet* was written in 1911, and is one of
the best things I have, but the old ladies (male and female) don't like

it anywhere at all. It makes them mad, etc. [I] think a description of
this better *Second String Quartet* (also [of the] Browning Overture)
was on p. 25—but can't [find it].[1]

m46v　　About that time (after Bass Brigham's call at 70 West 11th Street),[2]
and even before, it used to come over me—especially after coming
from some of those nice Kneisel Quartet concerts[3]—that music had
been, and still was, too much of an emasculated art. Too much of what
was easy and usual to play and to hear was called beautiful, etc.—
the same old even-vibration, Sybaritic apron-strings, keeping music too
much tied to the old ladies. The string quartet music got more and
more weak, trite, and effeminate. After one of those Kneisel Quartet
concerts in the old Mendelssohn Hall,[4] I started a string quartet score,
half mad, half in fun, and half to try out, practise, and have some fun
with making those men fiddlers get up and do something like men.
The set of three pieces for string quartet called: I. Four Men have Discussions, Conversations, II. Arguments and Fight, III. Contemplation
—was done then. Only a part of a movement was copied out in parts
and tried over (at Tam's one day)—it made all the men rather mad. I
didn't blame them—it was very hard to play—but now it wouldn't
cause so much trouble (see photo [of] sketch).

1 App. 3, #61. There is no such description on either side of T25—might Ives have
meant the paragraph below from 46v?
2 See §47, note 18—the address, 70 West 11, was good from 25 June 1908 to 2 May
1911.
3 Ives had been hearing the Kneisel Quartet for many years. In a letter to his father,
Wednesday 24 October 1894, he wrote: "I have bought a ticket . . . for the series of
chamber concerts this winter, [the] Kneisel [Quartet and the] Beethoven Quartet,
etc. . . ."
4 The concert hall of the Mendelssohn Glee Club is listed in Trow at 119 West 40th
Street.

28

T24　　　The *First Piano Sonata,* like many of the other things, had, as a
scherzo movement, some of the early ragtime pieces. Not all of this
sonata has been copied out in ink, although it is all there in lead pencil.
It was finished in 1909 or 1910. Not getting it into more legible shape
is one of the peculiar psychological things hard to explain.[1] When I
finished it, I had expected to get [going] right off and copy it out
plainly. Then, as in many other cases, I got started on something else,
T25m　　and I kept putting it off and putting it off, and for so long a time, that,
when I did look back at it, I had lost interest. And the result is, it's in

1 Ives may be shielding his old friend Griggs, to whom he had lent the unique finished
ink copy of the *First Piano Sonata* (App. 3, #24). After Griggs died at Palo Alto in 1932
(see App. 15), it couldn't be found. This probably started Ives on his photostat project.

the shape seen in the photostat copy. I had the lead-pencil manuscript put into this bound copy principally for my own reference,[2] and so that, if I ever did get down to copy it out, I'd know where to find it. I think that any musician, or at least anyone who is used to my music, could probably copy it out after a little study. Two of the movements used as scherzos are arrangements, from the theatre orchestra scores, of ragtime pieces for piano.[3] There are five movements—(seven movements counting 2a & 2b, 4a & 4b as separate)—and it's pretty long to put on a program. There are pages or sections that may be played, and have been played, as separate pieces or studies. For instance,

After this comma, the rest of the page is still blank (also the back of the leaf), as if Ives had meant to continue. The "instances" would have included Adolph Weiss's conducting *In the Inn* at the New School on Tuesday 16 February 1932, and a brilliant piano performance of it that this editor heard Jerome Moross play, also at the New School around that time.

There might have been something about the way Ives once described to the editor one possible aspect of the scenario: the family together in the first and last movements, the boy away sowing his oats in the ragtimes, and the parental anxiety in the middle movement. As Ives said of *Hawthorne*, "not something that happens, but the way something happens"—and the above is quite different from the memo on p. 7 of the second ink copy of the first movement (written after the negative q1436 was made):

"What is it all about?—Dan S. asks. Mostly about the outdoor life in Conn. villages in the '80s & '90s—impressions, remembrances, & reflections of country farmers in Conn. farmland.

"On page 14 back, Fred's Daddy got so excited that he shouted when Fred hit a home run & the school won the baseball game. But Aunt Sarah was always humming *Where Is My Wandering Boy*, after Fred an' John left for a job in Bridgeport. There was usually a sadness— but not at the Barn Dances, with their jigs, foot jumping, & reels, mostly on winter nights.

"In the summer times, the hymns were sung outdoors. Folks sang (as *Old Black Joe*)—& the Bethel Band (quickstep street marches)— & the people like[d to say] things as they wanted to say, and to do things as they wanted to, in their own way—and many old times . . . there were feelings, and of spiritual fervency!"

The indication "on page 14 back" probably refers to its other side, p. 15 (of the same copy), on which Ives sketched a rambunctious variant of the arpeggi in the 2nd and 3rd lines of page 3 of the Peer edition.

[2] Ives had several photostat copies of the *First Piano Sonata* bound, the most important one being his own, with many excellent changes. Unfortunately this set of positives was mostly too dark, on which the pencil revisions, grey on grey, can sometimes be read only by tilting the page to catch a reflection of light. It could never be satisfactorily photographed.

[3] App. 3, #20.

Ives uses Lowry's *Where Is My Wandering Boy Tonight* less often and less prominently in the sonata than Zundel's *Lebanon:* "I was a wandering sheep . . ." Normally, in Ives's larger works, their tunes are melodically related. These two start as each others' inversions, and in the clear statement of *Lebanon* at the end of the first movement, Zundel's cadence is colored by Lowry's.

See also Lou Harrison's perceptive foreword, *On Ives' First Piano Sonata,* in the Peer edition.

29

T26m

The idea of the *Second Piano Sonata* came originally from working on some overtures representing literary men—for instance, Walt Whitman, Browning, Matthew Arnold, Emerson—and I had in mind starting one (in a general way) on Whittier and [one on] Henry Ward Beecher.[1]

m20v

(The score of the second Overture, Matthew Arnold, probably has been lost—[for] a song from it see West London in 34 Songs. The overture, Browning (see the song, Paracelsus), was sketched [in] 1912, fully scored, and a good copy is in photostat. [For the] Second String Quartet see old sketches and good copy in the barn files. Descriptions [of] the three above for program notes are filed.)

T26m

These overtures[2] were not all finished in score—in fact I can't find any complete copies except the *Browning*[3] (have since found part of the

m26v

Browning score), which was called a Tone Poem, having got somewhat out of the overture shape. This—as far as I can see the notes in the score, which is hardly more than a sketch in some places—was never copied out in ink, as I remember. It is a kind of transition piece, keeping perhaps too much (it seemed to me) to the academic, classroom habits of inversion, augmentation, etc. etc., in the development of the first theme and related themes. But the themes themselves, except the main second theme, were trying to catch the Browning surge into the baffling unknowables, not afraid of unknown fields, not sticking to the nice main roads, and so not exactly bound up or limited to one key or keys (or any tonality for that matter) all the time. But it seemed (I remember when finishing it) somewhat too carefully made, technically—but looking at it now, most twenty years after, it seems natural and worth copying out.

T26m

I don't think that the *Whittier* or *Walt Whitman* ones got any further

---

[1] This is the one instance where editorial violence has been done to Ives's words. T starts: "The *Second Piano Sonata.* This was worked on mostly between 1911 [changed to 1904] and 1915 when it was finished, but the idea of it came originally from working on some overtures. . . ." But Ives has enough to say about the overtures to justify a separate section, so the opening has been made to do double duty, and the second sentence of section 30 serves also midway in the next-to-last paragraph of section 29.

[2] App. 3, #21.

[3] App. 3, #22.

than sketches. This overture infection (active from brass band days) was somewhere around between 1900 to 1912 or 1913. Some parts of these were made into songs—the Browning *Paracelsus* (#30, p. 71) [in *114 Songs*] and *Walt Whitman* (#31, p. 74)—some parts of these [songs] were new, and some old. I can find nothing left of the *Matthew Arnold Overture* but the first page—I have a hand-organ reflecting the London streets—a part of which is practically the same as the song, *West London* (#105, p. 244 [in *114 Songs*]).

The *Emerson,* which is the first movement of the *Second Sonata,* started (I think, not sure) with the first five measures later put into the song, *Duty* (#9[a], p. 18)[4]—(and was before that a male chorus with orchestra. This shows how one idea or set of ideas goes through so many transitions—for instance shows how a thing goes right on, starting (as this) as a male chorus, then overture or concerto for piano and orchestra, and finally a piano sonata.) It grew into more of a piano concerto, opening with several cadenzas, and gradually becoming more and more unified. The Emerson movement printed in the piano book is a partial reduction for piano from the sketch of this concerto. I can't now find all of this concerto sketch (about six or seven pages marked *Emerson Overture),* but it was originally in three movements: the first (the cadenzas)[5]—then the slow movement (starting with the theme at the top of p. 5 in the printed sonata)—the scherzo was about the same as from p. 8 to 11[6] (also not sure from the pages I find, think the scherzo was cut out or never started)—(but I think the scherzo was never written down, rather given up)—the last movement was about [from] the middle of p. 16 to the end, but this was much longer than in the printed copy.[7]

Some say "Why choose local authors for a reason for music?—people will say you are provincial. Why the local (which is national, and not universal and cosmic)?" I say "O Hell!" to this label monger! If a man is born in a sewer, he smells it and of it—(but he may be nearer a spiritual fragrance than the mayor). God lives somewhere in the Heavens—but ain't he universal?—Emerson lives in Massachusetts—and he's as universal as any writer, probably more so. His manner of speech, his signs, words, and symbols, will be in terms of what he knows (seen, sensed and lived). If he drawls like a Yankee and doesn't imitate an English up-inflect, but speculates ever on the Eternities, he may be as universal as Jupiter—but Arthur will just hear his drawl and put a nice label on it.

4 In the first extant sketch-page of the *Emerson Overture* (Q4450), the two measures that precede the opening of the piano movement have no resemblance to *Duty.*
5 The cadenzas were interpolated into the equivalent of pp. 1–2.
6 Pages 5 and 8–11 are the same in all editions.
7 Page 16 of the first edition corresponds to p. 17 of the revised edition.

There[8] has to be a tag on a bushel of potatoes to be shipped, and probably a label on a manner of talking, but the latter is harder to label—and [it's] not quite as necessary that it should bear a label. Labels in art are popular, easy to make, equally confusing, and usually wrong somewhere. Personally I feel like cussing [at] or at least side-tracking the inevitable tag "modern", "ultra-modern", etc. It has to be used till something else better is found, but just the same the necessity for its existence is too much like that of a nice tombstone (with the wrong dead man).

For instance just to show [how] easily it is to put to opposites, take modern music (as it is generally constituted today) and modern poetry. The trouble with modern music is that [it's] somewhat too intellectual —the brain has [been] working a little more than that bigger muscle underneath (what you may call it, spirit, inner blast, soul?)—while modern poetry (too much of it at least) goes in the opposite direction intellectually—it is putting poetry back where music was in the Suppé, Hérold, little-school-girl lingos—soft, easy entertainment—no brain or any other muscle of man required—(only lips, consonant and nice vowel sounds[9] strung along—and then some publicity agent dresses it up with nice, serious-sounding tags: "expression of experiences—the great subtle metre[10] here (3/8 please) must be felt sub-plus-con-sciously—

Bazoolta cripal   sot zwink!

Mam pleek, gradoggle bloe pleek–har churk!

but a resilto-expresso-equiblo-suo—
suo-freedo-expresso-baloozto—

(note [that] the 'o' is not the common 'o' as in 'medico'—but is the mystico interconnection from the self-experienco to the latent self and experienco-suo, [im]plying [that] the association of pre-imagos [is] but the association-self)

---

8 This "extra leaf, m27a," is on note paper of the Red Star Line (S.S. Pennland, New York to Southampton, 10–19 August 1934), and is headed: "Somewhere in Memos—'labels'." (See also §5, note 1.)
9 Ives wrote this word clearly as "songs"—it is tempting to conjecture that he meant "sounds," but he may very well have meant "songs" ironically.
10 Ives, who always spelled "theater", "center", and "meter", may have meant "metre" to look affected.

Mush, Swink, Plush,
Crush, Pansy, Mush.

then a croono ‖: a e i o u o i e a :‖

To communicate the self-essence of this true poetic-psalm is to transfer its pan-conscious message to the great, eternal Self!")[11]

m27a
p. 2
Yet Henry Cowell and Gertrude Stein are both labeled modern. I don't call Henry modern because I don't like to nod, but he is—one of the best of them—and I don't call Gertrude Stein modern because she isn't—she's Victorian without the brains. She has something she wants to sell, so perhaps in that she may get in on "modern." So you see how much the label is like the mouse Kitty has and has not!

[11] Though Ives mentions Gertrude Stein, neither the prose nor the "verse" lampoons her style directly.

30

T26m
The *Second Piano Sonata*—this was worked on mostly between 1911 and 1915[1] (when it was finished)—but the idea of it came originally from working on some overtures. The Emerson movement printed in the piano book is a partial reduction for piano from the sketch of the *Emerson Overture.*

T27m
The four transcriptions in the photostat copy[2] made a few years ago are nearer to the original and general plan—(and at the same time the inserts, and changed ways (some optional) of playing, etc.). This is, as far as I know, the only piece which, every time I play it or turn to it, seems unfinished. Even the photostat transcriptions, as they stand, are not exactly as I play them now. In these transcriptions, there are some things from the overture sketch that were not put in the printed copy— and there are several things in these (and especially in the way that I play them today) that were not in either. It is a peculiar experience and, I must admit, a stimulating and agreeable one that I've had with this Emerson music. It may have something to do with the feeling I have about Emerson, for every time I read him I seem to get a new angle of thought and feeling and experience from him. Some of the four transcriptions as I play them today, especially the first and third, are changed considerably from those in the photostat—and again I find that I don't play or feel like playing this music even now in the same way each time.[3] Some of the passages now played haven't been written

[1] Ives's playing the whole sonata for Max Smith in 1912 (see App. 7, §1) defines the date of composition as mostly 1911–12. See also App. 8.
[2] See App. 8. The "photostat copy" is from the copy by Emil Hanke (Q4921–34).
[3] In the Ives Collection there are five sets of positives with many changes in Ives's hand, all somewhat different.

out—(and some are in the short piano pieces and studies)[4]—and I don't know as I ever shall write them out, as it may take away the daily pleasure of playing this music and seeing it grow and feeling that it is not finished. (I may always have the pleasure of not finishing it) and the hope that it never will be—although shortly I think I shall make a record, perhaps playing each movement two or three different ways. This will be done more for my own satisfaction and study, and also to save the trouble and eyesight of copying it all out. After the record is made, Mr. Henry Cowell, Mr. Nicolas Slonimsky, or some other acoustical genius, could write it down for me—and probably better than I can.[5]

T28m

(Just [back] from 3 Abbey Road, London, June 12, 1933.[6] Machinery! —and what everything else is, and the other side of life as machinery, or as a result of its influence and fixtures—all of this, whatever the above means, I saw this a.m. I wanted to record (for my own observation) certain passages of piano things of mine. In the first place you have to be there at a certain time—so does Paderewski when he gives an 8:31 concert. How do you know at 8:31 that you are going to feel like playing note #92? Then you have to play what you have to play, which may not be exactly what you have to play. A bell rings—two bells—and a nice red light starts—and you start. You get going, going good maybe the first time, as I did this a.m. Then the nice engineer comes back and says you took over four minutes, and the last part was not recorded. As I remember, the last part was the only part of the above "going good" part. Then he played it over—it happened to be one of the best [times] that I've played it—so I told him that was just

m38v
tm

4 Among the *Studies* (now no longer complete), Nos. 2 and 9 (*The Anti-Abolitionist Riots*) are from two of the "centrifugal cadenzas" for the Emerson concerto.

5 Here Ives seems to betray a suspicion that, in the notation of his music, he may not always have found the best metric presentation. He must have been fully aware of his love for unduly prolonging a regular meter, just for the fun of the cross-accents, even if the rhythm had called for a metric shift. He is completely right, for instance, in *Hawthorne*, bottom of p. 34 of the revised edition, where the recurring 5/16 pattern is conceived within the 2/4 ragtime meter—but completely wrong in *General Booth*, mm. 42–46, where there is no justification for displacing the rhythmic sense of both words and music by one beat.

6 Among Ives's papers are two sets of bill-and-receipt, dated 8 and 13 June, 1933 from the Columbia Graphophone Company, Ltd., 102–108 Clerkenwell Road, London E.C.I. Since these offices are over three miles from the Abbey Road studios (N.W.8), one may presume from Ives's ms. date, "June 12—33," that both bills were one day later than the sessions in question, and therefore that Ives recorded two 10-inch sides on Wednesday 7 June, and two 12-inch sides on Monday 12 June. The matrices no longer exist, and pressings of only the two 12-inch sides survive.

The m and t versions differ greatly (m full of a fresh immediacy, t recalling other factors and details), but both describe a session involving more than only two sides, and may quite possibly be a complex of the two sessions. This editing combines whatever is most characteristic in both, omitting redundancies.

Henry Cowell recalled Ives's saying of these records that he could have played those things better with one hand tied behind his back. Ives obviously felt that they should be kept strictly confidential.

O.K., and I'd play some of the other passages. Then he says—"What?
—that recording is all gone—we didn't keep [it]—it was only to get
the time"—!! So I had to play it again—and it was awful this time—
sweaty fingers, short of breath, everything going wrong, wrong notes,
rhythm dying, mad inside, cussing under your breath. Then the man
comes in and says "This is all recorded"—even the cuss words. Then
just as I was going good again, the red light [goes out] and the buzzer
sounds, and the time is up. The next record has to start in the beginning
of the last measure—but how can you dive off a rock when you're in
the middle of the pool? So I told him I'd start all over again, and this
time I got started going wrong and kept it up perfectly, and it was
recorded perfectly! Now what has all this got to do with music?—this
is the business of music as it is today! It's all just music to make business, rather than the business to make music. A man may play to himself and his music starts to live—then he tries to put it under a machine,
and it's dead!)

T28m   The second movement, *Hawthorne*, as stated above, started principally with the *Celestial Railroad* idea—(in two pieces for piano, take-
offs: *The Celestial Railroad*, around pages . . . . . , *The Slaves' Shuffle*,
pages . . . . . , [also the] *Demons' Dance around the Pipe*,[7]—and were
written on our first vacation at Pell's, September 1909)[8]—and it was
thought of at first as a piece for two pianos, or two pianos and four
players. But in having the music published, it was reduced for one
piano—(at end of first [ink] copy, marked "Oct. 12, 1911"). For instance, on p. 25, published score, there are groups of notes which
originally were intended to be played by a second piano off the stage
or in another room. These were played by pushing down very lightly
with a strip of board 14¾ inches long with felt on one edge. It gives a
kind of sound of distant reverberations that one may hear in the woods
under certain conditions. Then, on the third staff, in the third measure,
from the eighth group of notes, this is played in the same way on the
first piano, but not struck, so that the lower piano part (which becomes
louder here) will start the strings vibrating.[9] The nine groups written
in the same way from here to the top of p. 26 are played in the same
way. It takes some practice to get this effect going just right, and the

7 In this balloon, Ives twice left spaces for page numbers, but never filled them in. In
Elliott Carter's copy, the 3rd line of p. 22 is labeled "Celestial Railroad"; one may
imagine the "Slaves' Shuffle" to be the second ragtime (starting on p. 37 of the revised
edition); in a marked copy, at the end of the 2nd line of p. 23, the right hand is labeled
"(demons)"———the left [Feathertop's] "(pipe rim)." But all this seems to suggest that
Hawthorne started out as a set of short pictures.
8 For Pell Jones's, see §20, note 2. According to *Our Book*, the Iveses left New York for
Elk Lake on Friday 20 August 1909, and were "home again" at 70 West 11th Street by
Monday 13 September.
9 The effect Ives describes here can hardly be satisfactory in a public hall—far better to
make these clusters sound at an appropriate volume.

T29m idea has been misunderstood by the great majority of people who have seen the music. It has also given some of the soft-ears a chance to get off the usual remark about this matter, "usual" because they all say it in the same way, with the same words and same looks, as though they thought that nobody else but they would say it. The footnote in English words at the bottom of this page is the only thing in the sonata that most of these dress shirts can read.

m28v The piano piece, *Celestial Railroad,* that Rovinsky played at concerts
tm a few years ago,[10] is an arrangement (and not any too good a one at that) for piano from parts of the Hawthorne movement of the *Second Sonata,* but mostly from the second movement of the *Fourth Symphony* (which was worked at about the same time and finished later when the last movement was made, winter 1913–14).

T29m *The Alcotts* (1913) and the *Thoreau* movement (1915) were both written[11] in a comparatively short time in the summer of 1913—(first summers we were in Redding—1913 and summer of '14). I did have [in mind], in connection with these, an organ, some strings, a flute, etc., but never got very far away from the piano. (Two passages, p. 61–64–63 from top, in the Thoreau movement, were from a slow movement of a string quartet, 1905,[12] but never finished or kept except this part. *The Alcotts* started as a short piece.)

m29 Some nice people object to putting attempted pictures of American authors and their literature in a thing called a sonata, but I don't apologize for it or explain it. I tried it because I felt like trying [it], and so, Good night shirt! Rollo! The attempt is more politely stated in the first page of the published sonata.[13]

T53m The Book of Essays, which was published at the same time as the Concord music, was written mostly while at Asheville in 1919,[14] and finished in New York in 1920. Some of these passages relating to Emerson, Thoreau, and some of the music [was] subject matter taken from

---

[10] Anton Rovinsky played it at Albany on 30 October 1928, at a Pro Musica concert in Town Hall, New York, on 14 November, and in his own recital at Town Hall on 20 November.

[11] More exactly "revised"—see note 1, above.

[12] Pages 61–64–63 of the first edition correspond to pp. 59–62–61 of the revised edition. See §26.

[13] Here Ives added: "Also see the attached sheet ⬙ "—but no leaf with this sign has showed up.

[14] The Iveses spent two months, January 16 through March 18, at Asheville. Various diary entries refer to the essays and the sonata (C = Ives's hand, H = Mrs. Ives's). In January, Monday 20 (H): "Charlie finishing up copy of Sonata Prologue"—Tuesday 21 (C): "C. worked at Thoreau, trying to write something to make people think Thoreau movement sounds like Thoreau"—In February, Wednesday 5 (C): "C. finishes Thoreau" —Saturday 8 (C): "C got his copies of his Thoreau from stenographer at B[attery] P[ark] Hotel"—Saturday 15 (H): "C . . . copying music"—Thursday 20 (C): "Emerson, Alcotts & Thoreau all finished & copied—3 movements"—In March, Thursday 6 (C): "Emerson refutes something by the whole and then unrefutes it by the same whole."

former papers. One, which (on p.   )[15] gives Emerson's influence, was from an article handed in to the Yale Literary Magazine when I was a Senior, and promptly handed back.

15 The page number was never filled in. One may wonder if he meant the story about the working woman, toward the end of the Emerson Essay.

31

T30m

The *First Orchestral Set,* called *Three Places in New England* (though before it had the nice name of *New England Symphony*),[1] was completely scored for a large orchestra in 1914[2]—but it has a varied history, or a life with a past. Some of the things in the second movement, *The Children's Holiday at Putnam's Camp,* were from, and suggested by, an overture and march for theatre orchestra or small brass band in 1902–03 (see old scores and sketches, some pages of which are [in] photostat copies, as the lead-pencil notes and paper were getting faint and worn and hard to make out). Some of these chords and rhythms came about, to a certain extent, from the habit of the piano-drum-playing referred to above. These pieces were called *March and Overture, 1776.*[3] The trio of the march was not used in this set, but was used in the *Fourth of July* score, which was finished before this piece, about 1911–12. It will be noticed in this trio that the tune *The Red, White and Blue* was set over chords of 4ths and 5ths, and that they don't go well together for some acoustical reason—and this trio was left out of this second movement. I first remember working on this when we had just built the little cabin on Pine Mountain,[4] Danbury, and the *1776 Overture* was started at the suggestion of Uncle Lyman, who had written a revolutionary play called *Benedict Arnold,*[5] and we were talking about making it into an opera. This must have been in the summer of 1903, for Uncle Lyman died in the spring of 1904. This second movement . . .

With these words p. 30 of T ends, and p. 31 is missing (both original and carbon), only m31v surviving in t. Ives would have given some of the program note to *Putnam's Camp* (on p. 20 of the Birchard and Mercury printings), the dreaming child being either himself or a composite including himself. It follows complete:

1 App. 3, #64. For still another title, *Three New England Places,* see §4.
2 The old full score on oblong paper (no longer complete) was for large orchestra: winds in pairs, 4 horns, 2 trumpets, 3 trombones and tuba, tympani and percussion, strings.
3 Ives leaves one in doubt whether he is referring only to "1776" (ms. title: *Overture and March "1776"*) or to both "1776" and the *Country Band March.* Both were apparently composed in 1903 (or 1903–04?) and were dovetailed in 1911 into *Putnam's Camp,* of which mm. 1–49 and 120–54 are from the *Country Band March,* 80–113 and 159–63 from "1776." The trio used in *The Fourth of July* is from "1776."
4 The cabin on Pine Mountain (3 m. SW of Danbury) was built in 1903 (see App. 17).
5 For this play and a note on Uncle Lyman see App. 20.

"Near Redding Center, Conn., is a small park preserved as a Revolutionary Memorial; for here General Israel Putnam's soldiers had their winter quarters in 1778–1779. Long rows of stone camp fire-places still remain to stir a child's imagination. The hardships which the soldiers endured and the agitation of a few hot heads to break camp and march to the Hartford Assembly for relief, is a part of Redding history.

"Once upon a '4th of July,' some time ago, so the story goes, a child went there on a picnic, held under the auspices of the First Church and the Village Cornet Band. Wandering away from the rest of the children past the camp ground into the woods, he hopes to catch a glimpse of some of the old soldiers. As he rests on the hillside of laurel and hickories, the tunes of the band and the songs of the children grow fainter and fainter;—when—'mirabile dictu'—over the trees on the crest of the hill he sees a tall woman standing. She reminds him of a picture he has of the Goddess of Liberty,—but the face is sorrowful— she is pleading with the soldiers not to forget their 'cause' and the great sacrifices they have made for it. But they march out of camp with fife and drum to a popular tune of the day. Suddenly a new national note is heard. Putnam is coming over the hills from the center,—the soldiers turn back and cheer. The little boy awakes, he hears the children's songs and runs down past the monument to 'listen to the band' and join in the games and dances.

"The repertoire of national airs at that time was meagre. Most of them were of English origin. It is a curious fact that a tune very popular with the American soldiers was *The British Grenadiers*. A captain in one of Putnam's regiments put it to words, which were sung for the first time in 1779 at a patriotic meeting in the Congregational Church in Redding Center; the text is both ardent and interesting."

[The captain's words have been re-discovered by the vigilant assistant town clerk of Redding, Miss Ebba Anderson, in the *Illustrated Guide to Putnam Memorial Camp* by Charles Burr Todd (1927), on p. 24. The meeting was a state dinner of the recently organized Redding Masonic Lodge on Thursday 25 March 1779. "After dinner the following songs were given for the entertainment of the company: *Hail America; Montgomery; French Ladies' Lament; The Mason's Daughter; On, On, My Dear Brethren; Huntsmen; My Dog and Gun.*"

Todd's footnote adds: "The song, *Hail America*, was the most popular in the army. We give it entire. It was sung to the tune of *The British Grenadiers*.

That seat of science, Athens,
 And earth's great Mistress, Rome,
Where now are all their glories?
 We scarce can find the tomb.
Then guard your rights, Americans,
 Nor stoop to lawless sway,
Oppose, oppose, oppose, oppose,
 My brave America.

Proud Albion's bound to Caesar
 And numerous lords before,
To Picts, to Danes, to Normans,
 And many Masters more.
But we can boast, Americans,
 We never fell a prey,
Huzza, Huzza, Huzza, Huzza
 For brave America.

We led fair freedom hither
  And lo, the desert smiled,
A Paradise of pleasure
  Was opened in the wild.
Your harvest, bold Americans,
  No power shall snatch away,
Assert yourselves, yourselves, ye sons
  Of brave America.

Torn from a world of tyrants,
  Beneath the western sky
We formed a new dominion,
  A land of Liberty.
The world shall own its Masters here,
  The heroes of the day,
Huzza, Huzza, Huzza, Huzza
  For brave America.

God bless this maiden climate,
  And through her vast domain
Let hosts of heroes cluster,
  Who scorn to wear a chain.
And blast the venal sycophants
  Who dare our rights betray,
Preserve, Preserve, Preserve, Preserve
  Our brave America.

Lift up your heads, my heroes,
  And swear with proud disdain:
The wretch who would enslave you
  Shall spread his snares in vain.
Should Europe empty all her force,
  We'd meet them in array,
And shout and shout, and fight and fight
  For brave America.

Some future day shall crown us
  The masters of the main,
And giving laws and freedom
  To England, France and Spain.
When all the isles o'er ocean spread
  Shall tremble and obey
Their Lords, their Lords, their Lords,
    the Lords
  Of brave America."

These words are indeed "ardent", their rhythmic character suggesting a slight variant of the tune, perhaps:

Ives must have found "interesting" the pronunciations of "America" and "Liberty" shown by the rhymes.]

Ives would also have given some of the background of *The 'St. Gaudens' in Boston Common*—Col. Robert Gould Shaw (1837–63) organizing the regiment of negro soldiers in the Union Army, and the monument by Augustus Saint-Gaudens (1848–1907) unveiled in 1897—perhaps using some words of the prefatory poem [variants below from sketches in Q0976]:

Moving—Marching—Faces of Souls!
Marked with generations of pain,
Part-Freers of a Destiny,

Slowly, restlessly swaying us on with you
Towards other Freedom!

The man on horseback,
Carved from a native quarry
Of the world's Liberty-rock
Your country was made from—

You—Images of a Divine Law,
Carved in the shadow of a saddened heart—
Never light-abandoned—
Of an Age and of a Nation!

Above and beyond that compelling mass
Rises the drum-beat of the common-heart,
In the silence
Of a strange and sounding afterglow—
Moving—Marching—Faces of Souls!

Ives would also have recalled his dismay at finding a leaf of *The St. Gaudens* tucked into the score of the *First Symphony* that he was showing to Walter Damrosch (see §14),—the first word of p. 32 of T being apparently the last word of a sentence quoted from a letter (no longer extant) confirming the reading session of 19 March 1910, at the regular time of Saturday morning's

T32m   rehearsal." The result of his playing it is referred to above. The first movement of this *First Symphony* was not shown to Wally, as it went into several different keys, and it had not been favorably received by Professor Parker.[6]

t31vm   This incident brings the mind back to the past, for everything that Wally said, and the way he said it—his looks, his manner, his motions, the stream of his voice, comment, and reply (by stick)—remind me of everybody of that breed (I mean mentally, not racially) that I had run into, before and behind, since and hereafter. They all run [true] to form when they talk about the same thing or anything. As an example, they have a glib hand-out—the label "workmanship" is one of their easy fall-backs. I don't remember one of them that fell back on the word "workmanship" that didn't mean just one and the same thing, "groove made technique," reflecting almost literally some sofa-cushion formulism which they've slept on for generations—the little, usual, tried-out, played-out expediences in harmony, melody, time—(rhythm is beyond them)—every right sound (sound or unsound) in just the nice way they've always seen it done, etc. etc.

So, after playing these three movements of *Symphony No. 1*, Wally

6 See §8, note 10, for the tonal mobility of this same theme in the song. T32: "Professor Parker."—m: "other 'well knowns.' "

turned to Mrs. Ives and said, "This instrumentation is remarkable, and the workmanship is admirable." (But even at that, he said it is too difficult in places, and will take too much rehearsal time—for his pocketbook). This music, at least the last three movements, is, if not the worst (No), one of the worst (No), poorest, weakest things (No) I've ever written. (The last time I played it over, a year or so ago, I felt more like it, I liked it well, and didn't feel the way I did once.) It was written ("written" is the right word) for a degree—that is, to complete my four years academic course at Yale. This was as a kind of an examination, as in the other courses, all of which had to be passed before the B.A. appeared. In other words, the better and more exactly you imitate the Joneses, the surer you are to get a degree. I know, because I got one— Yale '98 B.A.—titulo: "Artium Liberatium Baccalaurei."

m34vt
T32m

I also played this Black March (almost in the shape that it's in today) for Mr. Edgar Stowell, who was then violinist and Director (under David Mannes) of the Music Settlement School Orchestra in West 3rd Street. This was either in the fall of 1910 or 1911, the fall after we had stopped at Pittsfield at the Coolidges and met Mr. Stowell. [He] didn't let me finish playing the movement—said it [sounded] awful to him, and that I ought to write more in the "Geigermusik" style. So I showed him a part of the *Second Symphony* which could be played by string orchestra, and he tried it over. He liked this much better, and conducted it (the Introduction) at one of the school concerts.[7]

m32

There was another movement [of this *First Orchestral Set*] started but never completed, about the Wendell Phillips row and the mob in Faneuil Hall.

T32m

The last movement, *The Housatonic at Stockbridge*, (see photostat sketch) was suggested by a Sunday morning walk that Mrs. Ives and I took near Stockbridge, the summer after we were married. We walked in the meadows along the river, and heard the distant singing from the church across the river. The mist had not entirely left the river bed, and the colors, the running water, the banks and elm trees were something that one would always remember. Robert Underwood Johnson, in his poem, *The Housatonic at Stockbridge*, paints this scene beautifully. I sketched the first part of this movement for strings, flute, and organ shortly after we got home that summer (June 30, 1908).[8] It was scored

T33m

[7] Edgar Stowell (1879–1936) was a violinist in the New York Symphony, and later taught at the Settlement School on 3rd Street, at Bronx House, at Teachers College, and at Horace Mann School.

[8] *Our Book* outlines the Ives's honeymoon from their wedding, Tuesday 9 June 1908—a few days around Salisbury—Sunday 14, morning, church at Great Barrington—walking trip through Monterey, Tyringham, South Lee, Stockbridge, back to Great Barrington— Sunday 21, New Milford and New Preston—Litchfield, Washington, Newton—to New York, Thursday 25, "first night at home" (70 West 11th St.). The next item says: "Tuesday June 30, first meal at our own table—breakfast." (*continued overleaf*)

completely in 1914. In 1921 it was arranged for voice and piano, and put into the song book published that year. In 1929 the score was reduced a little to suit a chamber orchestra, but the difference in the scores was very slight (a tuba and three horns were cut out ad libitum, and the piano took on some of their parts). The photostat score that Slonimsky directed from included the tuba and horn parts, and is practically the same as the first copy (when I had full orchestra in mind). Some of the old score I have intact, but some places were cut out and pasted, to save time when Mr. Hanke made a copy for the smaller orchestra.[9]

Nicolas Slonimsky, upon seeing this score, felt that its derivations came more from America than from Europe. "As a boy in Russia, Slonimsky had read *Uncle Tom's Cabin,* Tales of Hawthorne, Mark Twain, and books of other American authors, and before coming here felt that there must be also some indigenous American music, something growing up from the soil, and that there must be something here besides that heard in Europe—jazz, and music strongly influenced by the European idiom." (Danbury Evening Times, August 6, 1931)

In this connection the following quotation is interesting, from an article, *The Real Frontier,* a preface to Mark Twain by Bernard De Voto (Harper's, June 1931):—"Susy had died and the world grew a more fitting habitation for the damned human race. He was in Lucerne, desperately trying to crowd work over the thought of her. Some of the Fisk singers came there, and he saw the well known chords pierce the apathy of Swiss and Germans who sat behind their beer mugs prepared to be bored. Hannibal could come to Lucerne,[10] and he wrote Joe

T34m

The likeliest date for the Sunday morning walk along the Housatonic seems to be the 28th, presuming that they went back to Stockbridge for the weekend and walked to South Lee, which Mrs. Ives thought possible, "though I can't remember accurately—there was a church all by itself in a field."

9 The full score of *The Housatonic at Stockbridge* in Ives's hand lacks the bottom two staves of each page, and a memo on p. 1 says: "(Mr. Price: Cello and Bass parts are OK and can be pasted on completed score with piano—CEI . . .)." This may set some kind of record for impracticality, but it leaves a tragic textual lacuna.

10 T34 has "would come home to Lucerne"—which changes the sense. The letter was published in Albert Bigelow Paine's edition of Mark Twain's letters (1917, Vol. 2, p. 645), and follows nearly complete:

"Lucerne, Aug. 22, '97.

Dear Joe . . . The other night we had a detachment of the Jubilee Singers—6. I had known one of them in London 24 years ago. Three of the 6 were born in slavery, the others were children of slaves. How charming they were—in spirit, manner, language, pronunciation, enunciation, grammar, phrasing, matter, carriage, clothes—in every detail that goes to make the real lady and gentleman, and welcome guest. We went down to the village hotel and bought our tickets and entered the beer-hall, where a crowd of German and Swiss men and women sat grouped at round tables with their beer mugs in front of them—self-contained and unimpressionable looking people, an indifferent and unposted and disheartened audience—

Twichell that, in the jubilees, America had produced the perfectest flower of the ages, and he wished it were a foreign product, so that she would worship it and lavish money on it and go perfectly crazy over it."

And also further in this connection, when the matter of indigenous or folk art in America brings up the question of the subject matter upon which the indigenous side of art may be based—whether it be backwoods tunes, country fiddlers, Gospel hymns, minstrel shows in music, or hillside or family portraits in painting—the following quotation from *American Folk Art* by Holger Cahill (in *The American Mercury*, September 1931) is also of interest: "Among the gems of American folk painting are the portrait of *Mrs. Freake and Baby* in the Worcester Museum, the *Portrait of a Child* in the Newark Museum, the *Girl's Portrait* which is owned by the Ives family of Danbury, Connecticut,[11] the *Portrait of a Woman* in pastel in the collection of Mr. and Mrs. Elie Nadelman, and the *Girl in Blue* in the collection of the sculptor, Robert Laurent. These portraits are as fine as anything in the world's folk painting, and they are of much more importance, as art, than the work of many a *petit maître*."

---

and up at the far end of the room sat the Jubilees in a row. The Singers got up and stood—the talking and glass jingling went on. Then rose and swelled out above those common earthly sounds one of those rich chords the secret of whose make only the Jubilees possess, and a spell fell upon that house. It was fine to see the faces light up with the pleased wonder and surprise of it. No one was indifferent any more; and when the singers finished, the camp was theirs. It was a triumph. It reminded me of Launcelot riding in Sir Kay's armor and astonishing complacent Knights who thought they had struck a soft thing. The Jubilees sang a lot of pieces. Arduous and painstaking cultivation has not diminished or artificialized their music, but on the contrary—to my surprise—has mightily reinforced its eloquence and beauty. Away back in the beginning—to my mind—their music made all other vocal music cheap; and that early notion is emphasized now. It is utterly beautiful, to me; and it moves me infinitely more than any other music can. I think that in the Jubilees and their songs America has produced the perfectest flower of the ages; and I wish it were a foreign product, so that she would worship it and lavish money on it and go properly crazy over it.

Now, these countries are different: they would do all that, if it were *native*. It is true they praise God, but that is merely a formality, and nothing in it; they open out their whole hearts to no foreigner.

The musical critics of the German press praise the Jubilees with great enthusiasm —acquired technique etc, included.

One of the Jubilee men is a son of General Joe Johnson, and was educated by him after the war. The party came up to the house and we had a pleasant time. . . .

"With love from us all.   Mark."

11 This must be the portrait (about 1790) of Sarane Taylor (1774–1827), later Mrs. Edward Wilcox. The story goes that, when the British were approaching Danbury on 26 April 1777, her family started to flee, but it took some time to find her—she was making mud-pies. Her daughter Sarah (1808–99) married George White Ives, and was Charles Ives's grandmother (see App. 13). Sarah's sister Sarane (1812–69), Mrs. Stevens, was the grandmother of Sarane Seeley (1870–1968), Mrs. Ralph C. Otis, through whose kindness the editor saw this portrait in Chicago in 1959. It is illustrated in Bailey's History of Danbury, facing p. 90.

32

m34
m34v
tm

m73v

m34v

m34v
tm

The incident of Walter Damrosch [talking about "workmanship"] brings to mind that the most recent example of this cushion-tire remark was from Lily-ear #199, Allie Stoessel.[1] He beat time through three little pieces of mine, two jokes and a water color (a thumbnail sketch), at a concert in New York, April 22nd, 1934, which I understood was to be rather an impromptu, semi-serious kind—none or few rehearsals, music fairly easy for players and audience. (The serious one of these two concerts[2] was given in Town Hall two weeks before.) So I picked three short, comparatively easy [pieces]—two of them but kinds of take-offs, *Halloween* (children's party) and *Firemen's Parade on Main Street*, two jokes—and one obvious picture, [*The Pond*]. Ally-boy Stoessel, Professor and Conductor (of old-lady societies etc.) conducts these three things. I didn't go to the concert. But more than one other who did, said (not exactly in these words), "Ally looked as if he didn't know what it was all about—stupid motions, stupid expression on his face, neck, and time beatin'—[he] looked bothered and surprised at the notes"—(all this over three little pieces that should be not difficult for a third-rate conductor—about all he'd to do is to smile and bow—the players have a little harder job, not much). He not only didn't see the joke, but didn't know they *were* jokes, and not nice music.

The first little piece is but a take-off of a Halloween party and bon-fire—the elfishness of the little boys throwing wood on the fire, etc. etc.—it may not be a good joke, [but] the joke of it is: if it isn't a joke, it isn't anything. Even Herbert Hoover could get it,[3] and the average listener always gets it. But Allie took it so serious, and beat time nice and regular, just as serious. I played this about thirty years ago with a little orchestra from a theatre just off the Bowery, in New York—and

---

1 Albert Stoessel (1894–1943), violinist, conductor, composer, was head of the music department of New York University 1923–30, and director of the opera and orchestra departments of the Juilliard School 1930–43.

2 Of these two Pan-American Association programs, the first was music, the second dance with music interludes.

Town Hall, Sunday evening 15 April 1934: Ruggles *Portals*, Roldan *Motivos de Son* (Judith Litante, soprano), Harris *4' 20"*, Salzedo *Harp Concerto* (Salzedo), Ives *The New River, December* (chorus), *In the Night*, Varèse *Ionisation, Ecuatorial*, Weiss *Andante* from the *Chamber Symphony*, McPhee *Piano Concerto* (Josef Wissow).

Alvin Theater, Sunday evening 22 April 1934: Martha Graham & company *Four Casual Developments* (music: Cowell), *Ekstasis* (music: Engel); interlude: Still *Three Dances*; Graham *Primitive Mysteries* (music: Horst).—Intermission—Graham *Primitive Canticles* (music: Villa Lobos; Judith Litante, soprano); interlude: Ives *Halloween, The Pond, The Gong on the Hook & Ladder*; Graham *Frenetic Rhythms* (music: Riegger); interlude: Revueltas *8 X Radio*; Graham *Intégrales* (music: Varèse).

Ives could hardly have referred to the second program as "semi-serious" if he had ever seen Martha Graham dance.

3 Ives was still a Wilsonian Democrat.

it was one of the few (or at least comparatively few) pieces that I remember sounded the first time exactly as I wanted it to sound. The players got it after a little trouble, and everybody seemed to. In this piece, I wanted to get, in a way, the sense and sound of a bonfire, outdoors in the night, growing bigger and brighter, and boys and children running around, dancing, throwing on wood—and the general spirit of Holloween night—(and at the end, the take-off of the regular coda of a proper opera, heard down the street from the bandstand). In spite of the subject matter, this was one of the most carefully worked out (technically speaking), and one of the best pieces (from the standpoint of workmanship) that I've ever done. The four strings play in four different and closely related keys, each line strictly diatonic. Then it is canonic, not only in tones, but in phrases, accents, and durations or spaces. I happened to get exactly the effect I had in mind, which is the only ([or] at least an important) function of good workmanship. Allie S. made some criticism implying that the workmanship was poor—the "four keys to once" didn't seem nice to him.

m36v
tm

So, ladies, you see, whenever now a properly dressed adding machine walks down the middle isle and gets off Western Union Platitude #22, "good workmanship"—I know there's something soft in that job. And if it happens to be any work of mine, then I know there's something wrong with it—at least I have a natural suspicion.

All of which—"on the whole"—"to sum up"—"in the final analysis"—"eleventhly"—"to conclude"—"in a brief summary"—these Rollos are like the chicken fancier who had seen nothing but chickens all his nice lifetime, and had never seen a lion. And so, on seeing a lion enter, he says, "He's built all wrong—no feathers, wrong color, too long, too many feet—he's not like a chicken." Creator, that's poor workmanship! You see above, Rollos, I rather seem to tend to compare my music to a lion, and the music you like to a chicken—which is quite all right, as the other way around would *not* be!—would it, Arthur?

33

T36m

The *Second Orchestra Set* starts with a slow movement which was originally an overture called *An Elegy for*[1] *Stephen Foster*. This was worked on about the same time as the Black March from the first set, and is something like it. The principal tune is no particular one of Foster's but just a kind of remembrance of his music in general. "Down in the cornfield" and other things are thrown in, off-key. According to a memorandum in the lead-pencil score, "37 Liberty Street," it must

[1] T has "of"—m has "to"—probably Ives dictated "for".

have been scored some time before May 1913, when our office was moved from Liberty Street to 38 Nassau Street.[2]

The second movement is but a rehash and combinations of some of the ragtime dances for small orchestra which grew up between 1902 and 1910–11, generally speaking. It takes a good pianist to play the piano part, and this movement is almost a piano concerto. This movement (it was marked [on] the back: "The Rockstrewn Hills join in a People's outdoor Meeting")[3] was completed and fully scored in 1911, the same time that the second movement of the *Theater Orchestra Set* was finished, and they were intended to be put together in one set called *Three Ragtime Dances*,[4] but they worked themselves into other movements instead.

The last movement, in my opinion, is one of the best—that's not the same as saying that it's any too good—it's simply saying that, as far as I'm concerned, I think it's one of the best that I've done. There's a personal experience behind it, the story of which I will now try to tell. We were living in an apartment at 27 West 11th Street.[5] The morning

T37m   paper on the breakfast table gave the news of the sinking of the Lusitania.[6] I remember, going downtown to business, the people on the streets and on the elevated train had something in their faces that was not the usual something. Everybody who came into the office, whether they spoke about the disaster or not, showed a realization of seriously experiencing something. (That it meant war is what the faces said, if the tongues didn't.) Leaving the office and going uptown about six o'clock, I took the Third Avenue "L" at Hanover Square Station.[7] As I came on the platform, there was quite a crowd waiting for the trains, which had been blocked lower down, and while waiting there, a hand-organ or hurdy-gurdy was playing in the street below. Some workmen sitting on the side of the tracks began to whistle the tune, and others began to sing or hum the refrain. A workman with a shovel over his shoulder came on the platform and joined in the chorus, and

2 This move can be dated exactly by a memo in Ives's hand: "Feb. 16, 1914—1st day of business in new offices . . . ." The New York telephone directory of 16 October 1913 lists Ives & Myrick still at 37 Liberty, that of 5 February 1914 already at 38 Nassau.
3 In both the score-sketch and the pencil score of this movement, the lower corners have been torn off the final pages. Perhaps one of these missing corners had the title. The version in App. 3, #82, has "in the" instead of "in a".
4 App. 3, #20.
5 In *Our Book* Mrs. Ives recorded: "1914 . . . October in Redding. Nov., took apartment at 27 W. 11th . . . 1915 . . . May 8th, to Redding."
6 The Lusitania was torpedoed Friday 7 May 1915 at 2 p.m., and sank by 2:30, only a few miles southwest of Queenstown (Cobh)—9:30 a.m. New York time. Ives's memory of the morning papers at breakfast must be of Saturday's, but the news would have spread quickly on Friday, and the scene described must have taken place late Friday afternoon (on Saturday, 8 May, the Iveses went up to Redding).
7 Hanover Square is south of Wall Street, where Stone and Pearl Streets come together in a triangle. The elevated trains, then so common in New York, have been replaced with bus lines and subways.

the next man, a Wall Street banker with white spats and a cane, joined in it, and finally it seemed to me that everybody was singing this tune, and they didn't seem to be singing in fun, but as a natural outlet for what their feelings had been going through all day long. There was a feeling of dignity all through this. The hand-organ man seemed to sense this and wheeled the organ nearer the platform and kept it up fortissimo (and the chorus sounded out as though every man in New York must be joining in it). Then the first train came in and everybody crowded in, and the song gradually died out, but the effect on the crowd still showed. Almost nobody talked—the people acted as though they might be coming out of a church service. In going uptown, occasionally little groups would start singing or humming the tune.

Now what was the tune? It wasn't a Broadway hit, it wasn't a musical comedy air, it wasn't a waltz tune or a dance tune or an opera tune or a classical tune, or a tune that all of them probably knew. It was (only) the refrain of an old Gospel Hymn that had stirred many people of past generations. It was nothing but—*In the Sweet Bye and Bye*.[8] It wasn't a tune written to be sold, or written by a professor of music—but by a man who was but giving out an experience.

This third movement is based on this, fundamentally, and comes from that "L" station. It has its secondary themes [and] rhythms, but widely related, and its general make-up would reflect the sense of many people living, working, and occasionally going through the same deep experience, together. It would give the ever changing multitudinous feeling of life that one senses in the city. This was completed and all scored (as it stands now) in the fall of that year, 1915.

About two or three years ago, Mr. Anton Rovinsky came up to the house and said that he was looking for a piano concerto, and asked if I had one. I played over this movement for him, and he said, "Why, that theme! Do you know what that is? That's the I.W.W. marching song."[9] He said he'd heard it sung in a Western city, and, the way it came to him, it sounded as strong [as], if not finer than, the *Marseillaise*. I didn't know, until Rovinsky told me, that the I.W.W. had also caught something from this remnant of American folk art that has been so long belittled and despised by too many nice, respectable, well-intentioned but unimaginative Americans with arrested muscles above the neck, especially those who have too much to say in musical and other circles today,—and who say, think, deride, or approve only what some busi-

[8] Written about 1867, words by Dr. Sanford Filmore Bennett (1836–98), tune by Joseph Philbrick Webster (1819–75), best known as arranged by Hubert P. Main.
[9] In the *Red Song Book* (New York, Workers Library Publishers, 1932), the tune of *In the Sweet Bye and Bye* appears on p. 12 as *The Preacher and the Slave* ("Music arranged by J. Schaefer. . . . Chorus: You will eat—bye and bye. . . . Tempo: brisk and mocking").

ness-man-musician-European (with a bigger reputation than anything else) has carefully told them to say, think, deride, or approve. The great trouble is that the commercialists are always (most always) on the side of the conventional and so sellable. They are just as unfair or stupid or lazy or musically limited as the nice talkers and writers who are against anything modern (so called) in music or any [other] part of Art. My experience with people like that is that they don't use their ears and minds any harder than a baby uses an axe.

m39v
tm

Since writing about this tune, we heard in June 1933, out of the window [at] 18 Half Moon Street in London,[10] a sound of men singing down near Piccadilly. It came nearer [and] nearer—they were Welsh miners, street singers. What were they singing (slowly, with dignity and reverence, and strongly beautiful)?—*In the Sweet Bye and Bye,* but with Welsh words. And as they passed and turned slowly away up Curzon Street, they began another song. What was that?—some famous old Welsh ballad? No, it was the American Gospel Hymn, *There's a wideness in God's Mercy* (Converse tune).[11] It was sung with an eloquent slowness, not evenly—not fast, precise, and "tinky", as so many nice church organists play it—but here there was a strength of accent, of phrase, of conviction. They sang it like great artists, not like great opera singers.

10 The Iveses lived at 18 Half Moon Street May 23–June 18 and July 14–20 in 1932, and April 29–June 14 in 1933.
11 The hymn, "There's a wideness in God's mercy," by Frederick W. Faber (1814–63) is most often sung to *Wellesley* by Lizzie E. Tourjée, but some hymnals link it with *Erie* (or *Converse*) by Charles Crozat Converse (1832–1918), which is the familiar tune for "What a friend we have in Jesus." Ives made eloquent use of this tune in the first movement of his *Third Symphony* and the middle movement of his *First Piano Sonata.*

34

T40
m40
tm

A set of pieces for orchestra called *Holidays* had its career from 1897 to 1913. These four pieces, movements of a *Holiday Symphony,* take about an hour, and although they were first called together a symphony, at the same time they are separate pieces and can be thought of and played as such—(and also, and as naturally, be thought of and played as a whole). These four pieces together were called a symphony, and later just a set of pieces, because I was getting somewhat tired of hearing the lily boys say, "This a symphony?—Mercy!—Where is the first theme of 12 measures in C major?—Where are the next 48 measures of nice (right kind of) development leading nicely into the second theme in G?" (second Donkey contrasting with Ass #1)—the nice German recipe, etc.—give it a ride, Arthur!—to hell with it!—Symphony = "with sounds" = my Symphony!

Also, there is no special musical connection among these four move-ments, and there is one—that is, I'm not conscious of any in particular —which leads me to observe that quite a number of the larger forms of instrumental music (symphonies, sonatas, suites, etc.) may not always necessarily form, or were originally intended to form, such a complete organic whole that the breath of unity is smothered all out if one or two movements are played separately sometimes. Some musicians have a reverence for doing certain things in a certain way, which is more the result of habit or custom than it is of reason or musical sense. I once suggested to a well known organist that some of the Brahms sympho-nies—some of those great movements (which seem to me to be of the finest and deepest religious import)—be played in church instead of so much of Mailly, Boellmann, Dubois, Lefébure Wély—even Guilmant is pretty weak sometimes ("you know, Eddie, that tinsel-pewed-organ-parfume")—it's about as appropriate to most religious services as a "false face on a corpse."[1] "But no!—why should I insult Brahms?" he shivered—"a symphony is a symphony and not a church organ piece." (He may be quite right.) "Thank you, damn you, thank you." But I am not so sure that Brahms would always feel that way. A horse race at Wells Cathedral Evensong[2] is not as sacred as Brahms's secular music.

The thing that started most of this trouble was some organ pieces for a Thanksgiving Service referred to on p. 7.[3] These pieces were put into a single piece for an orchestra (I am pretty certain) some time around 1904. I remember taking it to copy out when I went to Saranac Lake the following summer in 1905.[4] However, this made me think of making a kind of Holiday Symphony, each movement based on something of the memory that a man has of his boy holidays, rather than any present-day program of such. But this Thanksgiving movement is still in manu-script, and was never fully copied out in ink on score paper. I hope to do this this summer—but the order of each measure is marked in red ink on the different sheets, and it wouldn't be very difficult, after a little study, for anyone to copy this out in more legible shape and on separate score staffs.[5]

1 This sounds like a quote from Mark Twain (not yet identified)—?
2 This image suggests that Ives heard an evensong service raced through at Wells Cathedral (for his feelings about such things see the end of §33). For Monday 19 June 1933, the diary of the trip says: "Day at Wells!" They had been at Bath Saturday, and may have reached Wells Sunday in time for Evensong.
3 That is, on p. 7 of T—see §9.
4 One of the first items in *Our Book* is: "Sept. 1–8, 1905—Saranac Lake, Roberts Camp."
5 No score-sketch of *Thanksgiving* with indications in red ink has showed up. Might there have been one (marked in red), half way from the sketches toward the full score? Mrs. Ives recalled his writing out the full score at Taormina, where they stayed from 30 November 1932 through 14 March 1933. When Ives had it photostated, over the upper right corner of the last page he laid a card reading: "The Lord bless thee, and keep thee; the Lord make his face shine upon thee, and be gracious unto thee; the Lord

The other three movements are pictures of a boy's holidays in a country town: *Decoration Day, The Fourth of July,* and *Washington's Birthday.* In putting these movements together as a kind of a symphony, the *Washington's Birthday* (winter) would go first, the *Decoration Day* (spring) second, *The Fourth of July* (summer) third, and *Thanksgiving* (autumn) last. But these movements have been copied and bound separately, and may be played separately.

---

lift up his countenance upon thee, and give thee Peace." As a postface, he copied out two stanzas from the hymn, "O God, beneath thy guiding hand . . ." by the Rev. Leonard Bacon, written in 1833 for the bicentennial celebration of the founding of New Haven:

> Thou heard'st well pleased the Song of Prayer,
> Thy blessing came, and still its Power
> Shall onward through all Ages beam
> The memory of that Sacred Hour!
>
> Law, Freedom, Truth, and Faith in God!
> Came to those exiled o'er the waves,
> And where their Pilgrim feet have trod
> The God they trusted guards their graves.

35

T41m   The *Washington's Birthday* is for a kind of chamber orchestra: strings, 1 horn, 1 flute, a set of bells, and in the chorus a Jew's harp ad lib. I've always been a good Jew's harp player regardless of consequences, but I don't know exactly how to write for it. The notes on the Jew's harp are but some of the partials of a string, and its ability to play a diatonic tune is more apparent than real. And in this piece, from a half a dozen to a hundred Jew's harps are necessary—one would hardly be heard. In the old barn dances, about all the men would carry Jew's harps in their vest pockets or in the calf of their boots, and several would stand around on the side of the floor and play the harp more as a drum than as an instrument of tones.

The first part of this piece is but to give the picture of the dismal, bleak, cold weather of a February night near New Fairfield (for full description see program at back of music).[1] The middle part and the

---

1 The postface reads:
"'Cold and Solitude,' says Thoreau, 'are friends of mine. Now is the time before the wind rises to go forth and see the snow on the trees.'
"And there is at times a bleakness, without stir but penetrating, in a New England midwinter, which settles down grimly when the day closes over the broken-hills. In such a scene it is as though nature would but could not easily trace a certain beauty in the sombre landscape!—in the quiet but restless monotony! Would nature reflect the sternness of the Puritan's fibre or the self-sacrificing part of his ideals?
"The old folks sit 'the clean winged hearth about,
> Shut in from all the world without,
> Content to let the north wind roar
> In baffled rage at pane and door.'   (Whittier) [*Snow-bound*] (to p. 97)

shorter last part are but kinds of refrains made up of some of the old barn-dance tunes and songs of the day (half humorous, half sentimental, and half serious). As I remember some of these dances as a boy, and also from father's description of some of the old dancing and fiddle playing, there was more variety of tempo than in the present-day dances. In some parts of the hall a group would be dancing a polka, while in another a waltz, with perhaps a quadrille or lancers going on in the middle.[2] Some of the players in the band would, in an impromptu way, pick up with the polka, and some with the waltz or march. Often the piccolo or cornet would throw in "asides". Sometimes the change in tempo and mixed rhythms would be caused by a fiddler who, after playing three or four hours steadily, was getting a little sleepy—or by another player who had been seated too near the hard cider barrel. Whatever the reason for these changing and sometimes simultaneous playing of different things, I remember distinctly catching a kind of music that was natural and interesting, and which was decidedly missed when everybody came down "blimp" on the same beat again. The allegro part of this *Washington's Birthday* aims to reflect this, as well as to depict some of the old breakdown tunes and backwoods fun and comedy and conviviality that are gradually being forgotten. This was completed and scored out in the summer of 1913, though some of the barn-dance stuff had been used before.

If this piece is played separately, without outlining the program, it may give (and it has given) a wrong idea of what it is and what it was made for. These three holiday movements (perhaps less in *Thanksgiving*, which has some religious significance) are but attempts to make pictures in music of common events in the lives of common people (that is, of fine people), mostly of the rural communities. That's all there is to it. There is no artistic purpose—no message for the cosmic world of[3] Bibles—in fact, the more inartistic and unmusical they seem to Rollo, probably the better pictures they are. They could be played as abstract music (giving no titles [or] program), and then they would be just like all other "abstract" things in art—one of two things: a covering up, or ignorance of (or but a vague feeling of) the human something at

---

"But to the younger generation, a winter holiday means action!—and down through 'Swamp hollow' and over the hill road they go, afoot or in sleighs, through the drifting snow, to the barn dance at the Centre. The village band of fiddles, fife and horn keep up an unending 'break-down' medley, and the young folks 'salute their partners and balance corners' till midnight;—as the party breaks up, the sentimental songs of those days are sung half in fun, half seriously, and with the inevitable 'adieu to the ladies' the 'social' gives way to the grey bleakness of the February night."

2 Could this procedure be a popular survival of what is evoked in the three-orchestra scene in Mozart's *Don Giovanni?* Compare also the three deck-orchestras in Ives's sketch for *The General Slocum* (see §37).

3 Ives wrote what looks like "or" but probably meant "of."

its source—or just an emasculated piece of nice embroidery! So if *Washington's Birthday* were put on a program with no program-[notes], the D.A.R. would think it pretended to have something to do with Washington, or his birthday, or "These United States"—or some speech by Senator Blowout!

T46m   The *Washington's Birthday* score I played over, shortly after it was written, in a back room of Tam's Copying Bureau, either in 1913 or early in 1914, with some few men from a theater orchestra that Mr. Greinert or Mr. Price got for me. (This was played twice in the Globe Theater, New York, in Nov. 1914 and spring 1915.) We didn't have all the instruments—no cello nor bass—and, as I remember, we got through it fairly well. A few years later, I think in 1918 or 1919, Reber

T47m   Johnson, who was then Assistant Concertmaster of the New York Symphony Orchestra, arranged to bring some of the orchestra down to try this over for me, when we were living in 120 East 22nd Street.[4] He played one of the violins, Eddie Bachmann, La Prade, and a man whose name I forget, the other violins; Pollain and Harnisch, violas; Schmitt and Rosanoff, cellos; Mr. Possell, flute; and Mr. Reichard, a horn player. These were supposed to be the best men in the orchestra, and they were good musicians—but the old theater orchestra did as well, if not better. They made an awful fuss about playing this, and before I got through, this had to be cut out, and that had to be cut out —and in the end the score was practically emasculated. Harnisch (the viola) was the only one who was not more or less mad at the trouble the music gave them, and seemed interested (the first orchestra player who ever was). However, after four or five rehearsals, it was approximately well played, but only after some of the parts which seemed to me to be the best and strongest, were removed.

This score (as it stood originally with no simplifications) was played in San Francisco in September 1931,[5] Nicolas Slonimsky conducting. It was given then after three rehearsals, and [judging by] the reports from Henry Cowell (who looked over the score while they were playing), and [by] what the critics in the newspapers said (though that's no proof), it was well played. This shows what fifteen years of a little study and practice can do in turning impossibilities into possibilities. These things bring to mind another incident. According to the newspaper reports of this concert, neither the audience nor the critics were

4 The Iveses rented Henry Dwight Sedgwick's house at 120 East 22nd Street for almost nine years—fall 1917 through spring 1926. Elliott Carter retains the impression of a luxurious house—"they lived in great style."
5 On Thursday evening 3 September 1931, at the Community Playhouse, San Francisco, Slonimsky conducted: Riegger *Three Canons for Four Winds*, Stravinsky *L'Histoire du Soldat*, Ives *Washington's Birthday*, Weiss *Chamber Symphony* (first two movements), Prokofieff *Overture on Yiddish Themes* for piano, clarinet, and string quartet.

disturbed to the point of cussing. In fact a San Francisco paper said that the *Washington's Birthday* piece, next to the Stravinsky, was enjoyed most by the audience—(which doesn't mean, by any means, that these two were the best—in fact, from my experience, it would be a reasonable reason why they weren't. But I mention this to show [that] what professional orchestra players didn't like, ten or twelve years later an average audience *would* like, at least more than the old audience did.)

Either in the summer of 1913 or 1914, Mr. Sprague (Harmony's Uncle Albert) and Mrs. Sprague, with their daughter, Mrs. Coolidge, stopped to see us at Redding on their way to Pittsfield.[6] After dinner (before going) daughter says to writer, "Are you still keeping up your music?" Writer says, "Well, yes." So former asks writer to play some of it, and came into the little room with the piano, behind the dining room. I happened to have on the piano the score or the sketch of the Black March (*The St. Gaudens*). I started to play a little of this—daughter's face grew sour. "Do you like those awful sounds?" she said. So I stopped and played something that I thought might be a little less rough on her, which was the first part of *Washington's Birthday*. That made her walk out of the room. In getting into the car, headed toward Pittsfield, she said, "Well, I must say your music makes no sense to me. It is not, to my mind, music. How is it that—studying as you have with Parker—that you ever came to write like that? You ought to know the music of Daniel Gregory Mason, who is living near us in Pittsfield—he has a real message. Good-bye!"[7] The above nice lady has since become

6 Albert Arnold Sprague (1835–1915, Yale '59), son of a Vermont farmer-politician, was a classmate of Joseph Hopkins Twichell. He founded the very prosperous wholesale grocery firm of Sprague & Warner in Chicago, and became a director or a trustee of many Chicago institutions, but kept in touch with Twichell, occasionally visiting at Hartford, so that young Harmony (the future Mrs. Ives) grew up thinking of him as "Uncle Albert."

His daughter Elizabeth (1864–1953), who studied piano with Fanny Bloomfield Zeisler, and married Dr. Frederic S. Coolidge in 1891, devoted her large fortune to musical generosity (the Ives Collection is housed in the building she and her mother gave to Yale in 1917 as a memorial to her father).

7 In spite of the memory of this conversation, Ives probably included Mrs. Coolidge among the recipients of *Concord* early in 1921, and her puzzlement seems to have led to some correspondance with Mrs. Ives, including the following letter:

"The Laurel House, Lakewood, New Jersey,
March 15, 1921.

"My dear Harmony: In accordance with your request I sent a copy of your husband's music to a friend in Boston, who is very interested in new work and modern ideas, and who has given up writing in the European Idiom, and has recently been studying Asiatic music.

"I sent it to him because I did not in the least understand your husband's work myself, and I thought that I could not judge of anything which to me was so foreign. I must confess that I found nothing in it which I liked, but there is so much nowadays that I do not like because I do not understand it that I did not wish to express my opinion about it.

"I have today a response from this gentleman, and it is not encouraging to Charlie's work. I do not want to quote him because I think it would hurt you, but you see I am

quite a celebrated patron of music. Every year she gives somebody
something real nice for something—or something else.

I remember, while working on this *Washington's Birthday,* we went
to a usual symphony concert (sometime end of 1912, or spring 1913,
while living in Hartsdale),—and coming home with a vague but strong
feeling that even the best music we know, Beethoven, Bach, and
Brahms (played at this concert)[8] was too cooped up—more so than
nature intended it should be, or at least needed to be—not only in its
chord systems and relations, lines, etc., but in its time, or rather its
rhythms and spaces—blows or not blows—all up and down even little
compartments, over and over—2 or 3 (prime numbers and their multi-
ples), all so even and nice all the time—producing some sense of weakness, even in the great. And the conductor (I think Fiedler, or some
German—not sure)—what did he do but wear his nice permanent wave

---

trying to be honest in responding to your request, and feel that it is more friendly to
write in this way than not to write at all.

"I do not know whether you are still in Quebec, but I hope that this will ultimately
reach you and that your trip to Canada has proved a pleasant success.

"I sent you today an invitation to hear some of the Quartet compositions which
were sent to our competition last summer, and I thought perhaps that you would be
interested to come and hear them.

"I am still in Lakewood as you see, and am intending to stay here for a while.
With kind regards to your husband, I am, as always,

Affectionately yours,
Elizabeth S. Coolidge."

[The "friend in Boston . . . studying Asiatic music" must be Henry Eichheim (1870–
1942, violinist in the Boston Symphony 1890–1912), who conducted his *Oriental Impressions* at the fourth Coolidge Festival in October 1921.]

Ives's sketch for a reply is bluepencilled "Not Sent":

"Thank you for your letter to Harmony. If it isn't asking too much, I would like to
hear all your Boston friend has to say about my music (I *still* call it that). He can't hurt
my feelings—I've been called all the names in the criminal code. Favorable comment,
to a great extent, is negative—that is, in effect—it sends one up too many "blind alleys."
If I could see some of this man's music, any that is fairly representative of his main
beliefs, I could probably tell whether his criticism will be of value to me, as far as
future work goes. But whatever he says *won't* be discouraging—that can come from
only one source—you forgot that. However don't bother to tell me what he says or
who he is, if you'd rather not. The whole thing, of course, is but an experiment—and
it was not written primarily [to please.] I thought that would be generally understood.
However I was surprised to find so many men were interested in a thing so repellant
in form.

"We had an interesting trip to Quebec. Dave and Ella are much better. They are to
spend the summer with us in Redding. Harmony is well, and we hope to see you when
the Letz quartet plays the new pieces—though I still have to be careful, and can't go
out in the evening unless I can arrange to be away from the office during the day.

Sincerely yours"

[The "one source" is of course Mrs. Ives. The two words in brackets were accidentally
torn out, and are conjectural. The Iveses couldn't get to the quartet program.]

No further correspondence with Mrs. Coolidge was among Ives's papers.

[8] This must be the Boston Symphony, Muck conducting, at Carnegie Hall, Saturday
afternoon 22 February 1913: Mozart *Symphony in g,* Bach *Suite in D,* Brahms *Haydn
Variations,* Beethoven *Egmont Overture.* It was the only such program in New York at
that time, and the booklet of program notes was still among Ives's papers. He probably
went not with Mrs. Ives but with someone else; her father was still at Brattleboro,
and she recalled being there with him the whole time (see end of App. 16).

from I to IV—the ladies smiled nice, and renewed their subscriptions! Same old stuff! It came over me again at that [time] (as it had come over Father):—Is music an emasculated art? No, not all of it—but too much of it, even the best. And a wild idea came to me (it seemed wild then, but not now)—to make a piece that no permanent-wave conductor (of those days) could conduct. I stuck in some of my old piano cycle rhythm studies—2 - 3 - 5 - 7 - 11 - 7 - 5 - 3 - 2 - etc. (see photo—composed for string quartet and piano—"Studies in space, time, duration, accent, pulse" written on front page)[9]—if not good music (though today I think it is), at least good exercise for strengthening the muscles in the mind—and I'm not sure that it doesn't help some in the muscles of the heart and soul (wherever they are)!

Anyway, no mollycoddle mind (like O. G., A. S., W. M. G. D.) could like it, play it, or make any sense [out] of it—there's too much sense in it for that. The cycles grow, expand, ebb, but never literally repeat. When the string quartet are in the "unit" system, the piano is on the meter system, etc. When phrases with no accent [are at a] beginning, a grit chord on the strings starts the space. That "grit chord" (as chord sense) is to do the same thing [as] what, in other phrases, is done by accent, etc. Why should music be so even, so grooved in?—so smooth [that] our ears must become like unto feather beds, our muscles all drop out, and we have to have false-teeth ears to hear it with!

[9] This title became the subtitle of *In Re Con Moto et al,* the end of the sketch being dated: "Hartsdale, N.Y., Apr. 13, 1913" (a Sunday—see App. 3, #37).

36

Decoration Day, for full orchestra—it was started as a brass band overture, but never got very far that way. It was also finished and scored at about the same time the *Washington's Birthday* was.[1] The

[1] See App. 3, #56 and 57. The postface reads:
   In the early morning the gardens and woods about the village are the meeting places of those who, with tender memories and devoted hands, gather the flowers for the Day's Memorial. During the forenoon as the people join each other on the Green there is felt, at times, a fervency and intensity—a shadow perhaps of the fanatical harshness—reflecting old Abolitionist days. It is a day as Thoreau suggests, when there is a pervading consciousness of "Nature's kinship with the lower order—man."
   After the Town Hall is filled with the Spring's harvest of lilacs, daisies, and peonies, the parade is slowly formed on Main Street. First come the three Marshals on plough horses (going sideways), then the Warden and Burgesses *in carriages,* the Village Cornet Band, the G.A.R., two by two, the Militia (Company G.), while the volunteer Fire Brigade, drawing the decorated hose-cart, with its jangling bells, brings up the rear—the inevitable swarm of small boys following. The march to Wooster Cemetery is a thing a boy never forgets. The roll of muffled drums and *Adeste Fideles* answer for the dirge. A little girl on the fencepost waves to her father and wonders if he looked like that at Gettysburg.
   After the last grave is decorated, *Taps* sounds out through the pines and hick-

middle section (from G to about K before the march starts) was taken from an organ piece written some years before.[2] In my opinion this is the poorest part of the movement. (The melody of the march before the end is from Reeves's "Second Regiment Quickstep"[3]—as good a march as Sousa or Schubert ever wrote, if not better!)

T44m

The *Decoration Day* score was played (or rather "played at") by the National Symphony Orchestra, which had offered to give an invitation rehearsal-concert playing American manuscript compositions. This took place at Carnegie Hall in the spring of 1919 [rightly 1920].[4] Mr. Bodansky was the conductor of the orchestra, but did not conduct this piece, and I don't think that he saw the score. It was picked out by a committee of the orchestra, but I don't know who they were. I'm pretty certain that, had Mr. Bodansky seen the score, it would not have been played. At the concert, Mr. Bodansky's head was sitting right in front of us. He looked as though he didn't know what it was all about (that

T45m

is, the music), and always smiled at the wrong time.

We saw this generous offer by this orchestra in the newspaper,[5] and for the fun of it I sent them the score. As it was not a contest for a prize, etc., it seemed that I could send it without violating a "family tradition." Shortly after, I received a letter from the orchestra saying that the score had been accepted for performance, and asking to have the parts sent in, which I did. About a week or so later, I received another letter, sent by the Secretary, saying that, on studying the score more, they found it would be impracticable to play it—it was too difficult to read.[6] As I had gone to all the trouble of having the parts copied, etc., I wrote to them saying that I expected them to play it,[7] and I proposed to hold

---

ories, while a last hymn is sung. Then the ranks are formed again and "we all march back to town" to a Yankee stimulant—Reeves' inspiring *Second Regiment Quickstep*—though, to many a soldier, the sombre thoughts of the day underlie the tunes of the band. The march stops—and in the silence the shadow of the early morning flower-song rises over the Town, and the sunset behind West Mountain breathes its benediction upon the Day.

2 No such organ piece has survived. It may have been an organ version of the lost *Slow March* for band on *Adeste Fideles* mentioned in App. 2 at note 11. In *Decoration Day, Adeste Fideles* is quoted at letter I, *Taps* at letter J.

3 The *Second Regiment Connecticut National Guard March* by David Willis Reeves (New Haven, C. M. Loomis, 1877). George Ives's copy of the edition for piano contains some sketching in Ives's hand toward *Decoration Day*.

4 According to the letterhead of the letter in note 6, it was "The New Symphony Orchestra, Inc. of The Musicians' New Orchestra Society"—the offer was in the fall of 1919, the "reading" in the spring of 1920.

5 The newspaper printing of this offer has not yet been located.

6 "April 20th, 1920 [Tuesday] . . . After reading over your score carefully, I have come to the conclusion that it is absolutely impossible for us to play this composition at our rehearsals, as it is much too difficult to read at sight, and inasmuch as the time limit for our rehearsal period would not allow more than a reading.

"I trust, however, that the opportunity for us to play it will present itself in the future. Very truly yours, The New Symphony Orchestra, Paul Eisler, Ass't. Conductor."

7 "April 22nd, 1920 . . . My dear Mr. Eisler:—Your letter of the 20th was a disappointment. I doubt if the men will find the parts as difficult to play as the score indicates— all they have to do is to use their wits perhaps a little harder than usual during the first half dozen pages,—the rest should give little trouble. It takes about six minutes

them to it, and that, in their "public offer" asking for manuscripts, they said nothing about the grade of difficulty—whether it had to stop at Grade A or Grade B² or Grade F⁶. They wrote back saying that they would play it. (This correspondance is on file.)

The rehearsal was in Carnegie Hall. Mr. Eisler, an Assistant Conductor of the Metropolitan Opera, stood up and started them off with a nice baton in his hand. At the end of each section, one little violinist in the back row was the only one playing, all the others having dropped by the wayside. When they got to letter B, they all started together, and the back-line violinist was again the only survivor reaching C.[8] Section C was started in the same way, and so on till the march at the end came. At the end of that, a bass drum and the fiddler were the two survivors. I doubt if there was a single measure that was more than half played. As a player would get off and stop, he'd usually turn around and smile (one always spit in his handkerchief)—the same kind of a smile that a fat lady has when she runs for a trolley, half mad, half embarrassed, and half something else. After the "performance", at which some of the audience laughed, some of them cussed, and some did something else, Mr. Eisler was mad, came up, and handed me back the score saying, "There is a limit to musicianship." (But I didn't tell him, as I wanted to, [that] the greatest limits to musicianship are your [own] limitations. I heard only one between acts.)

This is a good example of how much water can run under the bridge in a few years time. This "performance" was in 1919 [rightly 1920], thirteen years ago, yet today this score could be picked up and played readily by any symphony orchestra with only a few rehearsals, and it has been. It was recently played by the Havana Symphony Orchestra, December 27, 1931, and with apparently little difficulty.[9]

---

to play it through. However, if you still think it impossible to play it next week, I will have to wait, as you suggest, for a better opportunity, which ought to be next Season. To change it to a more acceptable or practicable form would be possible, but I feel that as a matter of principle I cannot start in and work that way now. I'm afraid that I'll have to work things out in the way or ways which appeal to me, or not at all.

"I'm quite willing to pay for the extra time required to have an adequate rehearsal, but to do this seems hardly fair to the other composers who may not be in a position to do likewise—though this objection may not hold if the other numbers are longer than mine. As I remember, when the offer was made last Fall, there were no stipulations as to 'difficulty' or 'length.' Some such condition might be advisable in the future.

"Let me thank you for the interest already shown, and I'm glad the score was accepted —if not played.

"The orchestra is doing a much needed service in trying out this plan; it is to my mind a more wholesome procedure than that of 'prize competitions,' and I hope you all may discover some new music of value in the process—and that it will open up some ideas that will help us all.   Very truly yours, (C. E. I.)"

Eisler must have come to 120 East 22nd Street, because Mrs. Ives recalled in 1963: "I remember Eisler going over it with him at the piano, and Eisler said 'Why, you play like an artist!' Charlie's father had wanted him to be a concert pianist, but he was much too shy—he couldn't face that being-alone on the stage in front of an audience."

[8] It would be good to know who this back-row violinist was—he deserves some kind of heaven.

[9] Conducted by Amadeo Roldan (see §7, note 2).

37

T42   *The Fourth of July* was a thing that I'd had in mind for a good
while. It was finished, and the part that represents the explosions (or
other parts where the full orchestra is playing) was completely scored
T43m   in the summer of 1912.[1] Up to about letter I of p. 10, the score was
practically all in the sketch, which was completely finished before we
went to Brattleboro in January 1913, for I took it with me then to copy
it out in ink. (A doctor in the sanatarium looked at it strangely, and
assumed I was a patient.)[2] This is pure program music—it is also pure
abstract music—"You pays your money, and you takes your choice."[3]

Technically, a good deal of this movement was suggested by the old
habit of piano-drum-playing described above.[4] The string parts toward
the end, which are supposed to represent clouds of smoke, were originally in a group of notes playing all the tones together in the key of
B major. Later the two lower groups were arranged as they are in the
photostat score.

I remember distinctly, when I was scoring this, that there was a feeling of freedom as a boy has, on the Fourth of July, who wants to do
anything he wants to do, and that's his one day to do it. And I wrote
this, feeling free to remember local things etc., and to put [in] as many
feelings and rhythms as I wanted to put together. And I did what I
wanted to, quite sure that the thing would never be played, and perhaps *could* never be played—although the uneven measures that look
so complicated in the score are mostly caused by missing a beat, which
was often done in parades. In the parts taking off explosions, I worked
out combinations of tones and rhythms very carefully by kind of pre-
scriptions, in the way a chemical compound which makes explosions
would be made.

m43v   A piece that suggested some of *The Fourth of July* was a sketch made
tm

1 See App. 3, #58. Of the two versions of the postface, the shorter one is printed in the
New Music score—Ives may have felt a bit shy about the longer one:
"It's a boy's '4th—no historical orations—no patriotic grandiloquences by 'grown-
ups'—no program in his yard! But he knows what he's celebrating—better than most
of the county politicians. And he goes at it in his own way, with a patriotism nearer kin
to nature than jingoism. His festivities start in the quiet of the midnight before, and
grow raucous with the sun. Everybody knows what it's like—if everybody doesn't—
Cannon on the Green, Village Band on Main Street, fire crackers, shanks mixed on
cornets, strings around big toes, torpedoes, Church bells, lost finger, fifes, clam-chowder,
a prize-fight, drum-corps, burnt shins, parades (in and out of step), saloons all closed
(more drunks than usual), baseball game (Danbury All-Stars vs Beaver Brook Boys),
pistols, mobbed umpire, Red, White and Blue, runaway horse,—and the day ends with
the sky-rocket over the Church-steeple, just after the annual explosion sets the Town-Hall
on fire. All this is not in the music,—not now."
2 See App. 16, last paragraph.
3 From Mark Twain's *Huckleberry Finn,* end of Chap. 28.
4 See §11.

for a tragic tone poem written after the General Slocum steamboat disaster in the East River.[5] I don't believe I had a serious intention of finishing it. This awful catastrophe got on everybody's nerves. I can give no other reason for attempting to put it to music, and I'm glad to look back and see the sketch is hardly more than a page. It starts with several bands playing popular tunes on the boat, people singing— and then the explosion.

To get a composite sounding noise in some reasonable order was not hard to do. In this (see sketch, in *Thanksgiving*, old score-sketch, on empty p. 5–6)[6] the rhythms are used in a kind of chemical order:

The deep bells give	𝅝	(1)
Basses starting on C, up [by] half[tones]	𝅗𝅥　　　𝅗𝅥♯	(2)
Basses starting on C♯	𝅗𝅥　𝅗𝅥　𝅗𝅥	(3)
Cellos starting on D	𝅘𝅥　𝅘𝅥　𝅘𝅥　𝅘𝅥	(4)
Cellos starting on D♯	𝅘𝅥　𝅘𝅥　𝅘𝅥　𝅘𝅥　𝅘𝅥	(5)

and so on, all the way through the orchestra (one piccolo playing 15). Then when they all get up to their highest notes, they all hold *fff,* in their sound-area (covering, as a compact cloud of sound, from b[4] down in 4ths and 3rds, as far as there are number of players)—until the violins start the hymn of prayer *pp.*

I made *The Fourth of July* from this plan, but much better musically, as each group has a phrase of musical sense, not just an ascending chromatic scale as in *The General Slocum.* I remember playing the different instruments, the trumpet and the piccolo, and trying out the highest tones, and then jumping from a low tone (which is comparatively *pp*) to the highest tones (*ffff*). (In playing the cornet, scooping up with the breath from a low to a very high note, I remember, gave a different and stronger sound on the top note than if played without doing this.) Each part in these periods made (or at least I tried to have them make) a strain of musical sense by themselves—that is, when played by themselves—each part of the general explosion of noise having its own natural beginning and natural end.[7] It is not absolutely essential that these notes or rhythms be kept to literally. It would be very difficult to have it done this way. (The trumpets and trombones have the main outlines, and the others—sounding in, around, and with them—sounding in a cloud, so to speak.) It is the underlying gist that

T43m

T44m

[5] The explosion and burning of the excursion boat *General Slocum* with a church-outing crowd of passengers occurred, with tragic loss of life, on Wednesday 15 June 1904, near Randall's Island, New York City. Ives's sketch is dated "Pine Mt., July 1904."
[6] Of the score-sketch of *Thanksgiving,* the leaf numbered pp. 7–8 and renumbered pp. 5–6 was still blank in July 1904 and was used for the sketch of *The General Slocum* (negatives Q2833–34).
[7] There are two such explosions, shortly after letter M and after letter X, where the score-sketch says: "Town Hall fireworks blow up, skyrockets, firecrackers . . ."

is really the important thing. If one player should get to the end of an explosion-period first, he steadily holds until everybody reaches him, and the conductor wipes them out all together. Or in other words, the worse these places sound to Rollo, the better it is.

38

T49m   When we were in Keene Valley, on the plateau, staying in the fall of 1915[1] with Sue and Grossie—and with Edie (and Edie's second mother)[2]—I started something that I'd had in mind for some time (and [of] which some sketches were made a few years before—see mss.) —trying out a parallel way of listening to music, suggested by looking at a view (1) with the eyes toward the sky or tops of the trees, taking in the earth or foreground subjectively—that is, not focussing the eye on it—(2) then looking at the earth and land, and seeing the sky and the top of the foreground subjectively. In other words, giving a musical piece in two parts, but played at the same time—the lower parts (the basses, cellos, tubas, trombones, bassoons, etc.) working out something representing the earth, and listening to that primarily—and then the upper [parts] (strings, upper woodwind, piano, bells, etc.) reflecting the skies and the Heavens—and that this piece be played twice, first when the listener focusses his ears on the lower or earth music, and the next time on the upper or Heaven music.

m49t   This was suggested by a few pages of a sketch or general plan for a
m49v   *Universe Symphony* or "The Universe, Past, Present, and Future" in
tm   tones (see some marginal notes on back of old manuscript pages—see ms. page marked U s):[3]

    I. [Section A] (Past)   Formation of the waters and mountains.
   II. [Section B] (Present)   Earth, evolution in nature and humanity.
  III. [Section C] (Future)   Heaven, the rise of all to the spiritual.

T49m   I had this fairly well sketched out, but not completed—in fact I haven't worked on this since that time, but hope to finish it out completely this summer.[4] The earth part is represented by lines starting at different points and at different intervals—a kind of uneven and over-lapping counterpoint sometimes reaching nine or ten different lines
T50m   representing the ledges, rocks, woods, and land formations—lines of trees and forest, meadows, roads, rivers, etc.—and undulating lines of

1 One of the sketch pages with this place and date (Q4449) suggests that Ives was then thinking of the title: "The Earth and the Heavens."
2 "Edie's second mother" is of course Mrs. Ives, née Harmony Twichell, "Grossie" (short for "Grosspapa") her father (see App. 16), and Sue, her sister.
3 Might this be one of the missing pages?
4 That is, summer 1932.

m49

mountains in the distance that you catch in a wide landscape. (On p. 6–7 there [are] 15 separate lines, 11 in lower [parts], 4 in upper.)[5]

T50m

And with this counterpoint, a few of the (same kind of) instruments [as those] playing the melodic lines are put into a group playing masses of chords built around (various sets of) intervals, in each line.[6] This is to represent the body of the earth, from whence the rocks, trees and

m49v
tm

mountains rise. (From 5 to 14 groups of instruments or separate orchestras, each to know its own part before coming together in conclave, the various lines of[7] counterpoint [having one] primary and two secondary [voices]. Each "continent" has its own wide chord of intervals:—

m49v

(1) see sheet
(2) 5[ths] and 4[ths]
(3) 4[ths] and 5[ths] etc.
(4) 3rds
(5) 5[ths]
(6) 7[ths]—

(7) perfectly tuned har[monic intervals?]
(8) perfectly tuned overtones
(9) perfect 3-octave scale with no octaves
      (see quarter and eighth-tone[scales])
(10) quarter-tone chords, vio[lins?]
(11)

t49vm

Some perfectly tuned correct scales, some well tempered little scales, a scale of overtones with the divisions as near as determinable by acousticon, scales of smaller division than a semitone, scales of uneven division greater than a whole tone, scales with no octave, some of them [with] no octave for several octaves,—but all with their root in a fixed

m49v

tone, 32-foot, began [from] pedal A, 5th octave below. The pulse of the universe's life beat was by the percussion orchestra, who play their movement first, all through, before any of the other orchestras play.)

T50m

Between the lower group and the upper, there is a vacant space of four whole tones between B natural and E natural.[8] (I think this was not kept to, except in [a] general way.) The part of the orchestra representing the Heavens has its own chord system, but its counterpoint is chordal. There are 4 to 5 groups in some places divided [each] into four or five. On the lower corner of the 2nd page of the sketch,[9] this chordal counterpoint is broken by long chords, but stays this way for only a short time. These two main groups come into relation harmonically only in cycles—that is, they go around their own orbit, and come

5 In pp. 6–7 of Section A (Q3031–32), this could be true some of the time, depending on how much the indicated chord-types were filled in.
6 On p. 1 of Section A (Q3027), the middle staves have the melodic lines, and the outer staves have an elaborate chord forming a kind of background.
7 Here Miss Martin apparently skipped a line of her shorthand, and typed: ". . . the various line of each continent . . ."
8 Ives probably means between b and c1 (around middle c1). This would be more or less true of pp. 9–10 of Section A (Q3033–34).
9 This seems true of the lower left corner of p. 4 of Section A (Q3029), but not of p. 2 (Q4448).

to meet each other only where their circles eclipse.[10] (Written on the sketch and first page of score was[11]—"The wide valleys and the clouds are [of] one accord, and the horizon [of] distant hills (their roots from the earth) are as the clouds (their roots in the Heavens)—the soaring lines of mountains, cliffs, and pinnacles sent from the moving veins of rocks.")

The sketch of this is not complete, and I may extend it into a larger piece than I had originally intended (or put it into the *Universe Symphony*, to which it is related). But the themes and general plan are quite clearly indicated in the sketch. I want to work this out completely this summer. ([I] think [it] advisable staying on [this] job another year if possible.)

T51

I am just referring to the above because, in case I don't get to finishing this, somebody might like to try to work out the idea, and the sketch that I've already done would make more sense to anybody looking at it with this explanation.[12]

[10] This idea of large musical orbits relating at cyclic points suggests a parallel with classic Hindu music, of which Ives would have disclaimed any knowledge or experience.
[11] After "was", there is only the quotation mark but no words. These, from the middle of p. 1 of Section A (Q3027), seem the likeliest probability.
[12] This would be true if all the sketch pages Ives wrote toward the *Universe Symphony* had survived. But so many are missing that what he would like to pass on to a collaborator is tragically fragmentary.

39

T51m

The only other music that I might speak of is that in quarter tones, ([and] odds and ends of shorter pieces for piano,[1] some with string quartet[2] etc.—copy so blurred [that I] can't make all [the] notes out. Since [then, enlarged] photo[stats] (m[ore] easy [on the] sig[ht]) have been [made].[3] Some of these [pieces] are much better than they seemed at first—and [I] have had some copied out—see Chamber [Music] Sets.)

As stated above,[4] as a boy I had heard some quarter-tone experiments of Father, and this division or other divisions of the tone were not entirely unfamiliar to me. In the Sunday-School room of the Central Presbyterian Church,[5] New York, there were, for a while, two pianos

[1] The "shorter pieces" would be the *Three-Page Sonata* and *Studies* (App. 3, #18–19), *Waltz-Rondo* [to be published by Associated 1972], *Varied Air and Variations* [Merion 1971], and what the editor has called *Five Take-offs* (*The Seen and Unseen, Rough and Ready* or *The Jumping Frog, Song Without Words, Scene Episode, Bad Resolutions*).
[2] For piano and string quartet are *Halloween, In re con moto et al*, and the two pieces called *Largo Risoluto No. 1, No. 2* [Peer 1961].
[3] Ives had many enlarged positives made, hoping that they would be easier for his eyes to cope with. Unfortunately most of these were thrown away after he died.
[4] See §12.
[5] Ives was organist there from April 1900 through 1 June 1902.

which happened to be just about a quarter tone apart, and I tried out
a few chords then.

m51v   In this connection, and also referring to Father's glasses tuned in
different intervals larger and less than quarter tones, after hearing the
two pianos out of tune in Central Church (but as near as I could tell
by listening and with tuning forks, [they] were about a quarter tone
apart)—a scale (to knock the octaves and fifths out by wider intervals,
stretching [the] whole and half tones a little, but keeping the propor-
tions of the scale)—it was started or suggested by these two pianos, and
glasses between [the quarter tones]. But one piano was moved before
I could get it well grasped[6] in my ears. It was mostly worked out on
paper, which I have in part (see back of *The Indians* score)[7]—taking C
as basis, 5 quarter tones up = whole interval, and divided in [the]
middle by [a] glass = 2½ [quarter] tones—that is:

Notes in old scale

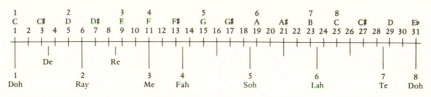

m52v   —(playing larger scale and then regular one alternately several times—
and it is quite an interesting sound difference and makes a kind of
musical sense).

New octaves, that is:

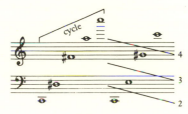

= no octaves nor 5ths during each four octaves, or no octaves nor 5ths
for 48 half-tones, and [the] only interval in common is [the] lower 4th.
But [the] trouble is:—[the] augmented 9th, taken as a scale length,
may be confused with [the] minor 3rd. I had some other division,

6 This word is hard to make out, but is quite possibly "grasped."
7 There are three copies of the following diagram differing only in minor details: (1)
on a rejected title page of "Last Chorus" of *The Celestial Country* (Q1718), back of
which is p. 1 of the score-sketch of *The Indians* (Q2838)—(2) in m51v—and (3) in
m52v.

m53v
tm

where the scale ended on a quarter-tone—can't find it. In this larger scale, there are but three intervals of even-ratio (so called): (1) the 4th [of the old scale] = [the] 3rd [of the larger scale]; or (2) from [the old] 4th to the top [of the larger scale] = minor 7th = [augmented] 6th; and [3] the sum of (1) + (2) = from C to E♭ top = minor 10th.

The other intervals are uneven—some way out from a simple ratio [as] 2/1—for instance 261/712 etc. This, at first, seemed very disturbing,—but when the ears have heard more and more (and year after year) of uneven ratios, one begins to feel that the use, recognition, and meaning (as musical expression) of intervals have just begun to be heard and understood. The even ratios have been pronounced the true basis of music, because man limits his ear, and not because nature does. The even ratios have one thing that got them and has kept them in the limelight of humanity—and one thing that has kept the progress to wider and more uneven ratios very slow—(it is said [that] for the power of man's ear to stand up against the comparatively uneven 3rds, [when used] to the very even octaves and 5ths, was a matter of centuries)—in other words, consonance has had a monopolistic tyranny, for this one principal reason:—it is *easy* for the ear and mind to use and know them—and the more uneven the ratio, the harder it is. The old fight of evolution—the one-syllable, soft-eared boys are still on too many boards, chairs, newspapers, and concert stages!

40

T51m

Of the *Three Quarter-tone Pieces* played at a Pro Musica concert in 1924 or 1925 (I forget which—see program),[1] the *Chorale* was little beside a study in quarter-tone harmony, having two pianos tuned together, one a quarter sharp (as they were in the Sunday school room). And also I tried out some of these chords when we first went to Redding, before the little piano (a quarter tone under the large piano) was moved into the back room.[2] These three quarter-tone chords were

[1] The second "International Referendum Concert" for 1924–25 of the Franco-American Musical Society (later Pro Musica) took place on Saturday evening, 14 February 1925. The announcement gave the fourth group ("For quarter tone Chickering Pianos") as Ives's *Largo, Allegro,* and *Chorale,* and the third movement of Hans Barth's *Sonata,* but with misplaced brackets imputing the *Chorale* to Barth. The program of the concert listed the Barth movement first, then only the *Chorale* and *Allegro* of Ives (as borne out in F.D. Perkins's review). They were played by Barth and Sigmund Klein, who had played the *Chorale* at Chickering Hall just the previous Sunday afternoon.

[2] The property at West Redding was bought in August 1912, the house and barn begun immediately, the cellar of the house finished in December, and the Iveses moved in in August 1913. Their neighbor William Ryder remembers that the addition was built in the winter of 1921–22, including the music room at the back, into which the little piano would have been moved later in 1922.

used also in the string passages, page 2, published score, second movement, *Fourth Symphony*. This is explained in some detail in my article,
Quarter Tone Impressions, in the *Pro Musica Quarterly,* March 1925.[3]

The other two pieces were written some years after the chords and
the *Chorale* were worked out, and are but studies in melodic and
rhythmic quarter-tone possibilities.[4]

I think a good many people hearing the quarter-tone concert (Aeolian
Hall, New York, Feb. [1925]) got the wrong idea of its purpose. I tried
to have both Mr. Schmitz, in the lecture,[5] and Mr. Barth, in the program, say that, as far as I was concerned, these pieces were not presented as definitely completed works of art (or attempts at works of
art). They were simply studies within the limited means we had with
which to study quarter tones. I must say that I think Hans Barth
went at the matter in the wrong way. I helped him build his quarter-
tone piano, and told him that it was with the idea of having an instrument that we could work on, rather than a something to exploit anything or anybody. Perhaps Barth misunderstood me,—but the concerts
he has given[6] and the way he has used the piano, to my way of thinking,
have done more harm than good in interesting people in quarter tones,
or developing a natural sense and use for them. (Besides, I think that
new scales (see article, p. 2)[7] will gradually be evolved in a natural
way probably, perhaps in centuries, and that their intervals will not be
(or all be) of the whole, half, or quarter tones known or so-called now.)

3 The three string chords in mm. 7–8 of the 2nd movement of the *Fourth Symphony*
appear in the same order but different spacing in m. 48 of the quarter-tone *Chorale*.
The first is the one in Boatwright's Note 57; the others are two different transpositions
of the one in his Note 60.
4 See App. 3, #76 and #88.
5 Perkins's review (*New York Herald-Tribune,* 15 February 1925, p. 8) reported: "The
Barth and Ives numbers . . . were prefaced by an exposition by E. Robert Schmitz, who
pointed out that another experimenter in this field, the late Ferrucio Busoni, aimed at
division of the whole tone into sixths, while Alois Haba is an apostle of the quarter.
The pianos were of the usual shape and appearance (Haba, it is said, uses a semi-
circular keyboard), but whether the subdivisions were obtained by tuning each in
quarter tones, or one a fourth of a tone above or below the other, was not stated."
6 On Friday and Saturday, 28–29 March 1930, Hans Barth played his *Concerto for
Quarter Tone Piano and Strings* with the Philadelphia Orchestra, Stokowski conducting,
in Philadelphia. Lawrence Gilman's program note consisted mainly of a long note that
had been "furnished to the annotator on behalf of Mr. Barth." It mentions Barth and
Sigmund Klein playing Ives's *Chorale* and *Allegro* in the concert of 14 February 1925,
but, "because of the difficulty of dividing themes, melodies, and chords between the
two players, the performance did not satisfy Mr. Barth. He immediately made arrangements to have Mr. George L. Weitz construct the invention he had formulated with
the assistance of a prominent firm of piano-makers." The note goes on to report that
this piano was finished in 1928, and the Friends of Music presented Barth in the first
quarter-tone recital in America on 9 April 1929, and that he gave similar recitals
at Buffalo and Providence, a series of recitals in the West in 1929–30, and one in Carnegie Hall, New York, on 3 February 1930. Throughout this note there is no mention
of Ives's having helped with getting the piano built.
7 This is the main burden of the first section of the article—see Boatwright.

41

m73v

Generally speaking, all of the above covers the things done mostly in the twenty years or so between 1896 and 1916. *([I] have, in most of these pages, purposely not gone into much of the chamber music, as most of this is filled with the technical laying out, some forms with numbered [sections][1], and plans of overtones, etc.)*

T52m

In 1917 the War came on, and I did but little in music. I didn't seem to feel like it. We were very busy at the office at this time with the extra Red Cross and Liberty Loan drives and all the problems that the War brought on. As I look back, I find that I did almost no composing after the beginning of 1918.

m52

The only music composed in 1918 were two songs or choruses for male voices[2]—but later turned into brass choruses. They were really just using brass as the older cornet sets did (some of them after[ward] had strings with piano accompaniment)—for or with the voice, as singers made such a fuss about singing [them]. The words could be handed to the listeners instead!

T52
T53m

In October 1918, I had a serious illness that kept me away from the office for six months, and I have not been since in my former good (very good) state of health, nor have I seemed to get going "good" in music since then. *(I'd start things, but they didn't seem to work out— [I] couldn't seem to keep them up and sailing. So [I] stopped and stopped etc.)* I don't know how to account for it except that what strength I had was used up during the day in what I had to do at the office, and it seemed impossible to do any work in the evenings, as I used to do.

During the last ten years or so, I've completed nothing.[3] A set of chamber music was started, and is fairly and mostly set down in a sketch[4] (some five or six years ago), and I've started a *Third Piano*

---

[1] Numbered sections appear in the sketch of the close of *Hawthorne* (but not always in the final order); (1) at p. 46 (revised edition), line 4; (2) at p. 47, line 2, 4th beat (or dotted-8th); (3) at line 4; (4) at line 5; (5) at p. 48, 2nd beat; (7) at line 4, last beat; (10) at p. 49, 6th beat; (8) at line 3, 5th beat; (13) at p. 50, 2nd beat; (12) at p. 51, line 3, 2nd beat.
The sketch of the *Chromâtimelôdtune* is in sections labeled A through H (see the score "reconstructed and completed" by Gunther Schuller in 1962 [MJQ music 1963]). But this usage seems to become rehearsal letters or numbers.
By "plans of overtones" Ives may mean the diagrams of quarter-tone scales and chords that led up to the quarter-tone pieces.
[2] Could these be male chorus versions of *General Booth* (1914), *Majority* (1914), or *He Is There!* (1917)?
[3] Fortunately this is not true—see Appendix 4, #123, 125, and 136–41, also *Sunrise* (1926).
[4] This must be the *Third Orchestral Set* (Appendix 3, #87).

Sonata,[5] which doesn't seem to get along very well. In 1919 and 1920, and especially 1921, I did write quite a few songs, and arranged songs for voice and piano from several for chorus—and also at that time made arrangements of songs from old scores, sketches, overtures, etc. Sometimes whole parts of these were put into a song, and sometimes they were revised, changed, or cut down to make a song. What these were is mostly spoken about above. *(I have several of these old scores.)*

[5] See Appendix 8, note 18.

PART THREE

Memories

42

T54m

The following is a kind of a general resumé of one thing or another, as I remember them, or as diaries, memos, letters, manuscripts, programs, etc. (or from talking things over with Mrs. Ives, family, and old friends) bring them back to mind.

43

One thing I am certain of is that, if I have done anything good in music, it was, first, because of my father, and second, because of my wife. What she has done for me I won't put down, because she won't let me.[1] But I am going to put this down at least:—After any of these musical friends of mine (mentioned above, and others) had left, she never once said or suggested or looked or thought that there must be something wrong with me—a thing implied, if not expressed, by most everybody else, including members of the family. She never said, "Now why don't you be good, and write something nice the way they like it?" —*Never! She* urged me on my way—to be myself! *She* gave me not only help but a confidence that no one else since father had given me. A free translation of most of the general advice that I always received from musicians, friends and otherwise (and also often from personal and family friends) was:—If you want something played, write something you don't want played. Mrs. Ives always said the opposite, and resented the above (free translated) advice.

m54v
tm

T54m

What my father did for me was not only in his teaching, on the technical side, etc., but in his influence, his personality, character, and open-mindedness, and his remarkable understanding of the ways of a

---

[1] This sounds like a verbal quote from the popular song, *Waiting at the Church* or *My Wife Won't Let Me,* by Fred W. Leigh and Henry E. Pether (Francis, Day, & Hunter, 1906).

boy's heart and mind. He had a remarkable talent for music and for the nature of music and sound, and also a philosophy of music that was unusual. Besides starting my music lessons when I was five years old, and keeping me at music in many ways until he died, with the best teaching that a boy could have, Father knew (and filled me up with) Bach and the best of the classical music, and the study of harmony and counterpoint etc., and musical history. Above all this, he kept my interest and encouraged open-mindedness in all matters that needed it in any way.

For instance, he thought that man as a rule didn't use the faculties that the Creator had given him hard enough. I couldn't have been over ten years old when he would occasionally have us sing, for instance, a tune like *The Swanee River* in the key of E♭, but play the accompaniment in the key of C. This was to stretch our ears and strengthen our musical minds, so that they could learn to use and translate things that might be used and translated (in the art of music) more than they had been. In this instance, I don't think he had the possibility of polytonality in composition in mind, as much as to encourage the use of the ears—and for them and the mind to think for themselves and be more independent—in other words, not to be too dependent upon customs and habits. (He even let me try out "two keys to once," as an Interlude in an organ piece, *Variations on America*, but didn't let me do it much, as it made the boys laugh—also in anthems, psalms, chords in more than one key; Psalms 67, 54, 130, 150, etc.)[2]

T55m

2 Ives crossed out the second part of this insert (after the dash), but it may be important as containing his only mention of a *Psalm 130*. Either this is lost (like *Psalm 23* in App. 2, at note 8), or else he meant the first sketch of *Psalm 135*.

44

When I went to New Haven, and took the courses with Professor Horatio W. Parker, in connection with the regular academic courses in Freshman year,[1] I felt more and more what a remarkable background and start Father had given me in music. Parker was a composer and widely known, and Father was not a composer and little known—but from every other standpoint I should say that Father was by far the greater man. Parker was a bright man, a good technician, but appar-

1 In T, Ives crossed out "in Freshman year"—probably remembering that, as a freshman, he couldn't "take" Parker's courses but merely audit them (see App. 6)—but this wording suggests that his work with Parker was more important in his memory than his strong filial sense liked to admit.

On the other hand, in 1969 the editor was surprised to hear an unconfirmed report that Parker had once mentioned Ives as one of the most talented young men he'd ever taught.

ently willing to be limited by what Rheinberger et al and the German tradition had taught him. After the first two or three weeks in Freshman year, I didn't bother him with any of the experimental ideas that Father had been willing for me to think about, discuss, and try out. Father died in October 1894,[2] during my Freshman year.

Parker's attitude, it seems to me (although I may be wrong), is the attitude (at least from my experience, which I'll admit has been limited) of most musicians, or at least the most that I'd met up to say about ten years ago.

m55v   An instance shows the difference between Father's and Parker's ways of thinking. In the beginning of Freshman year, and getting assigned to classes, Parker asked me to bring him whatever manuscripts I had written (pieces, etc.). Among them, a song, *At Parting*—in it, some unresolved dissonances, one ending on a [high] E♭ ([in the] key [of] G major), and stops there unresolved.[3] Parker said, "There's no excuse for that—an E♭ way up there and stopping, and the nearest D♮ way down two octaves."—etc. I told Father what Parker said, and Father said, "Tell Parker that every dissonance doesn't have to resolve, if it doesn't happen to feel like it, any more than every horse should have to have its tail bobbed just because it's the prevailing fashion."

2 See App. 13.
3 This e♭[3] is in m. 17 of *At Parting*. The manuscript version is a bit less dissonant than the published, but has the same skip of an octave and a minor ninth down to d'.

45

T55m   After Father's death, Dr. Griggs[1] (Choirmaster and baritone [soloist at] Center Church, New Haven—we were together four years there in the choirloft) was the only musician friend of mine that showed any interest, toleration, or tried to understand the way I felt (or what might be felt) about some things in music. The anecdote, given some pages
T56m   back, of the *Thanksgiving* organ pieces is typical of Dr. Griggs's attitude and open-mindedness.[2] He didn't like all the things I wrote by any means, but he was always willing to listen and discuss anything seriously. He had his own way of looking at things. A characteristic remark of his, that I remember, in speaking of the song, *General Booth* (which I played for him shortly after it was written in 1914 or so), was: "It's a good song—but not a song." I said, "It's not difficult vocally." He said, "No, it's difficult mentally. Unless the mind grasps and senses a tone from the ear, the voice can't sing it." And then he said, "It may be that

1 See App. 15.
2 See §9.

the grasping point of my ear and mind isn't up to what you expect it to be." (This he said with a smile when I told him, "If you can't sing it, nobody can.")

But he did better than most singers with difficult songs. He had a

m56v

better sense of intervals than he thought. My experience has been, not always but most always:—the more voice a man has, the less music he has. (See letter [from] Prof. [William Treat Upton], Oberlin, April 1932.)[3] Apparently in a singer's education the muscles of the throat get the training, and not the muscles of the ear and brain. ("Oh, those awful songs, impossible intervals, so unvocal!"— etc.) To sing intervals that lead away from the tonality and usual progressions is not physically impossible—any more than it is for a Hotel de Luxe lady to ride third class—it may be hard for her seat but good for her soul. What seems hard to start with—a "raucous interval"—after a while of labor for a generation, will become just a natural, if not the strongest, part of the armor. Perhaps more training by ear and less by paper—to what extent I don't know—but Father with a slide-cornet could strike any interval (containing even less than a half-tone), and in teaching children (also training the choirs and choruses), [he] would play the parts over several times before showing [them] the music.[4]

In writing some of the songs which seem to bother singers so, I got to putting them, in the voice part, first for cornet, clarinet, etc., so that

m57v

singers might hear them right first, at least as to intervals—but the solo parts keeping within a voice range. Even in some of the songs starting with this reason, I got to making short pieces as songs, but played by two, three, or more instruments—with the idea of giving the listener or audience the words, and letting them put them in, or follow along with them, as the solo instrument played (a kind of "songs without voices"). I have some of these old scores left. One set (only parts of which I can find) is: #[10], p. 19 (Charlie [Rutlage]), #2[?], [Evening],

---

3 Ives specifies neither "to" nor "from" nor any name—certainly Upton. His book, *Art Song in America,* had kept to older composers, and as part of his search for data about younger men, he sent Ives (from Oberlin) a mimeograph form, which he dated December 5, 1931, and a letter dated December 6, saying that Cowell had suggested his asking for the *114 Songs*—". . . I am intensely interested in the future of the Art Song, and welcome any constructive suggestions. . . ."

The sketch for Ives's reply (datable only by reference to Upton's letter) says: ". . . I can't say that I know much of the music of the younger composers . . . but from meeting occasionally some of the younger men, I should say that their lack of interest in songs is not a matter of decadence in their work . . . but rather that it is caused by—I won't say a decadence—but by a kind of musico-mental spiritual inertia, approaching an atrophy, on the part of singers in general . . . There are exceptions, mostly among the younger singers. . . ."

No further letter from Upton has been found among Ives's papers, and Ives might be referring to this letter *to* Upton and remembering the date wrongly, but more probably Upton wrote him again in April, agreeing with his view.

4 See §12.

[etc.][5] (see in the wooden box [on the] floor [in] my room [at] Redding).[6] *(Also photos, some [only] scraps, some whole.)*

[5] For other imagined Sets, see the list in Ives's hand which is given complete on pp. 52–53 of the catalogue of Ives's manuscripts:
    Suggested song-groups and instruments and about in this order of preference—
        "Three Poets and Human Nature" . . .
            Paracelsus . . . Walt Whitman . . . West London . . .
        "The Other Side of Pioneering" or "Side Lights on American Enterprise" . . .
            The New River . . . The Indians . . . Charlie Rutlage . . . Ann Street . . .
        "From the Side Hill" . . .
            Mists . . . The Rainbow . . . Afterglow . . . Evening . . .
        "Water Colors" . . .
            At Sea . . . The Swimmers . . . The Pond . . . Full Fathom Five . . .
[6] Any music mss. that might have been in this wooden box in the music room would now be in the Ives Collection.

46

T56m   The only other friend outside of the family (which I will be careful not to mention here), in the period running about twenty-five years after Father's death, who showed any willingness to try to get my music, or took any interest in it at all, was David Talmadge, Moss White's violin teacher. Talmadge, in his nice way, always liked to kid me more or less about those funny sounds, but he said that, the more he learned and studied the music, the more he thought there was something in it. He played the *First Violin Sonata*,[1] and also most of the *Second,* I think, and all of the *Third,* with me in 1914–15. He gave them serious, hard, and intelligent study, and played them well and in a kind of big way.

T57m   In 1917 he and Stuart Ross played the *Third Sonata* at a small invited concert in Carnegie Chamber Music Hall.[2] Talmadge played remarkably well, and Ross fairly well. Ross told me at the time that it was the hardest music he had ever played. To look at it now, in comparison with some of the other music, or with the earlier sonatas, or with much music that has been written since—that anybody could have felt that way seems incredible.

[1] See §22, note 5.
[2] For the date of this concert (probably Sunday 22 April 1917) see §24, note 1.

47[1]

This reminds me of other incidents or things that have happened on the other side of the fence. When I was living at 317 West 58th Street[2] with classmates who were then studying medicine in the College of

[1] For the term "soft-ears" (used in the table of contents as a heading for this section) see §30, after note 9.
[2] For Poverty Flat (first at this address) see App. 17.

Physicians and Surgeons, Dave Smith[3] came in one afternoon to call on Ned Park. I was then working on the *Abide With Me* organ and chorus piece, built around the tune in off-beats, and with the three keys used as the three triads of the main key (see above, last movement, *Theatre Orchestra Set*).[4] Dave said, "Why do you take a good tune like that and spoil it with a lot of burlesque?" At the time, I didn't know but what he might be right. But the last time I heard this played, not many years ago, I came to the conclusion that he was decidedly wrong. There was no sense of burlesque in it. In fact, the namby, nice-up-and-down, jumpy, precise little way in which I've heard some church organists play it (some of them "celebrated" so-called) approaches the burlesque more than the sounds which clothe the music in my piece.

T58m
Joseph Reutershan (who ran a little music store at 14th Street and was an insurance agent on the side doing business with Henry Hudson, when we were at Raymond & Co., 26 Liberty Street[5]—so it must have been somewhere between 1903 and 1906) got the afternoon orchestra playing at Keith's Theater, then in 14th Street, to play some of those small-orchestra ragtime dances. (As I remember, this was a part of the second movement of the *Second Orchestral Set*, and also a part of the movement of the *Theatre Orchestra Set* and the *First Piano Sonata*.) The pianist, as I remember, practised up and played it and liked it fairly well (so he said—or the beer said, one night at Luchow's),[6] [but] the rest of the orchestra didn't, and only played it because they were friends of Reutershan. At the second afternoon performance, the manager of the theater came out and stopped them, saying it made too much of a disturbance.

Later, some of these ragtime dances were arranged for piano by the above pianist (I forget his name), but he simplified and spoiled them. Some of the original small scores were lost, and I started to re-score some of them from his piano reductions about ten years ago. Jerome Goldstein[7] started to help me, but, as I remember, gave it up. A few

3 David Stanley Smith, b. Toledo, Ohio, 1877, Yale '00 (ΦBK), taught music at Yale 1903–46, organist at Center Church 1908–12, Dean Yale School of Music 1920–40 and conductor New Haven Symphony Orchestra 1919–46 (succeeding Parker in both), d. New Haven 1949. At Yale he roomed with Ned Park.
4 For this prototype of *In the Night* see §17.
5 Trow lists "Jos. Reuthershan, publisher, 19 E. 14th" and "Henry Hudson, ins., 32 Liberty"—also "Chas. H. Raymond & Co., ins., 26 Liberty." Ives apparently remembered the move of the Raymond Agency from 32 to 26 Liberty as being in 1903, but the Trow listing seems to prove that it was in 1902.
6 Trow lists: "August Luchow, German Restaurant; sole agent for the celebrated 'Wurzburger Hofbrau' and imported Pilsener Beer, 108 to 114 E. 14th."
7 Jerome Goldstein made his name as a champion of modern music in three sonata recitals at Aeolian Hall, New York: Wednesday 14 November 1923 (Huss 1st, Ornstein, Bloch), Tuesday 15 January 1924 (Tailleferre, Bartok 1st, Goossens), Tuesday 18 March 1924 (Milhaud 2nd, Ives 2nd, Pizzetti)—the third program with the collaboration of Rex Tillson. But when this editor met him some ten years later through Katherine Heyman, he was reported to be working as a janitor. He died not many years later.

years after this Keith experience, I think about 1909–10, Mr. Reutershan gave up his store and was made manager of Schirmer's retail department in Union Square.[8] When I was in there one day, he got laughing about the time the Keith manager threw my music out, and half in fun he buttonholed me and said, "Well, to tell the truth, I didn't blame him. That was the craziest lot of sounds I ever heard—(and your chords have so many intervals!" One of the things was a part of *Over the Pavements* —and some of the chamber-orchestra piece [I] worked on around 1905–1915 or so, *Tone Roads*.)

This reminds me of how all chords, most of two major or minor 3rds, and occasionally [of] three 3rds, chords of the dominant, subdominant, etc., were the only ones to use (in the classroom, slave-like blackboard, Rollo!). I remember, even on Stevens Street,[9] Father used to let me, half in fun and half seriously, make chords up of several 3rds, major and minor, going up on top of themselves. I remember one especially, which I sometimes would play in church, even in short interludes between verses in a hymn.[10] Harmony remembers going to Center Church with Sally Whitney[11] when I was in college and playing in Center Church (Sally's grandpa, Eli, invented the cotton gin, so Sal was used to invention!)—and after an interlude, [in] which probably one of these [chords with] four or five 3rds was used, Sally smiled and nudged Harmony.

For instance, [I remember] going over some of these chords with Father—one, which I played for fun etc. (often ever since), was C♮-E♮-G♯-B♮-D♮-F♯-B♭-D♮—and then Father saying, "Now if you will play this B♮ [as] B♭, and stop at F♯ [for the] top, there won't be any half-tone dissonance." But I remember we both liked the one with B♮ better, ([and some of] the various chords which could be made of: 3rds all and over, then 3rds and 2nds, then 3rds and 4ths, then 3rds and 4ths and 5ths, etc.—see in [ms. on] technical side of music, in office safe—this paper tries to keep away from as much technical stuff as possible.)

This boy's way—of feeling, if you can have two 3rds, major or minor, in a chord, why can't you have another one or two on top of it, etc.—

8 Schirmer's music store moved from Union Square to 3 East 43rd Street in 1910. Their records show no trace of Joseph Reutershan.
9 George Ives and his family lived at 16 Stevens Street, Danbury, from 1879 to 9 May 1889.
10 The chord-type Ives used in these interludes is given in §6—see note 2. There are sketches of interludes for *Nettleton* and *Bethany* (negative Q2208) and for *Woodworth* and another unidentified hymn (Q0974). The one for Bethany (as in Q3187) is given in Cowell, p. 35, omitting Ives's indications for upper staff, "Sw. Salicional 8 *ppp*"— and for lower staff, "Ped con Gt. 8 + 4 ft."—(the *mf* meant only for lower staff).
11 Sally Whitney was Harmony Twichell's roommate at Miss Porter's School, Farmington. In April 1900 she married Dr. Leonard C. Sanford of New Haven, but died in childbirth the next year.

[is] as natural to a boy as thinking, if three bases in baseball, why not four or five, Mr. Gumbo? A boy doesn't deserve much credit in anything like [this]—it's an obvious and natural way of having a little fun!

T59m   Another story and then I'd better stop. Max Smith[12] and Mary spent one Sunday with us in May 1912 or 1913 at the Whitman house in Hartsdale. I played over the *Third Symphony* and Max asked me how I had got so modern??!! (When this was being copied in, I think, Tam's office, Gustav Mahler[13] saw it and asked to have a copy—he was quite interested in it.) Then I played over the Black March (*St. Gaudens*), which I was working on then, and also some of the brass band stuff in *Putnam's Camp,* (and some of *Hawthorne,* and the third movement [of the] *Fourth Symphony* (I remember one particular spot!),[14] and some of the shorter piano pieces, parts of which were used in other things.) After I'd finished, Max, who had gone out on the stoop, said, "That first one was bad enough, but these were awful! How can you like horrible sounds like that?—(And it's even worse than you were ten years ago!"— for at the Yale Club in 1901 or '02, I showed Max a movement arranged for orchestra from an organ piece—(the arrangement was for the *Third Symphony*)—he got wild.) (Max was at that time, and had been for many years, the music critic on the *New York American.*)

Here is another. Reber Johnson,[15] about fifteen years ago—when the *Washington's Birthday* ([as] stated above) was played by the group from the New York Symphony which later went into the Barrère Ensemble (the players, not *Washington's Birthday*)—spoke about a program for one of their concerts. Harnisch, the viola, said, "Why don't we play a part of this piece of Ives?" Reber said "No—we must think of the audience."

m59v   Reber also got off another one, after I'd played over the *Second*
:m   *Violin Sonata* for him—that harmless piece. "After stuff like that"—he said—"if you consider that music, and *like* it, how can you like Brahms or any good music?" That is a very common attitude among almost all the well known lilies. They take it for granted—a kind of self-evident axiom, a settled-for-life matter, ipso facto, admitting of no argument. The classical is good for all time, the modern is bad for all time—so if you like one, you can't like the other. They don't always limit it to "good and bad." They, in a general way, throw (in their nice little minds) all

---

12 Thomas Max Smith, b. New York City 1874, Yale '98, LL.B '01 Columbia, married Mary Cowles at Seattle in 1909, music critic *N.Y. Press* 1903–16, *N.Y. American* 1916–23, d. at Keene Valley, N.Y., 1935.
13 See §16, note 1.
14 The "particular spot" must have been at No. 12.
15 For Reber Johnson see §35, at note 4. Mrs. Ives thought she probably had made a slip of the pen in the following entry in *Our Book:* "1918—Jan 26 [Saturday]. To Camp Upton. Played in Y.M.C.A. hut for soldiers. Mr. Robert [rightly Reber?] Johnson, violinist."

that fits into their accustomed habits of sound, technique, etc., all together into a classical idiom, good or bad. Everything not in it they throw out as non-existent as music, as such. Assuming that there are some good things among the latter class, that can in essence and substance compare with the better of the former, this type of mind then does the same thing as to say—"Now if you look out of that window and enjoy the mountains, how can you possibly look out of this window and enjoy the ocean?" (This is a very good simile—but all the above is.) Just to think—a dumb mind!

m66v
tm

Reber et al. (including David and Clara [Mannes] preach the gospel that "Music crawled into Brahms's coffin and died." They wouldn't think of saying that in so many words, but that is exactly what their attitude toward music is. (Their motto:—"All things have a right to live and grow, even babies and music schools, but *not* music!") Reber, in 1919,[16] looking out of the big window in Redding, lay back and groaned: "Music is now a lost art—it is going to the dogs." But some dogs (he didn't say this) can give it a better ride than some men. He did occasionally have a good word for some mild new music—a nice piece like Massenet with a G$\sharp$ in it somewhere, as I remember. Reber had his good points. He had a beautiful tone on the strings, and played Mozart perfectly. I'll have to admit I enjoyed playing Mozart with him, but a whole afternoon of Mozart is a whole afternoon of Mozart (I was going to say something worse, which I occasionally know how to do).

The same state of (mind?) is seen in some music professors in colleges —for instance, Dave Smith. He is the Professor of Music at Yale. His stand is exactly that of a Professor of Transportation who teaches up through the steam engine, and refuses to admit that any such things exist as electricity, combustion engines, automobiles, or aeroplanes. And his students would become Bachelors of Transportation knowing about as much about transportation as Dave Smith does of music.

A student and graduate of his at the Yale Music School, on coming to New York after receiving his liberal education and degree (and four years of the music classes) at New Haven, went to a concert, and heard something modern or comparatively new—at least something in music he had never heard before (Furness[17] told me, I think, but I don't remember the piece—I think it was something of Milhaud). Anyway, this young man's interest was aroused enough to make some study of the new things, and later he told Furness that he was beginning to feel

---

[16] m66v: "He Reber (1920)"—t59 & 66: "Riegger—1919"—*m:* "Reber—1919."
[17] Clifton Joseph Furness (1898–1946), A.B. Northwestern '21, while teaching music; A.M. Harvard '28, while teaching at Horace Mann (where Elliott Carter was a student, whom he introduced to Ives); from 1929 taught at Katherine Gibbs School and supervised academic studies at New England Conservatory;—known for Whitman editions and commentaries. The identity of the disappointed Yale graduate remains a mystery.

that he had been cheated at Yale, as in his courses there he had been kept safely away from knowing anything about what had been going on in the world of music except the convictions of former generations. A hard crack at Alma Mater, but somewhat deserved!

T59m   Still another. Bass Brigham,[18] Yale '97 and a violinist, called on us at 70 West 11th Street, which was sometime before the spring of 1911. I was then scoring *The Housatonic at Stockbridge* and played it for him. He said, "Well, that's a funny-sounding collection of sounds— your tonality and your chord relations are more wobbly than César Franck's, which are bad enough." I got him to play over the first violin part of the third movement of the *Third Symphony*. He got mixed up and called it N.G., but he seemed to like some of the *Second Symphony,*
T60   which we tried over. (Compare these two scores, and you can easily see why.)

One more incident and I promise to stop. Edgar Stowell[19] and family drove over to Hartsdale from where they were living then just north of White Plains. Stowell was then a teacher in the Mannes Music School Settlement. It was in the summer of either 1912 or 1913. I had the *Fourth of July* score on the desk. He looked at it and said, "That's the best joke I've seen for a long time. Do you really think anybody would be fool enough to try to play a thing like that?" We played over the *Second Violin Sonata* and started the *First*, but Stowell said it was too difficult and stopped. He said there were too many ideas too close together. We then played Daniel Gregory Mason's *Violin Sonata* (one with a nice theme like *Narcissus*).[20] Stowell said Mason's was better than mine because it was Geigermusik, but he did say that one page of mine had more ideas than Mason's whole sonata. Whether he meant this as advice in restraint and prudence I don't know.

18 Harcourt Brigham ("Bass"—pronounced like the fish, not the low voice), 1873–1953, Yale '97 (played violin in Parker's orchestra), New York Law School, admitted to the Bar in 1899, but spent most of his life as a gentleman of leisure, amateur musician, and cultured dilettante—never married.
19 See §31, note 7.
20 A copy of Mason's *Sonata in G Minor* for violin and piano, Op. 5 (Schirmer, 1913), is among Ives's papers. The opening phrase of the second movement (4/4, andante tranquillo) has the same contour and key notes as that of Nevin's *Narcissus*, Op. 13/4 (1891).

48

160v
n

And the thing that bothered Stowell, Wally [Damrosch], etc. most, next to dissonance, was to hear and try to play any rhythm except 1–2 or 1–2–3 and their variables. Rhythm is a thing perhaps more to be felt than tones are. To feel several rhythms together and hear them as such is not as difficult as it is for one man to play them. As a rule, probably more than three rhythms on the piano is ineffective—and perhaps three or four, in pieces for two players, as in a violin and piano sonata, or music for voice and piano. To have polyrhythm rise to its full strength, there must be one or a group of players to each rhythm— (by rhythm here I mean something which is only a part of rhythm in its bigger sense—various times of beats to one unit). And each group, if possible, should be of different tonal sounds—for example: strings, brass, drums, bells, wood, and the various kinds of percussion instruments, each to each meter.

t60vm   I remember my father using (in a brass-band comedy-piece taking off *A Trip to Coney Island*),[1] instead of some percussion instrument he didn't have (I forget which), some large water pipes, perhaps sewer pipes, made (as I remember) from some kind of cement or brick composition, and which gave quite a distinct sound if hit with a wooden hammer. The possibilities of percussion sounds, I believe, have never

---

[1] George Ives's entertainment, *A Musical Trip to Coney Island*, was performed on Wednesday 19 June 1889. Thursday's Danbury Evening News reported: "Such an aggregation of musical talent was never seen on the Opera House . . . stage before . . . everything was on a large scale. . . . The chorus numbered in the hundreds, the band in the thirties, and the orchestra in the twenties. . . .

"Promptly at eight o'clock the ten minute whistle sounded . . . faint music . . . that of a band . . . the 'Danbury and Coney Island Railway.' . . . The happy party were waving handkerchiefs from the windows. . . . Finally Conductor Barnum shouted "All aboard". . . .

"In the next scene the party was supposed to be on the iron, wood and cloth steamer, 'Signet.'. . . First chorus, band and orchestra appropriately sang Auld Lang Syne. . . . The Greylark quartette followed . . . singing *Serenade* by Van der Stucken. . . . F. Seymour's novel solos on glasses, bars, sticks and bottles. . . . The Trinity church boy choir . . . rendered *Peasant's Wedding March* by Soderman, then vocal quadrilles by Farmer. . . . *Ave Maria* by Gounod was sung by Mrs. Carrie Allen Baker . . . as an encore . . . *Rock Me to Sleep, Mother.* . . . Master Hans Kronold [cello, played] *Scotch Melodies* by Kuwner. . . . Master Gilmore of the Trinity church choir . . . sang . . . *Daddy.* . . . Mssrs. Pierpoint and Belden . . . the former picked the banjo and the latter the guitar . . . rendered old airs. . . . *Home, Sweet Home* was sung by the excursionists, when again the curtain fell.

". . . scene on the beach at Coney Island. . . . A musical storm now came up . . . wind, flashes of lightning and deep peals of thunder. . . . The music, after the storm had cleared away and the sun shone brightly, imitated the brass band at Paul Bauer's, while the great and only Levy rendered a cornet solo. The representations of the German and Scotch bands were unusually true to nature, and the Italian was also a good imitation. But it was the rendition of the *William Tell Overture* by Seidl's grand orchestra, that was the great feature. . . .

". . . then they 'took the cars to join the great Gilmore in his jubilee concert'. . . the *Anvil Chorus* from *Trovatore.* . . . The fireworks were a surprise. . . .

"The whole entertainment was concluded with the singing of *America.* . . . The party arrived home and poured from the cars past the row of hackmen, and all was over. . . ."

In the same issue was "A Card from Mr. Ives . . . What was intended in the first place as an instrumental concert grew to such magnitude, both vocal and instrumental— through the kindness of many friends—that the concert was more than one man could manage without some shortcomings being apparent. . . . To the many who kindly assisted in making the affair a success without previous notice my sincere thanks are given . . . although, in great part, an impromptu affair . . . a signal success and . . . an enjoyable occasion. . . . George E. Ives."

One may imagine that the "large water pipes" Ives mentions in the next line would have been just right for the *Anvil Chorus*.

been fully realized. (In the *Universe Symphony* I tried, for the percussion orchestra (Earth's motion and pulse), about a dozen different kinds—as Drums (8), Snare (2), Bells (11), Gongs (4), Pipes (2), Cymbals (3), Xylophones (2), Blocks of wood—all I could think of—it sounded (with eight players) better than I thought.)

m60v
tm
The listener, if he tries hard enough, will get the composite effect that's wanted, while each player concentrates on his particular meter, hearing the others as secondary sounds, at least while practising them. For instance, a piccolo playing a 13 over a 4/4 will be able, after a while, to get it fairly accurately, while a pianist playing 13 with one hand and 7 with the other will find it very difficult at first to get the effect, as the tonal sounds are so much the same—and I don't know, even if it's done accurately, how effective it is to the listener, unless he's had some practice in listening to and playing them himself. But if the different meters are each played by groups of different sounding units, the effect is valuable, and I believe will be gradually found an important element in deepening and enriching all of the depths of music, including the emotional and spiritual.

t60vm
I have with much practice been able to keep five, and even six, rhythms going in my mind at once, so that I can hear each one naturally by leaning toward it, changing the ear in each measure—and I think this is the more natural way of hearing and learning the use of and feeling for rhythms, than by writing them and playing from them on paper, which shows the exact position of each note in relation to each other, in the eye. The way I did it was to take, for instance, in the left hand a 5—with the left foot, beat a 2—with the right foot, beat a 3—with the right hand, play an 11—and sing a 7. Start with two, gradually add the others—perhaps to begin with, have a slow metronome with a bell play the one-beat, and think of the [measure] as a 2, then a 3, then a 5, then a 7, then an 11—([or] using several metronomes with bells, clicks, to get them going in the mind). (I've found an old set of exercises written for this practice, which I'll be glad to show to anybody who's interested.)[2] Various other rhythms can be held in the mind in this way, and after a while they become as natural as it is for Toscanini to beat down-left-right-up as evenly as a metronome for two hours steadily, and do it nice, with the ladies all tapping time with their feet.

160v
But it is very difficult and not worth the trouble. In piano pieces, songs, etc., two, sometimes three rhythms are all I find worth using.

2 This "old set of exercises" has not yet been found among Ives's papers.

49

T60m

    These instances, together with some of the others suggested above (a typical example is Professor Milcke), had something of the effect on me of a kind of periodic deterrent, something approaching a result of a sedative. Whether these musicians, in the above instances, were personal friends or not, the effect they had on me was the same. For instance, Dave and Max Smith[1] were old friends of mine, and real friends at that, whom I respected and liked and got along with, except

M13
T61m

when it came to music. But they, as well as the others, made it very evident that they didn't like my music—(that is, the parts of it I liked and felt the best, they didn't). And often that would get me thinking that there must be something wrong with me, for, with the exception of Mrs. Ives, no one seemed to like anything that I happened to be working on when these incidents came up. "Why is it that I like to use these different things and try out other ways etc. which nobody else evidently has any pleasure in hearing, seeing, or thinking about? Why do I like to do it? Is there some peculiar defect in me, or something worse that I'm afflicted with?" So I'd have periods of being good and nice, and getting back to the usual ways of writing, sometimes for several months, until I got so tired of it that I decided I'd either have to stop music or

T61m

stop this. Some of the results of these weak-minded, retrogressive moments I can spot every time I look at the first measure. For instance, some of the songs in 1908–09–10 are in this kind of a slump, while others a few years before, even as far back as 1901, are not—#58 [*Evidence*], #42 [*Serenity*], #52 [*Old Home Day*], #60 [*Autumn*], #61 [*Nature's Way*], #62 [*The Waiting Soul*], and #65 [*Spring Song*] are samples of the slump[2]—the *String Quartet* around 1905–06 (N. G., most of it destroyed or worked into something else)—some other pieces for strings (see back page 68)[3]—some of the *Third* and *Fourth Violin Sonatas*—and the *First Violin Sonata* in part was a kind of slump backward, although in some places it is quite the opposite. But more often, after these instances, nothing happened, good or bad, which is good.

m61v

    Another instance of how opinions, remarks, etc., which to the recipient seem either stupid or unfair, will cause one to do something that his better judgment knows it's not quite best perhaps to do—was

---

1 This wording seems to suggest that they were related, but Ives certainly knew that they weren't. See §47, notes 3 and 12.

2 These are the numbers in *114 Songs* (see App. 4). Ives later crossed Nos. 42 and 52 out of this list.

3 The back of T68 is still blank. For the String Quartet of around 1905–06 see §26, and App. 3, #60.

the way some of the "old ladies" purred out about playing the piano with a stick—"and how just terribly inartistic to have octaves of all white or black notes as chords of music!" The book of *114 Songs* was to start with the second one on page 6, Milton's *Evening*. But the "ta-tas" etc., above, made me feel just mean enough to want to give all the "old girls" another ride—and then, after they saw the first page of *The Masses* as No. 1 in the book, it would keep them from turning any more pages and finding something "just too awful for words, Lily!" I know for a fact that this is exactly what one lady did—and her wastebasket, not mine, was the one right place for that book!

50

Another thing that the songs remind me about, is that some of them were started for a solo instrument for the voice part with words written underneath, and for a small group of instruments as an accompaniment (about 3, 4, 5, 6, 8). The principal reason for this was because singers made such a fuss about the intervals, time, etc., and when they were arranged later for voice and piano, they were weakened in many cases, also simplified—which I should not have done. This is no way to write a song—but it's the way I wrote some—take it or leave it, Eddy!

Another [reason] also—Father could play, on his horn, a Franz Schubert or Steve Foster song better than many singers could sing it— he often taught songs and parts to singers or choirs etc. by playing. But he always insisted that the words should be known and thought of, while playing. That, I suppose, gave me the idea of "songs with or without voices."[1] Some [of these] songs were from the chamber music [pieces].

There were also some songs which ought to have gone in the book, but the "old ladies" again stopped it, I'm ashamed to say. There were some with wide jumps, 9ths, 7ths, almost two octaves, and almost impossible piano parts to boot (boot is good). Today these songs are quite reasonable, singable, and playable—for instance, one a Glory trance [*General Booth*], and a *Soliloquy* (study in 7ths and other things, taking off a Yankee drawl), one about bees [*Aeschylus and Sophocles*], and Keats, etc.[2]

n67v

1 Or had Ives found singers' words too seldom understandable? (The widespread notion that vivid words spoil vocal line tends to invalidate all song.) But Ives goes further in dissociating the music from the words by assigning to many of the instrumental versions abstract titles like: *Adagio sostenuto, Andante cantabile, Allegretto sombreoso*, etc. (see index of Ives's music).
2 Ives's only known Keats song is already in the book (App. 4, #26). But he mentions Keats also among the "Eleven Songs . . . 1922–27" (App. 3, #89). Either there was another Keats song, which is missing, or perhaps he meant Byron's *A Farewell to Land* (App. 4, #119).

51

T61m   There is another matter that I quite often think of and wonder about, to some extent. The last time I looked at the *Third Symphony*, it was brought back to my mind. This symphony, or at least part of it (as two movements were revised and scored from organ pieces [of] 1901 or so, the last movement from an organ prelude [on *Woodworth* by] Brad-

T62m bury), was finished about the same time [as], perhaps a little before, most of the three Holiday movements and parts of the other sets—and yet it's a kind of crossway between the older ways and the newer ways. And to a certain extent the same is true of the *First Violin Sonata*, though not as much so as the *Third Symphony*. And I sometimes feel that something like the following accounted for it.

I seemed to have worked with more natural freedom, when I knew that the music was not going to be played before the public, or rather before people who couldn't get out from under, as is the case in a church congregation—and a number of the themes and general subject matter had to do with religious themes—knowing that, if played at all, they would probably be played in church. Even after giving up the organ position in 1902, I substituted for an occasional Sunday service for several years after that at different churches,[1] and I would always take this opportunity of trying out things that I was working on, things of this character.

m62   And in playing them at a service, is one justified in doing something
m62v which, to him, is quite in keeping with his understanding and feelings —but [not] to the congregation, who [may be] unused to the idiom, or rather some of the sound combinations, and so naturally might misunderstand and be disturbed? The *Third String Quartet*[2] (not finished, I think for this reason) and the *Third Symphony* especially were to some extent boiled down, or rather suppressed, technically speaking. The last movement was fuller and more freely made than it is now in the final score, because I played it at some communion services, and got away from some of the things I had started with, and for so long a time forgotten—for instance, in the middle section and coda, there was a kind of an echo-organ effect that I played in practice when the church was empty, and didn't in the service. I can not find it written in any of the parts.

I remember particularly, in talking with Goldstein and some others about this, he said, "How far should a man consider his audience? You

1 No evidence has appeared of what churches or what dates.
2 This must be the so-called *Pre-Second String Quartet* (see §26). Compare the shifting numberings in §21–26 in the Table of Contents.

m63v

must have felt that your original way was the right one—do you think you are justified in changing it, because the audience might not get it?" —etc. No, not for the usual concert audience, unless they had paid admission to hear something which they knew in advance they would hear. But to a body of people who[3] come together to worship—how far has a man a right to do what he wants, if he knows that by so doing he is interfering with the state of mind of the listeners, who have to listen regardless, and are helpless not to?

M13
T62m

So, as I look back, I seem to have worked with more natural freedom, when I knew the music was not going to be inflicted on others. And this is probably one of the reasons that, not until I got to work on the *Fourth Symphony*, did I feel justified in writing quite as I wanted to, when the subject matter was religious.[4] So many of the movements in things used later were started as organ preludes and postludes etc. for church services, [and] I knew that they might be played. One has a different feeling in forcing your "home-made" on a public that can't help itself, than on a friend who comes to your house and asks you to play. (You have to finish at a public hymn, but a friend can walk out!)

M14
T62m

In other words, a congregation has some rights which an intimate or personal friend hasn't, in full. (At least, to friends a man has a right to say what he thinks, but before [a congregation not] quite the same right.)

M14
T63m

The last movement of the *Fourth Symphony* and the last movement of the *Second Orchestral Set* are built essentially on religious subject matter, but I didn't feel about them as I did with the music before that (for example, the *Third Symphony* and parts of the violin sonatas) in which religious themes are used. Why I felt that way, I'm not very sure. Was it for the reason just above, or for some other reason? Personally I don't believe that this was because of the following reason (which some too easily hold), that religious services have a tendency (as some say) to make a man conservative—that they restrict, in a certain way, freedom of thought and action. I feel differently, because it seems to me [that] most of the forward movements of life in general and of pioneers in most of the great activities, have been [the work of] essentially religious-minded men.

Anyway, in considering my music, the secular things—that is, those whose subject matter has to do with the activities of general life around one—seem to be freer and more experimental in technical ways. Com-

3 Ives wrote this word as "to" probably meaning "who".
4 This is not strictly true. If Ives's statement at the end of §43 be accurate, the field of his most wildly experimental music in 1893–94 was the choral psalm. But these psalms could hardly have been sung in church at that time. His father's "getting a choir in Danbury to sing [*Psalm 67*] without an organ" (see App. 5) was probably an informal reading.

pare the Holiday pieces written a year or so after the *Third Symphony*[5] (that is, after it was scored—as parts of it were from old pieces for organ), and about with the *First* and *Second Violin Sonatas*. (I realize I am talking a good deal about my own music, as though it was an important matter of interest, comparatively, to many—which it isn't[6]— but as this is a kind of personal diary, and as I happen to know more about my music than about anybody else's—and then one thing, good or bad, suggests another thing, good or bad.)

The Thanksgiving movement in this set is, in a way, an exception, because, when it was first written (played in Center Church, Thanks- giving Service 1897), it was quite experimental harmonically and, to a certain extent, rhythmically (Dr. Griggs said the chord, C major and D minor over it, gave something of the Forefathers' strength [that] a triad would not do), but heard today with the other movements in this set, it would seem quite conservative. But in considering the case of the Thanksgiving music as it is, a kind of paradox seems to appear. Dissonances, or what seemed to be dissonances at the time, had a good excuse for being, and in the final analysis a religious excuse, because in the stern outward life of the old settlers, pioneers and Puritans, there

M14
T64m

was a life generally of inward beauty, but with a rather harsh exterior. And the Puritan "no-compromise" with mellow colors and bodily ease gives a natural reason for trying tonal and uneven off-counterpoints and combinations which would be and sound of sterner things—which single minor or major triads or German-made counterpoint did not (it seemed to me) come up to. This music must, before all else, be some- thing in art removed from physical comfort.

The early ragtime pieces and marches, most of the *First Piano Sonata*, most of the *Theater Orchestra Set*, etc. seemed to get going "good and free"—and the hymn-tune sonatas and symphonies less so—until, as suggested above, the *Fourth Symphony* and the last movement of the *Second Orchestral Set* were reached.

[5] Ives often dated things by their last revisions or finishing touches. Here he is dating the *Third Symphony* as 1909 or 1910, but apparently it was mostly composed in 1904. (See §16.)
[6] Ives would have been surprised how many people were vitally interested in his music by April 1932.

52

m64

I might add one more matter, as some ask me about [it] and ap- parently don't get it all right:—why and how a man who apparently likes music so much goes into business. Two things:—(1) As a boy [I was] partially ashamed of it—an entirely wrong attitude, but it was strong—most boys in American country towns, I think, felt the same. When other boys, Monday A.M. on vacation, were out driving grocery carts, or doing chores, or playing ball, I felt all wrong to stay in and play piano. And there may be something in it. Hasn't music always been too much an emasculated art? Mozart etc. helped.[1]

m64v
(2) Father felt that a man could keep his music-interest stronger, cleaner, bigger, and freer, if he didn't try to make a living out of it. Assuming a man lived by himself and with no dependents, no one to feed but himself, and willing to live as simply as Thoreau—[he] might write music that no one would play, publish, listen to, or buy. *But*— if he has a nice wife and some nice children, how can he let the children starve on his dissonances—answer that, Eddy! So he has to weaken (and as a man he should weaken for his children), but his music (some of it) more than weakens—it goes "ta ta" for money—bad for him, bad for music, but good for his boys!!

[3] If a man has, say, a certain ideal he's aiming at in his art, and has a wife and children whom he can't support (as his art products won't sell enough unless he lowers them to a more commercial basis), should he let his family starve and keep his ideals? No, I say—for if he did, his "art" would be dishonestly weakened, [and] his ideals would be but vanity.

(4) Also other reasons, from experience, that to be thrown with people of all conditions all day long, for a good part of a man's life, widens rather than cramps up his sensibilities etc. (for instance, see Bellamann's *Musical Quarterly* article, January '33).[2] But others (many) feel differently, [that] writing sellable music part of the time doesn't disturb their better music. The way I'm constituted, writing soft stuff makes me sore—I sort of hate all music.

1 Ives's reaction to Mozart could very well be explained by the kind of Mozart performance that was fashionable when Ives was a young man—smooth and daintily smirking like Dresden china figurines. The Wagner cult had belittled all earlier music except Beethoven, but the twentieth century has found Mozart's music far more masculine than Wagner's.
2 Ives probably meant Bellamann's long quote from him in pp. 47–48 of the *Musical Quarterly* issue, pp. 96–97 in Cowell. Bellamann also says: "Mr. Ives' business success was founded on the same sort of daring experiment, together with an interest and confidence in human nature, that characterizes his music . . . the principles of this business were often radical and daring, but . . . were based really on . . . common sense . . . it brought him in close relation with thousands of men of all kinds and conditions. This association of over thirty years . . . gave him a high respect for . . . the average man's mind and character. This confidence . . . seemed too visionary and idealistic to many. . . . The young men were assured that this . . . would cause their failure within a year . . . but some of the plans that seemed the most visionary . . . worked out the best . . . as the business grew, the firm retained the respect and good-will of its competitors." Compare App. 9 (after note 21).

53

Just one or two more things, and then these memoranda, I hope, are about over. Exception has been taken by some (in other words there have been criticisms, often severe) to my using, as bases for themes, suggestions of old hymns, occasional tunes of past generations, etc. As one routine-minded professor told me, "In music they should have no place. Imagine, in a symphony, hearing suggestions of street tunes like *Marching Through Georgia* or a Moody and Sankey hymn!"—etc.[1] Well, I'll say two things here: (1) That nice professor of music is a musical lily-pad—(and also use the same remarks as about Aunt Hale in § 4). He never took a chance at himself, or took one coming or going.[2] (2) His opinion is based on something he'd probably never heard, seen, or experienced. He knows little of how these things sounded when they came "blam" off a real man's chest. It was the *way* this music was sung that made them big or little—and I had the chance of hearing them big. And it wasn't the music that did it, and it wasn't the words that did it, and it wasn't the sounds (whatever they were—transcendent, peculiar, bad, some beautifully unmusical)—but they were sung "like the rocks were grown." The singers weren't singers, but they knew what they were doing—it all came from something felt, way down and way up—a man's experience of men!

Once a nice young man[3] (his musical sense having been limited by three years' intensive study at the Boston Conservatory) said to Father, "How can you stand it to hear old John Bell[4] (the best stone-mason in town) sing?" (as he used to at Camp Meetings) Father said, "He is a supreme musician." The young man (nice and educated) was horrified —"Why, he sings off the key, the wrong notes and everything—and that horrible, raucous voice—and he bellows out and hits notes no one else does—it's awful!" Father said, "Watch him closely and reverently, look into his face and hear the music of the ages. Don't pay too much attention to the sounds—for if you do, you may miss the music. You won't get a wild, heroic ride to heaven on pretty little sounds."

I remember, when I was a boy—at the outdoor Camp Meeting services in Redding, all the farmers, their families and field hands, for miles around, would come afoot or in their farm wagons. I remember how the great waves of sound used to come through the trees—when things like *Beulah Land, Woodworth, Nearer My God To Thee, The Shining Shore, Nettleton, In the Sweet Bye and Bye* and the like were sung by thousands of "let out" souls. The music notes and words on

M15
T65

M16
T66m

---

1 Miss O'Meara (Librarian Emerita of the Yale School of Music) thinks that this must be Parker himself, who was known to say: "The hymn tune is the lowest form of musical life."

2 These may be baseball terms from the days when Ives played pitcher, fielder, short-stop, etc. A former Cornell varsity player, Jim Oliphant '68, suggests that "never took a chance at himself" could mean not risking a fastball that might rebound as a home run, and that "took one coming" could refer to a fielder catching a fly on the run that was dropping in front of him, and "took one going"—that was dropping behind him.

3 Is this Orrin Barnum? (see §12, note 11).

4 See §25, note 3, about Alfred Bell, the mason.

paper were about as much like what they "were" (at those moments)
as the monogram on a man's necktie may be like his face. Father, who

T66m   led the singing, sometimes with his cornet or his voice, sometimes with
both voice and arms, and sometimes in the quieter hymns with a
French horn or violin, would always encourage the people to sing
their own way. Most of them knew the words and music (theirs) by
heart, and sang it that way. If they threw the poet or the composer
around a bit, so much the better for the poetry and the music.[5] There

T67m   was power and exaltation in these great conclaves of sound from
humanity. I've heard the same hymns played by nice celebrated
organists and sung by highly-known singers in beautifully upholstered
churches, and in the process everything in the music was emasculated
—precise (usually too fast) even time—"ta ta" down-left-right-up—
pretty voices, etc. They take a mountain and make a sponge cake [out]
of it, and sometimes, as a result, one of these commercial travellers gets
a nice job at the Metropolitan. Today apparently even the Camp Meetings are getting easy-bodied and commercialized. There are not many
more of them here in the east, and what is told of some of those that
still survive, such as Amy McPherson & Co.,[6] seems but a form of easy
entertainment and silk cushions—far different from the days of the
"stone-fielders".

[5] This kind of freedom is described in a letter-sketch of 1945 as "the way, at an outdoor
meeting . . . with no instrumental accompaniment except a cornet . . . the fervor of the
feeling would at times, especially on reaching the Chorus of many of those hymns, throw
the key higher, sometimes a whole tone up—though Father used to say it [was] more
often about a quarter tone up—and . . . Father had a sliding cornet made so that he
could rise with them and not keep them down."
[6] Aimée Semple McPherson (1890–1944), Canadian evangelist, settled in Los Angeles
as the founder of an elaborately organized evangelistic association, and became a member
of the Chamber of Commerce.

54

M[18]   But the Camp Meetings aren't the only things that have gone soft.
T67m   How about some of the seed of 1776? There are probably several contributing factors. Perhaps the most obvious if not the most harmful
element is commercialism, with its influence tending towards mechan-
ization and standardized processes of mind and life (making breakfast
and death a little too easy). Emasculating America for money! Is the
Anglo-Saxon going "Pussy"?—the nice Lizzies—the do-it-proper boys
of today—the cushions of complacency—the champions of bodily ease
—the play-it-pretty minds—the cautious old gals running the broadcasting companies—those great national brain-softeners, the movies—
the mind-dulling tabloids with their headlines of half-truths and heroic

M[18]   pictures of the most popular defectives—the ladybirds—the femaled-
68m

male crooners—the easy-ear concert-hall parlor entertainments with not even one "god-damn" in them—they are all getting theirs, and America is not! Is she gradually losing her manhood? The Puritans may have been everything that the lollers[1] called them, but they weren't soft. They may have been cold, narrow, hard-minded rock-eaters outwardly, but they weren't effeminates.

Richy Wagner did get away occasionally from doh-me-soh, which was more than some others did. He had more or less of a good brain for technical progress, but he seems to put it to such weak uses— exulting, like a nice lady's purple silk dress, in fake nobility and heroism, but afraid to jump in a mill pond and be a hero. He liked instead to dress up in purple and sing about heroism—(a woman posing as a man.)

Music has been, to too large an extent, an emasculated art—and Wagner did his part to keep it so. What masculation he has in it, is make-believe. Even today probably about 83% of the so-called best musical programs—that is, of the large city symphony orchestras, of educational institutions, and of the opera—lean more to the molly-coddle than the rough way up the mountain. And 98¼% of all radio music is worse than molly-coddle—it's the one-syllable gossip for the soft-ears-and-stomachs, easy for their bodies, and is fundamentally art prostituted for commercialism.

Men (that is, women and men) are so constituted that they are at first more inclined to buy the easy (to hear and look [at] it) than the difficult. Toward art in general, especially music, they are like the five year old boy who comes down to breakfast. He sees two tables in the dining

room: (1) nice lollypops, (2) oatmeal. He goes to #1, if he has his way. But most of them don't always have their own way (as everybody does on the radio). For that reason most boys go to #2, and they grow up strong, more or less. But towards music, and to a certain extent towards literature and art in general, the majority still go to table #1 (lollypops etc.), because the president, the directors, and stockholders of the Rollo companies are weak sisters, and not strong fathers and mothers— for there is more money in selling #1, because it's easier to sell. Look at the faces of the people who go every night to the movies, the next A.M.

When I think of some music that I liked to hear and play 35 or 40 years ago—if I hear some of it now, I feel like saying, "Rollo, how did you fall for that sop, those 'ta tas' and greasy ringlets?" In this I would include the *Preislied*,[2] *The Rosary*,[3] a certain amount of Mozart, Mendelssohn, a small amount of early Beethoven, with the easy-made

---

[1] Ives probably meant no particular group but the lazy or carefree in general. (The Lollards were in another century and had much in common with the Puritans.)
[2] From Act 3 of *Die Meistersinger*—for Ives's disappointment with Wagner see also the letter of 1 April 1894 in Boatwright, note 41.
[3] For another reference to Nevin see §47, note 20.

Haydn, a large amount of Massenet, Sibelius, Tchaikovsky, etc. (to say nothing of Gounod), most Italian operas (not exactly most of the operas, but most of each opera), some of Chopin (pretty soft, but you don't mind it in him so much, because one just naturally thinks of him with a skirt on, but one which he made himself). Notwithstanding the above slants, which many would say are insults, it seems to me, as it did then and ever, that still today Bach, Beethoven, and Brahms (No) are among the strongest and greatest in all art, and nothing since is stronger or greater than their strongest and greatest—(not quite as strong and great as Carl Ruggles,[4] because B., B., and B. have too much of the sugar-plum for the soft-ears—but even with that, they have some manhood of their own). I won't say that their best is better or worse than any music before or since—I won't say, because I don't know— and nobody knows, except Rollo!

m33v   My brother[5] says, "That's rather conceited of you, isn't it, to criticize the great men (as Mozart, Wagner, etc.), especially when [you] do some composing yourself. Some might say that you imply that your music is greater, less emasculated, and more to the point[6] than any of the so-called great masters!" I don't imply any such thing—I don't have to—I state [that] it is better! Ask any good musician—those who don't agree with me are not good musicians—but if some of the poor musicians (that is, Ossip, Arthur, and Kitty) should agree with me, then I'd begin to think I was wrong.

m50v   (Sep. 4 [rightly 5], '34—in London (18 Half Moon St.). Last evening Harmony, Edie, and singer [Laurence] Holmes, and Daddy went to a Promenade Concert [at] Queen's Hall—a Sibelius program.[7] The music on the boats and Green Park[8] didn't bring it home to me more strongly and hopelessly surely, than sitting there for an hour or so and

---

4 Ruggles was a year and a half younger than Ives, but they seem not to have met until 1930. Ruggles had often been told by his friends in the International Composers Guild that Ives didn't amount to anything. So a first-hand acquaintance with Ives and his music must have been like a revelation of a yet unknown glory of New England. Conversely Ruggles and his music were enormously appealing to Ives's Yankee independence. They soon became each other's favorite living composers. Their earliest extant correspondence is Ives's telegram of Friday 26 February 1932 (the day after Slonimsky had conducted *Sun-treader* in Paris): "We are all elated that Paris is up with you treading the sun." See also §56, at note 1, the end of App. 19, and the chronological index, item of 26 February 1932. Ruggles died Sunday 24 October 1971, age 95.

5 See App. 13.

6 The word "point" is a guess in the dark at the meaning of "II X T."

7 Tuesday evening, 4 September 1934, at Queen's Hall, Sir Henry Wood conducted a BBC Promenade Concert with the following program: Sibelius *Karelia Overture, 7th Symphony, Luonnotar* (Helmi Liukkonen, soprano), *Pohjola's Daughter, 1st Symphony;* Franck *Le Chasseur Maudit;* Tchaikovsky *The Battle of Poltava (Mazeppa).*

    The Iveses had met Laurence Holmes, baritone, on the S.S. Pennland (sailing from New York, Friday 10 August 1934, to Southampton). The program of his recital of Tuesday 16 October 1934 at Wigmore Hall and three reviews of it are in one of Ives's scrapbooks, but Ives had already sailed back to New York.

8 Green Park is between Buckingham Palace Gardens and Piccadilly, from which Half Moon Street runs northwest to Curzon Street. Mrs. Ives recalled that Green Park had a bandstand.

hearing those groove-made chewed-cuds (those sound-sequences tied to the same old nice apron-strings, which have become greasy in the process),—that music (and all art, like all life) must be a part of the great organic flow, onwards and always upwards, or become soft in muscles and spirit, and die! I was never more conscious of the vapidity of the human minds that accept anything, round, soft, fat, or bazoota, which somebody else with a nicer silk hat than theirs hands them— commercial silk hatters[9]—music conservatories (the better known the worse)—the paid newspaper critics—the prima donna monopolists— and perhaps the lowest of all, the publishing, the broadcasting, and recording for profit. The *Valse Triste* (as brown-sugar-coddle as it is) is bigger than what [we] heard last night—for the first is a nice lollypop, and it doesn't try to be something else—but these symphonies, over-tures, etc. are worse because they give out the strut of a little music making believe it's big. Every phrase, line, and chord, and beat went over and over the way you'd exactly expect them to go—even when it didn't go as you'd expected, you didn't expect it would—trite, tiresome awnings of platitudes, all a nice mixture of Grieg, Wagner, and Tchai-kovsky (et al, ladies). But the worst part—a thing hinting that music might some day die, like an emasculated cherry, dead but dishonored— was to see those young people standing downstairs, seriously eating that yellow sap flowing from a stomach that had never had an idea. And some of them are probably composing, and you can see them going home, copying down those slimy grooves and thinking they are creating something—helping music decline—dying—dying—dead.)

55

T68m   These memoranda started as an attempt to put down in some definite shape some of the things I'm asked about concerning my music, and also some of the things I'm not asked about, but which occasionally appear in newspapers or articles purporting to give information about me or my music—which are more information to me than to anyone else (samples of the above are given [in Part One]).

I find that most musicians, critics, etc., take it for granted that a man who composes music must, as a result, be conversant with all the music that has been written in the world up to last night. So many apparently seem surprised, and can't understand why I don't know this piece or that piece of this composer or that composer, especially if it had just been played by the last conductor from Europe who had appeared on the scene with the score in his vest pocket.

9 Anybody from 19th-century Danbury would know at first hand some of the varied aspects of big business as represented in the Danbury hatting industry.

As I see it, there are only about two reasons why I don't. One is that, being in business for so many years, I had only evenings, Saturday afternoons and Sundays, and summer vacations of two or three weeks, in which to work. For this reason, as far back as twenty or so years ago, I got out of the habit of going to concerts, especially in the evenings. I always seemed to have something I was working on, and it was this, and the fact that my time was limited, that kept me from going out much.

The other reason—(and I remember being conscious of this as far back as 1910 or '11, a particular instance after coming from a concert of the Philharmonic which I think Gustav Mahler conducted)—[was] that, on account of having only a limited time in which to work, I got into the habit of carrying things in my mind which were not put down, or only partly put down, on paper. As this was the case most of the time, I found that listening to music (especially if in the programs there were things with which I was not familiar) tended to throw me out of my stride. I'll admit it may have been a kind of weakness on my part, but I found that listening to concert music seemed to confuse me in my own work, maybe not to a great extent, but enough to throw me off somewhat from what I had in mind or purposed. Hearing the old pieces that I'd been familiar with all my life (for instance, the Beethoven and Brahms symphonies, Bach, or even the *William Tell Overture,* etc.) did not, as I remember, seem to have this effect. I remember hearing something of Max Reger—I forget what it was—I think Fiedler played it with the Boston Philharmonic about twenty years ago[1]—and when I got back to what I'd been working on, I was conscious of a kind of interference or lapse (something as you feel when writing a letter and someone butts in [and] reads his letter to you when you're trying to write yours).

At any rate, I found that I could work more naturally and with more concentration if I didn't hear much music, especially unfamiliar music. To make a long story short, I went to very few concerts. I suppose everyone is built differently and works differently. It just so happened that I felt I could work better and liked to work more, if I kept to my own music and let other people keep to theirs. I don't by any means say this as a recommendation to others—in fact, if I'd had more time

---

1 This must be the concert of Thursday evening, 11 November 1909, at Carnegie Hall, conducted by Max Fiedler: Reger *Symphonic Prologue to a Tragedy* Op. 108, Thomas *Air from Le Caïd* (Charles Gilibert, baritone), Brahms *Second Symphony,* Massenet *Air from Grisélidis* and Bordes *Dansons la Gigue!* (Gilibert), Strauss *Till Eulenspiegel.* Ives was then in New York, at 70 West 11th Street, and the booklet of program notes is still among his papers. The Boston Symphony gave two other Reger performances at Carnegie Hall around this time, on 9 November 1911 and 9 January 1913, both Thursday evenings, but Ives was living at Hartsdale both times, and, as Mrs. Ives remembered, he would not have stayed in town for an evening concert.

for my own music, quite probably I wouldn't have felt this way. But when people take it as a matter of course that I know such and such music, or such and such a symphony, and I tell them I don't, they seem so surprised, and can't understand why anybody who is really interested in music shouldn't be familiar with everything that's going on in the world of music.

I never thought much about this habit until articles were sent to me saying that something of mine was influenced by so-and-so, giving names of composers whose music I hadn't heard, and in some instances whose names I hadn't heard of. For instance, it wasn't until about 1919 or '20 that I first heard any of Stravinsky's music. At that time I did hear a part of *Firebird*,[2] and I thought it was morbid and monotonous. (The idea of a phrase, usually a small one, was good enough and interesting in itself, but he kept it going over and over, and [it] got tiresome.) It reminded me of something I'd heard of Ravel, most of whose music, that I've heard, is a kind I can't stand, weak, morbid, and monotonous—pleasing enough if you want to be pleased. Now in 1923 or '24 I heard one of the symphony orchestras play Stravinsky's "Chinese Rossignol".[3] I've never heard or seen the score of the *Sacre du Printemps,* yet I've been told (and shown notices of critics etc., saying) that some of my music—for instance, *Putnam's Camp* (second movement, *First Orchestral Set*)—had been strongly influenced by the *Sacre du Printemps*. Personally I don't believe they have anything in common. The places in this movement which some say come from Stravinsky were written before Stravinsky wrote the *Sacre* (or at least before it was first played), and came direct from the habit of piano-drum-playing.[4]

T71m

2 The first New York performances were both by Damrosch and the New York Symphony: Sunday afternoon 31 December 1916: Dvorak *New World Symphony,* Saint-Saëns *2nd Concerto* (Samaroff), Stravinsky *Firebird* (original suite);—Thursday afternoon & Friday evening 10–11 February 1921, Russian program: *Volga Boatmen's Song* (arr. Stravinsky), Glinka *Russlan* overture, Rimsky-Korsakoff *Scheherazade* (ii & iii), Stravinsky *Firebird* (revised suite), Rachmaninoff *2nd Concerto* (Rachmaninoff). Both times Ives was in New York, in 1916 at 142 East 40th St., in 1921 at 120 East 22nd St. Thursday afternoon 10 February 1921 seems most likely, in view of Ives's writing, the next month: "I still have to be careful, and can't go out in the evening unless I can arrange to be away from the office during the day." (see §35, end of note 6).
3 The first New York performances were by Damrosch and the New York Symphony, Thursday afternoon & Friday evening, 1–2 November 1923: Franck *Symphony,* Fauré *Pelléas et Mélisande* suite, Sibelius *Finlandia,* Stravinsky *Le Chant du Rossignol* (first time in New York). Then simultaneously by Damrosch on Thursday afternoon & Friday evening 27–28 March 1924: Stravinsky *Le Chant du Rossignol,* Brahms *Double Concerto* (Kochanski, Salmond), Skryabin *Le Poême de l'Extase;*—and by Mengelberg and the New York Philharmonic, Thursday evening & Friday afternoon 27–28 March 1924: Stravinsky *Le Chant du Rossignol,* Goldmark *Negro Rhapsody,* Beethoven *4th Symphony.* Both times Ives was in New York, at 120 East 22nd Street.
    It was Damrosch's performance that Ives heard (probably Thursday afternoon 27 March 1924), which Furness refers to in a letter of Sunday 6 April 1924 (discussing performances of Skryabin's *Extase*) as "the one we heard last week."
4 See §11.

m71v

As an example, on page 37 [of the] photostat [score of] *Three Places in New England,* the middle measure[5] has been picked on as coming from Stravinsky. Whether it sounds or looks like Stravinsky I don't know, because I don't know him or his [music]. But when people make an absolute and definite statement that it is from Stravinsky, they lie. This measure is directly from the old piano-drum habit. In this particular case, it happens that, as far as its rhythm goes, it is a third measure from a set of three common-time measures used in an early march and one overture, "1776" (see *Overture and March "1776"*, photostat score, on page 1, lower line, at bottom[6]—also *Country Band March,* p. 2, also p. 6).[7] The two rhythms going together (in the piano-drum part) are nothing but a beat or pulse on the first of [each] four 16th-

m70v

notes, and one on the first of [each] three 16th-notes. Say, if a band is marching at 120 = ♩ = ♬♬ , the next fastest marching (keeping the ♪ unit the same) will be stepping to three 16ths or ♫ , and if two bands feel like marching on these accents,

one is:

other:

(see also Chamber Music, *Tone Roads,* etc.—also see last part of coda of organ variations [on] *America,* 1892—see photo). Then, for three 4/4 measures, if the top band stops playing, the second one is playing [off-]accents—[in the 3rd measure] it is simply:

n71v

[This] will be the measure on p. 37 cited above (here the first two measures are just cut out). It doesn't take much musical intelligence to see that (or to do that, for that matter). The basis of the plan is so simple [and] obvious that it is a "truth." In putting these two rhythms together, the 16th-notes don't have to be struck all the while. They will [be] played in various phrases, omitted [in others]. The more they are in, the more variants will occur, etc. I'll bet 1000 people have

70v

---

5 That is, m. 124, the middle measure of p. 37 of the score by Emil Hanke, corresponding to p. 49 of the Birchard and Mercury printings.
6 In the sketch of "1776", p. 1 (Q2407), the piano-drum part is continued in a kind of shorthand under the bottom staff, and m. 18 (m. 93 of *Putnam's Camp*) has the rhythm of the first of the three measures notated below.
7 In the sketch of the *Country Band March,* p. 2 (Q2057), threes overlap fours in mm. 44–45 (which correspond to m. 27 of *Putnam's Camp*), but the figure in the cello is different and an octave higher, and the beams make groups of three: b♭–b♮–c¹, a–b♭–c♭¹, b♭–c¹–c♯¹, etc. On p. 6 (Q2061), mm. 128–29 (m. 124 of *Putnam's Camp*—see note 7 above) have the rhythm of the third of the three measures notated below.

thought of this, perhaps played this—yet, because they don't know [what] it is, they say it is meaningless, or influenced by Orcus from Australia!

m71v
m70v
The above is a good illustration of how much fuss the Rollos make about some things their little ears are not used to. They make their grand, unqualified pronunciamentos—for one reason (and a good reason)—they don't know that what they are talking about is not what
m71v
they are talking about. So they call [these things] unnatural, unmusical, un-meaning, based on no laws of art, nature, or humanity—when as a
m72v
matter of fact they're based on deductions from quite simple premises, suggesting other logical premises from similar processes, but almost too self-evident to need explanation.

For instance Father used to say, "If one can use chords of 3rds and make them mean something, why not chords of 4ths? If you can have a chord of three notes and [one of] four, alternating and following, why not measures of 3/4 then 4/4, alternating and following? If the whole tones can be divided equally, why not half tones? That is, if one has twelve notes in an octave, why not more or less? If you can learn to like and use a consonance (so called), why not a dissonance (so called)? If the piano can be tuned out of tune to make it more practicable (that is, imperfect intervals), why can't the ear learn a hundred other intervals if it wants to try?—and why shouldn't it want to try? If the mind can learn to use a two against (or rather with) a three, why not nine vs. eleven?—or even better (or worse)? If the mind can learn to use two rhythms together, why can't it [use] five or worse together?—and the measure referred to above? If the mind can understand one key, why can't it learn to understand another key with it?" A nice old lace-capped professor says—"because it is all against the natural laws of tone underlying music!"—in other words, he uses a nice nickname for something his aunt has taught him to sleep on "comfortable"!

56

T71m
Just one more thing and then I promise to stop. "This can't be played"—"This makes no sense"—or (as one critic said after hearing, at a concert here in New York, one of the great pieces in the history of music, Carl Ruggles's *Men and Mountains*) "It's meaningless to me— all of this modern music just bores me."[1] (To the one-syllable boy,

1 This remark was probably overheard at one of the few concerts one can be sure Ives attended—at Town Hall, New York, Saturday evening, 10 January 1931—Slonimsky conducting the Chamber Orchestra of Boston: Mozart *First Symphony* in E♭, K16, Ives *Three Places in New England*, intermission, Ruggles, *Men and Mountains*, Robin Milford

stories in two syllables = meaningless, that is, boring.) The pianist who says "This isn't pianistic, it can't be played, it's meaningless"—the singer who says "This can't be sung" (for the same reason) "it's meaningless"—the critic who says he doesn't like it, "it's meaningless"—are, in my opinion, in the same state of mind and are in about the same relation and the same attitude towards music as a six-year-old boy is [in] towards literature when he tells his mother "Now when you read stories to me, give me real stories, those in one syllable. There is nothing in two syllables, it is meaningless—I don't understand them, and it is not literature. Give me words of one syllable and not many of them."

Not all, I am glad to say, but a good many of the most celebrated musicians in all lines are in about the same class with this boy—also the flannel-mouth editors who write articles in trade papers condemning all modern music. They are not quite in the one-syllable boy's class yet—just a little bit more effort on their part—just a gradual learning how to use their ears, brain, souls a little more—[and] they will get a little less feeble and be able to sit up a little each day—in other words, musically, when they know just a little more, they will be almost half-witted, and perhaps even in the one-syllable class.[2]

I know a piece of music that a famous violinist said couldn't be played, and which was played not many months after by men who made it the business of their minds and hearts to find out how to play it.[3] Instrumental prima donnas are bad enough, but vocal prima donnas are worse. I won't say all of them, but a good many of them (especially the older and more celebrated ones) are so limited in their knowledge of intervals (orally and mentally) that any song that doesn't parallel the boy's one-syllable story they can't sing and call [it] unsingable. I will admit that in a good many of my songs there are intervals which, without acquaintance [or] without thorough study, seem unsingable and not grateful to the voice.

In this connection, there are a few songs [which], because of the very wide and mean intervals to locate, for singers whom I had shown them to, and also because the piano parts seem to be especially annoy-

Suite, Cowell *Marked Passages*, Mozart *A Musical Joke*, K522. Two of the Ives movements were repeated (see end of App. 17).

Some years later Ives sketched an insert for Lucille Fletcher's article about him: "He seldom goes to concerts nowadays . . . one of the last ones he went to [was] about ten years ago. . . . Ives is a great admirer of his old Yankee friend, Carl Ruggles, and his powerful music. At this concert he sat quietly through the boos and jeers at his own music—but when that wonderful orchestra work, *Men and Mountains*, of Carl Ruggles was played, there were some hisses near him—and Ives jumped up and shouted You god damn sissy . . . when you hear strong masculine music like this, get up and use your ears like a man!'"

2 For an elaboration of this image, see App. 12.

3 Ives must be thinking of Milcke and of Talmadge and Ross—see §24.

ing to both singers and pianists, were left out of the book of *114 Songs*.
Most of them are, I think, in the safe at 46 Cedar Street. But since
writing this, I've had photostats made from some of the old manuscripts. Among these are manuscripts not much good and left out of
the book, but which are probably better than some in the book. Most
of them are old, and one or two [of the] better ones but with mean
intervals (1910–   ) were taken from the "Humanophone", an idea of
Father's—others [were] later. These songs of wide leaps were to be
sung [with the] different notes by different voices—not a duet, quartet,
etc.—but one voice taking a high note, a middle voice, and another
man taking [a] low note, etc. For instance, a theme of one ("Aeschylus"):[4]

T72m   Whether they are grateful to the voice in one way makes little difference, but when the song has to be sung, it has to be sung. But with
one or two exceptions there are no songs in my book of *114 Songs*
which I haven't sung and couldn't sing, especially when I was writing
them. I will admit that, if I haven't seen them for some time, as is the
T73m   case with many of them, it takes a little practice and effort to get them
back in the ears and mind. But there are but few of the songs that I
can't (after a few hours of renewing acquaintance) sing, although I
don't want to infer here that I'm a singer. I have a rough voice, but I
can make a noise on the right note at the right time and on the right
interval—and, in spite of the piano, get the song going somewhere.
Any singer can do the same thing if he makes up his mind to it, unless
he is a congenital musical defective, or with about the same musical
mentality that is sometimes the possession of famous operatic stars.

There is nothing that I have ever written for a piano that I haven't
been able to play. Give me a day or so *(but sometimes a year or two
too)* of practice and I can always get the music back into my fingers.
Not that I can play as well as I'd like to, but at least I can convince
myself that it's playable.

[4] Only a few of these notes occur in *Aeschylus and Sophocles* (a in m. 11, g^2–$a\flat^1$ in m.
15), but the sketch, of which pp. 1–2 are missing, may have had more of them.

Extant leaves of the *Memos,* concordance with the Cowell book

Just for the record, and because experience has shown the advantages of putting things in order, to make them readily available, this first appendix includes three lists that might come in handy for reference.

M The preliminary leaves earlier than M are all missing (see Preface), but fortunately most of the leaves of M (on ruled legal-size foolscap) have survived, and are here listed showing the corresponding page of T, M11–12 being an outline table of contents for Part II.

p. 1 (T1)—verso blank	p. 13 (T61–62)—patches (T31, 48, etc.)
p. 2 (T1–2)—verso blank	p. 14 (T62–65)—verso blank
p. 3 (T2–3)—p. 4 (T3–4)	p. 15 (T65–66)—p. 16 (T66)
p. 5 (T4–5)—p. 8 (T9–10)	[p. 17 missing]
p. 6 (T5–8)—p. 7 (T8–9)	p. [18?] (T67–68)—verso blank
p. 9 (T10–11)—p. 10 (T11–13)	[the rest missing]
p. 11 (T13–29)—p. 12 (T30–54)	

T & t Miss Martin's first typings (T) and carbons (c) from her shorthand notes of Ives's dictation (see Preface) are listed below, showing which leaves are extant for her numbered pages (boldface type = those that Ives lent to the Cowells, lightface type = those that he couldn't find). The first plus indicates that Ives added something on the front of the leaf, the second plus on the back (these additions being called m in the Preface). Wherever the addition is to be inserted into a page other than the one it's written on, the intended page number follows the plus in question (within parentheses where Ives's placement is definite) and [brackets where his indecision required an editorial guess]. In the same way, pp. 45–48 are inserted into p. 42, in order to keep together his discussion of each movement of the *Holiday Symphony.*

Similarly, for Ives's dictating from m, Miss Martin's typings (t) and carbons (c) are listed to the right of the listings for the page in question of T. Before each t, r indicates that the interpolated material was on the front (recto) of the leaf of T, v (verso) on the back, rv on both. Again the first plus indicates material Ives added on the front of this new leaf, the second plus on the back (these being called *m* in the Preface). Apparently none of these *m* interpolations were dictated or typed. In view of the variety of places (the houses in New York and Redding, and the barn) in which all these leaves were found, one may be thankful that only 23 out of some 200 are missing, the only serious textual lacuna being T31.

Leaves of T	and carbons	Leaves of t		and carbons	Pages of this editing
1. **T**++(4)	c+	v	t(4)+	c+c c	26–27, 30–31
	["separate sheet",		{t(4)+	c c c	31–32
	*m*la(4), missing]		{t(4)	c c c	32
			extra leaf, *m*lb(4), 2 pages		30
			ext. leaves, *m*lc(4), 4 pages		omitted (redundant)
2. **T**++	c	v	t+	c	27–28
3. **T**++	c	rv	t+	c	28–29
4.	c+				29, 32–33
5. **T**++	c+				33–34, 35–36
6. **T**++(5)	c				36–37, 34
7. **T**++	c				37–39
8. **T**++	c				39–40
9. **T**++	c	v	t+		41–42
10. **T**++	c+	v	t+	c	42–43
11. **T**++		r	t+	c	43, 45–49
		v	t++	c	
12. **T**++		r	t+	c	49–51
	extra leaf, *m*12a	v	t+	c	50
13. **T**+ {(13) + {[11]	extra typed copy of above[11]	r		c[11]	51–55, 46
				c c c	
		v	{	c	
			{ t	c	
14. **T**++(13)	c	v	t+	c	55–56, 54
15. **T**++ {(12) {[10]	c	v	t {(12)+ {[10]	c	56–57, 50, 43
16. **T**++[21]	c	v	t[21]+	c+	57–58, 67
17. **T**++(18)	c				58, 61
18. **T**++	c	v	t++	c	58–62
			*m*18a—4 pages		62–64
19. **T**++	c	v	t+	c	64–66
20. **T**++ {(20) {[26]	c				66–67, 76
21. **T**++	c+				67–69
22. **T**++(23)	c+				69–70, 70–71
23. **T**++(24)	c				70–72
24.	c+	r	t+	c·	72–74
25. **T**+					74–75
26. **T**++					76–77, 79
27. **T**++	c	v	t+	c	77, 79–80
			*m*27a, 3 pages		78–79
28. **T**++ {[29] {[18]	c	v	t++[11]	c	80–81, 63, 47
29. **T**++[11]	c				82, 43–44
30. **T**+	c+				83–84
31.			{t("34a")+		86–87
	(31v, 34v, 36v)	{	t("34b")+	c+	87, 90–91
			{t("34c")+	c	91
32. **T**++[68]	c		{t[68]+	c+	86–87, 134–35
		(32v-33v)	{t[68]+	c	
33. **T**++[68]	c	v	[see 32]		87–88

Leaves of T	and carbons	Leaves of t	and carbons	Pages of this editing
34. T + +		v[see 31]		88–89
35[?].				
36. T + +(34)		v[see 31]		91–92
37. T + +[11]				92–93, 47
38. T + +[28]		v t[28] +	c +	93, 80–81
39. T + +	c	{r t+ / v}	/ c +	93–94
40. T + +	c	rv {t+ / t+}	c + / c +	94–96
41. T + +(42)	c			96–97, 100–01
42. T + +	c			97–98, 101–02, 104
43. T + +	c	v t + +[18]	c	104–05, 63
44. T {(44)/[42]} + +(11)	c			105–06, 102, 44
45. T[42] + +[42]	c			102–03, 101
46. T[42] + +[24]	c			103, 98, 74
47. T[42] + +(1)	c			98, 25–26
48. T[42] +	c			99–100
49. T + {(49)/[50]} + {(49)/[50]}	c	v t{(49)/[50]} +	c	106, 107
50. T + +[68]	c			106–08, 135–36
51. T + +	c			108–11
52. T + +(51)	c			111–12, 109
53. T {(53)/[29]} + +(51)	c	v t +(51)	c	112–13, 82–83, 110
54. T + +	c	v t +	c	114–15
55. T + +	c			115–16
56. T + +	c			116–18
57. T + +(56)	c			118–19, 117–18
58. T + +	c			119–21
59. T + +	c	(59v, 66v) {t+ / t+}	c + / c +	121–23
60. T + +	c	v {t+ / t+}		123–26
61. T + +	c +			126–28
62. T + +				128–29
63. T + +(62)	c			129–30, 129
64. T + +	c			130–31
65.	c			131–32
66. T + +(59)	c	v[see 59]		132–33, 122–23
67. T + +(61)	c			133, 127
68. T +	c			133–37
69. T +	c			137
70. T + +(71)	c			137–38, 139–40
71. T + +	c			138–41
72. T + +(71)	c			141–42, 140
73. T + +(72)	c + +[52]	v t + +[34]	c	142, 141–42, 112, 90

The following list gives the locations of those parts of the *Memos* which are in Cowell. Many of the textual differences are due to the Cowells' not having had all the extant sources at their disposal, other differences due to editorial choice or paraphrase. Indented numbers refer to the indented sections in Crowell, otherwise to the main text (L = line).

Page in Cowell:

13	in pp. 79–80	70, L9–10	118
21–22	45	L15–18	59
22	45–46	L19–23	123
23–24	132–33, 132	71, L1–4, 7–15	126
25–26	42–43	71–72	71
28, L12–29, L2	38	72, L6–9	70
29–30	114–15	72	70
32–33	49–50, 49	73	71
33, L1720, 2–24	51	73–74	114
33–34	51, 115–16	74, L14–16	71
34, L1–17	39, 38–39	75–76	112–13
34	39	80	56–57
36, L5–7	83	88	134
L17–20	41	89	135
37	130–31	130, L3	130
40–41	136–37	130–131	29
42	55	131–132	138
43–44	128, 129, 128, 129	132	28–29
65, footnote 1	87	157, L23–24	127
66–67	126, 121, 122, 121, 122	169, L2–3	55
68, L5–6	51	201–202	106–08
L16–20, 23–25	98	202, L29–30	108
68–69	98, 121	203	106
69, L10–20, 25–26	123		
L30–32	87		

Ives's earlier Lists of Works (1929–35)

The only extant manuscript list earlier than the typed lists in App. 3 is an incomplete one that Ives started in ink on the back of an Ives & Myrick calendar for December 1928. Although it contains questionable datings, it is valuable in many ways and is given below in full.

(for my own information, not for publication)

Songs (about 200) from 1886 to date: 114 printed in book [from] 1888 to 1921, 8 in 1923, 3 [in] 1924, 2 [in] 1925, 1 [in] 1928.[1]

Anthems, Hymns, etc.: *"As Pants the Hart" [42nd Psalm]* 1885 (father's help),[2] *Communion Service,* 1886–87 (Sung at St. James' Episcopal Church, Danbury),[3] *Te Deum, Benedictus,* Baptist Choir, Danbury, 1888–89,[4] Solo—low contralto, Isabelle Raymond—*Rock of Ages,* 1890.[5]

Since then, two complete morning and vesper services, St. Thomas' Church, New Haven, 1893–94.[6]

1 That would make 14 songs composed (or finished) after the book. Counting backwards, the "1 in 1928" must be *In the Mornin'*, "2 in 1925" are probably *Johnny Poe* (an unfinished sketch for male chorus and orchestra) and *Sunrise* (rightly 1926?), for "3 in 1924" there are only *A Sea Dirge* and Edith's *Christmas Carol*, for "8 in 1923" only *Aeschylus and Sophocles, On the Antipodes, The One Way, Peaks* and *Yellow Leaves*. A later Keats song may be lost (see §50, note 1), which with the above 10 would make the "Eleven Songs . . . 1922–1927" specified in App. 3, #89.

2 The handwriting of the two extant copies is not before late 1890, one of them bearing two later memos: "C E I June 1888 or 1886 [changed to 1887]"—and "Methodist Church Jn 1887." In the diary with musical programs of the Baptist services, the morning anthem on Sunday 12 April 1891 was "As pants the Hart—Ceal Klein" (a cryptogram for C. E. I. when little?).

3 The only complete *Communion Service* is sketched in George Ives's copybook, the first Kyrie dated "1890 Jan 8" [almost certainly 1891]—a later copy being dated "Mch. & Apr. 1892." There is also an incomplete *Gloria,* the handwriting suggesting 1890 or 1891.

4 No *Te Deum* has come to light. The *Benedictus* (in E, 3/4) has a memo: "July 27— Aug. 5, '90." Another anthem from 1890 is *Turn Ye, Turn Ye* [Mercury 1952].

5 The one existing copy is in a handwriting not before 1892, but on a margin it bears a pencil address, "16 Stevens St." (good only to 9 May 1889). Either the address was there first, or this may be a revision. After "1890" Ives wrote "Psalms"—but probably realized he was ahead of himself and put the Psalms further down.

6 No "complete morning and vesper services" have come to light, beyond the possibility that the morning service might have included the *Te Deum,* and the evening service the separate *Gloria* or the *67th Psalm* (see App. 3, #8).

Since then, about 20–25 Anthems, responses, and hymn-anthems (alla
Harry Rowe Shelley and Dudley Buck) during four years at Center
Church.[7]

About 10 Psalms—100th, 24th, 90th—*23rd Psalm* (Center Church and
Newark Presbyterian, Bloomfield Presbyterian) 1897–98—(*90th
Psalm* 1923–24).[8]

Cantata, *The Celestial Country*, 1898–1900, given at Central Church
concert, 57th Street, New York, April 18, 1902.[9]

Brass Band: *Holiday March*, 1885–86, Wooster Band Danbury,[10] *Slow
March* (Adeste Fidelis, cantus firmus) '86 or 87, played by Danbury
Band, Decoration Day, and Carmel, N. Y., Band about '87–88.[11]
Circus Band.[12]

Fantasia (or Paraphrase) on *Jerusalem the Golden* (before leaving
Stevens St., Danbury, 1888).[13]

Intercollegiate March, 1895, New Haven Band and Washington
Marine Band, McKinley Inauguration 1897—Published by Pepper
& Co., Philadelphia, Pa.[14]

[7] This quantity of anthems is a tragic gauge of how much is lost. When Ives resigned as
organist from the Central Presbyterian Church (then at Broadway and 57th Street), he
left all his best choir and organ music there, and in subsequent moves it was all thrown
out. Beside the Psalms, there are only four extant anthems which Ives might have assigned to his Yale period: *Easter Carol, Lord God Thy Sea Is Mighty, The Light That Is
Felt,* and *All-Forgiving*—and possibly the response, *Search Me O Lord* [Ives's music?].
[8] Beside *Psalm 42* and *Psalm 67*, there are eight others: 150th and 54th (1894?), 25th
and 24th (1897?), 100th (1898 or 99?), 14th and 135th (1899 or 1900?), and 90th
(1894–1901?, recomposed in 1923–24). No trace has showed up of the *23rd Psalm* beyond the possibility that an organ interlude might belong to it. Nothing among Ives's
papers indicates any Newark church—he probably meant Bloomfield.
[9] See §6.
[10] This march (composed Christmastime 1887) survives only in a set of parts in George
Ives's hand (piccolo, 2 cornets in A, 2 violins, piano), which must have served for the
performances on 16 January 1888 by George Ives's Theatre Orchestra, and on Christmas
Day 1888 at the Methodist Sunday School (see §12, note 11). On the piccolo, cornet,
and piano parts, the title is *Holiday Quickstep*.
[11] This *Slow March*, of which no trace survives, may be the source of the *Adeste fideles*
episode in *Decoration Day*.
[12] These two words are written above the preceding date, with no caret showing where
they belong. They seem to imply an old band version of *The Circus Band* (App. 4, #56).
George Roberts's orchestration (from the *114 Songs*) was made later, around 1934.
[13] "Danbury" is a guess at Ives's over-hasty writing.
Might this missing band piece have had something in common with the organ variations
on *Jerusalem the Golden?*
[14] The name here copied as "Pepper" (from the later lists) looks more like "Peter"—
Gopsill's Philadelphia Business Directory for 1897 does list James W. Pepper (Music
Store, also Publisher) at 234 S. 8th, but no Peter nor any similar name in that trade.
A manuscript score of this march (with the air *Annie Lisle*) bears a memo: "(played at
Danbury Fair Grounds by Danbury Band, Oct. 1892)." The Ives Collection has negative
photostats (y6001–8) of a set of 16 parts that was lent by the late Julius Mattfeld from
the library of the Columbia Broadcasting System in 1957, lacking any title page or cover.
On the solo cornet part is printed: "Copyright 1896 by C. E. Ives"—with no mention of
Pepper & Co.

Several Quicksteps[15] and 1 Overture (alla *Zampa*), etc.[16]

Small (Theater) Orchestra:[17]

From 1935 on, Ives had various lists of his works typed up, at first by Miss Martin, which may be dated by their omission or inclusion of dated publications. The earliest is different from all the others in being numbered and in chronological order, according to the dates Ives was then using or the starts of various date-ranges. It lists *Three Places in New England* as Birchard [1935], but not yet the *18 [19] Songs* (New Music, October 1935). The text below is slightly simplified wherever it would duplicate App. 3.

COMPOSITIONS OF CHARLES E. IVES

1. Organ pieces, songs, brass band marches,   about 1886–96
      anthems and hymns
2. About Two Hundred Songs   1888–1921
3. Album of Thirty-four Songs (New Music Pub. Co.)   1889–1921
4. Manuscript church anthems,   about 1890–1900
      glee-club male choruses, piano pieces, etc.
5. Organ and other fugues,   1891 to about 1902
      concert and church-service pieces
6. Marches, short pieces,   about 1894–1904
      overtures, etc., for orchestra
7. March *Intercollegiate* for full military band   1896
      (pub., Pepper & Co., Philadelphia, Pa.)
8. For a "Revival Service"—Prelude, Offertory, and   1896
      Postlude—String Quartet   20 min.   (manuscript)
9. *First Symphony*   50 min.   1896–98
10. *Take-offs* (academic, athletic, anthropolitic,   about 1896–1916
      economic, tragic) for large and small orchestras
11. Chorals from a "Harvest Festival"   1897 (1 & 2), 1902 (3)
      for double chorus, organ, trumpets, trombones   10 min.   (ms.)
12. From Orchestral Set, *Holidays—Thanksgiving*   1897–1904
      15 min.   (manuscript)
13. Cantata, *Celestial Country* (St. Bernard)   (manuscript)   1898–99

[15] The only surviving quickstep for band, beside the two already mentioned, is the *March* with the air, *Omega Lambda Chi*, the score of which is dated January 4, 1896.
[16] In the score-sketch of the 4th movement of Ives's *Second Symphony* there is a memo on p. 1: "(from Overture *Town, Gown, and State* in *These United States*, for Brass Band, 1896, played [at] Savin Rock, New Haven, Ct.)" This is lost, but it might have been the one Ives called "alla *Zampa*". For Ives's general view of Hérold (1791–1833), the overture of whose *Zampa* (1831) has long been a semi-popular classic, see §29, before note 9. However, Ives's untitled and incomplete student overture in G minor for orchestra has a ryhthmic vigor that may be partly indebted to *Zampa*, and makes one regret all the more the loss of *Town, Gown, and State*.
[17] Ives may have hesitated to start listing this category—how small?—which theater?— and the *Holiday Quickstep* already under "Brass Band"—a great pity he didn't.

14. *Second Symphony* (a new largo added   1899–1902
    around 1909 or 1910)   40 min.
15. Ragtime Dances (about a dozen)   about 1900–1911
16. Single piano pieces, studies, etc.   about 1900–1915
17. Overtures for large and small orchestras   about 1901–1912
18. *Allegro* and *Adagio* (started as a   1902–1907
    First Violin Sonata and never completed)
19. *Second Violin and Piano Sonata*   25 min.   (photostat)   1902–1909
20. *First Piano Sonata*   1 hr.   (6 movements)   1902–1909
21. Sets for basset-horn, trumpet, cornet, or English-   1902–1917
    horn solos, with small orchestras, some called *Cartoons*
    and *Songs without Voices*. Of these some were arranged
    (1921) for voice and piano.   (see published song albums)
22. *Seven Songs* (Cos Cob Press, 209 W. 57th St., New York)   1902–21
23. 1st Orchestral Set, *Three Places in New England*   1903–14
    20 min.   (C. C. Birchard & Co., Boston)
24. Pieces for small groups—strings, woodwind,   about 1904–14
    etc.—a few with voice, some with choruses
25. *Second String Quartet* (two movements   1905
    used in later pieces for orchestra)
26. *Set for Theater or Chamber Orchestra*   15 min. (New Music) 1906
27. *Third Violin and Piano Sonata*   30 min.   (photostat)   1907–14
28. *First Violin and Piano Sonata*   25 min.   (photostat)   1908
29. *Fourth Symphony*   40–45 min.   (New Music)   1910–16
30. *Third Symphony* (1st & 3rd movements partly from   1911
    organ pieces, 1901)   30 min.   (manuscript)
31. Preludes and sectional movement from a   1911–16
    Universe Symphony (uncompleted)
32. *Second Piano Sonata*   (pub. 1919)   1911–15
33. *Second Orchestral Set*   20 min.   (photostat)   1911–15
34. Three pieces for unison chorus and orchestra: [1]   1912
    A Man—Lincoln the Great Commoner   5 min.   (New Music)
35. *Second Set* for trumpet, woodwind, violin and piano   1912–21
    10 min.   (manuscript)
36. From Orchestral Set, *Holidays—Fourth of July*   1912
    10 min.   (Edition Adler, Berlin)
37. 1st movement from Orchestral Set, *Holidays* (strings,   1913
    flute, horn, and bells)   12 min.   (photostat copies)
38. Quartertone music—*Chorale* for strings   1913–14
    (arranged for two pianos)
39. From Orchestral Set, *Holidays—Decoration Day*   1913
    10 min.   (photostat copies)

40. Three pieces for unison chorus and orchestra: [2]   1915
    The Masses   10 min.   (photostat copies)
41. *Fourth Violin and Piano Sonata*   20 min.   (lithograph)   1916
42. *Third Orchestral Set*—two movements (uncompleted)   1919–26
43. A book of *One Hundred Fourteen Songs*   published 1921
44. Three pieces for unison chorus and orchestra: [3]   1921
    An Election   5 min.   (manuscript)
45. A book of *Fifty Songs* (from #43 above)   published 1922
46. Eleven songs   1922–27
47. *Largo* (quartertone—two pianos)   1924
48. *Allegro* (quartertone—two pianos)   1924
49. [*Third*] *Piano Sonata* (one movement, uncompleted)   1928

Ives's later Lists of Works (1937–50)

The order of the above list remained, in some degree, a framework for Ives's later, fuller lists, even when he lumped groups together, separated them into individual titles, or recombined pieces into different groups. Generally, the problem of dating Ives's music is complex enough to warrant giving all the evidence offered by his lists, of which the different versions are outlined below, A–D being typed by Miss Martin, E–G by Mrs. Christine Loring (now Mrs. Valentine of Refugio, Texas).

a—1929?—is the manuscript list in App. 2.

A—1935 (3 pages, 2 carbons)—is the typed list in App. 2.

B—1937? (5 pages, original and carbon)—has *Washington's Birthday* as New Music [1936], not yet *Psalm 67* as Arrow (1939). The original has many corrections, most in Ives's hand, a few in Miss Martin's.

C—dated March 1, 1943 (5 pages, original and 2 carbons of a different original but with same text)—includes corrections from B and publications of 1939 and 1942. The original has corrections, most in Ives's hand, one in Miss Martin's.

D—1943? (6 pages, 3 slightly different carbons)—has the corrections from C. On a cover, in Mrs. Ives's hand (to Mrs. Loring?): "Can you get it all onto five sheets?"

E—1945? (5 pages, 12 slightly different copies). Two copies have added pencil indications of the Arrow score of the *Third Symphony* (1947).

F—1947? (5 pages, one carbon)—has *Third Symphony* as Arrow 1947.

G—1949? (7 pages, 17 slightly different copies)—includes the publications of 1949, but lists the *Four Songs* (Mercury 1950) as "Six Songs."

g—1949?—is a manuscript list of "Principal Works" and "Recordings" including the Columbia record of *Concord* (issued 1948). Still clipped to it is a note from Mrs. Loring about details of typing from it.

The following is the complete text of G, except for redundant addresses (mostly now obsolete). The numbering is editorial, and the footnote immediately below each item takes account of significant variants in the other lists and from other sources.

COMPOSITIONS OF CHARLES E. IVES

* Published music. Unless marked otherwise, the music
is in manuscript only, some of which are in photostat.

1   A Book of *114 Songs,* printed 1921   1888–1921
     All lists give "printed 1921"—but proof sheets are dated June 1922, and
     the book, on p. [263], has: "C. E. Ives / Redding, / Conn. / 1922"
     The earliest song, *Slow March* (App. 4, #114), might be 1887. For
     contents see App. 4.

2   A Book of *50 Songs* (from the above edition)
     A: "published 1922." BCDEF: "published 1923" [copies ready April '23].
     This smaller book is the result of an indiscreet review of *114 Songs* in
     the *New York Evening Sun* of Tuesday 29 August 1922, announcing
     that Ives would send the book to all who asked for copies (see Boat-
     wright, p. 132). The sketch of Ives's letter says: "In order to keep good
     faith . . . I shall have another edition of some of the songs of more
     general interest printed, particularly those of the verses of some of the
     poets mentioned in the Sun's article." For contents see the numbers with
     asterisks in App. 4.

3   **Seven Songs,* published 1932 by Cos Cob Press,   1902–21
     c/o American Music Center, 250 W. 57th St., New York City
     "B" in App. 4 [Cos Cob Press 1932, now Associated]. The American
     Music Center is now at 2109 Broadway.

4   **Album of 34 Songs* (from the above edition),   1889–1921
     published by New Music Edition, San Francisco, Cal.,
     and c/o American Music Center.
     "C" in App. 4 [*New Music,* Vol. 7/1, Oct. 1933, now Merion, with order
     changed for better page turnings].

5   **Album of 18 Songs* [rightly 19], pub. by New Music   1894–1925
     "D" in App. 4 [*New Music,* Vol. 9/1, Oct. 1935, now Merion, with order
     changed for better page turnings]. The wrong number was due to the
     last-moment inclusion of *Feldeinsamkeit.*

6   *Six Songs, published by Mercury Music   1898–1920
     Corporation, 47 West 63rd St., New York City
     By "Six" Ives probably meant the *Four Songs* ("E" in App. 4), the
     Chanson de Florian, and *The Light That Is Felt* [all Mercury 1950].

7   Organ music for church service and recital, anthems,   1886–1902
     hymns, psalms, songs, glee club choruses, brass band pieces
     and marches, pieces for theater orchestra, and some dance
     music. Among these are:
     For the anthems etc. see App. 2, notes 2–8, for the band pieces notes
     10–16. By "dance music" Ives seems to mean the *Ragtime Dances* (#20
     below). No routine dance music by him is known—at least none has
     survived.

8   **67th Psalm* for unaccompanied chorus, published   1898
     by Arrow Music Press, 250 W. 57th St., New York City

If the memo in App. 5 is correct, *Psalm 67* was composed in 1894 [Arrow 1939, now Associated]. The only other psalms in print are *Psalm 24* [Mercury 1955], *Psalm 90* [Merion 1970], *Psalm 54* and *Psalm 150* [Merion 1972].

9   *March, *Intercollegiate*, for full military band,   1895
     published 1896 by Pepper & Co., New York City
     See App. 2 (note 14), where both lists mention Philadelphia, not New York.

10   Fugues for organ and strings   1892–95
     See §9, note 6, and §13, note 4.

11a *Variations on *America* for organ ⎫ published by   1891
11b *Adeste Fidelis*,   ⎬ Music Press, Inc.,   1897
     in an organ prelude   ⎭ 130 W. 56, New York
     BCDE: "Variations for organ on 'A National Hymn' "—see §9. Even the edition throughout has "Fidelis" [Music Press 1949, later Mercury].

12   *Three *Harvest Home Chorales* for mixed voices with piano accompaniment (orchestra versions available on rental), published by Mercury Music:
     Harvest Home, text by   1898
          Rev. Geo. Burgess (1839)

     Lord of the Harvest, text by   ⎫   dates uncertain,
          John Hampton Gurney (1802–1862)   ⎬   some time
     Harvest Home, text by   ⎭   before 1902
          Rev. Henry Alford (1844)
     BCDE, last line: "before 1912"—which Ives changed in E to "before 1902". Ives changed B to read: "2nd 1898, 1st and 3rd dates uncertain . . ."—compare App. 2, 2nd list, #11 [Mercury 1949]. Varèse wrote Ives in 1944 (hoping to perform the Chorales with his Greater New York Chorus) that the 2nd one would be more practicable renotated and conducted in 3/2.

13   Cantata, *Celestial Country* (St. Bernard),   1898–99
     mixed chorus, quartet, soli, strings, brass, and organ
     The text is Henry Alford's *Processional Hymn*, "Forward! be our watchword" (all but the first two lines), which Ives wrongly imagined to be derived from the *De Contemptu Mundi* of Bernard of Cluny (who is not to be confused with Saint Bernard of Clairvaux). See §6 [to be published by Peer].

14   Prelude, *Let There Be Light*, for male chorus   1901
     (or trombones), strings, and organ   (photostat)
     Of the two sketches (n2356–57), the one for mixed chorus (n2357) may be earlier. The dedication reads: "To the Choir of the Central Presbyt. Church, New York, Dec. 1901." [Peer 1955.]

15   *First String Quartet, A Revival Service*,   1896
     Prelude, Offertory, and Postlude   20 min. (photostat)
     Originally *Chorale—Prelude—Offertory—Postlude*, numbered I-II-III-IV in all earlier sources. But the *Chorale*, a fugue, was revised for orchestra

in 1909 and transferred to the *Fourth Symphony,* and the numbering of II-III-IV changed to I-II-III. [Peer 1961, all four movements.]

16   *First Symphony* for large orchestra,   1896–98

4 movements, about 40 min.   (photostat)

At the end of the full score of the 1st movement, Ives wrote: "finished . . . May 29, 1895." See §14 and §8, note 10 [Peer 1971].

17   *Second Symphony* for large orchestra, 5 movements,   1897–1901

about 35 min., published by Southern Music Publishing Company, Inc., 1619 Broadway at 49th St., New York City.

The last movement is partly from an early overture called the *American Woods* (Brookfield). The part suggesting a Steve Foster tune, while over it the old farmers fiddled a barn dance with all of its jigs, gallops, and reels, was played in Danbury on the old Wooster House bandstand in 1889.

BCDEF: "(The slow movement was replaced by another 1909–1910)" —but by the time Mrs. Loring was typing G, he probably realized that this replacement happened to the *First Symphony* rather than to the *Second* (see §14 and §15). "1909–1910" may be the date of some revision. The end of the last movement was originally normal tonic chords (Q0294), the final dissonant flourish dating apparently from the 1940s. [Southern 1951.]

18   Single piano pieces, studies, etc.   about 1900–14

(some in photostat), material from some parts of these used in piano sonatas and some of the chamber music.

See §39, note 1.

19   *Three piano pieces, published by Mercury Music Corp.:

19a   *The Anti-Abolitionist Riots in 1830s and 40s*   1908–09

19b   *Three-Page Sonata*   1905

19c   *Some Southpaw Pitching*   1908

The *Anti-Abolitionist Riots* and *Some Southpaw Pitching* are Studies #9 and #21. The *Three-Page Sonata* was written at Saranac, September 1905 [all three, Mercury 1949]. On a bit of music paper Ives wrote a memo to "put on top [of the] 3-page Sonata:—'made mostly as a joke to knock the mollycoddles out of their boxes and to kick out the softy ears!' "

Study #22 was printed in *New Music,* Vol. 21/1, October 1947, but with a misprint that is not obvious: in m. 8, 1st beat, the two top notes are db^3 and g^3, not bb^2 and e^3, as in m. 7 [revised edition, Merion 1972].

The numbering of the *Chromâtimelôdtune* as "#27" suggests that, even though it was apparently conceived for piano and brass quartet, it may have been included as the last item in a take-off of Chopin's 27 studies [orchestration by Gunther Schuller, MJQ Music 1967].

20   Ragtime dances (about a dozen), mostly for small   1900–11

theater orchestra. Some of these were arranged for various combinations of instruments, some for piano and used as scherzos in some of the piano, and violin and piano, sonatas and orchestral sets later. Of these, some have the same themes, strains, etc., but used somewhat differently. Thus they do not all stand as different pieces.

> Three of these ragtime pieces are in the *First Piano Sonata* (see §28— one of them, *In the Inn,* also in the *Theater Orchestra Set,* see §17), and another is in the *Second Orchestra Set* (see §33).

21   Overtures for large and small orchestras.   about 1901–12
Some of these had to do with the lives and works of literary men (and are not all complete). Parts of these were made into songs and shorter pieces called *Songs Without Voices.* Some were arranged (1921) for voice and piano (see published song albums).

> See §29.

22   Overture, *Browning,* for symphony orchestra   1911

> See §29 [Peer 1959]. In C (in item 21) Ives added: "Browning (only complete score) found—started in 1908, finished in full score in R. 1911 summer." By "R" Ives usually meant Redding, but summer 1911 they were living in Hartsdale, and the Redding property was not bought until August 1912, not lived in until September 1913. Page 12 of the score has a memo for Price with the address "70 W 11" (good only to 2 May 1911). See also chronological index, 1912 July.

23   *Allegro* and *Largo* for violin and piano,   1901–02
started as a *First Violin Sonata* and not completed. The *Largo* was originally for violin and organ (solo stop), and later for violin, clarinet, and piano.

> g: "Allegro for violin and piano, 1903." The *Pre-First Violin Sonata* (see §21) was not only completed but bound in buckram. For a performance of the original instrumentation of the *Largo* see §6, note 4 [Peer 1967, for violin and piano, edited by Paul Zukofsky]. The trio arrangement is #26.

24   *First Piano Sonata*, 7 movements, about 50 minutes,   1902–09
published by Southern Music Pub. Co.

> ABC: "about one hour"—which Ives changed in C to "50 mins." See §28 [Peer 1954]. See also Dennis Marshall's perceptive article, *Charles Ives's Quotations: Manner or Substance?* (*Perspectives of New Music,* Vol. 6/2, 1968).

25   Sets for various small groups of instruments or chamber orchestras, some with voice ad lib. (all in photostat):

> After this colon, in B, the indentations go through #51, thus defining as sets #26–27–28, 29, 30–31–32, 34–35–38, 39, 41–42–43, 44–45–47, 48a–b–c, and 49–50–51. In CDEFG the indentations are less clear, and other inserted titles change some of the groupings. See §18.

26   *Largo* [for] violin, clarinet, and piano   1901

> An arrangement from #23 [Southern 1953], and the probable nucleus of #29.

27   Scherzo, *All the Way Around and Back*—   before 1908
piano (two players), violin, clarinet, bells or French horn

> All these lists leave out the most important instrument, a bugle (or

trumpet). One page of the sketch has an address "c/o Raymond & Co." (good only through 1906). [Peer 1971.]

28   Andante con spirito, *The Rainbow*—   1914
       flute, basset or English horn, strings, piano
       Ms: "To H.T.I. on her first birthday in Redding, June 4, 1914" [Peer 1959]. Song arrangement, App. 4, #8.

29   *Trio* [for] violin, clarinet, and piano   about 1902–03
       So far, no trace has showed up of this trio, beyond the probability that the *Largo* (#26) served as part of it, and the possibility that a few fragmentary sketches may belong to it (n1135c, n2534, n2780b, n3227).

30   Largo cantabile, *Hymn*—string quartet & basso   1904 ⎫
31   Scherzo—string quartet (middle section   1903 ⎬ May be
        finished later, some time before 1914)   ⎬ played
32   Adagio cantabile, *The Innate*—string quartet   1908 ⎬ together
        and piano (arr. for piano and voice 1916)   ⎭
       For a group title to #30–31–32 see the end of §6. #30 [Peer 1966] was part of #60 (see §26)—song arrangement, App. 4, #20. For #31 [Peer 1958] see App. 17 at note 2. #32 [Peer 1967] was later than #60—song arrangement, App. 4, #40.

33   *Three Outdoor Scenes*, to be published by Bomart Music Publications, 40–03 Broadway, Long Island City 3, N.Y.
       [Bomart 1949, the group title dating hardly earlier.]

34   *Allegro vivace, *Halloween*—string quartet and piano   1911
       Ives dated the sketch "Halloween (on the 1st of April!)"—adding "Pine Mt" and also the address "34 Gramercy Pk" (good only to early June 1908). Ives would have been at Pine Mountain in April only on a weekend, but in 1908 the 1st was a Wednesday, in 1907 the Monday after Easter—so Sunday 1 April 1906 is probably the right date.

35   *Largo sostenuto, *The Pond*—flute, harp, 2 violins,   1906
       viola, cello, bass, piano, medium voice
       The song arrangement is *Remembrance*, App. 4, #12.

36   *Central Park in the Dark Some 40 Years Ago*   1898–1907
       for orchestra
       In BCDEF, this was included in the "Cartoons or Take Offs" (see #52 below), whose group dating is misapplied here. The right date is in the second sketch: "Runaway smashes into fence . . . heard at 65 C[entral] P[ark] W[est], July—finit Dec . . . 1906, with J. S. M[yrick] . . ." It was originally paired with *The Unanswered Question* (also 1906—see #47 below), the postface of the score by George F. Roberts ending: "These two pieces were first entitled: I. 'A Contemplation of a Serious Matter' or 'The Unanswered Perennial Question'   II. 'A Contemplation of Nothing Serious' or 'Central Park in the Dark in the Good Old Summer Time'."

37   *In re con moto et al*—string quartet and piano   1908
       In C, Ives wrongly dated this "1908" in pencil (followed in DEFG). At the end of the sketch: "Hartsdale, N.Y., Apr. 13, 1913" (a Sunday—see §35, notes 8–9). [Peer 1968.] In C, up the left margin, Ives wrote "This [is] a separate piece and shouldn't have been put in [here with the sets] as the others." But DEFG keep it in the same place.

38   Allegro moderato, *The Gong on the Hook and Ladder,*   (date
      Firemen's Parade on Main Street, for strings,   uncertain,
      flute, clarinet, bassoon, 2 trumpets, trombone,   some time
      piano and drums;—triangle, bass drum and   before
      cymbals ad lib.   1912)
      See §19, at note 5 [Peer 1960].

39   *Trio* [for] violin, cello, and piano   1904–11
      The memo on p. 5 of the sketch—""New Haven, June . . . '04"—suggests
      that the second movement was started (or outlined) during the sexennial
      reunion of Yale '98. The sketch for a title page reads: "Trio . . . Yalensia
      et Americana (Fancy Names)—Real name: Yankee jaws at Mr. Yale's
      School for nice bad boys!!" A first version may have been finished in 1905,
      later revisions being mostly in the 3rd movement. [Peer 1955.]

40   Allegro, *From the Steeples and the Mountains*   1901
      for strings, brass, and bells
      Title at end of copyist score: "From the Steeples—the Bells!—then the
      Rocks on the Mountain begin to shout!" Neither the sketch nor the final
      version mentions strings. [Peer 1965.]

41   Allegretto sombreoso, *Incantation,*   (date uncertain)
      for trumpet, flute, 3 violins, piano
      This is No. VI in what Ives once called "Set #1" (*See'r, Lecture, New
      River, Sick Eagle, Calcium, Incantation*), "made in 1906"—see §18,
      note 1. [Peer 1958.] Song arrangement, App. 4 #18.

42   Scherzo, *Over the Pavements*—clarinet, bassoon,   1906–13
      trumpet, piano, drum;—piccolo and trombones ad lib.
      The memo on the sketch of mm. 44–50—"2 Bands! C[entral] P[ark]
      W[est], D[ecoration] D[ay], May 1906"—suggests that this was com-
      posed mostly in 1906. See §19, at note 7. [Peer 1954.]

43   Adagio sostenuto [*At Sea*]—string   (date uncertain, some
      quartet, English horn or flute, piano   time before 1914)
      The earliest extant sketch is in a set (*At Sea, Luck and Work, Premoni-
      tions*), the first piece having a memo: "arranged for E[nglish] h[orn] . . .
      from song for organ and violin . . . played at Hartsdale, Dec. 1912"—the
      2nd: "(Redding, Oct. 20, 1916)"—and the 3rd: "(120 E. 22, Jan. 1917)"
      [which has to be 1918, because the move to 120 E. 22 was in late October
      1917]. Any "song for organ and violin" would probably antedate Ives's
      resignation from his last church job in June 1902. [Peer 1969.] Song
      arrangement, App. 4, #4.

44   Andante cantabile, *The Last Reader*—   1911
      English horn or clarinet, strings, 2 flutes
      The earliest extant sketch is in a set (*Indians, Gyp the Blood, Last
      Reader*), with a memo at the end: "(Hartsdale, N.Y., June 4, 1911)"—
      Mrs. Ives's birthday. [Peer 1967.] Song arrangement, App. 4, #3.

45   Scherzo, *The See'r*—   before May 30, 1913
      clarinet, trumpet, alto horn, piano and drum
      For a hint that *The See'r* came from a projected Beecher overture
      (1904?), see App. 8, note 25. For the date (1906) of the set in

which it first appears, see §18, note 1. The copyist score (made under George Roberts's direction) shows how Ives sometimes entered a revision only the first time, expecting it to be followed the other times. He apparently realized that, at the "moderately fast" tempo, the many 16th-note appoggiaturas would sound too leisurely, and changed the first one to a 32nd, but never got around to explaining this to Roberts (at that time, in the mid 1930s, his health was precarious and unpredictable, and cataracts were beginning to form on his eyes). Song arrangement, App. 4, #29.

46   *Autumn Landscape from Pine Mountain*   1904
       for strings, woodwind, and cornet

Ives added this item to C as: "An Autumn Landscape from Pine Mt. 1904. Strings, woodwind, Cornet (muted) is heard from Ridgebury." [Ridgebury is roughly two miles west of Pine Mountain, which is about three miles southwest of Danbury.] No music with this designation has showed up.

47   Largo to Presto, *The Unanswered Question, A Cosmic*   some time
       Landscape—trumpet, 4 flutes, treble woodwind,   before
       and string orchestra, published in Pan American   June, 1908
       Bulletin of Music, Washington, D.C.

The sketch bears the address "c/o Charles H. Raymond & Co., 26 Liberty" (good only through 1906). See #36 above. [Boletín Latino-Americano de Música, Vol. 5/5, October 1941, as *La Pregunta Incontestada*. Southern 1953.]

48a *Fast   ⎤ Tone Roads et al. (Chamber orchestra) ⎤   1911
48b *Slow   ⎬ Published by Southern Music Pub.   ⎬ 1911–1919
48c *Slow & Fast   ⎦ Co., Inc.   ⎦   1915

See §19. The second of these three pieces seems to have been lost, except for possible fragments of sketch on a page with sketches of the other two and of *Over the Pavements* and *All the Way Around and Back* (Q2790). [No. 1, Peer 1949. No. 3, Peer 1952.]

49   Largo molto, *Like a Sick Eagle*—   1909
       English or basset horn, voice ad lib., strings, piano

For the date "made in 1906" see §18, note 1. In that ms., above the sketch of this, is a memo: "H.T.I. in Hospital—Sally singing, 70 W. 11, April 29, '09"—which cannot be the date of composition (though Ives later thought it was), but must have been added through association or correspondence of mood. Song arrangement, App. 4, #26.

50   Allegro—Andante, *Luck and Work*—   1916
       English or basset horn, flute, violins, piano and drum

See #43 above. The ms. of the song version (App. 4, #21) bears the address "37 Liberty St." (before February 1914), so this score-sketch was probably orchestrated from it.

51   Adagio, *The Indians*—English or basset horn or trumpet,   1912
       bassoon, strings, piano, and Indian drum

See #44 above. Song arrangement, App. 4, #14.

             (All of the above [#26–51] are in photostat.

Arrangements for voice and piano of some
of these pieces are in the song albums.)

52   Pieces for orchestra, *Cartoons or Take-offs*—   1898–1907
      Undergraduate and other events (academic, anthropic, urban,
      athletic, and tragic)—among them, Calcium Light Night
      (photostat)
      See §19. The group dating, 1898–1907, has been applied wrongly both to
      Calcium Light Night and to *Central Park* (#36 above). By "academic"
      Ives probably meant *A Lecture* (*Tolerance*)—by "anthropic" *The See'r*
      or *Rube trying to walk 2 to 3*—by "urban" *Over the Pavements* and
      Central Park—by "athletic" the *Yale-Princeton Game* and *All the Way
      Around and Back*—by "tragic" *The General Slocum* and possibly *The
      Unanswered Question* and *The Pond*. Two other "athletic" take-offs of
      1907 are incomplete and are not in Ives's lists: *Mike Donlin—Johnny
      Evers* and *Willy Keeler*.

53   **Third Symphony* (1st and 3rd movements from organ   1904
      pieces, 1901—recopied score with a few revisions, 1911), about
      18–20 min., published by Arrow Music Press
      ABCD: "1911"—EFG: "1904" [more realistic]. See §16. [Arrow 1947,
      now Associated.] See also App. 4, #47.

54   *First Violin and Piano Sonata*—   1903–08
      3 movements, 20 min. (photostat)
      See §22. [Peer 1953.] See also App. 4, #44.

55   A Symphony, *Holidays:*
      See §34.

56   **1st movement, *Washington's Birthday*,   1909,
      for strings, flute, horn, and bells,   rescored
      about 11–12 min., pub. by New Music Editions   in 1913
      On p. 1 of the score-sketch: "started Oct. 22, 1909, at 70 W. 11." See
      §35. [New Music 1936, now Associated.]

57   2nd movement, *Decoration Day*, for full orchestra,   1912
      about 9–10 min.   (photostat)
      ABC: "1913"—corrected by Ives in C to "1912". See §36. [To be pub-
      lished by Peer.]

58   **3rd movement, *Fourth of July*, full symphony orch.,   1912–13
      6–7 min., pub. by New Music and Edition Adler, Berlin
      On p. 1 of the score-sketch: "Started 1911 from chords in 'Cage' 1905— +
      in Whitman's little house, Hartsdale—Sally came out—hot 4th of July—
      Rocket sick." ["1905— +" probably means "1905 plus or minus."] See
      §37. [New Music and Edition Adler 1932, now Associated.]

59   4th movement, *Thanksgiving*, for full orchestra,   1904
      about 20 min.   (photostat)
      On a cover: "put in this piece Aug. 1904." See §9. None of these lists
      mention that *Thanksgiving* is for orchestra and chorus. [To be published
      by Peer.]

      (These movements may be played as separate pieces.)

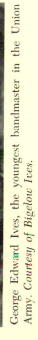

Charles Edward Ives at West Redding (about 1935?).

George Edward Ives, the youngest bandmaster in the Union Army. *Courtesy of Bigelow Ives.*

Charles Ives and his brother Moss outside their grandmother's wood house, in which they played store. Though faded, the three signs to the left of the door read: "CANDIES," "EGGS—20¢ per Doz.," "PYLE'S PEARLINE for easy washing." On the wagon on the left: "Ives Bros. GROCERY." Above the door: "IVES BROS." Beyond the window, half hidden by the grapevine: "165—IVES BROS.—167" (the _____ of Bigelow Ives fresh negative by Bill Ioli._

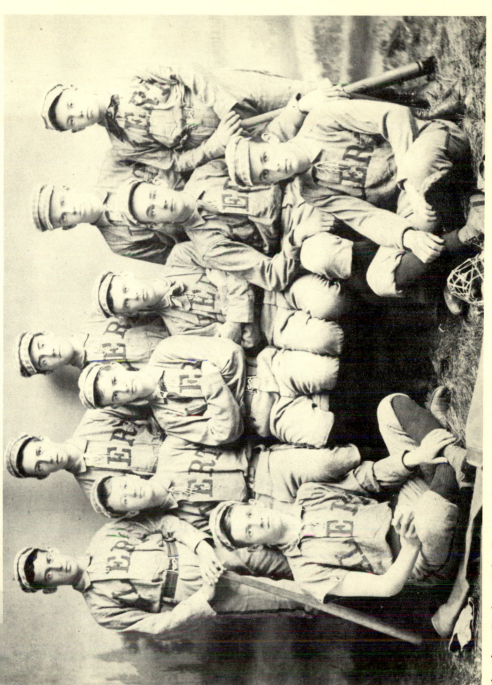

The Alerts, Danbury, July 1890. *Standing*, Art Ballard, Roy Millard, George Clark, [Holland?], Herb Wildman; *on bench*, Charlie Ives, [Archer?], Bill Reed, Clarence Nowlan; *on grass*, Robert Alexander, Leroy Andrews. *Faded original print, signed on the back "Geo. Ives," courtesy of the Scott-Fanton Museum, Danbury, fresh negative by Bill Joli.*

Julian Southall Myrick, from a baseball team picture (about 1897?).

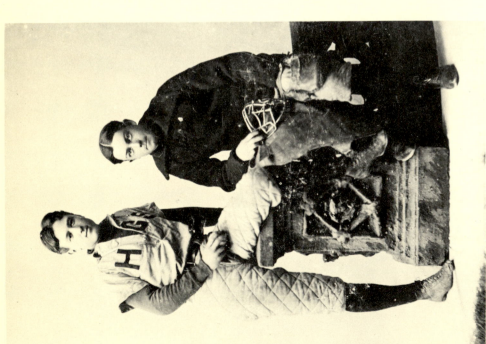

Ives and Franklin Hobart Miles (1876–1954), spring 1894, battery of the Hopkins team that defeated a team of Yale freshmen. *Photograph by H. Randall, New Haven.*

George Edward Ives (about 1885?). *Photograph by J. H. Folsom, Danbury.*

John Cornelius Griggs.

Charles Ives at Battery Park, with passers-by, newsfan, pigeon, and the Whitehall Building. Julian Myrick thought that this snapshot may have been taken around 1913. *Fresh negative by Bill Joli.*

Mrs. Ives and Edith, 1915. Mrs. Ives remembered it was taken by "Harrison, a free lance photographer—he used to bring pictorial backgrounds with him."

– some in church terms, as "Thanksgiving pieces. Father kept me on Bach & counterpoint, from a child till I went to college – & then with Parker, I went over the same things – even the same Harmony (Jadassohn) & Counterpoint text books – & I think I got a little "fed up" on too much counterpoint exercise – and I did sometimes things that "got me in wrong" – for instance: a couple of Fugues – one C e – 4 subjects in 4 diff Keys C, G, D, A – + another C, F, Bb, Eb – it resulted when all got going, in the most dissonant sounding counterpoint – Parker took it as a joke – (he was seldom mean – & I didn't bother him much after the first few minutes – he would just look at it for a page or so, & hand it back with a smile or joke about hogging all the keys etc. & talk about something). I had & have great respect & admiration for Parker & most of his music – but he was absolutely tied to German rules, & some what "hard-boiled":

The first S. was written while college

I at movement changed –

too many keys. Done later etc. – made another 1st – the

"L. Sy Party in coll" — last 1901 (deny)

(Overture Habil for orga pieces

14 Hymn – 2nd mvmt – 1st children day 1905

last I & III later 1910–1, mvmts)

theatre B. Act I but [...] manage [...] Central Park holding [...]
[...] his complete — [...] ago Tapes [...] in 1906 — [...] 4th
5th [...] times in no Pacific. Key — now fancy name at oval
"Rags" 1900 — [...] about 1916. II able form it [see back of p.]

IV Sym. States 1910–16. Something
[...] used in other things, which I
was working on about same time
i.e. Pre- (Vio. Sonata — Celestial R [p=24]
parts as in Hawthorne I Piano. modern
[...] last movement (slow march) on [...] Hz Bay
started in 1901 — (McKinley death) — a personal
experience (not given here)

Vio. Sonata — 1st. 2nd movt 1901 — only
not finished

2nd called 1st 1907–8
3rd " 2nd — 2nd movt early 190-2–3
finished about 1909–10

4th called 3rd (after milk-...) [...] 1914 — 2nd early
[...] 4 (shows how one goes about [...]) NG. [...]
5. Children's Day [...] Mass W.) NG.

2 String Quartets — 1st in [...] N.G. — destroyed
is really 92nd Eden — 2nd "Salvation Army" 1,904–16
"Russwar Sermon" 1896. It had movement [...]
P[...] Sonata I, 1911 & 15. [...] — concerts
Hawthorne — 45 [...]
2nd M.

" " II 1902–9–10
(explain Rag Time Dances.)

Other tunes — mostly turned into other things
for College to [...] after 2–4–[...]
i.e. songs. "P[...] Whitman" [...] etc.

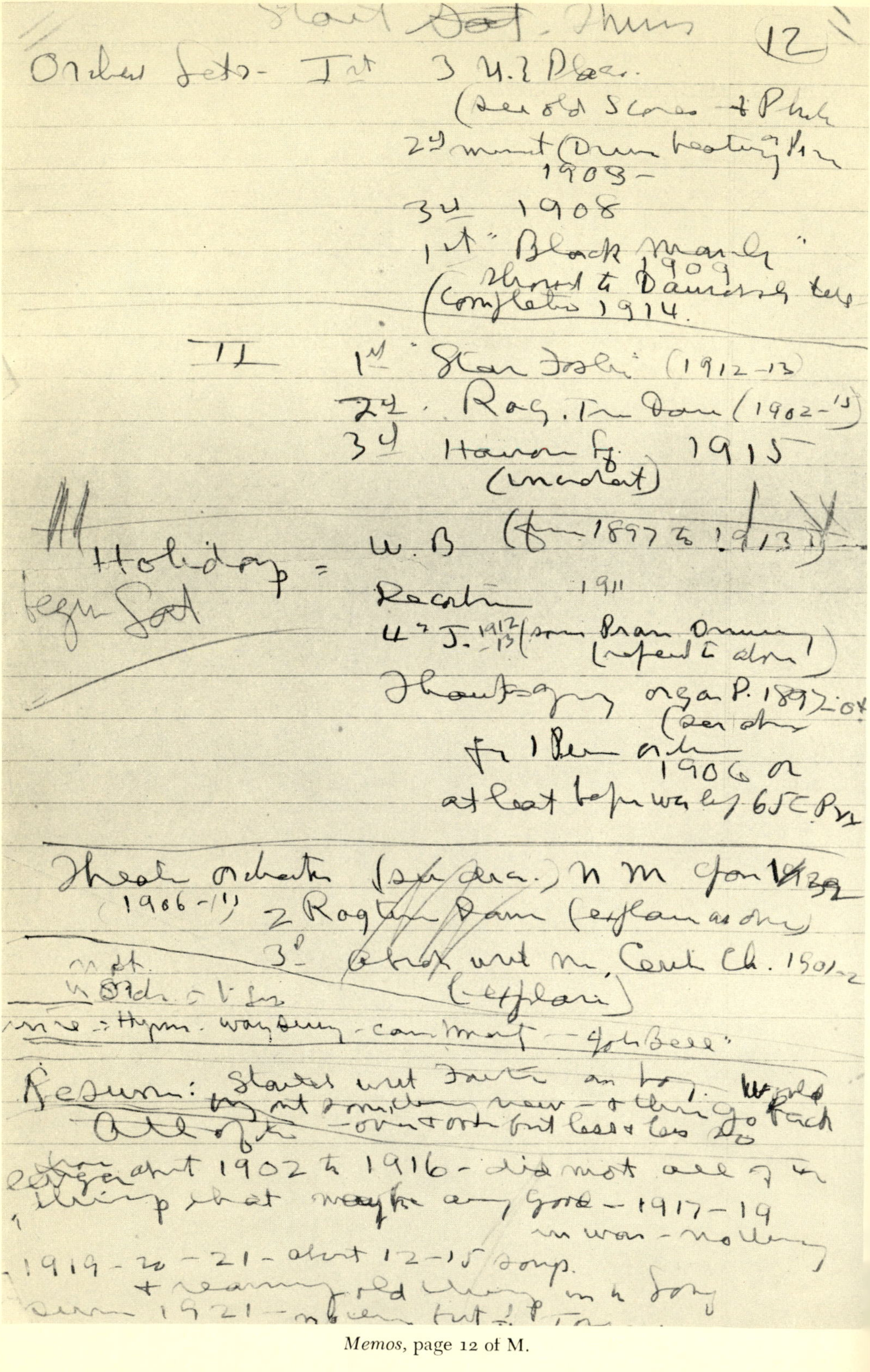

Orches Sets — I   3 N.E. Plac.

(see old Scores + Phs

2�ᵈ mvnt (Drum beating)? in
1903 —

3ᵈ 1908

1ˢᵗ "Black March"
1909
(Completes 1914.

II   1ˢᵗ "Star Isle" (1912–13)

2ᵈ Rag. In Dam (1902–13)

3ᵈ Hamon fg. 1915
(incident)

III Holiday =   W. B (from 1897 to 1913)

begn Sat   Recotion   1911

4ᵗʰ J. 1912–13 (some from Drum
(refers to abov)

Thanksgivg orga P. 1897? ot
(see abov
for 1 Bem o lim
1906 or
at least before was by 65 E Prs.

Theate orchestra (see abov) N M from 1899
(1906–11) 2 Ragtm Dam (explan as abov)
n pt.   3ᵈ Chof wrt m, Cent Ch. 1901–2
n 8ᵗᵈs o 1 fns   (explain)
mve = Hymn. waydmy — cant mvmt — of h Bell.

Resume: Started writ Fourts on to
ny nt a million now — + thing go back
All ofte — over t ort but less + less so
etra abt 1902 to 1916 — did not all of n
thing that may be any good — 1917–19
in war — nothing
1919–20 –21 – abt 12–15 songs.
+ reamng old thing in h Song
sum 1921 – no vim but of

Back of Pages 32 and 33 (continued)

Beethoven, with the easy made Haydn, a large amount of Massenet, and his like, and

most ~~European~~ operas - not exactly most of the operas, but most of each opera;
        Italian

most of Chopin (pretty soft, but you did not mind it in him so much, because one

naturally thinks of him with a skirt on him, but one which he made himself).

Notwithstanding the above slants, which many would say are insults, it seems to me

as it did then, and ever, that still today Bach, Beethoven and ~~Brahms~~, are among

the strongest and greatest, as anything that is or is to be, is stronger or

greater than the strongest and greatest. I will ~~not~~ say that their best ~~is~~

better or worse than anything in any art, before or since - I will not say,

because I do not know - and nobody knows - except Rollo.

....

Memos, page 33v of t.

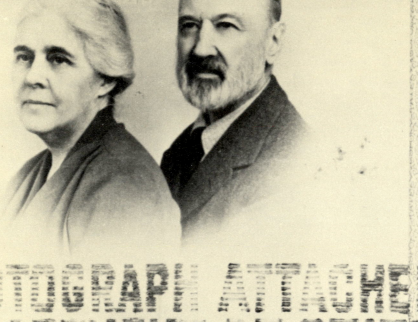

Passport, spring 1938.

60   Two movements started as a *Second String Quartet,*   1905
     uncomplete, parts of which were used in later pieces
     for orchestra
     This is the Pre-Second String Quartet—see §26.

61   *Second String Quartet* (2nd movement 1907) (photostat)   1911–13
     See §27. No 1907 sketches of the 2nd movement have survived. In the
     existing sketch, the end of the 2nd movement is dated: "Jan. 1, 1911,
     70 W. 11 . . . before Mike's weddin—1st anniv." [Julian Myrick was
     married on New Year's Day 1910, and the Iveses always went to the
     wedding-anniversary party—see App. 18.] [Peer 1954, corrected reprint
     1970, based on the editor's comparison of sources and additional data
     contributed by Malcolm Goldstein and Wayne Shirley.]

62   *Set for Theater or Chamber Orchestra*   1906–11
62a   *In the Cage* ⎤
62b   *In the Inn* ⎬ about 10 min.
62c   *In the Night* ⎦   pub. by New Music Editions
     See §17. Except for some revision, it must have been almost entirely
     composed in 1906. [*New Music,* Vol. 5/2, January 1932, now Merion.]
     Song arrangement of *In the Cage,* App. 4, #64.

63   *War March,* for chorus, orchestra,   1917
     full brass and drum corps
     The earliest sketch is apparently the first state of y6100–6103, as for
     voice and piano. A band score implied by the memo—"from Score,
     D[ru]m parts & 2 pianos"—is missing. The pencil full score for orchestra
     (1919 or later) is no longer complete. The text of this 1917 version, *He
     Is There!* (App. 4, #50), is to be published by Peer 1972.
         In 1942 Ives rewrote the words, to bring them up to date with the
     Second World War, and changed the title to *They Are There!* or *War
     March.* Lou Harrison completed a full score, restoring the missing
     measures [Peer 1961, also App. 4, #126].

64   *First Orchestral Set, *Three Places in New England*   1903–14
     3 movements, about 20 min.
     See §31 and App. 11, note 12.

64a   I.   [*The St. Gaudens in*] *Boston Common*
     Score-sketch dated: "Hartsdale, N.Y., 1911, July–Aug."

64b   II.   *Putnam's Camp*
     Score-sketch dated: "(Whitman's House, Hartsdale, N.Y., Oct. 1912)"

64c   III. from *The Housatonic at Stockbridge*
     Score-sketch page with address 70 W. 11 (before May 1911). Song
     arrangement, App. 4 #15.
     (This set has been referred to, at times, as a "New England
     Symphony"—pub. by C. C. Birchard & Co., Boston, Mass.)
     [Birchard 1935, later Mercury.]

65   *Second Violin and Piano Sonata, 3 movements, 15 min.,   1903–09
     to be pub. by G. Schirmer, 3 W. 43rd St., New York City
     A: "1902–1909"—B: "1907–1910" (changed by Ives to "1904–1910")—
     C: "1904–1910"—DEF: "1903–1910". At the end of the ink copy of the

first movement: "July '03, Oct. '07 . . . played 1911 [with] Ed. Stowell.
No go. He didn't like it." At the end of the second: "1902, 1907 Nov."
At the end of the third: "1906, 1909–10, III m[ovement] finished 70 W.
11." See §23, also #86 below. [Schirmer 1951.] See also App. 4, #46.

66   Pieces for various groups of instruments or
       chamber orchestra, with voice or chorus
          *(arrangements for voice and piano published in song albums):
          See §50.

67   1. *The New River*—chorus and chamber orchestra   1912
       For the date "made in 1906" see #41 above (in that set it is called *The
       Ruined River*). In the sketch of the voice and piano arrangement of July
       1913 (App. 4, #6), there is a memo—"back from Zoar's Bridge, June
       9th[?], 1911—Gas machine Kills Housatonic!"—which cannot have been
       added as date of composition, but for association of idea.

68   2. *December* (Rossetti-Folgore)—   1912–13
          male chorus, brass, and woodwind
       [Peer 1963.] Song arrangement, App. 4, #37.

69   3. *General William Booth's Entrance into Heaven*   1914
       (Vachel Lindsay)—chorus or single solo voice,
       originally with brass band (arranged for chamber
       orchestra by Dr. John J. Becker, 1934)
       The first sketch seems to be as for voice and piano (App. 4, #120).
       [Orchestration by Becker to be published by Merion.]

70   4. *Duty* (Emerson)—   date uncertain,
          male chorus and orchestra   some time before 1914
       Duty and *Vita* (with a group title *Two Slants—Christian and Pagan*)
       were composed at Hartsdale on the same Sunday that Ives heard the
       Rev. Daniel Ernest McCurry (1875–1957) preach a sermon contrasting
       Christian faith and Stoic pessimism. This would have been in the summer
       of 1911 or 12 or 13. Song arrangement, App. 4, #9.

71   5. *Premonitions* (Johnson)—voice or chorus with flute,   1917
          oboe, clarinet, horn, strings, piano, and drums
       For the January 1918 date, see #43 above. Song arrangement, App.
       4, #24.

72   6. *Aeschylus and Socrates*—   1922
          with piano, string orchestra or quartet
       For *Aeschylus and Sophocles* see App. 4, #123.

73   7. *On the Antipodes*—   1915–23
          with two pianos, organ, and string orchestra
       See App. 4, #125.

74   **Second Pianoforte Sonata*, 4 movements, published 1919. 1909–15
       (This Sonata is an attempt to present one person's impression of
       the spirit of the literature, the philosophy, and the men of
       Concord, Mass. of over a half century ago. This is undertaken in
       4 Movements: 1. "Emerson"; 2. "Hawthorne"; 3. "The Alcotts";

4. "Thoreau". The first movement was to be a piano concerto and was partially written as such. There are 4 transcriptions of this for piano. There was an Alcott Overture, 1904, with a theme and some passages used in the sonata.)

2nd Edition (1946) published by Arrow Music Press.
ABC: "1911–1915" (which Ives changed in C to "1910–1915")— D: "1910–1915"—EFG: "1909–1915." ABCDEFG: "published 1919"—but on p. [73]: "C. E. Ives / Redding, / Conn. / 1920" [the copies not ready until January 1921]. In C, after "as such," Ives added "1907," and wrote the date of the Alcott Overture as "composed on Pine Mt. around 1902–04."

Apparently the sonata was mostly composed in 1911–12, or rather recomposed from the *Emerson Concerto* of 1907, possible sketches toward a *Hawthorne Concerto* of September 1910, the *Orchard House Overture* of 1904, and whatever orchestral sketches toward *Thoreau* are meant by the memo on the ink copy: "finished May 30, 1915, from some ideas— Walden Sounds—Ch[urch] Bells, flute, Harp (Aeolian) to go with Harmony's *Mist* . . . Elk Lake 1910."

For Ives's playing the whole sonata for Max Smith in 1912 see App. 7, §1. Probably only a few details remained to be finished in 1915. See §29–30 and App. 7–8. [Privately printed 1920, revised edition Arrow 1947, now Associated.] See also App. 4, #48.

75 *Third Violin and Piano Sonata*, 4 movements,   1905–14
    20 min.   (photostat)

A: "1907–1914"—BCDEF: "1902–1914." On p. 1 of the first movement: "1st . . . 2nd and 3rd Verses and Refrains from organ Preludes played . . . Nov. 1901."—"2nd movement from Theater Orchestra score played 14th Nov. 1905" [a Monday]. On p. 1 of the 2nd sketch of the 2nd mvt.: "(started as Organ Toccata for Central Pres. Ch. concert May 8 [18?], 1901 . . ." On p. 1 of the 3rd mvt.: "mostly from organ Prelude . . . played 1901, Nov."
The indication "4 Movements" may be explained by a memo on *Tom Sails Away* (App. 3, #51): "(Sketch for a Violin Sonata . . . was to put in 3rd—Didn't . . . put into this song Sep. 1917)." See §24. [New Music, Vol. 24/2, January 1951, now Merion.]

76 Quarter-tone music, *Chorale* for strings,   1903–14
    arranged for two pianos   (photostat)

ABCD: "1913–1914"[?]. EFG: "1903–1914." See §39–40. [Peters 1968, ed. George Pappastavrou; conjectural realization for strings by Alan Stout to be published by Peters.]

77 Prelude and sectional mvt. from a *Universe Symphony*   1911–16
    (uncompleted), the underlying plan of which was a
    presentation and contemplation in tones, rather than in
    music (as such), of the mysterious creation of the earth
    and firmament, the evolution of all life in nature, in
    humanity, to the Divine.

Ives says, in §38, that it was started in the fall of 1915, but the oldest address on the mss. is 37 Liberty (before February 1914).

78   Unison choruses with large orchestra:
       For a group title see App. 2 (2nd list), Nos. 34, 40, 44.

79   *Lincoln the Great Commoner*   1912
       (from Edwin Markham's poem), pub. by New Music Editions
       Score dedicated "To Dr. David Cushman Twichell." [*New Music* 1932
       (with a cover design by Carl Ruggles), now Merion.] Song arrangement,
       App. 4, #11.

80   *The Masses*—10 min.   (photostat)   1915
       Piano arrangement (in part) in song album
       Page 9 of the pencil full score is dated: "Dec. 28, '14—27 W. 11." On
       p. 10 Ives began Verse 6 ("As the tribes of the ages wandered and fol-
       lowed the stars—whence come the many dwelling places of the world")
       in a style pointing forward to the twelve-tone row. But he apologized in
       a marginal memo: "The plan of this, in the orchestra parts, is to have
       each . . . complete the 12 notes (each on a different system) . . . and
       hold the last of the 12 . . . as finding its star. Occasionally something
       made in this calculated, diagram, design way may have a place in music,
       if it is used primarily to carry out an idea . . . as in the above, but
       generally . . . or alone . . . it is a weak substitute for inspiration or music.
       It's too easy—any high-school student (unmusical) with a pad, pencil,
       compass and logarithm table, and a mild knowledge of sounds and instru-
       ments (blown or hit) could do it. It's an artificial process without
       strength, though it may sound busy and noisy. This wall-paper design
       music is not as big as a natural, mushy ballad."

81   *An Election* (score in photostat only)   1920
       Piano arrangement in song album pub. by New Music
       The beginning and end are borrowed from *Lincoln* (#79 above). Song
       arrangement, App. 4, #22.

82   *Second Orchestral Set,* for symphony orchestra,   1912–15
       3 movements, about 15 min.   (photostat)
       See §33. [To be published by Peer.]

82a   I. *An Elegy to our Forefathers*
           EF: "An Elegy"—Ives adding in F: "to our Forefathers." But see §33
           for the title, *An Elegy for Stephen Foster.*

82b   II. *The Rockstrewn Hills Join in the People's Outdoor Meeting*

82c   III. *From Hanover Square North, at the end of a Tragic Day,*
               the Voice of the People Again Arose

83   *Fourth Symphony* for large orchestra, 4 movements   1910–16
       1st and 2nd movements published by New Music Editions
       BCDEF: "2nd Movement published . . ."[correct]. See §20. For the
       chronology of many elements from earlier pieces which went into the
       Fourth Symphony, see the preface to the printed score [Associated 1966],
       though the date given there for *The Celestial Railroad* is probably wrong
       (see below).

84   An arrangement for piano of a part of the 2nd movement
       of the *Fourth Symphony* was made later and called a Fantasy
       for Piano, *The Celestial Railroad*   (photostat)

The most plausible date is revealed in a letter of Thursday 3 September 1925 from Schmitz to Ives: ". . . I am much interested in seeing the transcription you are doing of the Hawthorne movement . . ." Jean Lunn has found that certain patches that Ives pinned to pages of his ink ms. of *The Celestial Railroad* had been sketches for the *Fourth Symphony*.

85   An arrangement for piano by John Kirkpatrick of the 3rd mvt. (a Fugue) of the *Fourth Symphony*   (photostat)

Ives's inclusion of this arrangement of 1937 was all out of proportion to its makeshift character.

86   *Fourth Violin Sonata,* 3 movements, about 10 min.,   1914–15 pub. by Arrow Music Press

See §25. This piece has a baffling chronology. In the 1940s, Ives gave the editor a copy of the lithograph printing with the 4th movement torn out, saying that it got in by mistake—(this explanation was taken with a grain of salt).

After he died, and one could sort his manuscripts, the many disclosures were equalled by the many questions one could no longer ask him—the only consolation being that it had always been next to impossible to get a definite answer out of him to a definite question—not only would he go off on new tangents, but he hated to be pinned down to anything he preferred being reticent about (see §20, note 8). But the disclosure that the torn-out movement of the *Fourth Sonata* was the earlier version of the end of the *Second Sonata* looked like history through a surrealist lens.

This movement, *The Revival,* is variously dated "1906–9" or "1906, 1909–10"—the earlier version therefore 1906. In the sketch page, Q2321, sketches toward the second movement of this *Fourth Sonata* clearly ante-date those of *In the Night* (1906). The first movement incorporates most of his father's *Fugue in B flat* and owes something to a lost sonata for trumpet and organ from 1900—and the third movement is based on a lost score-sketch of 1905—but there are no datings of their adaptations into the *Fourth Sonata.*

When he wrote this sonata "quickly within two or three weeks in the fall of 1916" (as told in §25), he certainly had an earlier version of the 2nd movement from 1906, perhaps of the others too. He may have been correct in saying that the 4th movement got in by mistake, but it hardly could without having been somehow associated with the others. [Arrow 1942, now Associated.]

87   *Third Orchestral Set,* 3 movements   1919–26 (one movement uncompleted)

It is a fair heartbreak that Ives never finished this set. The first and third are hymn-tune movements, and the second is a comedy of Danbury reminiscence—for instance, "In middle of march . . . train at Bethel Station stops parade . . . whistle . . . [conductor] yells 'All aboard!' . . ."

88   *Largo* and *Allegro,* quarter-tone music for two pianos   1923–24 (photostat)

See §39–30. The *Allegro* is derived mainly from the *Ragtime Pieces* (#20 above) and from *The See'r* (#45 above). [Peters 1968, with #76.]

89   Eleven songs—among these are some from Aeschylus,   1922–27 Landor, Keats, and passages from "Native Poets"

By "Aeschylus, Landor" Ives meant Landor's *Aeschylus and Sophocles*. Keats is not represented in the extant songs of this period—has one been lost?—or is he absent-mindedly referring to Byron's *A Farewell to Land*? (see §50, note 2). "Native Poets" is probably a facetious grouping of Bellamann (*Peaks* and *Yellow Leaves*), Benjamin R. C. Low, Yale '02 (*Johnny Poe*), the anonymous negro (*In the Mornin'*), Edith (her *Christmas Carol*), and himself (*On the Antipodes, The One Way, Sunrise*).

The *114 Songs* and their reprints

Since the most accessible part of Ives's music, the songs, is the least satisfactorily treated both in the *Memos* and in Ives's Lists, this comparative neglect justifies giving the contents of the *114 Songs,* with sources and available reprints, and going on to include all the other published songs. Many of the sources are Ives's student essays on standard song texts, which started a habit of putting new words into old music—sometimes with impressive results, as in *Rough Wind*—sometimes betraying that the new words did not evoke the music—but always bearing out, by the web of correspondence, Ives's idea that "the fabric of existence weaves itself whole." The following volumes will be referred to by letter (the *114 Songs* being A):

B = 7 *Songs* (Cos Cob Press, 1932; later Arrow; now Associated), none revised.
C = 34 *Songs* (New Music, Vol. 7/1, Oct. 1933; now Merion), 3 new, 25 revised.
D = 19 *Songs* (New Music, Vol. 9/1, Oct. 1935; now Merion), 5 new 9 revised.
    (The Merion issues of C and D are in better order for page turning.)
E = 4 *Songs* (Mercury Music, 1950), 2 from C revised, 2 from A not revised.
F = 10 *Songs* (Peer International, 1953), none revised.
G = 12 *Songs* (Peer, 1954), none revised.
H = 14 *Songs* (Peer, 1955), none revised.
 J = 9 *Songs* (Peer, 1956), only one revised.
K = 13 *Songs* (Peer, 1958), one new, 12 from A not revised.
L = [12] *Sacred Songs* (Peer, 1961), from F, G, H, J, and K.
M = 11 *Songs and 2 Harmonizations* (Associated, 1968), none from A, all new.

Numbers with asterisk appeared in *50 Songs* (whose pages kept the page numbers they had in A); H.T. or H.T.I. is Mrs. Ives; the first date given is from A; ar = arranged; ad = adapted; > = derived from; < = developed into; r (at end of line) = revised.

1   *Majority* or *The Masses* (Ives), [ar]1921 [omitting verses 5–6]
                                        D16r
        > score-sketch, 1914–15 (App. 3, #80). See the end of §49. The poem, in antiphonal psalm form, is in numbered verses.
2*   *Evening* (Milton), 1921   B1, Arrow 1939 (now Associated)
        From *Paradise Lost,* Book 4, lines 598–604. Ives's idea of putting it first suggests that it was probably the most recently composed.
3*   *The Last Reader* (Oliver Wendell Holmes), [ar]1921   C20
        > score-sketch dated on Mrs. Ives's birthday, 4 June 1911 (App. 3, #44).

4*   *At Sea* (Robert Underwood Johnson), [ar]1921   C3r
      > score-sketch [1912?] (App. 3, #43),
      > "song for organ and violin" [1902?]

5*   *Immortality* (Ives), 1921   C5r
      Mrs. Ives told how, in early spring, Edith was very sick with an infected
      ear—"screaming with pain—two doctors."

6*   *The New River* (Ives), [ar]1921 [ms: ar July 1913]   C19r
      > score-sketch, 1906 (App. 3, #67).

7*   *Disclosure* (Ives), 1921   G12, L12

8   *The Rainbow* or *So May It Be!* (Wordsworth), [ar]1921   C16r
      > score-sketch dedicated to H.T.I., 4 June 1914 (App. 3, #28).

9a* *Duty* (Emerson) ⎫   ⎧C1a r, E1r
9b* *Vita* (Manlius) ⎬ [ar]1921   ⎨C1b r, E2r
      > *Two Slants* or *Christian and Pagan*, score-sketch, summer 1911 or '12
      or '13 (App. 3, #70). In §26 Ives says that *Vita* was derived from part of
      the *Pre-Second String Quartet*—surprising in view of the medium (unison
      chorus and organ) but by no means impossible.

10*   Charlie Rutlage (D. J. O'Malley), n.d.[1920 or '21]
                           B2, Arrow 1939 (now Associated)
      Ives's text was the 1920 printing of *Cowboy Songs* collected by John A.
      Lomax, for whom it was "nameless poetry." But see the revised edition
      of 1938, also John I. White's article *D. J. "Kid" O'Malley* (*Montana*,
      Vol. 17/3, July 1967, p. 60). For the tune O'Malley had in mind, *Lake
      Ponchartrain*, see a western version in Margaret Larkin's *Singing Cowboy*
      (Knopf 1931, Oak Pub. 1963, p. 46).

11   *Lincoln, the Great Commoner* (Markham), [ar]1921 Peer 1952
      > score, 1912 (App. 3, #79). The 1921 dating is probably of a slight
      revision—the sketch of the arrangement bears the address, "37 Liberty"
      [good only to 16 Feb. 1914].

12*   *Remembrance* or *The Pond* (Ives), [ar]1921   G9
      > score, 1906 (App. 3, #35).

13*   *Resolution* (Ives), 1921   D17

14*   *The Indians* (Charles Sprague), [ar]1921   B3
      > score-sketch, 1912 (App. 3, #51).

15   *The Housatonic at Stockbridge* (Robert Underwood Johnson),
      [ar]1921   G11
      > score, 1908–14 (App. 3, #64c). See §31 at note 8.

16*   *Religion* (Lizzie York Case), [ar]1920 [ms: ar before May 1911]
                                      G8, L10
      > a lost anthem. The 6th stanza of the poem *There Is No Unbelief* was
      quoted in James Thompson Bixby's essay, *Modern Dogmatism and the
      Unbelief of the Age.* Ives's ms. has two redundant memos, the gist of
      which is: "Mrs. Browning wrote this—Rev. Wilton Merle-Smith handed
      it to me to put to music—but he didn't like the music—we sang it in
      church Feb. 16, 1902 (made into song later at 70 W. 11)." [address
      good only to 2 May 1911]

17*   *Grantchester* (Rupert Brooke), 1920   J9
        Through a delay in receiving permission, the pages for this song are blank
        in the first printing of *114 Songs* (bound in light green).

18   *Incantation* (Byron), [ar]1921   C8r
        > score-sketch, 1906 (App. 3, #41).

19*   *The Greatest Man* (Anne Timoney Collins), 1921
                                        C7r, Arrow 1942r (now Associated)
        The poem appeared in the *New York Evening Sun*, 7 June 1921. Mrs.
        Collins wrote another portrait of her father, Frank Timoney, in the
        article *The Tender Gaoler* (*The Ave Maria*, Vol. 84/4, 28 July 1956).

20*   *Hymn* (Tersteegen, tr. John Wesley), [ar]1921   C25r
        > score-sketch, Aug. 1904 (App. 3, #30), omitting mm 1–6.

21   *Luck and Work* (Robert Underwood Johnson), 1920   C12r, E4
        The 1920 dating is probably of a revision—the sketch of the arrangement
        bears the address, "37 Liberty" [good 1909–Jan. 1914]— < score-sketch,
        20 October 1916 (App. 3, #50).

22   *Nov. 2, 1920* or *An Election* ⎫   D12r
        or *It strikes me that . . .* ⎬ (Ives), [ar]1921 ⎰ Mercury 1950
        > score, 1920 (App. 3, #81).

23   *Maple Leaves* (Thomas Bailey Aldrich), 1920   B4

24   *Premonitions* (Robert Underwood Johnson), [ar]1921   C11r
        > score-sketch, Jan. 1918 (App. 3, #71—see also #43).

25   *Ann Street* (Maurice Morris [pen name of Morris W. Pool]), 1921
                                                                     C2r
        The poem appeared in the *New York Herald*, 12 January 1921. See §18.

26*   *Like a Sick Eagle* (Keats), [ar]1920 [ms: before 1914?]   C22r
        > score-sketch, 1906 (App. 3, #49). The 1920 dating is probably of a
        revision—the sketch of the arrangement is on the same leaf as #21
        (coeval?). The words are the first five lines of the *Sonnet on Seeing the
        Elgin Marbles* (first word changed from "My").

27   *The Swimmers* (Louis Untermeyer), 1921 [C: 1915–21]   C14r
        The poem appeared in the *Yale Review*, Vol. 4/4, July 1915, entitled
        Swimmers. Ives set only part of it. After 1922 he tried orchestrating a
        measure ("Filled with the sense of . . .").

28   *On the Counter* (Ives), 1920   H14

29   *The See'r* (Ives), [ar]1920 [ms: ar July 1913?]   B5
        > score-sketch, 1906 (App. 3, #45). Arrangement on same leaf as #6
        (coeval?).

30*   *Paracelsus* (Browning), [ad]1921 [D: 1912–21]   D14r
        > *Browning Overture*, 1908–12 (App. 3, #22), m. 42–55, 38–41, 7–10.
        From Scene V, lines 803–06, 845–46, 853, 855–57.

31*   *Walt Whitman* (Whitman), [ar]1921   C4r
        > score-sketch, 1913. From *Song of Myself*, section 20.

32   *The Side Show* (Ives quoting Pat Rooney), [ad]1921   G10
        Pencil memo on the sketch: "(for △ K E show, clarinet and piano, 1896,
        spring show—put into song)"—added in ink: "words 1921—changes."

33*   *Cradle Song* (Augusta L. Ives), 1919   D4

Elam Ives, Jr. (1802–64), the hymn composer, was a fourth cousin of
Isaac Ives (1764–1845—see App. 13). His *Musical Spelling-Book* (1846)
contains three poems by "Miss A. L. Ives," who must be his daughter
Augusta (later Mrs. Charles Langdon).

From Early Italian Poets

Ives's bracket includes only #35–37 (in deference to Rossetti's title for
his book of translations), but he would have meant it as including also
#34.

34*   *La Fede* (Ariosto), 1920   D5r
      (*Orlando Furioso*, canto 21, stanza 2.)

35   *August* (Folgore da San Geminiano, tr. D. G. Rossetti), 1920   G7
36   *September* (Folgore, tr. Rossetti), 1920   C9r
37   *December* (Folgore, tr. Rossetti), [ar]1920 [ms: 1913?]   C18r
      > score-sketch, 1912–13 (App. 3, #68). Arrangement on same leaf as #6
      (coeval?).

38   *The Collection* (Kingsley and another hymn writer), [ad?]1920

                                                K12, L11
      [> a lost anthem, say around 1892?]
39   *Afterglow* (James Fenimore Cooper, Jr.), 1919   C10r
      See App. 19 for "Jimmie" Cooper (1892–1918).
40   *The Innate* (Ives), [ar]1916   D9r
      > score-sketch, 24 November 1908 (App. 3, #32).
41   "*1, 2, 3.*" (Ives), [ad]1919   E3
      > sketch, *Rube trying to walk 2 to 3*, 1906.
42   *Serenity* (Whittier), [ar]1919   B6, Arrow 1942 (now Assoc.)
      > score-sketch, before May 1911. From Whittier's *The Brewing of Soma.*
43   *The Things Our Fathers Loved* (Ives), [ad]1917   H12
      > a lost score-sketch of about 1905.

4 Songs Based on Hymn-tune Themes

44*   Watchman (John Bowring), [ad]1913   H11, L8
      > *First Violin Sonata* (App. 3, #54), iii., 1907
         > "organ and soprano song" of 1901 [lost].
45   *At the River* (Robert Lowry), [ad]1916   C13r
      > *Fourth Violin Sonata* (App. 3, #86), iii., [1906? or 1916?]
         > "cornet and violins qu[artet] piece, 1905."
46   *His Exaltation* (Robert Robinson), [ad]1913   J7, L7
      > *Second Violin Sonata* (App. 3, #65), i., 1907
         > *Pre-First Violin Sonata* (App. 3, #23), iii., 1903.
47   *The Camp Meeting* (Ives quoting Charlotte Elliott), [ad]1912

                                                K10, L6

> *Third Symphony* (App. 3, #53), iii., 1904, mm. 12–17, 0–5, 29–36, 44–62, > a lost "organ piece for Communion Service", 1901.

48   *Thoreau* (Ives quoting Thoreau), [ad]1915   C15r
     > *Second Piano Sonata* (App. 3, #74), iv., 1910–15.

3 Songs of the War

49   *In Flanders Fields* (John McCrae), [revised]1919 [composed
       1917]   H13
     > a lost "march for Dewey Day", 1899.
50   *He Is There!* (Ives), 30 May 1917   Peer 1972
     < full score, partly lost (App. 3, #63)
         < *They Are There!* or *War March*, words revised 1942 (#126 below)
           < full score [Peer 1961].
     The Chorus has an added part, "Obligato ad lib Violin, Flute or Fife."
         Of the 1917 text a typed memo says: "The second verse was inserted
     in the realization of the added strain that American soldiers of German
     descent are under. The forbears of many of them were exiled from Ger-
     many after the revolution of 1848, and came to the United States as the
     country where their ideals could be realized. Carl Schurz was an example
     of this type of patriot; like him, many of them fought under The Stars
     and Stripes against slavery in this country. The hope of a 'free Germany'
     was always with them, and now their boys are fighting for the fulfillment
     of that hope." [Ives may have been thinking of Greinert—see §20, 2nd
     paragraph.]
51   *Tom Sails Away* (Ives), [ad September]1917   D7r
     > a rejected sketch (lost) toward the *Third Violin Sonata* (App. 3, #75).

5 Street Songs and Pieces

52* *Old Home Day* (Ives quoting Virgil), [revised?]1920 [ms: before
       February 1914]   K13
     The Chorus has an added part, "Obligato (ad lib) fife, violin or flute,
     only with 2nd verse."
53   *In the Alley* (Ives), 1896 ("After a session at Poli's")   K4
54   *A Son of a Gambolier* ("Traditional"[of Irish derivation?]),
       [ad?]1895   J1
     > March for piano or orchestra [1892–95?]. Words only in second strain.
     At end: "Kazoo chorus, flutes, fiddles and flageolets."
55   *Down East* (Ives), [ad?]1919   K11, L9
     [> *Down East Overture?*—1897?]
56* *The Circus Band* (Ives), 1894 [words later?]   F3
     > March for piano or band (App. 2, note 12), 1894?
         < Orchestration by George F. Roberts, about 1934.

57* *Mists* (H.T.I.), 1910 (second setting)   C21r
  > first setting, September 1910 (see App. 19).

58 *Evidence* (Ives), [ad]1910   J6
  > *Wie Melodien zieht es* (Klaus Groth) [1898?—compare Brahms, Op.
  105/1].

59 *Tolerance* (Kipling), [ar?]1909   C23r
  > score-sketch, *A Lecture*, 1906 (see App. 3, #41). In A & C, below:
  "(Adapted, from a piece for orchestra, to the above words, 1921)" [not
  true—composed directly to those words in or before 1906]. Stanza 7 of
  Kipling's *The Fires*, as quoted in President Hadley's *Some Influences in
  Modern Philosophic Thought.*

60 *Autumn* (H.T.), [ad]1908   J5
  > *Autumn* (other words—lost), 1902 or before. See App. 17, after
  note 1.

61* *Nature's Way* (Ives), [ad]1908   H10
  > *Holder klingt der Vogelsang* (Ludwig Hölty), ms: 1892[?]—compare
  Schubert.

62* *The Waiting Soul* (William Cowper), [ad]1908   G6, L5
  > *The Ending Year* (whose words?), [ad]1902
      > a lost song (Kipling?), [1898?]
  This music was clearly not for *The Ending Year*, and might be the lost
  first song in a group of three (with *Tarrant Moss* and *The Love Song of
  Har Dyal*, Ives's and Price's copies both lacking the title page and the
  first one). If these were *Three Poems of Kipling*, Ives may have requested permission to publish and been refused (Kipling was notoriously
  difficult). It looks as if Ives lost patience in 1902, and adapted this to
  The Ending Year, *The Only Son* to *Harpalus*, and (perhaps later)
  Tarrant Moss to *Slugging a Vampire*. The orientalism of *The Love Song
  of Har Dyal* resisted adaptation. Later on, *Tolerance* was presented as an
  anonymous quotation in Hadley's lecture.

63 *Those Evening Bells* (Thomas Moore), [ad]1907   H9
  > *The Sea of Sleep* (whose words?), ms: 4 January 1903. See §8, note 15.

64 *The Cage* (Ives), [ar?]1906   *New Music* 5/2, January 1932r, H8
  > *In the Cage* (App. 3, #62a), 1906. See §8, note 14, and §17.

65* *Spring Song* (H.T.), 1904 [ms: ad 14 August 1907]   G5
  > a lost song of 4 July 1903, which Ives designated illegibly.

66* *The Light that is Felt* (Whittier), 1904[ms: 1903] Mercury 1950
  > anthem version, 1895[?]—ms: "put into Song . . . Nov. 1903."

67* *Walking* (Ives), [ad]1902 [ms. suggests 1900–02]
                                                    B7, Arrow 1939 (now Assoc.)
  > a lost anthem of April 1898.

68* *Ilmenau* (Goethe, and tr. H.T.), 1902 [ms: before 1902] Peer 1952
  Compare Schubert, Op. 96/3.

69 *Rough Wind* (Shelley), [ad]1902   C27
  > *Judges' Walk* (Arthur Symons), say 1893–98. See §8, note 10.

70* *Mirage* (Christina Rossetti), [ad]1902 [ms: "put in *Mirage* . . .
  Dec. 14, '02"]   F10

> *Like Unfathomable Lakes* (whose words?), ms: "Nov. 5" [year torn off, restored by Ives in pencil as '92—probably too early].

71* *There Is a Lane* (Ives), [ad]1902   J4
> *Widmung* (Wolfgang Müller), say 1897?—compare Franz, Op. 14/1.

72   *Tarrant Moss* (Kipling), 1902[1898?] (only first four words printed)   K9
< *Slugging a Vampire* (Ives), [ad?]1902, #124 below. See §8, note 8, and #62 above. Footnote in A: "Permission to use this verse had not been obtained from Mr. Kipling at the time of going to press."

73   *Harpalus* (from Percy's "Reliques"), [ad]1902   C26
> *The Only Son* (Kipling), say 1897?—see #62 above.

74* *The Children's Hour* (Longfellow), 1901   C28r

75* *I travelled among unknown men* (Wordsworth), [ad]1901   F9
> *Frühlingslied* (Heine), ms: 8 November 1896—compare Franz, Op. 20/1.

4 French Songs

76   *Qu'il m'irait bien* (tr. Moreau Delano, from whom?), 1901   G4
The ink ms. bears Ives's Yale address, good only to June 1898.

77* *Elégie* (Louis Gallet), 1901   J3
Compare Massenet.

78   *Chanson de Florian* (Florian), 1901 [1898?]   Mercury 1950
Compare Godard.

79   *Rosamunde* (Wilhelmine von Chézy, tr. Bélanger), 1898   H4
First composed in German, 1895?—compare Schubert.

4 German Songs

80   *Weil' auf mir* (Lenau, and tr. Westbrook), 1902 [earlier?]   H7
Compare Franz, Op. 9/3.

81   *The Old Mother* (Vinje, German tr. Lobedanz, English tr. Corder), 1900   K8
Ives's second setting—compare Grieg, Op. 33/7.

82* *Feldeinsamkeit* or *In Summer Fields* (Almers, and tr. Chapman), 1900[ms: 1897]   D19
Ms: before November 1897—compare Brahms, Op. 86/2. See App. 6.

83   *Ich grolle nicht* (Heine), 1899 [ms: before 31 March 1898]
                                                                         C30r
Compare Schumann, Op. 48/7. See App. 6.

84* *Night of Frost in May* (Meredith), [ad]1899   D13r
> *Ein Ton* (Cornelius), say 1895?—compare Cornelius, Op. 3/3.

8 Sentimental Ballads

85   *Dreams* (Baroness Porteous, tr. by whom?), 1897   J2
        Compare Strelezki's *Träume.*
86   *Omens and Oracles* (whose words?), about 1900 [ms: August
        1899]   F8
87   *An Old Flame* (Ives), 1896 [ms. title: *A Retrospect*]   K3
88   *A Night Song* (Thomas Moore), [ad?]1895   Peer 1952
        > an unfinished song-sketch (whose words?), say 1894?
89   *A Song* ⌈ O have mercy, Lord, on me (Tate & Brady) [1889?]⌉
      —for ⌉   ms. title: *Hear My Prayer, O Lord*   ⌉
      Any- ⌉ When the waves softly sigh (Ives?) 1892   ⌉ H1
      thing ⌊ Yale, Farewell! we must part (Ives?) [1898?]   ⌋
90   *The World's Highway* (H.T.), n.d. [H.T.I.: 1906?]   K2
        See App. 19.
91*   *Kären* (Parmo Carl Ploug, tr. Clara Kappey), 1894 ['95?]   G1
        Compare Heise.
92*   *Marie* (Gottschall, tr. Elisabeth Rücker), 1896   H3
        First composed in German—compare Franz, Op. 18/1.

93*   *Berceuse* (Ives), 1900 [ad 1903?]   K7
        > *Wiegenlied* (1st stanza: *des Knaben Wunderhorn;* 2nd: G. Scherer),
        say 1900? Compare Brahms, Op. 49/4.
94   *Where the Eagle* (Monica Turnbull), 1900[HTI: 1906]
                                              Cos Cob Song Vol. 1935, K5, L4
        > *Grace* (whose words?), ms: before April 1899.
95   *Allegro* (Ives), [ad]1900   K6
        > *Sehnsucht* (Christian Winther, Ger. tr. Lobedanz), [ad]1900—compare
        Kjerulf.
              > *Rosenzweige* (Karl Stieler), 1900[?]—compare von Fielitz.
        The only sketch of this music has, above the voice-staff, *Rosenzweige*
        (which fits it beautifully), and below the staff *Sehnsucht* (which fits it
        very badly).
96   *Romanzo di Central Park* (Leigh Hunt), 1900   H6
        Ives gave this song no title—it is taken from his introductory note. There
        is also a postscript: "Some twenty years ago, an eminent and sure-minded
        critic . . . told a young man that —— was one of our great composers. . . .
        The above collection of heartbeats would show the influence, on the
        youthful mind, of the master in question." A leaf from the book reveals
        that the composer represented by the dash was "Victor Herbert!!—lily-
        white hands and diamonds!"
97*   *Die Lotosblume* (Heine) 1899[?]   ⌉   C29
        and *The South Wind* (tr. H.T.), [ad April 1908]⌋
        Compare Schumann, Op. 25/7.

From a Cantata, *The Celestial Country*

⌈98* *Naught that Country Needeth* ("Alford, from St. Bernard"), 1899
⎜   H5, L3
⎣99   *Forward into Light* ("Alford, from St. Bernard"), 1898   F7, L2
       These two arias are #2 and #6 of the seven movements of the cantata
       (App. 3, #13). The text, by Henry Alford, is not derived from Bernard of
       Cluny, who was not Saint Bernard.

100* *A Christmas Carol* (Ives), n.d. [December 1897?]   D15r
       In preparing D, Ives added below: "(before 1898)"—which is not in D.

101   *My Native Land* (Heine, tr. by whom?), 1897 [ms: before June
       1895]   G3
       Ives's first setting—compare Lassen's *Es war ein Traum.*

102   *Memories, A—Very Pleasant, B—Rather Sad* (Ives), 1897   F6

103* *The White Gulls* (from the Russian, Maurice Morris), 1921 C6r
       The translator (Morris W. Pool, see #25) wrote Ives that the poem
       was "published in the *Herald* when it was the *Sun*"—that is, when the
       Sun temporarily absorbed the *Herald* in February through September,
       1920. Search through microfilms has not found it, but the films consulted
       lacked Sunday–Monday 22–23 August 1920, where it might still be found.

104* *Two Little Flowers* (H.T.I. and Ives), 1921—see App. 19.   D11
105* *West London* (Matthew Arnold), [ad]1921   C17r
       > *Matthew Arnold Overture,* December 1912—see §29.

106* *Amphion* (Tennyson), [ad?]1896   F5
       > *In April-tide* (Clinton Scollard), say 1895?

107* *A Night Thought* (Thomas Moore), 1895 [ad about 1903?]   C31
       > *In My Beloved's Eyes* (W. M. Chauvenet), [1895?]
       A memo in Ives's hand, "for Giles, in D, *My Beloved's Eyes,*" suggests
       that, when Ives was Giles's choirmaster (1900–1902), this song still had
       its original words, and that the adaptation may have been after 1902.

108* *Songs My Mother Taught Me* (Adolf Heyduk, tr. Natalie
       Macfarren), 1895   H2
       Compare Dvorak, Op. 55/4.

109   *Waltz* (Ives), 1895 [ms: 1893 or '94]   G2
110* *The World's Wanderers* (Shelley), 1895 [adapted later?]   F4
       > *Leise zieht durch mein Gemüth* (Heine), 1895?—compare Franz, Op.
       41/1. Memos, on Ives's copy with German words, for ordering copyist
       copies and transpositions suggest that this was still a German song while
       Ives was a choirmaster.

111   *Canon:* Oh, the days are gone . . . (Thomas Moore), [ad?]1894
       [adapted later?]   D8
       > *Canon:* Not only in my lady's eyes . . . (whose words?), ms: January
       1893.

112* *To Edith* (H.T.I., 28 January 1919), ad 1919   F2
       > a lost song of 1892.

113* *When Stars are in the Quiet Skies* (Bulwer-Lytton), 1891 [ad
       about 1893?]   C33

> *Country Celestial* (Neale, from Bernard of Cluny), [1891?]
< *Du bist wie eine Blume* (Heine), ms: after January 1896
  Compare Schumann, Op. 25/24.

114   *Slow March* (the family and L. D. Brewster), 1888 [ms. summer
       '87 or '88]   F2
       Memo on ms: "Found by mother in mss. [in the] cellar, May 16, 1921."

Other Songs Published before the *114 Songs*

115   *William Will* (S. B. Hill), 1896
                              Willis Woodward & Co. 1896—out of print
       Campaign song for McKinley. Susan Benedict Hill finished James M.
       Bailey's *History of Danbury* after his death. Her letter to Ives of 20
       August 1896 is about publication of "*our* song."

116   *A Scotch Lullaby* (Charles E. Merrill, Jr., Yale '98), 1896
                                          Yale Courant 1896, M4
       Facsimile in the *Yale Courant*, Vol. 33/5, Dec. 1896, pp. 125–27, with
       the music in Ives's hand and the words in Merrill's.

Other Songs Published since the *114 Songs*

117   *Soliloquy* (Ives), 1907 (accompaniment meant for 4 hands)   C24
118   *Song for Harvest Season* (G. Phillimore), 1894 [1893?]   C32
       Accompaniment for instruments or organ. Memo on ms: "This piece was
       played about when the new Baptist Church in Danbury was opened,
       either in summer of 1893 or 1894. Father played the cornet, Mrs. Smyth
       tried to sing, and I played the lower parts." [The church was dedicated
       on Sunday 16 April 1893.]
119   *At Parting* (Frederick Peterson), 1889   C34
       See § 44, at note 3.
120   *General William Booth Enters Into Heaven* (Vachel Lindsay),
       1914   D1
       Ives's text was apparently the reprint of lines 1–23 and 30–37 in a
       review of the poem in *The Independent* for 12 January 1914. The earliest
       sketch seems to be for voice and piano, the sketches of instrumentation
       being later (these may constitute the "brass band" score mentioned in
       App. 3, #69). The ink copy for voice and piano is dated 26 September
       1914.
121   *A Farewell to Land* (Byron), D: 1925 [ms: December 1909]   D2
122   *Requiem* (Robert Louis Stevenson), November 1911   D3
123   *Aeschylus and Sophocles* (Landor), 1922 (App. 3, #72)   D6
       Accompaniment for piano and string quartet, mm. 1–8 (quartet) >
       "Greek Fugue" [1897?], mm. 11–15 (piano) > *Pre-Second String
       Quartet,* 1905 (App. 3, #60, and §26).
124   *Slugging a Vampire* (Ives), D: [ad?] 1902   D10
       > *Tarrant Moss* (Kipling), #72 above. Footnote in D: "This was orig-
       inally to Kipling's *Tarrant Moss* ('I closed and drew,' etc.), but as per-
       mission was not obtained, the nice poetry above was written later (not
       by Mr. Kipling)."

125   *On the Antipodes* (Ives), 1915–23 [ms: partly 1904] (App. 3, #73)
                                                                        D18

   Accompaniment for one piano, 4 hands, and organ pedal at the end (no
   sketches or parts specify two pianos or string orchestra as in App. 3, #73).
   For a sketch page dated 17 March 1904 see App. 17, page 265. Some
   of the chords may be either > or < the *Universe Symphony* (App. 3,
   #77, and §38).

126   *They Are There!* or *War March* (Ives), words revised 1942
           (see #50 above)   J8r

127   *Abide With Me* (Lyte), 1890 [1891?—older ms. '92?—new acc.
           later]   K1, L1

   Compare William Monk's *Eventide.*

128   *Vote for Names* (Ives), November 1912, acc. for 3 pianos.
                                                                     Peer 1968

   Ives's hasty, incomplete sketch (Q2636) has no indication of speaking
   the title, etc., but does imply an ostinato accompaniment—"same chord
   hit hard over and over—Hot Air Election Slogan."

129   *Flag Song* (Henry Strong Durand, Yale '81), November 1898
                                                                     Peer 1968

   Words written possibly for a Yale alumni dinner, music (Q2518–19)
   probably not composed to these words—perhaps adapted from a song
   listed in the program of a Hopkins Grammar School fraternity show of
   1894 with words by E. E. Garrison ("From the lands where they are
   dwelling . . ."—chorus: "Here's to Pi Sigma Tau . . .") and music by
   Ives which is lost.

130   *Rock of Ages* (Augustus Montague Toplady), [1889–92?]   M1
   Compare Thomas Hastings' *Toplady.*

131   *Far From My Heav'nly Home* (Henry Francis Lyte), [1890–92?]
                                                                        M2

   Compare Lyte himself, and Wilkes's *Lyte.*

132   *There is a certain garden* (whose words?), 1893   M3

133   *God Bless and Keep Thee* (whose words?), [1897?—ms: before
           December '97]   M5

134   *No More* (William Winter), December 1897   M6

135   *Pictures* (Monica Peveril Turnbull), H.T.I.: 1906   M7

136   *The One Way* (Ives), [May 1923?]   M8

137   *Peaks* (Henry Bellamann), [September 1923?]   M9

See
p. 179

138   *Yellow Leaves* (Henry Bellamann), [late 1923?]   M10

139   *A Sea Dirge* (Shakespeare, *The Tempest,* Act 1, Sc. 2), January
           1925   M11

   Compare Purcell and Parry.

140   *Christmas Carol* (words and tune by Edith Osborne Ives, De-
           cember 1924, accompaniment by C. E. Ives, November 1925)
                                                                       M12

141   *In the Mornin'* (negro spiritual, before 1850, accompaniment by
           C. E. Ives, 1929)   M13

Ives's note on the *67th Psalm*[1]

This is a kind of enlarged plain chant, the fundamental of which is made of two keys (but to be felt [or] heard as one)—G minor, with C major superimposed. The chords standing for the other relations [to these] fundamentals keep a similar tonal relation.[2]

I remember Father saying that this (as a basic formation, and among some other combinations we had worked out) had a dignity and a sense of finality—quite a different effect from the dominant 9th. But when the lower parts take the major, and the upper parts the minor—for example in measure 5, page 1—it forms a kind of dominant 9th.

Harmonically the fundamental could be (would be in harmony books of nice professors) catalogued as an inversion of the 9th. But whether an inversion or not, it seems to me to be a stronger chord than the 9th—which makes one feel that all inversions are not inversions, not always. A wider distribution of the same notes (so called, in terms of one octave) will bring out, to some extent, not exactly the same thing, if measured by the difference of overtone vibrations—beats— ratio of vibration numbers—and the ear feels this, but not in the class-room! To have the ear bossed all day long by Jadassohn may not be the only way or the best way of growing—at least not in the morning.

Father, I think, succeeded in getting a choir in Danbury to sing this without an organ[3]—but I remember I had difficulty in the New Haven choirs. The two keys gave trouble. It seemed for some reason more difficult for the ladies to hold their key than the men. Why—I couldn't quite make out—possibly because it is either low pitches, or the lower parts are closer to the root,—and then perhaps because the

---

1 Just as soon as Ives was in insurance, and had some money of his own to spend, he started having copyist copies made of his songs, and had two of the first ones bound to-gether with a few gatherings of music paper, with the idea of copying others into the book—he was that impatient for something that would at least feel and look like a book of his songs. Eventually many of the blank pages were used for sketches, pp. 13–14 (at the end of the first song) for this memo, which is undated.

2 In the first four measures the two harmonic strands are exactly parallel with one excep-tion at the end of m. 3—minor mediant below, and lowered mediant above.

3 Ives always dated this psalm 1898, but George Ives died in early November 1894. See also §51, note 4.

ear is more accustomed to feel the fundamental note primarily, and to think in its terms—and perhaps not. Occasionally it was sung by the men, while I played the upper staff on an enclosed manual.[4]

4 The "upper staff" probably refers to Ives's score-sketch on two staves (neg. no. n2248–49), which he might have played from (no choir parts or other copies of this psalm have come to light). This kind of performance may have been an ancestor of the hovering choir of violins in the *Fourth Symphony*, or of the Earth-and-Heaven idea in the *Universe Symphony*.

Postscript to Appendix 4, (#137–138–139, p. 177)

The editor would like to point out several errata in the first printing of his own edition of M, which are not all self-evident:

Peaks, m. 25, 2nd beat: a♯1 and c♯2—m. 27–28: slur from "dri-" to the note before "–ven".

Yellow Leaves, m. 5, last 8th: 32nd and dotted 16th (not 16th and dotted 32nd) —m. 13: the last chord lacks an arpeggio sign.

A Sea Dirge, M. 3, 2nd beat: the a♭ should be preceded by a [—m. 12, seventh 8th: the tied b2 lacks an 8th-flag—m. 17, third 8th: ♭ before e1—m. 21, sixth 8th, voice: ♭ before d1—m. 22, fifth 8th, voice: ♮ before d1.

Also #141, *In the Mornin'*, has appeared previously as *Give Me Jesus*.

APPENDIX 6

Ives's scholastic record (1894–98), Chadwick's visit to Parker's class (1898), and the footnote to *Ich Grolle Nicht*

Since various things Ives wrote about his work at Yale must be checked against the courses he actually took, it is best to start with his official record. The gradebooks of that period are large ledgers, each accounting for five classes, this one for '96–'00. Each student has four columns of thirty-one lines: the first six for his four (more restricted) underclass terms, the next twenty-one for his four (more elective) upperclass terms, and the last four for his averages. In the twenty-one upperclass lines each grade is preceded by the number of hours and followed by the course number, but the underclass courses were not numbered—here the Modern Language grade is usually followed by either Gr. (German), Fr. (French), or by the initial of the instructor. The listings for '98 also give a breakdown of the freshman year into three sections (Abbott to Fuller, Gage to Myers, Neale to Young), naming instructors for each section—but none for the sophomore year— and also the complicated methods of determining averages.

In Ives's day, grades were on a basis of 400 with 200 passing, instead of the now familiar proportion of a passing 60 out of 100 (an outline of 1959 shows equivalents in the two systems). The listings below are filled out from the course descriptions in the catalogue of the year in question, and the grades for the two terms with the recommended percentile equivalents.

Freshman year, 1894–95—average 223 (65).

Greek—Homer *Odyssey* v–viii; selections from Herodotus and Thucydides; Plato *Apology*—
 Carleton L. Brownson, Tutor.   205 (61), 214 (63).
Latin—Livy xxi–xxii; Cicero *de Amicitia, de Senectute;* Horace *Satires;* Composition; History of the Roman Republic—
 James J. Robinson, Instructor.   221 (64), 216 (63).
Mathematics—textbooks: Chauvenet's *Geometry*, Richards's *Trigonometry;* projection of figures; triangles and surveying—
 Asst. Prof. William Beebe.   198 (59), 185 (57).
German—Gustav A. Andreen, Instructor.   297 (79), 254 (71).

English Literature—Brooke's *Primer;* Shakespeare three plays; Milton
minor poems—
William Lyon Phelps, Instructor.   Second term, 275 (75).

Sophomore year, 1895–96—average 226 (65).

Greek—Aeschylus *Prometheus;* Sophocles *Antigone;* Euripides *Iphi-
genia in Tauris;* Aristophanes *Frogs;* lectures on Greek drama and
theatre.   246 (69), 234 (67).
Latin—Terence one or two plays; Horace *Epodes, Odes;* Tacitus
Agricola, Germania; reading Latin at sight.   220 (64), 225 (65).
Mathematics—applications of trigonometry; algebraic equations;
analytical geometry; map projection.   226 (65), 260 (72).
French (beginning)—Robert L. Taylor, Insrtuctor. 260 (72), 150 (45).
English (2 hr.)—Shakespeare *Tempest, Lear, Hamlet;* Spenser *Faery
Queene;* Milton *Paradise Lost* i–ii; Addison *Spectator;* Swift *Gulliver;*
etc.—William Lyon Phelps.   275 (75), 245 (69).
Rhetoric (1 hr).—essays, conferences.   275 (75), 175 (53).

Junior year, 1896–97—average 243 (69)

Logic, Psychology, and Ethics 1 (3)—nervous system, general psych.,
Profs. Geo. T. Ladd, G. M. Duncan, E. H. Sneath; experimental
psych., Dr. Edward W. Scripture.   240 (68), 200 (60).
Political Science 20 (3)—Hadley's *Economics;* financial and industrial
problems of the day—Prof. Arthur Twining Hadley, Asst. Prof.
Irving Fisher.   200 (60), 220 (64).
History 41 (2)—Europe from the Reformation to the French Revolution;
the state system; political and intellectual movements—
Prof. Edward G. Bourne.   250 (70), 240 (68).
French 60 (3)—standard French authors; syntax, exercises in composi-
tion, oral practice—Robert L. Taylor, Instructor. 220 (64), 225 (65).
Music 271 (2)—Counterpoint (see below)—
Prof. Horatio Wm. Parker.   270 (73), 325 (85).
Music 274 (2)—Instrumentation—Prof. Parker.   300 (80), 300 (80).

Senior year, 1897–98—average 259 (72).

Philosophy 4 (2)—History of speculative thought from Descartes to
the present; readings from Descartes to Kant—
Prof. George M. Duncan.   230 (66), 230 (66).
Political Science 40 (2)—The Science of Society—
Prof. William G. Sumner.   270 (74), 255 (71).

History 53 (2)—Europe since 1789—
    Prof. Arthur M. Wheeler.   240 (68), 240 (68).
History 61 (2)—The American Colonies—
    Prof. Bourne.   275 (75), 260 (72).
French 71 (2)—Short masterpieces: Chateaubriand, Voltaire, J. J.
    Rousseau, Molière, Pascal, Montaigne—
    Robert L. Taylor, Instructor.   265 (73), 240 (68).
English 115 (1)—American Literature of the past 100 years—
    Asst. Prof. William Lyon Phelps.   295 (79), 250 (70).
Music 272 (2)—Strict Composition—
    Prof. Parker.   325 (85), 300 (80).
Music 274 (2)—Instrumentation—Prof. Parker.   340 (88), 280 (76).

Four-year average 238 (68).

Only in music did Ives ever rise above a "gentleman's C"—his overall average being D plus. His classmate, Julien Ripley, told how he had been rather surprised when Ives graduated—"he was a little casual about some of his studies."

When Ives entered Yale, Parker, as the new Battell Professor of the Theory of Music, reorganized the music curriculum into six principal courses (electives open only to upperclassmen) and a seventh comprising instruction in practical music. These appear three times in each catalogue: in the undergraduate and in the graduate courses, and in the statement of the Department of Music (their descriptions hardly changing from year to year)—but in different order and numbering in the three places. Perhaps Parker revised the Department statement but not the other listings, and the inconsistency remained. In the list below, the three sets of left-hand numbers are: Department (graduate, undergraduate)—and the abbreviated descriptions are followed by the official registrations during Ives's four years.

1 (1, 270).   Harmony (2 hours)—intervals, chords, modulations, suspensions, harmonization of melodies, figured bass; Jadassohn's *Harmony*.   12, 13, 7, 7.

2 (2, 271).   Counterpoint (2)—accompanying chorales and canti firmi, orders [species], imitation, simpler composition.   2, 5, 3, 2.

3 (4, 273).   The History of Music (1)—lectures, earliest stages, church music, opera, oratorio, development of forms to culmination in Beethoven.   0, 9, 10, 0.

4 (3, 272).   Strict Composition (2)—triple and quadruple counterpoint, fugue, canon, free treatment of different kinds of thematic material.   0, 2, 1, 2.

5 (5, 274).   Instrumentation (2)—lectures on instruments illustrated from great composers, exercises in practical orchestration.   0, 0, 2, 1.

6 (6, 275).   Free Composition (2)—part songs, glees, pieces for piano and other instruments, sonata.   0, 0, 1, 0.

[7](7, 276).   Practical Music.

Beside Parker, the music faculty included Samuel S. Sanford, Professor of Applied Music, Harry B. Jepson, Instructor in organ (Ives's predecessor at Center Church), and Isidor Troostwyk, Instructor in Violin, who was concertmaster when Parker organized the New Haven Symphony Orchestra early in 1895.

Music 3 (History) was announced as a public lecture series, Wednesdays at 5, with titles appearing in the *Yale News* the Monday before. This suggests that, in other courses too, Parker might have welcomed qualified underclassmen as auditors (if they had time) or even individually (if he had time). If so, this explains Ives's "four years with Parker" in §13, and Parker's criticism of *At Parting* before November '94 (see §44). If the date on the full score of the first movement of the *First Symphony* is correct—"Finished 76 So. Middle, Yale . . . May 29, 1895"— Ives was doing very advanced composition as a Freshman. The amount of music he wrote at Yale (the symphony, several overtures etc., marches for piano and for orchestra or band, the *First String Quartet* and its prototypes, several fugues, the Thanksgiving organ pieces and many others, some of *The Celestial Country*, various anthems and partsongs, music for fraternity shows, and around fifty songs) would help explain his mediocre grades.

The following conversation probably took place at the time of Parker's performance of Chadwick's *Melpomene Overture* on Thursday 31 March 1898. Music 4 (Strict Composition), which Ives was then taking, met Tuesdays and Thursdays at 2. Apparently Parker hurried back from lunch at Heublein's, but Chadwick took his time. Parker may have considered the re-setting of famous song texts as part of strict composition. The memo appears on margins of a copy by Price of Ives's *Ich grolle nicht,* but the first classroom scribblings from which it was copied are missing.

Geo. W. Chadwick came into class this afternoon (on [his] way back from Heiblein's),[1] sat down behind me and Puss[2]—Lord! [what a] beer breath! When Chadwick came in, Parker [was] objecting to the too many keys in the middle [of *Summerfields*][3]—Geo. W. C. grinned at it and [at] H. W. P. Of this song, Prof. Horat[io] P[arker] said it [was] nearer to the G[rolle] of Schumann than the *Summerfields* was near to Brahms.

But Chadwick said the *Summerfields* was the best. C. said "The melodic line has a natural continuity—it flows—and stops when [rounded out][4]—as only good songs do. And [it's] different from Brahms, as in the piano part and the harmony it takes a more difficult and almost opposite [approach][5] to Brahms, for the active tranquillity

1 See §9, note 9.
2 The Yale '98 class book gives "Puss" as one of the nicknames of Grenville Parker (1873–1924), who entered in the class of '97 and shifted to '98, being in the Freshman Glee Club two years and in both the University Glee Club and the College Choir four years. He was David Twichell's roommate. He never signed up for a music course, but had come with Ives to audit.
3 Ives's translation-title for *Feldeinsamkeit.*
4 Ives, in copying, skipped the word or words after "when" (end of a line)—"rounded out" seems plausible.
5 Ives wrote this word as "aspect? (can't make out word)"—"approach" seems the logical solution.

of the outdoor beauty of nature is harder to express than just quietude. In its way [it's] almost as good as Brahms." He winked at H. W. P. and said "That's as good a song as you could write."[6]

[This was] written on the sides of the ms. of this and [of] the *Summerfields* sketch copy after I got back [to] 76 S[outh] M[iddle], after class in Tr[umbull]—carefully on the margin, as at that time (1897–8) Chadwick was the big celebrated man of American Music.

Footnote to *Ich grolle nicht* in *114 Songs*
(lacking in the later reprints)

The writer has been severely criticized for attempting to put music to texts of songs which are masterpieces of great composers. The song above and some of the others were written primarily as studies. It should be unnecessary to say that they were not composed in the spirit of competition; neither Schumann, Brahms, or Franz will be the one to suffer by a comparison,—another unnecessary statement. Moreover, they would probably be the last to claim a monopoly of anything— especially the right of man to the pleasure of trying to express in music whatever he wants to. These songs are inserted not so much in spite of this criticism as because of it.

[6] Such classroom indiscretion on the part of an experienced administrator might be explained by Chadwick's having been Parker's teacher, and now (after a good German lunch with plenty of beer) lapsing absent-mindedly into a practice-teaching-session attitude.

APPENDIX 7

Memos About the *Concord Sonata* (1913–29)

When *Concord* and the *Essays* were sent around to those who Ives hoped would be interested, the reactions varied, both in character and articulateness, all the way from Bellamann's lectures to various waste-baskets. Ives's counter-reactions had already been equally articulate, and are preserved in three manuscripts jotted down hastily to unburden his feelings, and with no thought of publication. But they reveal almost as much about the principles of composition he was using in *Concord* as the *Essays* do about the philosophy expressed. All three are datable: 1913, 1923 or later, and January 1929. The first (of which only pp. 3–6 are extant), the third (pp. A–B–C with a patch for p. C), and the patch for the second one are all on sheets of ruled yellow foolscap. But the second was partly written into a copy of *Concord* which has a history.

When the first complete public performance of *Concord* was announced for January 1939, Lawrence Gilman wrote Ives asking for the loan of a copy to study. The one referred to above may have been the only extra one Mrs. Ives could find, and before sending it to him, she started to tear out the back flyleaves that had the memo, but realizing that these included the title page etc., she copied it all out instead. Gilman's letter of thanks to Mrs. Ives says: "I am greatly indebted to you and to Mr. Ives for your kindness in sending me the copy of the 'Concord' Sonata and the other material—but I have an uncomfortable fear that I put you to a good deal of trouble. I shall take care of this copy of the music, and return it promptly. . . . Naturally I remember you as Harmony Twichell—you represented to me in those days a number of ideals!"

Afterwards Mrs. Ives thanked Gilman for his review of the sonata in the *New York Herald Tribune,* and he wrote back: "You were very kind to write as you did about my article, and the message from Mr. Ives moved me deeply. It is I who should thank him—for one of those experiences that bring new worlds about us. . . . I have not forgotten that you lent me Mr. Ives' score of the Sonata! You shall have it back in a short while. (I don't like to let it go!)"

In answer to Gilman's questions about other music, Edith wrote him (Mrs. Ives being then in Danbury), and he replied: "Thank you for your gracious letter . . . I wish I might have everything that he has composed, and also, whatever commentaries he has written on his music. If I seem to be greedy, he is to blame! . . .— to whom my obligation is already so immeasurable."

Gilman showed the same care in preparing to review the Ives concert planned as a repeat of *Concord*, and asked if he might hear Mina Hager rehearse the songs. She said afterward, "When he came in, he made my little apartment seem like a palace!" But before the day of the concert he suffered a heart attack. Though he was up and around by spring, he died in September. His daughter wrote Mrs. Ives: "My mother has asked me to write and thank you and Mr. Ives for your very lovely letter of sympathy. . . . You both know, I am sure, that the experience of studying and hearing Mr. Ives' scores was one of the notable events of last winter for father, and you will treasure, as I do, the remembrance of his deep enjoyment of it." Eventually much of Gilman's library was sold.

Years later, in 1965, Harold Schonberg (to whose perceptive reviews Ives enthusiasts have reason to be grateful) was surprised by an offer of a gift of the second movement of Ives's *Fourth Symphony* in the *New Music* printing—a copy which had once been part of Gilman's library. Indeed he would be delighted. When it came, along with it was the first edition of *Concord* with scribblings inside. After recognizing their importance and finding out what they represented, he generously sent this editor reproductions of the pages that had writing in Ives's hand. Later on, in a joint attack on some of the textual puzzles, he offered not only helpful guesses but the kind of searching interest that made "two pairs of eyes see better than one." So it is partly through his kindness that this text can be based on all extant sources.

The editing follows the procedures outlined for the *Memos*. M = pages in Ives's hand; m = pages in Ives's patch for the second one; H = pages in Mrs. Ives's copy of the second one.

1

(1913, pages 1–2 missing)

M3

. . . of it, whether transposed higher or lower. This attitude is, or at least it seems to me that it is, one that has helped to restrict music— that is, its processes of growth—so that in too many musicians, critics, listeners, players, etc., the ear muscles have been used too weakly, or at least too little—so that they only like and approve music (call it musical sounds if you like) if it is something they are used to—they don't have to stand up like men and do anything but sit down in the easy-lace easy-chair and purr.

The same or similar attitudes and arguments, or rather protests, the Hawthorne (second) movement came in for. For instance, I played the whole sonata to Max Smith last year (1912)—the Hartsdale piano didn't help!—though the last [movement], *Thoreau,* in the middle section, I played partly from the sketch and with a few improvisations in a few places, as it was not all written out fully completed (but it was practically as it is now, though there are a few places I'll have to clean up). Max said the Alcott movement was by far the best—by "best" Maxie meant (but didn't know it) the easiest to listen to—that is, for his nice ears. But his ears were so tired when it came to *Thoreau*—he

M4

just changed the subject. And it was the same (about the same only in detail) with the *Hawthorne* as the *Emerson*—he didn't try to get it, made him half sore, half cuckoo, etc. Now the *Hawthorne* is fundamentally a scherzo, a joke—and I explained that—a kind of program and take-off music—the opposite of *Emerson,* which is serious, goes to the deeper things (I like to think it does—it did as far as I was concerned), and for that reason not as clear to get. [It is] more difficult to sense and feel its substance than the *Hawthorne,* but less difficult to play—that is, *Emerson* is more difficult mentally, perhaps spiritually, but *Hawthorne* is more difficult physically. The hands and fingers have to practise more and harder, something as a hurdler has to get up his muscle and keep at it every day until his feet can make it right —hard and fast, and land right—muscle training—and the *Hawthorne* requires as much of the player's muscles, even his feet. Sometimes he has to jump two or three octaves and land right—fast.

M5

Max did get the Drum Corps chords,[1] and smiled at the Rollo's moaning question, which I had to play twice and take off—the "what's all this?"[2] It isn't a program of events exactly, but just a general take-off of things funny, fairylike, wild, real and unreal—I've forgotten some of the stories or incidents, as the Demon's pipe, the frost pane, Railroad to Heaven, etc.—Dr. Griggs got it immediately, but Stowell didn't like not having a nice key in every room. He'd point to this place— "Now what chord is that?—What key does that chord belong [to] there?—a C♯ and then D♭ [in the] next chord!"—etc. etc. He couldn't see that if there isn't (in the whole or only a section) a key—that is, when the notes are not used in the tonal relations that a key superimposes on the substance—that signs which would suggest that tonality should not be used as such—they are more or less misleading, first the eye, then the ear. And why not in music—yeah Art!—in serious music too, a something which comes up from the life of a day, perhaps something that nature does to an Elm Tree, something as of old-time humor, or a sense of hilarity, a jump-upward feeling a boy may have on an early winter morning—why not?

M6

The "Magical Frost Waves" on the Berkshire dawn window—to me the *Hawthorne* movement starts with that, first on the morning window pane, then on the meadow. Perhaps some morning I feel like playing the frost lines moderately fast and *pp*—and then a boy lands on the stoop faster, and plays it *presto* and *fff*—why not Art?—and then he gets riding on the railroad—perhaps (but not every day) on the Celestial Railroad—then he jumps over the castle wall with Feathertop, but not quite exactly the same jump every time—some days it's more of a hurdle, and some days a high dive. Then one day he gets agoing so high up and fast like, another boy helps him—why not, Art? Then

[1] This must be the stylized roll-off ending the march in *Hawthorne.*
[2] The question "What's all this?" is exactly the way Ives once explained the high f-sharps in *The Alcotts* to the editor.

all of a sudden he is in the old churchyard—he hears the solemn old hymn, the distant bells—his old ghost friend greets him—he feels suddenly reverent in an honest boylike way—why not Art? And then he gets hit and jumps on the railroad train again and is off—he forgets the dead and dances on the Demon's pipe bowl—why can't that all be a natural part of serious music?—and the serious part may stand up and shake hands, Art!, with that rollicking scarecrow, so solemn and . . .

[the rest missing]

2

(1923 or later)

M1H1 (see letter from Dr. Paul Stoesher[?],[3] harping—July 1921)—And many others say—"Why this?—What is this?—What's the nice key?—Where's—etc.—etc.?" They want nice straight lines to lean on—"How can you play without counting 1–2–3–4 ♪·♪·♪·♪· , Rollo?" Rhythm is a bigger thing than a nice little ticking watch. And Ethelboy says—"Why that fellow doesn't understand music at all—he writes B♯,[4] then he doesn't know he must go nice to C♯ minor—he doesn't know that a half note equals two quarters, etc. etc., Rollo ♪·♪·♪·♪·♪· ."

They want to have Ralph Waldo Emerson or Henry Thoreau sing Do–Me–Soh   —but those men were men—they didn't sing Doh–Me–Soh—they knew the Doh–Me–Soh, but they didn't sell it to the ladies all the time, they used it as one of the windows, not the whole parlor, etc. etc.

Some do [see it], but a good many (mostly teachers, professors, etc., in nice colleges and conservatwaties) don't—even after having it explained (see Program and Prologue) that this is not a nice sonata for a nice piano player, but something that the writer had long been thinking about.

M2H2 Time—♩ = ♩—to help bring through the eyes the spirit of what the sounds or lines try to represent. The notes hold into the next general thought, as thoughts do—every thought hasn't a clothes-pin between it [and the next]—they go on and up. Emerson's thought was usually a part of the before and afterward—not little miniature ideas in frames, to be read easily and put down, etc. It was bigger and

---

[3] Ives's writing of this name was hasty and vague, and the reading given is anything but certain. Unfortunately no such letter (even from a name remotely similar) has showed up among Ives's papers—a great pity, since he apparently wrote the start of this memo on the letter itself. Or might this be the Dr. Stoehr whom Ives mentions in *Some Quarter-tone Impressions* (Boatwright, p. 112)?

[4] This "B♯" is probably the same one as at note 7 below, or possibly the one ending line 4 of p. 34 of the revised edition.

greater and higher than a one-line picture on paper. These longer notes on the lesser beats, of course, are helped by the pedal, but

M2½H2   ped . . . .* underneath is a poor substitute for what I had in mind— (that is, what Emerson, Thoreau, etc. had in mind, and what I tried to get out of my system in "tones" or in "sounds" if you like—call it music or not, it makes no difference)[5]—and then the pedal, unless used in long or whole-phrase passages, when lifted, stops the thought-sounds, which ought to be thought of continuing to their natural ends. So to write them, usually the more fundamental themes, somewhat in this

M3H3   way is nearer to what the music (?) should be to the ear and the in-mind than the limited but more conventional (more proper) way. In fact, as soon as music goes down on paper, it loses something of its birthright!

Though the Emerson movement started as a kind of piano concerto, the orchestra [was] the world and people hearing, and the piano cadenza was Emerson (especially had the "thrust and dagger").[6]

Then another complaint from Prof. $5000 is the combination of notes in the chords. If he can't get his Jadassohn out and check it up, then it really isn't nice music etc. etc. "He puts notes in a chord that don't belong in it—and he usually has too many notes—he doesn't understand harmony—for instance, on page 3, there is a B♯ and B♮ in the same chord[7]—that is wrong" (Grandma Prof. says). It is not, you g—— d—— sap!—takin' money for emasculating music and students. I suppose I should explain by footnotes for soft-feeted, for those who can't see or do anything unless they have been "learned to" nice in some music kindergarten for grown-ups in legs. The twelve notes in a nice well-tuned piano are "twelve notes"—machine-made almost—but

M4H4   at present the best instrument, that is, the widest sound implement we have, for only one man to use. But the mind, ear, and thought don't have to be always limited by the "twelve"—for a B♯ and a C♮ are not then the same—a B♯ may help the ear-mind get higher up the mountain than a C♮ always. It has another use, perhaps a more important [use] than a nice little guide in a resolution—it makes a chord, in some cases, more a help and incentive for the ear and mind to say (nearer to) what it feels. For instance, in the key of C, B going up to C, sometimes under certain moods, is sung (regardless of the piano) nearer to C than the B on the piano—and, going down from C to B, farther away. Now when both the two B's are used in a chord, there is a practical, physical, acoustical difference (overtonal, vibrational beats) which makes it a slightly different chord than the B's of an exact

5 Here Ives may be referring to the letter from Goetschius (see note 12 below).
6 This sentence is an afterthought sketched in between paragraphs. For other versions of "thrust and dagger" see App. 8, note 9.
7 In the first line of p. 3.

octave—and [even] on the piano the player sees that and feels that, it goes into the general spirit of the music—though on the piano this is missed by the unimaginative.

M5H5

Some of the chords in this, but more often passages from the *Second String Quartet* and some of the Chamber Sets—one I remember in pages 3–6 of *The St. Gaudens*[8]—I copied out and had played by six violins at Tams, playing in a kind of chord-system made—that is, assuming that a Db was nearer down to C, and that C♯ was nearer up to D. After the players had sensed this difference in playing the passage —say B–B♯–C, D–Db–C (to remember the B♯ and C, and the D and Db etc.)—to me they usually sounded nearer to each other than a quarter-tone, though in the upper and the lower movements I noticed very little difference. Then [I] would try to have the player think and so play the Db as it had been played in going down to C, and the C♯ as it had [been] played in going up to D, and then play with the others in a chord—and this had its own way [of being] different to the usual.

For instance, I don't remember this particular chord Prof. S. remarked on page 3—but a passage marked page 15 (see end of fourth brace)—in left hand, two lower notes of the chords, a G♮ goes up to Ab (though in the sketch marked G♯),[9] and the B♮ to Cb, and Cb to C♮, —the B♮ (when played by strings) went up from B, and the Cb went

M6H6

almost to C♮. And when this passage is played on the piano, this difference can be sensed, if not actually heard—that's the piano maker's or tuner's fault, not the ear's. That is, as the G goes to Ab, the B♮ is sensed as going to Cb—in the strings the chord Ab–Cb–G♮–Bb[10] is a different chord from Ab–B♮–G♮–Bb (see typewritten copy sent to Bellamann of technical plan etc. of Sonata, with tone-vibration tables etc.)—the difference in its overtonal beats (actually measured vibrationally), especially if hit rather hard, is evident.

Thus, when a movement, perhaps only a section or passage, is not fundamentally based on a diatonic (and chromatic) tonality system, the marked notes (♮, ♯, or b) should not be taken as literally representing those implied resolutions, because in this case they do *not* exist. The eye mustn't guide or enslave the ear too much or entirely in all cases—any more than the hand should too readily ("easily" better word), by the ways of its anatomy, physiology, and its life, limited too much by custom and habit and bodily ease, should narrow (enslave?— soften?—dwarf?—emasculate?) pianoforte music—Zat's right, Rollo?

8 Measures 13–18 of *The St. Gaudens* would seem to lend themselves particularly to this kind of experiment. Ives probably means pp. 3–6 of the score by Emil Hanke.
9 Page 15, fourth brace, of the first edition is p. 16, third brace, of the new editions. The g♯ of the sketch is in a parallel passage on p. 5, first brace.
10 Though Ives uses all capital letters, he obviously means the third chord from the end of the third brace of p. 16 (new editions).

Often, what is called awkward is easily called unmusical—a good hurdler doesn't have a pole to help him over—let the muscles of the hand get as strong as the Concord muscle of 1840, et al—and perhaps the muscles of the ear and soul will join in.

Another remark (made not to me or in a letter from a friend) was made by a rather overrated, celebrated piano player—it was, to me, typical of that sap—he said somepin' like this—"In the third movement, on the first page, a chord of A♭, E♭, and C is played in the left hand, but the signature is A♭—now the signature of E♭ would do just as well for A♭ and E♭ and C—and the right-hand part is in the signature [of] B♭—though running between E♭ and sometimes way out. This man", he said, "doesn't understand tonality—the A♭ signature is wrong, and so is the right hand." That is a typical get-off of a lily-eared softy. That first page is one of the simplest and most obvious things in the whole book. When Rollo says that the E♭ would be better than A♭, he says the subdominant chord is exactly the same as the tonic in its relation to the nice scale. Almost any conductor of the Philharmonic or the Boston Symphony could see even that. The left hand is in A♭—in that key—no other key—keeps that key—is that key —it intends, does, [is] meant to do that, couldn't do anything else, and will always put the player's left-hand-mind in that nice key of A♭ and nothing else (for old man Alcott likes to talk in A♭, and Sam Staples likes to have his say over the fence in B♭)—and the nice soprano sings in B♭. No, Rollo, the subdominant and tonic are not the same chords.

Especially in *Hawthorne,* it's more important to get the "gist and swat" agoing than to slow up to get the written notes. Thus some notes are detail and may be made . . . (see △).[11]

And some ask, "What do you mean by not to play literally?"—etc. Several reasons—but Rollo never tries to think what. One [reason is] that [it's] better not to—or [you] don't have to (which is the best [reason]) play every thing and piece and measure the same every time —not as Josey Hofmann et al play Beethoven, this nice little note just this way, etc.—Ta ta—making Beethoven a lady-bird etc.

> Play it before breakfast like ——!
> "   "   after   "   "   ——!
> "   "   " digging potatoes "   ——!

In fact, these notes, marks, and near pictures of sounds etc. are in a kind of way a platform for the player to make his own speeches on. And as I tried to infer in the book, in various places, that Emerson, Thoreau especially, and the others perhaps less so, weren't static,

11 These few words are another insertion between paragraphs. The extra leaf with the triangle-sign has not showed up.

rule-making, do-as-I'm-told professors,—to me their thoughts, substance, and inspiration change and grow, rise to this mountain, then to that, as the years go on through time to the Eternities. It was the attempt to catch this, to give one man's impression, reflected as it might be through sounds—inadequate enough probably to others— but not to let the music get the best of it, of them or the ideals. If the music is just taken as such, and by itself, it shouldn't mean the right something, or anything much—at least I hope not!—if it does, then it would show that my theory was all wrong—or rather I might say, if it were not for my years of friendship with Emerson, Alcott, Thoreau, [and] Hawthorne, the music, whatever it is, wouldn't be whatever it is!

The general stand taken, the remarks caused, and I might say the persistant fundamental misunderstanding—or should I say lack of discernment, aural, mental, and human, especially from professors, teachers, theorists, etc., with the exception of Prof. Goetschius[12] of Columbia and a Professor in Wellesley (I forget for the moment his name)[13]—are caused principally [by], or rather their tenets are based on, an aural limitation. They assume that fundamentally all of this (music?) ought to be and supposedly is based (and therefore limited, and so weakened, but they don't say that) on their tonal habitudes, or call them the normal scales, the diatonic, tempered, major and minor scale platforms. And these resulting uses, by years of custom and habit, these chordal progressions, modulating tones growing around them, systems of suspensions, etc., etc., assume something that in this Sonata

M8H10

M9H10

12 Percy Goetschius wrote Ives from New York on 20 May 1923: "I owe you an apology for not having sooner acknowledged your kindness in sending me a copy. . . . The Sonata excited my deep interest, and the more I saw of it, the more I wished to see, before writing to you about it. . . . The recent receipt of your *114 Songs* jogged my spirit. . . .
"I wish you to know that I do not take your work lightly. I say, frankly that I do not *like* this manner of sound-association, for I am too fully grounded in the habits (I admit that they are, to some extent, 'habits') of the classic methods. . . .
"But I am not, in conviction, a heartless and brainless Conservative, who recognizes the 'Last Word' in anything that Bach, Beethoven or Brahms have said in tone—no, nor Ives. . . . I am absolutely convinced of your sincerity, and see many admirable evidences of that *logic*, which is a part of my pet Physical Law, in your work—note that I hesitate to call it 'Music'. . . . As to your book, it is magnificent. . . .
"With sincere thanks, and very best wishes for your success, I am cordially yours, Percy Goetschius."
13 Clarence G. Hamilton wrote Ives from Wellesley College: "I want to thank you for the copy of your sonata, together with the prefatory book. I have not yet had time to study them with the requisite care, but am impressed with the high ideals of your work, and its novelty of presentation. I welcome the daring of those who, like yourself, are making incursions into new harmonic fields, since it is only by such incursions that new musical materials are to be developed.
"With much appreciation of your courtesy in sending the copies, I am
Yours very truly, Clarence G. Hamilton."
Hamilton dated this letter "March 10, 1920"—meaning 1921. Henry F. B. Gilbert had thanked Ives for the *Essays* on 26 May 1920, and Ives's sketch for an answer, dated 28 May says: ". . . when the *Concord* copies are finished, I'm going to send you one . . . But you'll be spared this for some time, as it takes longer to correct proofs than I imagined. . . ." Gilbert thanked Ives for the sonata on 17 February 1921.

is *not* assumed, except in a relative (analogous better word here) or occasional way.

m1

(I won't say a lack of discernment[14]—that would imply that there was something very important to discern—as for example the Hawthorne movement is supposed to be a kind of Scherzo—and that name doesn't mean (though perhaps it should) a serious moan—even Rollo knows that. So when the raised-solemn-brows say, "He doesn't [put] any marks of expression in—doesn't he know that it must be *p* or *f*?—doesn't he understand the difference?—Why, he doesn't even have a key!—doesn't he [know] that all serious music must have a nice key?—He says in a footnote 'Don't play it literally'—what does he mean by that?—He says four 32nds is not twice as fast as four 16ths—he certainly does not understand musical notation—he has some chords with all the notes in the scale in—he ought to learn good harmony nice! —He simply doesn't understand music!"—though I don't say or mean to say, Nancy, that the *Hawthorne* is as funny as *Huckleberry Finn*—

m2

but most of the chatter of the above old lady throats reminds me [of] that old Mrs. Jermimah Nichols, who would always have a morning moan on Grandmother's doorstep. She said, "Sarah Ives, you should be thankful for all the blessings you've got." (Jerminah had more to eat, less to do, more help in the kitchen, less trouble good and bad than most of the housewives then in Danbury, those days.) And Grandmother one day said to that moan, "Yes, Jermimah Nichols, I'm thankful for all the blessings I have—and I'm thankful for all the blessings I haven't!"

And so, when I get these letters, comments, and ree-marks of the above old-made-male-ladies, it sore of reminds [me] of what Jermimah said to Father (or Uncle Lyman, I think) after reading *Tom Sawyer*— "I don't believe half he (Mark Twain) says—he's nothin' but foolin' all the time. He ought to be more serious—he ought to learn to write good!")

M9H10

Thus here the music naturally grows, or works naturally, to a wider use of the twelve tones we have on the piano, and from (ever in an aural kind of way) building chordal combinations which suggest or imply (and of course to the aural imagination only, when played on a

M9H11

piano) an aural progression which physically is not in the piano strings, [but] may be implied by the mind [and] ear as a thing [of] musical sense. A part of or different parts of a movement may be based entirely on the major or minor tonal scales as we know [them] in our usual tonality system—then just as naturally, as soon as the ear has had some

14 This long balloon apparently started as a counter-qualification to be inserted somewhere early in the preceding paragraph, but its placement becomes a problem of compromise between continuity of the general thought and closeness of the key words.

acquisition and use, this and other tonal groups may be used together in other passages, and find their natural part in the general expression —then the other tonal groups may be used only—the ear, with practice in listening and hearing, making reasonable and natural chordal and melodic ways of expressing what is underneath the music.

M10H11 As to the matter of implied changes in the tone of a note (usually only one or two in a chord say of from six to eight notes) which when played on a piano does not change, but which the player can think of aurally as going higher or lower, as the case may be (see typewritten chart of measured or tonal-difference beats, etc.)—in many cases (as in the example above, p. 1)[15] the accidental mark (call [it] key index—

M10H12 though really not an accidental, [but] a sign for a different ratio of overtonal vibrations) is made to suggest and conform to the above theory—in other places so as not to bring to mind a tonality which does not exist, and so not [to] feel or think about not having a key. This is so it won't mislead the eye first, then as a result also the ear and the mind et al.

Of course all this leads back to whether a man's ear, mind, etc. is naturally willing or not naturally willing—rather whether he feels that the system as we know it, that of tonality, is a field too closely fenced in to be all it might be (that is, not entirely natural)—whether the laws we all learned, to the point almost of saturation, from Jadassohn, Goodrich, Richter, Riemann & Co. didn't gradually cave in and seem to grow into nice apron-strings—as a kind of feeling that the field is getting smaller and smaller and with more and more fences. As a specimen of just one fence, the picket—of the leading tone, so called —instead of a leading tone, often more of a withdrawing tone—its

M10H13 importance in the treatises was not (though called so) because it was a natural process of tonal science, but because it was easy for the ear to be led thusly. How thoroughly we learned the nice rules and obeyed them (but sometimes didn't and played hooky) or was it submitted to

M11H13 them, until one day, when a man becomes of age, the ear begins to sit up and think some for itself—and somehow that imperfect triad seems to grow less imperfect, and those two leading tones (or rather being led by tonic supremacy) get tired of that, some of that, semitone groove back home, etc.—and the melodic tendency scolds, for the smoothness and correctness of the whole resolution is endangered. But the ear begins to look for more trails up the mountain. Thus it's now more than a resolution that's endangered—all music is endangered!—Rollo told me so.

So two notes standing alone a whole tone apart seem (to the nice

---

15 That is, on p. 1 of the manuscript—see note 4 above.

classroom) to be a nice sign that they are a part of the dominant
seventh, and must act obediently—but the ear sometimes doesn't feel
exactly that way—so we must be fair and change that sign. Suppose
two curves, an up and down, start on E♭ and D♭, and are held down
hard through the arpeggios and back, and we don't land in A♭ major—
that sign isn't fair, Rollo, it points us the wrong way—so the sign-
maker makes it C♯ and E♭, and the music via the ear takes its own
way up the mountain better, and feels better about [it]. For instance,
just as an illustration or instance [of] wrong signs made nearer right,
or at least away from a misleading tendency—see *Thoreau*, page 61,
2nd brace, chord [at] beginning of 6th quarter-note beat—this is L H.:
C♯–F♯–E♮,[16] R.H.: G♯–F♮–B♭—if the right-hand G♯ had been put
an A♭, the eye would probably, to most, have suggested a resolution
to a nice E♭ major tonic chord, even in spite of the C♯ in the left hand
with F♯ and E over [it] which may seem to lean towards a B♮ gate—
but it doesn't get there, Rollo!

This is just one technical explanation of why certain notes have been
written as they have, in the Sonata and other music. No more technical
notes and explanations today, Rollo, for Edith and Susanna have their
own and better notes in the back yard!

Then, to my way of hearing and thinking, a sharp is a kind of underlying sign of, or senses and reflects or encourages, an upward movement, tonal and more perhaps spiritual, at a thing somewhat more of
courage and aspiration-towards than the flat carries or seems to—the
flat is more relaxing, subservient, looking more for rest [and] sub-
mission, etc.—often used as symbols as such, when they're not needed
as the signs of tonality in the usual way.

3

(January 1929)

The continuity of this music is more a process of natural tonal
diversification and distribution than of natural tonal repetition and
resolution. Often the roots or the beginning and end of a passage or
cycle are not literally the beginnings or ends—but combinations of
tone that can and do stand for them, if not to the eye, to the ear and
mind after sufficient familiarity.

For the most part, the Sonata was decided and sensed to a great
extent by the ear and mind (to say nothing of the left side of the
breast) before much went down on paper. It has seemed to me for a

M11H14
M12H14
M12H15
M1

16 Ives absent-mindedly wrote D♮ instead of E♮, but he refers to it correctly further on.
In the new editions, this chord is on p. 59, in the middle of the second brace.

long while back that too much went down on paper too soon. The pen and eyes are inclined by habit and custom to make the music somewhat more static than it should be—that is, more in the customary conventions than the ear and mind would agree to, or like enough to use (if they had more chance to hear and think about new fields, substances, and visions in music, which they are not used to, as the pen and eyes help the ear and mind keep too easily and steadily to their nice old customs and habits.)

M2   Maybe that may be some of the reason of some musicians who've written me or made some remark and criticism, [and] said that the music wasn't quite as awful as it looked. And a few musicians who took enough trouble and time to try to be fair enough to get into it in some ways at least, and went at it somewhat seriously, said that it sounded (after some study and familiarity by ears) better [and] more logical than it looked on that nice paper!—and more musically understandable —one man even [said] quite eloquent, though I didn't mean it to be especially.

And when the Nice Old Ladies say "no design—formless—all music should have design and form"—Yes, Sarah, but not your designs and forms—No, Sirree! In this Sonata they're spitting about, there is design —somewhat more than there should be, it seemed to me—and the form is obvious, but it isn't drabbed on every milestone on the way *up* or *to* or *on*—it takes care of itself, so to speak, and isn't yanked back every thirty-two measures by those nice apron strings hanging on the classroom scroll.

M3   A natural procedure in a piece of music, be it a song or a week's symphony, may have something in common [with]—I won't say analogous to—a walk up a mountain. There's the mountain, its foot, its summit—there's the valley—the climber looks, turns, and looks down or up. He sees the valley, but not exactly the same angle he saw it at [in] the last look—and the summit is changing with every step— and the sky. Even if he stands on the same rock at the top and looks toward Heaven and Earth, he is not in just the same key he started in, or in the same moment of existence.

m   (That a symphony, sonata, or jig—that all nice music should end where it started, on the Doh key, is no more a natural law than that all men should die in the same town and street number in which they were born. The academics—"$50 please"—fall back over the nice waste basket and say "natural laws"—that's an easy excuse. Anything their ears (and that above their ears, wherever that is) hasn't heard for thirty-three years or before, don't like, don't understand, etc. etc. etc. etc. ⅄. ⅄. ⅄. —they scold and say "not a (or against) natural law"—in other words anything that isn't easy to play, hear, or sell.

The more one studies and listens and tries to find out all he can in various ways, technically, mathematically, acoustically, and aurally, [the more] he begins to feel (and more than that, actually know and sense) that the world of tonal vibrations, in its relation to the physiological structure of the human ear, has unthought of (because untried) possibilities for man to know and grow by—greater and more transcendent than what has too easily and thoughtlessly [been] called a natural law! Just a few months' study of what can be found in the tables of acoustical vibrations—pure, tempered, differences of overtones, beats, etc.—as found in Helmholtz et al—and it will be realized that nature's laws are greater than a mere plagal cadence.)

M3 So, Sarah, let the music move as the mountain does, and it will be a

bigger thing than A—C Mus. Dock!

The above is to explain something that Cuckoo couldn't see. As I remember, Max Smith said someone (I think Pitts Sanborn, wall-paper man!), after Rovinsky had played *The Celestial Railroad* in a concert [in] Town Hall, November 1928, [said] that that (*The Celestial Railroad*) had a design and form that he followed, but the rest of the Sonata didn't.

P. S. (not Part Sixth) couldn't have seen that anyone could follow the design and form etc. of the sonata, after they take off their silk stockings, silk hat, and nice Dress Suite.

I read this to A. Rovinsky—he said "Righto!"   Jan. '29.

Questionnaires about the
Concord Sonata (1935)

A kind of supplement to App. 7 may be furnished by two communications addressed in 1935 to this editor. In 1927, in Paris, I got to know Katherine Ruth Heyman's copy of *Concord*. She knew Ives and told me to write him, which I did on 7 October, and he promptly sent me the *Sonata* and the *Essays*. Penetration was gradual. In 1932 I was playing *The Alcotts,* and correspondance with Ives (more exactly with Mrs. Ives and Edith, writing for him) resumed in 1933. In January 1934 I wrote him that I'd decided to learn the whole sonata, and he sent me the *Emerson Transcriptions.* In July I wrote him that "yesterday in town I played George Antheil as much of *Emerson* as I could remember, and he confessed he didn't know that American music that wonderful existed." In March 1935 I played *Emerson,* and wrote Ives in July that comments ranged "all the way from the lady who muttered 'absolutely inexcusable!' to the gentleman who told me he felt as if he were looking face to face at times into your soul and at times into Emerson's."

All this time Ives had been in precarious health (some of the time in Europe), and I hadn't yet met him. So on 28 September 1935 I wrote him: ". . . I want very much to play the whole sonata some time. . . . In the meantime could I bother you about a bit of documentation? 1. Would my recital be the first public performance in New York of *Emerson?* 2. Could you let me have the dates of composition of the various parts of the sonata? . . . (perhaps an accompanying questionnaire would simplify some of the bother.) 3. Are there any sketches of *Emerson* which antedate the version printed? The *Epilogue* indicates a conception for large orchestra, which leads me to suspect a first sketch of clearer polyphonic intention, taken down for two hands for the printed version . . . The later *Four Transcriptions from Emerson* . . . seem to me an exposition of certain substances which don't properly form part of the actual musical texture, but which hang about the music in no less necessary a way. The printed version is so strongly organized a lyric and rhythmic continuity that what remains is to plumb its nature and evolve a manner of presentation. The transcriptions offer invaluable clues to the musical intention, but provide more additional notes than can well be taken care of. . . . 4. Does *Emerson* contain any examples of melody built on preexisting words? I suspect this from the way your songs are often quite indifferent about vocal or instrumental presentation—the horn solo in *In the Night*—etc. . . . I should love to know if I'll be playing any quotations from *Compensation* or *Self Reliance.* . . . 5. Have you any other piano works beside the first and second sonatas? . . ."

Mrs. Ives wrote me a long detailed answer to all the above questions. After Ives died, the sorting of his manuscripts turned up four different sketches toward her letter, in his own hand. The text given below is Mrs. Ives's letter with some of the variants as footnotes. The "questionnaire" mentioned above follows after Mrs. Ives's signature.

West Redding   Connecticut   Oct. 11th 1935

Dear Mr. Kirkpatrick,

Mr. Ives wants to thank you for your letter. He says he always respects the interest of a man probing the foundations of things—even of a sonata.[1] He will try to answer your questions as briefly as possible, though the letter will have to go into some detail. I will take down what he says.

The Emerson movement did start, as you ask, with an orchestra in mind. It set out to be an overture with piano, but it was never fully scored or finished. Since your letter came, I have been looking through the music here, but as yet have found but one page and part of another of this sketch. It is hard to make out, and I doubt if it is worth much study. There may be more of it among my things in New York, and I will look when we get back later in the fall,[2] and will be glad to let you have whatever there is.

You ask if there are any examples of melody built on pre-existing words or certain essays—No. In neither the Emerson or Thoreau movements are there any quotations or attempts to picture any particular essay or saying or philosophic part.[3] They try rather to reflect the underlying definite and indefinite things in the authors' characters and works—or, as suggested in the preface, but composite pictures, or an impression. But the Hawthorne and Alcott movements try to suggest something in the tales, incidents, or more definite characteristics of the authors. For instance,[4] the Alcott piece tries to catch something of old man Alcott's—the great talker's—sonorous thought.

1 First sketch: "he says it's good to find a musician who is as much interested in the things of the substance as [in] the notes."
2 First sketch: "probably the latter part of November." Actually it was early in November that Ives wrote John J. Becker: "We're back in Babylon—just happen to be in one of those slump-attacks—so will write more when I can get up again."
3 In one of the marked copies of the first edition, a memo on p. 13 (Y6449) refers to the fugato starting in line 4: "This movement . . . and for the next two pages or so, attempts to suggest the struggle that seemed to go on in Emerson, in reconciling . . . the influence of the old Puritan canon, dogma, etc., with his individual growth—that is, theology vs religion (see page 20–21 [of the] Essay) [Boatwright, pp. 18–19]. In fact the whole movement has more to do (and more than I intended) with the struggles of his soul than [with] that peace of mind which he commands even in his struggles— though the music tries to end with that feeling."
    In conversation Ives once told me that the theme in clusters on p. 2, in lines 4–5 "had something to do with the idea of tolerance"—though it was only after he died that my slow mind appreciated the way he suggests this idea by voicing the theme in three keys at once.
4 First sketch: "for instance the demons dancing around the pipe [in *Feathertop*], *The Celestial Railroad*, etc."

You ask about the transcriptions. The first[5] was mostly from a sketch of an *Emerson Overture* for orchestra and piano, referred to above. Around that time, 1910–11, I seemed to have the overture habit and started out to make a series of them on "Men of Literature." But they either were not completed or ended up in something else. Some of the things in the Emerson score went into the Sonata the next year. The other transcriptions are but short pieces made from the printed sonata, with some lines from the old score in some measures, and in others some supplementary details—for instance, the coda at the end of the third transcription.[6]

It seems to me usually (perhaps not at every time of day) that the printed movement is nearer Emerson[7] than either the first score or the transcriptions by themselves, and I think you are right in keeping to that.[8] The transcriptions seem to grow away from Emerson in some places. They may have too much of the "dash and dagger"[9] which he had, and which he missed in some of his contemporaries, and not enough of his other fields of action and contemplation—though some of the fuller measures in the transcriptions, when they don't interfere with the general line of the sonata, it may be well to play. For example,[10] the middle staff in the top brace, page 11, 3rd transcription, which in the book is on page 15;[11] and some of the measures in the last two or three pages of the last transcription, on pages 17 and 18 in the book.[12] As I remember, I did something of this kind when I used to play the movement.

However, do whatever seems natural or best to *you*, though not

---

[5] Second sketch: "The first . . . was arranged shortly after the Sonata was finished . . . the three others were made a year or two after the Sonata was printed."
[6] Second sketch: "a coda that was neither in the sketch or sonata, nor suggested in the sketch, as far as I can recall."
[7] First sketch: "nearer the real Emerson (that is, of course, his real Emerson) . . ."
Third sketch: "nearer the real Emerson—just homely thinking, meditation and contemplation—little or nothing to please the bodily senses (easy listening)—little . . . reference to the custom and habit of mind and ear. . . ."
[8] Second sketch: "The transcriptions (which are partly from the Overture and partly a later growth) had too much of the centrifugal manner, too constantly active." [Ives had called the cadenzas for the concerto-overture "centrifugal cadenzas."]
[9] First sketch: "grit[?] & dagger . . ."
Second sketch: "jilt & dagger, which Emerson lamented that Washington Irving, [James Russell] Lowell, and other friends of his didn't have."
Third sketch: "dig[?] & dagger . . ."
Fourth sketch: "urge[?] & dagger . . ."—changed to: "———— & dagger . . ."
[10] First sketch: "for instance, in the top right hand line, in the last half of the second brace on the first page, the chords in the sketch were left out [of the sonata]—apparently [I] thought, according to a marginal note, [that they] were rather too sensuous for Emerson—they might cause it to please the ladies too easily." [These chords are in the revised edition.]
[11] These extra notes are in the revised edition, p. 15, first two lines.
[12] The fourth Transcription corresponds to the revised edition, last two lines of p. 17 through p. 19.

necessarily the same way each time.[13] The music, in its playing as well as in its substance, should have some of Emerson's freedom in action and thought—of the explorer "taking the ultimate of today as the first of tomorrow's new series."[14] It is said that Emerson seldom gave any of his lectures in exactly the same way, and that the published essays were not kept to literally. Sometime in the 1850s[15] my grandmother heard Emerson lecture on the New England Reformers. I remember her saying that she was startled (perhaps somewhat put out) to find that the printed text, which she knew almost by heart, was hardly more than an outline in his lecture. Apparently Emerson liked to trust to the mood of the moment—perhaps too much.

As to performance of this movement in New York:—About five years ago Oscar Ziegler played one of the transcriptions in the New School.[16] In 1929 Keith Corelli played the whole movement in a studio concert in New York.[17] I think it was in connection with a lecture—am not certain —I couldn't get out to it. At an impromptu church concert in New York in the spring of 1914, I played the Emerson and part of the Hawthorne movements.[18] There have been one or two concerts in which some of the sonata was played, whether Emerson or not I can't remember or find programs. But yours will probably be the first concert in New York of importance in which this movement is played. Sorry I can't be more definite.

You ask about other piano music besides the first and second Sonatas. Sometime in the winter of 1926–27 I finished a one movement piece which I called the *Third Sonata*. The last time I played it over it didn't seem satisfactory.[19] There are some shorter pieces. Most of them are old and, I think, of doubtful value. Others went into chamber music pieces. Of these some are in legible photostat copies, and I will be glad to have them sent you.

13 First sketch: "as long as it seems natural to you and doesn't disturb the line of the whole sonata—I haven't played it for some time, but I remember that I didn't play it or didn't feel it exactly this same way all the time—sometimes more of the transcriptions seemed better, far more often they didn't."
14 This is altered from the first paragraph of the Emerson essay, which quotes Emerson's *Circles* (as pointed out in Boatwright, p. 11, note t).
15 First sketch: "he came to Danbury to lecture once—my grandmother heard him— after his essays were published . . ." The family tradition is that, on this occasion, Emerson was a guest at the Ives house—see App. 13, 4th paragraph.
16 The "Largo" that Ziegler played in a recital at the New School on 6 January 1931 must be the Third Transcription. Ziegler had played *The Alcotts* in New York on 1 May 1928.
17 Among Ives's papers are programs of Keith Corelli's recitals in 1928–29, showing that he played *Emerson* at Santa Barbara, Charleston, Spartanburg, New Orleans, Chattanooga, and Montreal.
18 Mrs. Ives had no definite recollection of when this might have been, nor does the church have any record of it.
19 Third sketch: "it didn't seem to go—not exactly a thing I would want played . . . and I put it away, to season." [No manuscript called the *Third Piano Sonata* has showed up; Ives probably destroyed it.]

I appreciate greatly the trouble and work you have given this music, especially when you knew that it is liable to disturb some people or do something else that nice music won't do.[20] I remember, just after finishing the Emerson movement, playing it to an old friend of mine. He said, "That music is homely, awkward, and lanky—so was Emerson. It won't please the ladies much—neither did Emerson."[21] Be that as it may, it takes at least some courage[22] and, I am afraid, some labor and patience, and you have my sincere thanks for playing it!

We hope it won't be long now before we have the pleasure of seeing you. With best wishes from us both, I am,

Sincerely yours,   Harmony T. Ives

Music:	Emerson	completed in the summer of 1912[23]
	Hawthorne	" October 12, 1911[24]
	The Alcotts	" 1915[25]
	Thoreau	" 1915
Essays:	Prologue	all 1919—printed when the sonata was engraved
	Emerson	in the fall of 1919
	Hawthorne	
	The Alcotts	
	Thoreau	
	Epilogue	
Four Transcriptions		1st arranged for piano sometime after 1915 and
from Emerson		before 1918, mostly from an uncompleted score for orchestra (1911). The other transcriptions were made a year or two after the Sonata was printed, and the four were copied and put together as in the photostat copy.

After other letters, I wrote Ives again on 20 November, not knowing that he was in unusually bad health: "I can't help becoming more and more impatient about collating *Emerson* with the remains of the old overture . . . there are two passages

---

20 Third sketch: "and which does not lend itself toward making a 'hit'."
21 This sounds like Dr. Griggs—see App. 15.
22 Third sketch: "as well as bodily strength [and] a strength of fingers."
23 Second sketch: "Shortly after 1911, at Pell's, I got the idea of a Concord sonata—and finished Emerson as a sonata [movement in] 1912—took the common themes from the Alcott [overture] and 'Fate knocking'." [The Iveses were at Pell Jones's on Elk Lake, 18 miles west of Port Henry, New York, 16–26 September 1911, but not in 1912, when they went to Saranac in September.]
24 Second sketch: "The first, 1907, was 'take off' ('Scarecrow dance', 'Celestial R.R.')."
25 Second sketch: "Alcott—(more of old man Bronson)—to go with Henry W. Beecher —'old man with straw in mouth' (not kept)." [This seems to imply that *The See'r* is derived from sketches toward a Beecher Overture.]

that worry me:—the first line on page 6, and the Beethoven chords on page 17 (I don't think their inner voices have found their final or most appropriate spacing)— and I suspect and hope that the overture will throw some light on the polyphonic intentions involved. Everything else is perfectly satisfactory and reveals more and more new beauties with each performance. Only those two bits seem sketchier and sketchier. . . . By the way, was Hawthorne one of those Men of Literature overtures, and is there a surviving score of him?"

The answer came in Edith's hand, and the sorting of Ives's manuscripts again disclosed three sketches. The first sketch is very different from and longer than the letter, outlining the things Ives meant to explain later. It follows the letter here, all but the parts that would be redundant.

164 East Seventy Fourth Street, New York City

December 30th, 1935

Dear Mr. Kirkpatrick:—

Under separate cover the remains of the old overture, which you asked Father for, are being sent. About half a dozen pages are all that are found. These are quite indistinct in places and difficult to make out. Father thinks they won't be of much help, and doubts if they are worth spending much time over.

The other matters in your letter Father will answer in more detail as soon as he is better. He has not been at all well, and has not been able to attend to things. Father greatly appreciates your interest and the hard work you have shouldered.

With all best wishes for the New Year, I am, sincerely yours,

Edith Ives for Charles E. Ives

[First Sketch]

The Overture . . . seems more like a Piano Concerto with sort of cadenzas.[26] Quite a little of the Overture [is] not in the Sonata. Because [it's] not in the Sonata may not mean that it ought to be—or that it was left out by mistake . . . . The Overture (what is left) and the Sonata (in the book) are, in some ways, more like two separate and different pieces on some of the same texts, than the same piece in different forms.

In the two places you speak of, the first line [of] page 6, and the "Beethoven chords" [on] page 17:—The first may have been in the Overture, but is not in the pages that I can find—but it probably was— as, in the copy from which the sonata was engraved, there was a lower set of notes in the left hand which was crossed out of the engraver's copy—I can't make them out exactly, but [they were] probably cut out as some other things were—probably or perhaps because they didn't seem quite essential enough to pay for the difficulty in playing and listening that they might cause.[27] Am enclosing this and other pages

26 Second sketch: "a concerto with an overdose of cadenzas."
27 These extra notes have small note-heads in the revised edition, p. 6, first two lines.

from the engraver's copy—do whatever you think best.

The second place you speak of, the Beethoven chords on page 17:—
You find a part of this page in the score, beginning ⌀ etc. as marked.[28]
These chords are but the knocks on the portal, and are played more as
such, as bang more than as music. They have no inner counterpoint,
but I remember there was a kind of a blur up in the middle of the
second chord—and why the F was let out in the second time I don't
know.[29]

You can see, at the beginning of the overture page here, that the
orchestra gave some of these knocks, and then the piano, and then
another time the Clarinet and Trumpet gave it in unison and the piano
had an off figure, which was suggested from the score in the [Fourth]
Transcription, page [13], but is not the same.[30]

You ask if Hawthorne is an arrangement from a score—No. It was
first as it is in the book, for piano only—though at times, I had another
piano or player in mind—but I don't remember his putting in an appearance.

But I was working on a Symphony about this time, and in the
scherzo I put some of the Hawthorne movement in, mostly the parts
having to do with *The Celestial Railroad.*[31] Later on I made a short
fantasy for piano from the symphony score, which had some of the
Hawthorne. This piece, as I remember, didn't seem quite satisfactory,
and I have no copy.[32]

No transcript of this first sketch was communicated, and I didn't meet Ives
until May 1937. In the meantime the Beethoven chords had disclosed their voice-
leading, and I didn't remember to bring it up again, nor did he (it was much later
that I learned how he hated to be pinned down). So it was quite a surprise to find
that the intended effect was "a kind of a blur."

[28] In all the extant sketches for the *Emerson Overture,* this sign occurs only at the top of
p. 5, in a crossed-out memo: "for rest of these measures see back p. 4—at   " But p. 4
is missing. Either Ives still had it in 1935 and never got around to having a photostat
made of it, as he evidently intended, or else he was absent-mindedly confusing whatever
was on the back of p. 4 with the leaf he goes on to describe in the next paragraph. This
leaf is still numbered 10–11 (blank pp. 10–11 at the end of the score-sketch of the third
movement of the *Third Symphony,* from which Ives tore it), but in the *Emerson Overture*
it may have been pp. 12–13. These two pages (negatives n1675–76) correspond, in the
revised edition, to lines 2–4 of p. 18, and from the last line of p. 18 through the first
measure of the third line of p. 19.
[29] The "F" may be the right-thumb f1 with which the "Beethoven chords" start, on both
p. 6 and p. 18, and which is soon changed to g1.
[30] Part of this "off figure" is the rising fourth, f1–b♭1, early in the second line of p. 18.
[31] That is, having to do with Hawthorne's story *The Celestial Railroad.* Ives's piano piece
with the same title is mentioned in the next two sentences. Se App. 3, #84.
[32] Ives had given the copy by George Price to Becker in 1931 (now at New York
Public Library, Lincoln Center, with Becker's mss.). He still had his own ink copy but
probably couldn't find it.

George's Adventure and *The Majority* (1919)

After returning from Asheville and finishing the clear copy of *Concord* and the *Essays,* Ives set about giving an appropriate form to a set of ideas which had been on his mind since 1916, probably before. The final result was *The Majority* (included in Boatwright's editing of the *Essays Before a Sonata and Other Writings,* with a list of sources). Apparently Ives started it in a form borrowed from Plato, but then forsook dialogue and rewrote it as a long essay. Later he reworked some of the dialogue into the following short story, and had it typed (directly from his ms., not from dictation). But he must have found the story too cryptic, and wrote a six-page insert with some of the meat of *The Majority,* finally referring to "p. 20" of the dialogue-manuscript itself (of which only pp. 20–41 now survive).

Since the insert and the old ms. cannot be inserted without wrecking the story, these three elements are here strung along one after the other, complete. Even though many thoughts appear substantially as they do in *The Majority,* the dialogue-context not only gives them quite a different flavor but includes several autobiographical details not found elsewhere. Editing procedure is exactly as for the *Memos,* S being a four-page preliminary sketch, M the ten-page ink ms., T the seven-page typed copy.

M1T1

George's Adventure

or

A Study in Money, Coherence, Words, and Other Things

(a good model for a poor story)[1]

A man was walking along a dark street one night—or rather along a street one dark night—when a man, whom he did not then recognize

---

[1] S has no title. M1, above, has various stabs at title and subtitles, all crossed out, the final version being up the left margin. On the top of T1 Ives wrote: "This is just to show how a man should write who considers himself a nice author and whom everybody else considers crazy."

And on the back of T1: "This story was written after a man had listened three hours to a debate by all the members of Congress (or a meeting of politicians). They were talking about something when they started, but when it was all over, they all looked around as though they did not know what it was all about. Their sentences, interruptions, personal remarks, shaking first fingers, all were very logical sounding—especially the 'sounding'—like 'George' and his wife.

"This story has nothing to do with politics or the Senate. It is just a picture of the 'mind in a mess' after reading or listening to a politician working (his mouth)".

as a friend,[2] asked him what time it was. But he (the 1st man) had not carried a watch for many years, because he found it easier to look at clocks or ask other people the time, and also because the face of a watch never gave him much confidence—though he was often conscious of a selfishness in bothering other people—and though he believed in the beauty of poverty, he was sometimes afraid that, because he did not carry a watch, he might by some be considered poor, when as a fact he was quite rich and had two nice watches home. So, when asked for the time, he usually fumbled in his pocket to give the impression that it was natural for him to carry a watch, when, as we have seen, it was unnatural.

And now he fumbled in his pocket—but when this man (2nd man) saw that he (1st man) had no watch, he (2nd man) said, "Have you any money?" Then the 1st man knew what to do and hit the 2nd man, and the 2nd man hit him at the same time. Then the 1st man fell down, and no one knows whether the 2nd man did or not—anyway he was not around to help when the policeman came.

M2T1   The 1st man had a nice ride in an ambulance, and when he woke up in the hospital bed, he found himself looking up at a smart young nurse

M2T2   whose face was very ugly. This (the last four words) was a part of the efficiency and good management of this hospital (which was always crowded, no matter how many people died)—and it might be said here that this particular nurse had bought this hospital and given it to the city fathers (and mothers), and had become a nurse in it, not only for the joy of serving but because of certain idealistic convictions—for had she not said publicly, "Many can buy, but few can nurse."

Anyway the 1st man, George by name, got well very soon—at least he did not stay at the hospital long. When he got home he felt lonesome, and as he looked around his room and saw no wife or children, he decided to get married—and also the thought occurred to him that, if he didn't get married pretty soon, his oldest children would be younger than his younger brother's grandchildren.[3] George was then over fifty. So he went right out and asked a beautiful grey-haired[4] lady to marry him, and she was glad to do so, as she was over sixty. But this is better than having the bridegroom ninety-two and the bride twenty-three, as happens in real life.

M3T2   A short time after the wedding day they began to talk to each other. "Would you have asked me to marry you," said George's wife, "if I had been rich and you poor, and if you had had no younger brother?" "I would not," said George, "as I think it wrong for a man to marry for

2 S: "a man whom he thought a stranger because he could not see his face"
3 When Ives was married at thirty-three, his oldest nephew Richard was six.
4 The words "beautiful" and "grey-haired" are only is S; M has "good" crossed out.

money." "But," said his wife, "does that mean that you think it wrong for a woman to marry for money?" "No," said George, "until women have an equal chance with men to make money." George's wife (as a wife) was pleased to hear this, but (as a woman) she said, "If women had the chance, they could, being brighter, make more money than men." But George said, "That being the case (viz, being brighter), they would make less money than men."

M3T3   "Now George . . ." said his wife, but George went right on talking. "There never was (and there never can be) a bright and successful business man (that is, one who has accumulated much wealth, say $50,000 or over)[5] who was or is not fundamentally stupid—predominantly bright but fundamentally stupid. Well, one certain characteristic of those who are both predominantly bright and fundamentally bright is that they never make money." "I can believe that they never make money," said George's wife, "but I can't believe there are any such

M4T3   persons—name just one." "I'll name several," said George, "Harry Thoreau, Diogenes, Oliver Goldsmith, St. Paul, Abe Lincoln, Beethoven, John Brown—they all would have been successful in business if they only had had that stupid streak at bottom." "But these men weren't in business," said George's wife. "Yes they were," said George, "they were in business and could have made lots of money if they had only been fundamentally stupid as well as predominantly bright." "How could they have made lots of money?" said George's wife. "By *doing* what they did, but *being* what they were not—Diogenes by selling his tub, Thoreau by making not using pencils, John Brown by owning not freeing slaves, Lincoln by being a politician not a statesman, Goldsmith by being ungenerous not generous, St. Paul by being a lawyer for a corporation and not for the Gospel, Beethoven by writing symphonies for the people and not to the people, composing for the human-ear and not for the human-soul. They all had the same chances, they were all in the same business, the same business that we are in,

M5T3   the business of life. But along comes that basic streak of stupidity in us and changes it in quality not in kind, and makes it a business *for* life. But the business *of* life lies not in the visible facts of the choice of a calling, or an acquisition of an office and the like, but in the silent

M5T4   thought by the wayside as we . . ."

    "You're tiresome," said George's wife, "so just tell me if you mean that, when the world reaches that high state of social and moral consciousness when women shall have an equal chance with men in developing or using that basic stupid streak so that they can make money

[5] One must remember the relative value of the dollar in 1919 and 1972. The differences in prices of familiar staples are not at all consistent—but if one triples Ives's figures, one will not be too far off.

(big money)—that then it will not be wrong for a man to marry for money." "That is a very obvious deduction," said George, "and hence probably more wrong than right. But since you have brought on this discussion, I will tell you a truth (which is *not* making a confession)— I *did* marry for money." "Then you committed a wrong," said George's wife. "I did not," said George. 'But you said a little while ago that you

M6T4 thought it wrong for a man to marry for money." "Yes," said George, "wrong under the conventional (or misunderstood) meaning of the term money."

Here George started to get all wrought up as the conversation (his) began to lead up to his pet theme: The Philosophy of Terms in the Essence, or The Futility of Words as such. "Words are the one invention of man that has done more to cause war and retard civilization than the discovery of gunpowder—and it is man's fault, not God's. God is justified in putting words, gunpowder, and even whiskey around for man to discover, but man is *not* justified in not knowing what they mean. Now whether or not the ability of learning (or I might say of experiencing) their true meaning is a problem of objective or subjective contemplation, best determined by a-priori or empiric methods, is . . ." "George!" interrupted his wife, "you are getting so vague, I hardly . . ."

M7T4 "Ah vagueness!" went on George, "vagueness is the sublime stimulant of literary inspiration, the source of its perennial hope! When the Great
M7T5 Tennyson told the Great Browning, after he (the Great T.) had finished *Sordello* for the twenty-ninth time, that even then he (the G. T.) could not tell whether Sordello was a city, a woman, a patent medicine, or a book![6] Imagine what a wonderful hope welled up into the heart of the Great Browning at that!" "The hope of what, George?" "The hope that he himself would some day know what it meant! Perfection in genius," continued George, "is not its strongest influence, but the hope which this perfection inspires—the hope of ultimate and universal perfection when the individual soul becomes identical with the super-soul and finally . . ." "*You* told me," shouted George's wife, "that you did marry for money. I have no money. Now go ahead and tell me what you

M8T5 mean." "Well," said George, "to do that I must use words or terms— then I am again at the mercy of civilization's greatest error, for I *cannot* speak without using words."[7] "Never mind," said George's wife, "I must know, regardless of what the words mean."

"Well then," said George, "money is the measure of the unit of comfort. It is its equivalent and can be exchanged for it, and in this ex-

6 The publication in 1840 of Browning's *Sordello* was greeted with uncomprehending dismay, Mrs. Carlyle saying she couldn't make out whether Sordello was a man, a city, or a book—Tennyson writing that he understood only the first and last lines and these were lies. It was years later that Tennyson and Browning met and became good friends.
7 S: "for when I tell you the truth, you will understand the direct opposite."

change it produces this unit, hence the possession of any substance *without* or any inherent quality *within* (a person) that produces this unit *is* money, and it measures in the same way. Now the economists say that the unit of comfort is the measure of that which satisfies a definite material, physico-social need (per man or family-group), but here is where the economists begin to err and mankind begins to suffer. The meaning of the word 'comfort' is its only meaning and hence all its meanings. It thus extends beyond the qualifications of the 'need' in the sense above. It is more comprehensive than tangible. A lower part may help a higher part, but that relation does not make them identical. The satisfaction of a material want (or need) may be an *aid* to the intangible part—for instance a hungry man after receiving food has more power (or is more susceptible) to experience an ecstatic thought for instance, or a spiritual emotion, or the sublimity of a product of a high moral sense—but this aid is more an attribute than a primal cause, or even always essential, because a dying man who hasn't taken food for a week may have such an experience. Likewise an ultra-emotional sense which . . ."

Just then George saw his wife's hand reach for a book, and so he said, "When that man knocked me down, I was on my way to ask a young girl who was worth $26,000,000 to marry me, but when I woke up in the hospital and found her nearer than I was accustomed, I saw a look in her face (near that little yellow mole on the lower jowl) which suggested a furious sense of duty, the fanatical color that will cause one to lay down his life, especially after he has been locked up for murdering everybody who didn't agree with him. The ideal duty (in her case) was to give $1,000,000, and not a cent more, to this hospital, so that the surplus, the remaining $25,000,000, would go absolutely intact to her idiotic nephew, who would have more sense than to give any of it away. At that moment, strange to say, a perception came to me, a product of some innate intuition—the origin I do not seek—it passed instantaneously from sub-consciousness to consciousness. I knew then that she could not furnish *my* unit of comfort."

"How did you know that I could?" said his wife. "I didn't know that you could, but I didn't know that you couldn't." George's wife was made happy upon hearing this, for she was poor by her measure (which now she accepted as wrong), and George was rich by her measure (which now she accepted as wrong)—and as she didn't like him very much, she was glad to know that *she* at least didn't marry for money. And as she was a generous and high-minded person, she wished there was something she could do to recompense the kind, bad man who knocked George down, and also the true, efficient management of the hospital. But she did not know the address of the kind man. And, as is often the

M8T6

M9T6

M9T7

M10T7

case with high-minded characters whose contemplation of life is inspired or measured by deep moral values, her sense of justice was so
acute that she could not bring herself to discriminate against the kind
bad man, and so the hospital didn't get any of George's money.

End

Ives gave no indication, in p. 3 of M, where he intended to insert the following,
which he wrote on the backs of pp. 3-5-6-7-2-4 of M. It has a two-page insert of
its own (here called m) to replace the bottom of M2v and the top of M4v.

M3v

"This basic streak of stupidity is not a part of moral or immoral
qualities—(for instance *honesty* is one of the most common traits in a
successful business man's character)—it is not a part of a mental, intellectual or unintellectual quality, except insofar as the mind has to do
with the lower development of the individual soul—but it has to do
with that dulness of the soul's life which keeps it from seeing through
its door to the universal-soul (or the over-soul as Emerson calls it), or
even keeps it from seeing that there is a door—a dulness clarifying the
sense of proportion in pragmatism, but obscuring it in the spiritual, for
instance not perceiving that one man, or a few men, should not accept
the opportunity which the disparity offers (or take an advantage
which the lack of proportion offers) between the natural evolution of
nature (of God, if you like) and the social evolution of man—or, to be
more definite still, a dulness which prevents a man who has made
$2,000,000, made it, not inherited it, made it 'from shirtsleeves' honestly,
as men say, and legally, as men say"—(George said $2,000,000 because
he himself has made $1,800,000)[8]—"a dulness which prevents this man
from seeing that he has no inherent or natural right in this congestion

M5v

from attrition, no more than a farmer would have in feeling that it was
due to his personal industry and intrinsic ability as a planter that the
rain fell on his field and not on his friend's in the next town, or that it
was in his virtue as a carpenter or cattle raiser that lightning struck his
barn after he had sold it and not before.

"God put men in the world for the same reason that he put trees,
oysters, coal, worms, etc., etc.—so now you, when the gong rings, up
and take your regular stand!—all to take their natural part and share
in the permanent benefits or temporary perils of his natural evolution
or universal progress or whatever you prefer to call it. There are not
more trees than there is land, there are not more oysters than there is
water, *and* a few trees do not get most of the rain, and a few oysters do
not get most of the ocean. Because the tentative agreements of ex-

---

[8] In the second of these numbers, Ives added an extra zero, but there would be no reason
for his imagining an amount different from the $1,800,000 in the old dialogue-manu-
script.

pediency between man and man (call it Social Order, if you like) has not yet caught up to the natural order, is the reason that the earth has not yet been handed back to all of those to whom it belongs—that is, to those who have to live on it—but, I may say, it is on its way, and coming too fast for some.

"Well," said George, "as long as I am on the subject . . ."—"and you are long on it," said his wife—"I can't help," said George, "mentioning a few other instances which appear to me to reflect this so-called funda-

M6v   mental stupidity. A successful Wall Street Christian gentleman, upon entering the service of a semi-godlike institution, thought among other things that he could in this way combat the German idea of God, but forgot apparently that *his* idea of God, carried to the most brutal extreme, was what had brought Germany, or rather the old-fashioned part of it, to the front-of-hell (how many entered it we will never know in this life, and if we know in the next one, we hope it will be only by a process of elimination).

"Just one more instance," said George, "then I'm through. This same 'basic streak of dulness' favors logic over intuition. A soldier-boy risking his life and giving it, asking for nothing in return, doesn't understand why the Y.M.C.A. do not *give* him, for nothing in return, a box of matches. They say, if he will reason it out, he will see that they are right—but *he* has something *better* than reason, hence he is *wrong*.

"I believe," said George with feeling, "that a national and even economically scientific process of bringing social evolution up to that of evolution in nature (where for the good of mankind it ought to be) lies in a liberation of wealth-congestion by means of a limited personal property right. The details of working out this plan I will explain

M7v   later," said George, as he saw his wife scowl and throw down the *Atlantic Monthly* which she had been reading—"I really would reduce my own fortune to $100,000, even to $50,000," said George, "if I were sure I wouldn't be the only one to do it, but . . ." "Remember," said George's wife, "the saying of Thoreau, 'The actual example of one man is better than the noble philanthropic devices of a thousand.'" George was so imbued that he heard not, and his wife smiled as she admired George's weakness.

"Be that as it may," said George, and then almost stopped. But his wife, being interested in her magazine, which she again turned to, said, "But if this limitation (of personal property per unit) is so natural or necessary, why don't the governments or the people do it?" "Is that one question," said George, sort of startled, "or an investigation?—'why don't the governments or the people?'—do you know what you are asking? Don't you think the governments have all the trouble they want on their hands now?—and don't you know that it's the business of government to proceed in the series of inverse ratios, for the direct benefit of the individual or localized details, and not for indirect benefits to universal fundamentals? Do you think that Senator Fall or Mr. Hearst would be interested in pushing a bill that would reduce his personal millions in copper mines to $50,000, in order to watch the phenomenon of social evolution coincide with your natural evolution?[9]

M2v —or how many other great men, who have our and the people's interests in the hollow of their hearts, would be interested in playing this kind of a Samson?"

"It would be almost a confiscation, wouldn't it?" said George's wife, "it would seem like that horrid radicalism, anarchy, or Bolshevism we hear about." "It might be radicalism," said George, "but everyone is radical at times. It depends upon our diet, or subconscious experience, our mother-in-law, the pleasure or sorrow we have in making out our income lists, our blood pressure, the price of gasoline, etc., etc. Was it Carlyle? who said that every man is a radical in the morning upon hearing a strain of music and a conservative in the evening after dinner. Radicalism nowadays is not so much a matter of going to the 'root' as making someone go with you and then making everyone think that you're there. It is the degree of this quality rather then the quality of a principle that leads us to call a thing or a person 'radical.'

M2vm1 "For instance, you believe in beauty as a principle, and if you go out to look for a beautiful hat, you are an enthusiast—but if you look
M4vm1 for the most beautiful hat, you're a radical. If you should come home with a new hat on and say, 'Isn't this the most beautiful hat you've ever seen?'—and I say 'No'—and thereupon you, by strength of character, control your temper and try to prove it to me by arguments (the kind that only suffragists know how to make), and you convince me, you're a radical, and you will win. But if you come in and say, 'Isn't this the most beautiful hat you ever saw?'—and I say 'No'—and you get hysterical and throw a saucer at my head, then you're more than a radical, you're an anarchist, and you will lose.

m1 "As for Bolshevism, I haven't yet found out what it is. Those that come from Russia, and try to tell us in the newspapers, apparently don't know. It must have started from some good idea and ideal— but as soon as they started to get effeminate and throw things around, I imagine some of their ideals got effeminate too. Still it may work out
m2 in Russia and thereabouts, where everybody is used to having things thrown at him—but a Yankee wants a stronger argument than a bomb —the hysterical-woman saucers and the anarchist bombs to him are

9 See Boatwright's notes on Senator Fall on his pp. 180 and 257.

merely a sign of a bad loser who hasn't brains and isn't strong enough to fight like a man. If a man or woman has a plan with any virtue in it, that virtue will come out in time, if it's presented in an open, manly way to the rank and file. If it is presented with a threat, it will meet the same fate that Hohenzollern met.

"The 'Soviet,' as far as I can learn, is a crude form of our old-fashioned New England town meeting, where the farmer and the blacksmith and the storekeeper looked at everything through their farm, smithy, or store eyes—and the Russian Soviet government leaders, Lenin and Trotsky, are rather 'back numbers' who still hold, as far as we can learn, reactionary views regarding the function and ability of the proletariat. They have still to learn that there is no hope for any social progress until the social-machinery government (or what-you-will-call-it government) not only trusts but is guided by the 'brain' of the proletariat—that is, until each man and woman has a direct say in the fundamental things their government does—that the government must have no 'will,' but that the people (the majority) must have and be all 'will,' the government simply an organic machine to work out the command of this 'majority will.'

M4v
"The most hopeless part of the Hohenzollerns and Bolshevism is not their brutal atrocities (any man, if he deadens his natural sensibilities long enough or drinks unnatural drinks long enough, will become so brutal that society will suppress him)—the hopelessness of it is its fundamental stupidity. The Hohenzollerns, starting with low ideals and many bad ideas, became the greatest brutes in history. The Bolsheviks, starting with high ideals and many good ideas, also became the greatest brutes in history. What hope is there for a man who shoots off your legs in order to make you walk over and shake hands with him?" "I suppose," said George's wife, "he might be shooting to make your brothers come over and shake hands." "That," said George, "is a sign of an even lower degree of stupidity. It is the assumption that the majority of men are physical cowards, and that mental processes can be changed by force. Physical cowardice is as rare as a flower that is afraid to blossom. There are plenty of mental cowards, some moral cowards, comparatively speaking, but no physical cowards."

———

At the bottom of M4v Ives wrote "(see p. 20)." This can mean only the fragment of the old dialogue-manuscript (here called M), of which pp. 20–41 survive. Here also there are long inserts (as indicated on the left margin by backs of pages).

M20
"History is always consistently against that view. (A police commissioner told me that he wished for at least one p.c. among his thousands of policemen, just for variety, companionship, and because

he had such a fine speech ready, but he never can.) Physical cowardice seldom exists except in subnormal mentalities, and then it is a disease. (Cowardice (and success) is difficult to estimate, it is probably never estimated exactly. Your level worst and your level best are things that no one but you can estimate—and more likely you'll have to turn to God for the solution.) I venture to say that, of the millions of soldiers we sent to France, there are not a dozen cowards and these dozen would be found to be anomalies. (Foolhardy bravery may be a sign of cowardice—a man who refuses to jump off Brooklyn Bridge may be braver than the one who does.)

"Intimidation has not turned back one transcendent thought or one valuable idea from going where it was destined to go, and doing what it was destined to do. It may be temporarily delayed, or its species may revert only to propagate in a related form, but brute force (the world's greatest idiot) has never kept the germ from its divine order. A black eye never reformed a drunkard, a czar never stopped a free thought. All the bulls in the world could not affect the manufacture of china— even to the extent of one teacup. No natural reform, destined to be because it was natural, was ever accomplished or ever prevented by brute force per se—it may have been hastened or delayed by it, but 'time' is one of the most negligible of elements in any great department of progress. (The circumstance of our Civil War of the '60s freed the slaves, but if that circumstance hadn't happened at that particular time, other circumstances perhaps more natural, perhaps more generous, perhaps with broader reconstruction feelings etc., would have freed them. The story of the butterfly and the chrysalis was just as true in 1890 as it will be in 1960—and the year 8163 will find it true.")

George's wife, upon hearing the words "brute force" and "cowards," several times looked up from her book and asked if George thought that his remedy by a "limited property right" would cause any disturbance. "Yes and no," said George, "a mental disturbance on the part of a few, and hence naturally a certain amount of uncertainty in some lines of business for a while, great apprehension in some quarters, but no underlying economic disturbance. Property will always take care of itself in the same way that the ocean will." (Quote Emerson: "Things have their laws as well as men, and things refuse to be trifled with.")[10] "(Of course I do not mean property in the sense of estates, stocks, etc. only, but everything on the continents except men's bodies.) The measure of property may be out of plumb for a moment, the form of exchanging it may be inconvenient by the new way, but the process of exchange is bound to be simplified. The reduction would probably

M21

---

[10] From *Politics* (sixth page) in the *Essays, Second Series*.

be best effected by a graduated scale for a period of years, allowing for liberal marginal fluctuations, but valuations would be easier to appraise, as there would be less manipulation, and because the law of averages could come into fuller play (= stability). There would be more minds at interest and naturally less haste, and hence more care and thoroughness in material and business and scientific development. (Bright, quick minds, if they have too great an ascendancy, as they have had in the U. S., may be [their] own undoing.)

M22

"The principal objection or criticism would be in the relation of this plan to dynamics—fear that the tune of life would always be played mezzo-forte—symphonies but with no great climaxes—no sublime passages from barefoot to silk hat, or from Rivington to Riverside overnight—no Diamond Jims or the bishop's immortal sermon on The Dying Railroad King[11]—[fear] that enterprise, enthusiasm, incentive for great things will be gone, and the like. They *will* be gone, *some* of them—the enthusiasm or incentive to great things may go—but not for *greatness*. Greater things will be possible for a greater number. It will tend to open up, in the hearts of all, hopes that can come near fulfilment.

"The plan is but an analogy of the plan Darwin showed us. His theory of evolution was attacked from many sincere Christian pulpits —that it took away the hope, the very life, of the Christian religion. But the church sees now that Darwin told but another of God's parables, that his discovery (or revelation, if you like) but demonstrated the wideness of God's mercy,' and supported the hope of the Christian, of all religions—the hope not only that our souls will have immortality, but that some time all of God's creatures will have *souls*—a thought that will give hope to a worm is indeed transcendent.

M23

"(No, it will distribute and stimulate the purest kind of enterprise, initiative, enthusiasm, and incentive for the truest 'great'—not prostrate it.) If Edison had known, when he made his first experiment, that, no matter what he discovered, he could never make more than $100,000, would he have stopped experimenting? He may say that he would, but he wouldn't—he *couldn't*. There has never been anything done in business or science (that has been worthwhile) that hasn't been done for the same reason Beethoven wrote the *Fifth Symphony*—and Beethoven was so rich that he almost starved. The men that will lie down because they can't become millionaires are not strong enough to stand up and

11 New York's Rivington Street, way downtown, was a haven for thousands of immigrants, whereas the most conspicuous residence on Riverside Drive was the "chateau" of the self-made steel magnate Charles Schwab, which occupied a whole city block.

James Buchanan Brady, the gaudy but generous railroad-supply millionaire called "Diamond Jim" (also self-made), died on 13 April 1917, age 60. The funeral was on the 16th at St. Agnes' Church, New York, with a eulogy by the rector, Monsignor Brann.

be counted. Great discoveries like great fortunes are stumbled upon, but God directs the stumbling in one and man directs it in the other.

M23v   "The concentration of wealth in a few is not so much an economic harm in itself—in fact it doubtless has had some practical advantages (unity of organization, etc.)—but it is the power that this concentration gives a few that is making it an economic evil. And not necessarily either that this power has always been used wrongfully or unwisely (for that has not been always the case)—it is the state of mind at large it generates, the public resentment that such a thing *can* occur in a republic, even if only representative. This congestion is the modern cradle of the tyrannical spirit, a subtle thing of insidious growth, almost without the owner's knowledge—it becomes organized brutality, Hohenzollernism for instance.

    "Its ancient cradle lay in the minds of the two apes who thought there was only one coconut tree in the world—so one ape killed the other. Its modern cradle lies in the minds of the apes who know there are enough trees but who want to possess them all, not for the pleasure or need of eating the coconuts, but for the pleasure of giving away some of their own (perhaps ten percent) to others, provided they will eat them in their (the owners') way, provided they will use the milk in their (the owners') way—they are permitted to come into the grove if

M24v they will admire it in their (the owners') way—the children may blow their noses if they do it in their (the owners') way—but as soon as any shadow comes over the 'will' or the 'divine right,' as soon as they (the people) want to *be good* in their own way, then the tyrannical spirit becomes brutality, sometimes legal, sometimes not. At first it is a kindly, bland-faced tyrannical spirit, patronizing the arts, as all the arts patronize them—doing all kinds of good if it can only be done in their way—but once they lose their way, their compass is self-will—and brute force if necessary.

    "A non-laborer says that labor's great error lies in thinking that wealth is limited. This conception confuses the absolute and relative, or rather substitutes the absolute for the relative. Wealth is *limited* in the same way as a man's choice in the preference of sunlight to moonlight, or land to water—it is limited by the law of supply and demand, by the velocity of the earth around its axis, by the number of miles around the equator, by the distance from the top of Mt. Marcy to the center of the earth. This man meant to have said the measure of wealth

M25v is unlimited (if a man thinks his cheese worth $1,000,000, he can list it at that in the market and refuse to sell for less)—he meant that there were gold mines still to be discovered, and experiments and discoveries for the good of mankind still to be made. But economic wealth *is* limited—if he was talking about the wealth of the soul, he was undoubtedly right, but he was talking about economic wealth, and that *is* limited."

"But," said George's wife, "your equalizing wealth per unit is so liable to make life monotonous. Your levelling of great fortunes is liable to level greater things in life. Plutocracy has been prolific, and her children have not all been degenerate. Refinement, felicity, and gentility of mind have some place. Art needs personal as well as impersonal patronage. Your plan may take much that is picturesque out of life, perhaps a certain vivacity, pomp, or elegance." "Perhaps pomp," said George, "will be gone, but nothing picturesque will be lost. Would Beethoven have taken any less pleasure in getting up at midnight and shouting at the Prince's window 'Fool of a Lobkowitz! Ass of a Lobkowitz!' if the window of his patron had happened to be that of the head-clerk of the people (the majority) instead of an archduke's or margrave's? Do you think the White House any less beautiful because you own it, than a state senator's house because you don't own it? Is not the architecture of West 50th Street as monotonous as Hester Street?[12] The difference *is* rather between 100 actual patrons and 100 future patrons perhaps."

"Oh George, your hyperbolic mind is more amusing to you than to anyone else—but I suppose you attribute it to unselfish sparing others that trouble," said his wife, wearily. "Well all right," she continued, "if this plan is so necessary as you say, why don't the people adopt it?" "They would if it was put up to them," said George. "Then why doesn't the Government put it up to them?" said George's wife. "Don't ask me irritating questions. You heard what I said about Senator Fall and Mr. Hearst." "Well why don't they vote for it?" "Well how *can* they vote for—and even if they *did* vote for—You bring back embarrassing thoughts."

"Pardon me, George, I forget about your voting for Governor Partial[13] last fall; but don't you think his sudden change of attitude about your two favorite plans of (a) broadening the educational function of the state, and (b) a scientific budget and auditing system (instead of a scientific party spoil system)—aren't you charitable enough to think that this sudden change, the day after election, might have been due to a sincere conviction, to another but as true a command from the innervoice of his social-consciousness, to a broader conception of expediency, to a high-minded sacrifice to his friends and rather enemies) who stood by him with something stronger than voices in the campaign, or to

12 In 1919, the part of West 50th Street near Fifth Avenue was an elegant neighborhood, and Hester Street was part of the ghetto, but the façades of the houses in both were unrelieved brownstone.
13 Elected in 1918, Alfred E. Smith served as Governor of New York in 1919–20 and later in 1923–28.

the amen religion of compromise, or some similar principles of nobility inherent to all great men—of politics?"

"It *might* have been," said George. "God knows, but not quite as fully as the Governor—but I am inclined to think it was—yes 'twas an inner voice all right, perhaps of his campaign manager, who didn't tell him but merely breathed something about the state finances not being able to stand the brick trade schoolhouse when Queens needed three marble courthouses, and that there couldn't be a budget system as Senator ———— had never heard of a budget and pronounced them unconstitutional and a symptom of socialism, because he (as majority leader of the Senate—23 men) knew what the people wanted. And he knew what the people wanted because in his great campaign speech" —(which George had written for him)—"he said '*I* am a true American' and 'for am I not like Washington and Lincoln?!' and this always made (some = the) people cheer and sometimes made the band play *Hail to the Chief.*"

"Oh George," interrupted his wife, "if you wouldn't try to be funny but just be natural and ridiculous, you'd be so much more impressive." "But the thing that makes me sore," continued George rather excitedly, "is that, when I thought I was voting for the new schoolhouse, I was just voting for the Governor and his party. I don't mind being a fool, but I hate to be fooled. I woke up the other night and began to think how little I had to say about anything. I've tried to be a good and loyal citizen, I've always voted the *right* way, I never spit on the sidewalk— I gave $1,000 to the Red Cross, when Uncle Henry (who is worth $20,000,000 against my $1,800,000, and President of the Welcome Home sign committee, for he put up the sign at his own expense) only gave $5,000. And unless I get into politics (and I can't because I haven't a big voice and can't make a speech, and I haven't the faculty of jollying people up, that is, lying to them in a hearty, honest, friendly way, and I don't care for money or fame), [then] I haven't a thing to say, not a damn thing!"

"Oh George," said his wife, "how ridiculous! How can you, when you're under a government of, by, and for the people—" "That's an elliptical sentence!" cried George. "What is the ellipsis, pray?" said his wife. "Almost everything that ought to be in it." "Name just one word," said his wife. "Representation—Some—Indirect—Few." "Stop!" said his wife, "that's almost treasurable." "An honest man," said George, can be neither treasurable nor patriotic, for the same reason (old Mr. Taylor[14] said) that a true Christian could never be 'praised or insulted.'" "Anyway," said his wife, "don't you have a chance to vote

M25

M26

_____
14 This sounds like Jeremy Taylor (1613–67).

for the man who you think represents your principles, or for the party whose platform represents your principles?" "Yes I have the chance to vote for the man and the platform, but *not* necessarily for the principle. I've voted for free trade presidents and parties and elected them —but did we have free trade? If Cleveland tried to live up to his platform, all of a sudden the senate would go republican, and you know the result—rows, talking, speeches, compromise, then a short prayer— the pork barrel and congress adjourns—all because a shoemaker in Massachusetts wants to make more money from his shoes than a man in Servia makes—and the Boston shoemaker goes to church on Commonwealth Avenue and sings 'Peace on *earth*' (not only in Massachusetts), 'Good Will to men.' "

M27

"But George, you trust your representative in Congress, don't you?" "I trust his honesty, but not his brains." "But," she said, "in a representative government what else can you do?" "But," said George, "why a representative government?" "But," said his wife, "why not a representative government?" "Are the years 1876 and 1919 the same or different years? Are there ends to a circle? Do parallel lines meet? Are the absolute and relative identical? Does effect come before cause? That five-year-old boy knows why direct government is as possible now as it was impossible 100 years ago!—because he knows that a choo-choo goes faster than a horsey—because he sees his mother telephone in the morning and he has crackers for lunch.[15] The Democrat party, the Citizens party, the anarchist party, the Republican party, the Socialist party, the conservative party, the radical party (any political party) are as useless today and as unnecessary in society as a horsewhip is in an automobile! What have I had to say about any fundamental principle? What have I, what have you, what has anybody had to say about the great things that vitally concern all? What have we had to say about high tariff, low tariff, war, national resources, international relations even of the simplest kind—about taxation, peace, public money, conscription, government ownership, league of nations, prohibition, unlimited or limited property right, free trade, civil service, and the like, and other problems?"

128

"But George," said his wife, "these problems are so full of intricate phases and collateral problems . . ." "They are all as simple in their essence," said George, "as any of your household problems, sometimes simpler. You put your hands under the water to clean them—you don't put the water under a microscope. I sometimes feel like making the rest of my life a perpetual stump speech or shouting at society: If you (the majority) want the minority to say what you shall do, to direct

[15] These observations sound typical of Edith, then five, though they are not among the things she said that got written down.

every move you make, to run your world for you, to run your affairs, say so—and you'll have that privilege. If *you* (the majority) want peace on earth, *you* can have it. If you (the majority) want war, it's yours for the asking. If you (the majority) want a few murderers to take charge of your government and turn your daughters over to the state to breed public families, you can have them. If you (the majority) want your daughters to be free to marry whom they wish, if you (the majority) want to turn the murderers over your knee, say so and it is done. If you (the majority) want middlemen to make your laws, they can't do it unless you *say* so. If you (the majority) want mediaeval, national prejudices—high tariffs breeding race jealousies, hatred and war, and standing armies and mass murder—just say so and you can have it, it's all yours for the asking.

M29

"But," said George furiously, "do you suppose that, if I could put squarely and visibly and simply before all the people who have to live on this earth, or make all governments put squarely and visibly and simply before their people a simple referendum no larger than a postal card, and ask but for a no or yes—don't you know that some of mankind's troubles would start to clean up forthwith? Suppose something like the following should be put up to the people of all countries, provinces, communities free or unfree, from Back Bay clubs to the tribes of Sahara, to all grown men and women (say over 18, for if we can draft boys of 18 to fight, we can draft them to *think*)—make everyone (after a certain period of reflection, *not* agitation) register his convictions by answering this:[16]

(1)   Do you (or do you not) want the world to be governed by the people (the majority) and *not* by the non-people (the minority)?   Yes or No.

(2)   Do you agree, if the people (the majority) of all countries do away with (absolutely and forever) armies and navies, to do away with yours?   Yes or No.

(3)   Do you agree that, if the people (the majority) of all countries agree to a free, unrestricted intercourse, in all relations or functions of mankind, whether of commerce, business, religion, art, literature, science, etc.—whatever idea, virtue, or genius God has given man, he will share it unrestricted with all—if they all (the majority) agree, will you do it?   Yes or No.

M30

(4)   If the people (the majority) agree that it is best (for a more natural program of social evolution) to have a right to own enough and only enough personal property to furnish (to family units) a com-

---

16 Compare the following with the final versions of the questions (Boatwright p. 151).

fortable material existence (with a little marginal surplus to satisfy the hope of man's nature, details and figures to be voted upon later)— say measured by an income somewhere between $2,500 and $7,500 a year (or by a measure of the minimum and maximum unit that a man's service is worth (or what he can put into society), the maximum of which cannot be over $10,000 per annum (probably considerably less) —a scientific examination by the law of averages (or the law of evolution) into all the natural, social, economic, moral phenomena (and the life) would probably show that the maximum is nearer $1,000 than $10,000)—according to the judgment of the people (the majority) in each country or community—do you agree to this? Or, to put this question more simply, do you agree to a limited personal property right? Yes or No.—and what limit?

(5)   Do you agree that the answers to these constitute your conviction and will in the matter and a *command* to your government to organize its machinery so that it (together with the other governments of the world) can gradually learn to carry out in details the will of the people (the majority)?   Yes or No.

(6a)   Do you consider it necessary (until the time that universal social consciousness is a little more developed) that the people (the majority) establish a world police, to suppress (physically if need be) those mental and moral reactionaries (the *minority,* the non-people) who try to oppose *with force* the will of the people (the majority)?   Yes or No.

(6b)   Do you agree that no one who owns the maximum amount of property shall have an active participation in or hold a government position?   Yes or No.

A30v

"Article (6a) I personally feel," said George, "may be unnecessary. It is put in as relief, or it will appeal only to the timid. For my part," said George, "I'd rather trust in the strength rather than the weakness of human nature—that is, in the common decency of man. I'd rather defend my household, if it came to that, by a club or piano stool or anything I could grab, rather than the protection of paid artillery. There is something of a cowardly intimation in the words 'protection and security.' However, there are many who will think I'm wrong, and the article had perhaps better go in." "And I think," said his wife, "there are many women and children who had rather defend themselves, and die if necessary, than live in luxury and be defended by mediaeval laws and modern guns. But as you are eliminating 'power by property' (the basic cause of greed and brutality), women and children will be safer without the brute's security leagues." "Aren't you going a little too far?" said George cautiously. His wife smiled and continued her book.

M32v

"The (6b) article will hardly be necessary either," said George, "or rather, whether it is necessary or not will depend upon the maximum limit. It will be almost impossible for $100,000 or $50,000 to form monopolistic combinations without the majority knowing it, while if the limit is $1,000,000, a score of millionaires could cause some serious inconvenience (to say the least) for the people (the majority), though under our procedure it could be only temporary. The fact that there are (in the U. S. Senate, the House, and in State Legislatures, and in leaders of political parties) men who are worth considerably over $1,000,000 is more ridiculous than amusing in a democracy. However," said George, "that won't worry us much longer. Some will defend large property owners' participation in government on the ground that their property is a symbol of 'brains' and hence ought to be used for the public good. But, as we have seen, it is more a symbol of chance environment, uneven opportunity, haphazard traditions, and due as much to fundamental stupidity as to predominant brightness—in other words there is a larger percentage of men who haven't accumulated property, that could render efficient public service, than there is among the so-called successful class. Another thing—with $50,000 or $100,000 maximum right, a laborer (if skilled and industrious) may make his $50,000 quicker than a capitalist. As there will be little need of personal capital, the stimulant to industrial progress will be in the inspiration of many—the public surplus *will be* the capital—or rather call it the people's (the majority's) industrial foundation fund."

M31

"Illiteracy," said George's wife, "(even in our own country isn't it about 16 percent?) might spoil your scheme." "The questions are [so] vital that they are simple—and oral presentation and verbal affidavit could easily be taken. Some of the most thoughtful men in the world are illiterate. (Education is more dependent on truths than on lead pencils, though a pencil makes it easier.)"

"Well," said his wife, "how many do you think of the majority would subscribe 'Yes'?" "The majority would, they already *have* in their hearts and minds. There are two classes of people (the minority) who would write 'No'—(a) those who have or want to get more money than they need, and (b) organic cowards. Fear causes the restrictions referred to in clause (3)—fear and his campaign managers, suspicion, prejudice, ignorance, etc. How do you know that we cannot learn more from the Chinese than they can from us? At least we can offer each other our best—it will not only be best for each but best for both. One of the most perfect personal characters (intellectually, morally, spiritually) I have ever known was half Chinese and half

M31v

Connecticut.[17] There seemed to be a supreme species. The Yankee wit

17 Bart Yung's father was Chinese (see App. 17), but his mother was Mary Louisa Kellogg of Avon, Connecticut.

and oriental fatalism produced a serious sense of humor and a different philosophic-practical turn of mind than ever came out of Concord.

"Anyone who has to live on this earth cannot sidestep the earth's problems. (A few elderly Republican Senators would like to sidestep them—why?—for the same old reason—fear!) National sovreignty has been an idiosyncrasy since 1418 (discovery of gunpowder). It was a part and never a whole—from an essential it became a delusion, and now almost an impossibility (not to say an impracticality). Senator Jones (or is it Smith?—the law of averages will make it either) talks about it and then buries his head in its sand. I've seen a porter on a Pullman train pull out his watch with dignity and say that 'his car' was going 58 miles a minute (but he didn't say how fast the rest of the train was going).

M31 "Prejudice is the bad part of good traditions. Is it necessary for a red-head boy who sleeps in the north room to hate his black-hair brother who sleeps in the south room? If it is, then it's necessary for M32 the Tasmanian to hate the Australian. (Race-inertia (the moving-in-a-straight-line part) is, says Henry Adams, but a local condition—therefor it isn't a constant essential and man can change it, and ought to change it occasionally—as against other inertias, for example sex-inertia, which is a vital condition—therefor man cant't change it.)

"The difference between the negroe and the sun-browned white man is only of degree, not kind. The negroe has happened to live nearer the sun. He has been sunburned for centuries upon centuries. Because there is no more difference between the stars than [between] the dust particles in the sun's rays, space and time are man's small ways, not God's. [In] the almost hourly depression of the casualty list, there is a slight undercurrent of hope—the names of boys from all countries of the earth—does it not suggest this universal infusion—that it may symbolize or be the physical substratum of the Emersonian universal mind and Oversoul? (This mixture or social infusion has of course always been at work, we see it in all mythology and history and biology, we see the idea at least in the Tower of Babel, we see it in Herodotus.) Pure blood, if left to stand long enough alone, will like milk become sour and decomposed."

"But George," said his wife, "won't the process of putting all this into effect make it a slow, delayed . . . There are so many obstacles, complications." "The obstacles, complications, and delays will be legal, not physical. If 20,000,000 men can be registered for military service in twelve hours, it won't be a bigger or longer job to register their opinions on a few fundamentals—it will be simpler than you think, because it is vital to all." "I didn't mean the physical registering—that part will be easy enough—I meant from a constitutional standpoint, even in this country." "A fairly competent law clerk," said George, "could straighten out that detail in three days. I think it can be done without changing the constitution. There is an article or preamble: 'We, the people of the United States, in order to form a more perfect Union, establish justice, insure domestic tranquillity, provide for the common defense, promote the general welfare, and secure the blessings of liberty to ourselves and our posterity, do ordain and establish this Constitution for the United States of America.'

"If not, an amendment could easily be drawn up—that is, unless it gets in the hands of Senator Barnacle and the circumlocution office. If a committee of legal lights for the Senate and House begin to sit on it, together with 100 corporation lawyers or acute and brilliant minds (and above all precedent-loving), then for every four reasons for doing it there'll be forty-two reasons for not doing it—rights of habeas-corpus (of body politic) may be invoked—or the shades of Washington or Lincoln might be presented, forgetting that Washington kicked King George in the shins and Lincoln several others."

M34   "All right," said his wife, "but how about those in the minority who conscientiously think they're right too?" "You've heard of Murphy's one alternative[18]—well, I'll give you three: 1st, to stand up like a man and present these ideas with perseverence, enthusiasm, and intelligence, and if there is virtue in the plans the majority will eventually accept them, they can't help it (the best and quickest way to repeal a bad law is to obey it literally and furiously)—2nd, to go to another country or community whose laws coincide with these views—3rd, to become cowards and put a fuse behind someone's back and blow up the man *possibly* but eventually *themselves* and kill what virtue their ideas have. Such mental degenerates (members of the minority) force the people (the majority) to treat them in exactly the way a farmer treats a skunk who has lost his self-control."

M35   "I see," said his wife, "but many people will say your ideas are too transcendental, too visionary." "The fundamental doctrine," said George, "of transcendentalism (the innate goodness of man) may be visionary, but if it was not true, there would never have been not only a world but a universe. The most practical thing I've ever done was to go into business and in twelve years make $1,800,000.[19] But the idea that made it possible was called not only visionary but that it would ruin us within a year. They were sorry for us—no other firm had ever been so ridiculous (even my partner, though interested and open-minded

---

18 Murphy was a name that Ives loved to use facetiously. In his last illness, one of the nurses met Mrs. Ives in the hall, alarmed that his mind was going—"He's calling me Murphy!"
19 That is, twelve years from the start of Ives & Co., at the beginning of 1907.

about it, was not enthusiastic until he saw actual results beginning).[20] But I remember Thoreau's advice: 'Whenever an old man tells you you can't [you try and find that you can]'.[21]

M35v

"I assumed that the law of averages was divine, and that the average man . . ." "There's no such thing," said George's wife, "as the average man." "Very well, Sophist! the majority then—most men. I assumed that *most* men were honest and most men were intelligent. Therefore, if your goods had as much good in them and truth in them as you knew how to put in them, the more salesmen (by salesmen I mean men, experience, letters, anything) that can help to put the 'truth of your goods' before the people (the majority), the less (and in the inverse ratio) will be the force of dishonesty and unintelligence against you. This attitude, of course collateral essentials, [was] easy to develop, viz one price to all, big and little buyers, one commission and open contracts to all agents, brokers, etc., and as much courtesy and service and *sympathy* (which is as important to men as to women).[22] Our business grew from a few thousands to 15,000,000 in twelve years— and these good old experienced, practical minds in the other firms, with the identical goods to sell and 100 times more capital to start with—if they didn't fail, they didn't grow over 25 percent. The largest one, who did 2,000,000 when he told us what failures we would be, has made an increase to 4,000,000 (with the same goods to sell). He invariably believed, as soon as a man bought for him, 'look out'— as soon as he sold for him, 'look out, he might be a crook.' He limited his vision, tried to save one eye, and so became almost blind."

M36v

"But," said George's wife, "you're inconsistent." "Thank you!" said George. "Excuse me," said his wife, "I didn't mean to insult Emerson[23]— but I don't get you, for you said a while ago that great fortunes were stumbled upon, that intrinsic personal ability, etc., had little to do with it, in fact you needed a little fundamental stupidity." "I'll admit the 'stupid streak' but not the rest," said George. "(1) Nine men out of ten, if their fathers had brought them up on the great transcendental doctrine (as mine did me),[24] would have done the same as I did. (2) Nine

20 This is apparently the only hint of any skepticism on the part of Julian Myrick.
21 Ives wrote only the first clause of Thoreau's sentence from memory, indicating the rest by dashes. In the copy of *Walden* which he inscribed: "to Harmony, in Deerfield and Vermont, Feb. 1913"—on p. 7 this sentence is underlined: "What old people say you cannot do you try and find that you can." For another adaptation see *The Majority* (Boatwright, p. 158).
22 All this sounds like Ives lecturing the training school for agents.
23 George's wife is obliquely referring to Emerson's famous dictum in *Self-Reliance:* "A foolish consistency is the hobgoblin of little minds."
24 Ives's father had evidently brought him up also on that aspect of transcendentalist thinking that was to seem one of Ives's own contributions—faith in human nature to the point of accepting what others might contribute to one's own work. Clarence Nowlan (see §25, note 2) told the editor in 1960 that, as a boy, he could never understand how George Ives could bear to sit down in the orchestra playing violin and being conducted by Harry Biddiscombe, who was so much less a musician.

men out of ten, if they had, plus (1), the opportunity of observing (as I did), in a certain clerical job,[25] the possibilities in that business, would have observed them and done the same as I did. And (3) principally and most important, the $1,800,000 that I made, though made openly, legally, and in accordance with rules etc. of the business, was all out of proportion to the 'idea,' to the service that I rendered society. A blacksmith who has made a shoe so that a horse will slip less, and incidentally $18 per week, has come nearer *earning* that $1,800,000, than I did."

M35

"But I do hope," said George's wife, "that I can get one tour on the Mediterranean[26] before your limited property plan goes into effect." "Well, I don't expect to live forever," said George, "so I'm not worrying." "And," said George's wife, "what will you do with the money that will come to the people from the plan?" "It's the principle more than the money. But personally I'd first divide a good part of it among the maimed soldiers—they are by no means the only sufferers from this fundamental stupidity, but they are the worst. Then," said George,

M36

"it could be used as government expenditure (for taxes would be less) under the direction of the majority."

"Well," said George's wife, "after the government has learned to become an efficient organism—a clerical machine (as it were) with the President as head clerk, and assistants chosen as one chooses a good dentist, a good grocer,[27] etc., to carry out (as long as they do it well

M37

and to the satisfaction of the majority)—in a word, when this scientific machinery is running perfectly, so that it will function accurately and carry out effectively the ideas and will and wish of the people (the majority), how do you know the people will act wisely and rightly?"

"Do you believe," said George, "the stomach is a part of the physical human body?" "Yes." "Do you believe that a brain is of the physical human body (some people have no brains, that is true, but that isn't the point)?" "Yes." "Then put 100 men (chosen at random) down to a dinner (good or bad, it makes no difference as long as it is the *same* food)—90 men, 90% of those men's stomachs will digest normally, that is, act wisely or rightly. Put 100,000 men down to the same food— 95% of the stomachs will act rightly. Put 1,000,000[28]—98% will act rightly. The brain will function as any other organ, its results will parallel our stomach percentages above. In other words, if the same

25 Even though Ives was not well fitted for the actuarial department of Mutual, that introduction to the principles and procedures remained invaluable to him. But "George" may be lumping this together with Ives's job in the Raymond Agency.

26 In 1919 Mrs. Ives had been to Europe twice (see App. 19), Ives not yet. After "Mediterranean" the ms. seems to read: "in M Utata"—apparently an unfocussed sketch toward a take-off of a ship's name.

27 After "grocer" Ives included a third trade-designation, but illegibly.

28 Ives wrote only five zeros but put the comma clearly after the "1."

M38 kind of the right kind of food is put before enough brains, they will function normally—that is, act wisely and rightly."

"What is the right kind of food, George?" said his wife. "Truth in all its aspects," said George, "and universal education is fast supplying it. And on the consignees and distributors of this foodstuff rests a greater responsibility than on the officers of the world's largest industrial units. A teacher of the humblest country school has a greater trust than can ever rest on the world's greatest railroad president. That these captains of the world's most important industry have never been adequately paid is one of the most acute signs of the aforesaid fundamental stupidity. It is the primary, the common and public high school teachers we must look to for the base of supply, rather than some of the traditional-minded guides in some of the larger universities, whose course in economics is guided more by what has been in the past rather than what has been in the future, whose law of supply and demand is inspired if not determined rather by the alumni dinner than

M39 by a freshman. The latter (universities) tend to distribute 'Truth' with too much rigidity. If it is received by this consignee, it is too well boxed up and labeled, or it is too often handed down unboxed. Educational sensibilities are not as insensible as the seats in the college chapel. Innate perceptions, if the term may be used here, are not all trigonometric. Enthusiasm to find the natural in universal education must be one of its greatest services.

"I remember," said George, "that before I went to college I was interested. I found a pleasure in browsing in my father's library that I never found in college. My mind seemed to stop, at my first freshman recitation, as soon as I felt smothered by the compulsory constant proximity of 300 classmate minds[29]—compulsory ideas of tutors, compulsory traditions of professors, compulsory courses, compulsory freedom of thought, compulsory chapel—I learned not a thing that I ought. Whatever thoughts I had came out of some others' mouths, or didn't come out at all. I learned not to have a 'shy foot' in batting (at

M40 the plate), and that the Freshmen could always rush the Sophomores at Thermopylae—valuable, but all four years in complete dulness of mind.[30] But after receiving the sheepskin (the most appropriate thing I had received for a long time), I felt free to think again, and I'm gradually getting straightened out.

"On the other hand," said George, "over-stimulation, over-encouragement, which tends to create an artificial mind, is an opposite problem

29 This sounds like one of the ways in which Ives's shyness would occasionally take hold of him, becoming almost pathological.
30 What Ives describes here as "dullness of mind" may have been largely due to his father's death. In the sketch of 1930 to Griggs (end of App. 15), he calls it "that awful vacuum I was carrying around with me."

for other consignees. More geniuses have been started on the path of subsidy by writing a poem or an opera for a $1,000 prize, more master-pieces have been perverted than blossomed in this wise. A cocktail will make a man eat more, but will not give him a healthy normal appetite (if he had not one already). If a Bishop should offer a $100,000 prize (or a living) to the curate 'who should love God the hardest for fifteen days,' whoever got the prize would love God the least.[31] But, broadly speaking, our consignees of truth through universal education

M41 have distributed better and more nobly than some of the consignees of more material goods, and have, at the same time, been less well dis-tributed unto.

"Yes," said George, "universal education is well on its way to carry out its God-destined plan—(It is the plan that has always been with us. It is restated in nature, in science, in the soul of man. Its mark is found everywhere. Science gives a simple example—'For the greater the num-ber of risks exposed, the greater the number of exhibits under observa-tion, the less the mortality, the more accurate the deductions.'—Huxley) —the plan, in a way, that Channing, Pascal, Epictetus, Darwin, and many other agents, fragments of the universal mind, have shown us. It is the plan that Christ has shown us—'I die not for you but for all.'

"Yes," said George, "the people (the majority) will act rightly if they are given the chance." "And if they do fall down a manhole occasion-ally," said his wife, "they will know whose fault it is." "It will be a little amusing to see them throwing mud at themselves instead of at the 'innocent but fat official,' wildly knocking themselves, and writing anonymous letters through the newspapers to themselves."

"Well," said George's wife, looking up from her book, "you have shown to me (and I hope to yourself) the evil effects of social progress of an honest but fundamentally stupid streak—how about the pre-dominantly bright *and fundamentally bright* people?—but I don't believe there ever has been one."

After the above sentence, Ives directs one "(to bottom p. 3)"—but since this p. 3 is no longer extant, one can do best by directing the reader to the final version of *The Majority*.

[31] Compare this paragraph with the next-to-last paragraph of section V of the Epilogue, in the *Essays Before a Sonata* (Boatwright, p. 93).

Broadway (1922)

Among various materials by which Ives taught the school for life insurance agents, the most vivid is the following story. It was reprinted as a pocket-size booklet by "Ives & Myrick, Managers The Mutual Life Insurance Co. of New York, 46 Cedar Street, New York" (address good from May 1923)—but the title page specifies: "Printed, by request, from Agency Bulletins July–Sept., '22" (the three chapters appearing in those three months).

Ives's ink sketch and clear copy of an earlier version have a preface: "The two illustrations of selling talks below were taken from reports of actual interviews . . . turned in by agents on the back of their canvass cards. The first is a composite of several reports. The second is one of the few complete and literal records of interviews we have, and for that reason may be less useful than the first. We find that it is difficult for an agent to make a literal report of an entire interview. The agent remembers the effect of a few words more vividly than the phraseology and the order in which they were used. . . . The presentation-platform is a pretty constant factor, but there are almost as many successful talks as there are agents, and as varied as their temperaments (that is saying a good deal!) . . . The important thing is the knowledge and conviction behind the talk." [The last sentence, only in the first sketch, is equally typical of Ives's music.] In this earlier version the characters are called simply "Prospect" and "Agent" with no names.

Ives's scrapbooks also contained the final ink ms. of Chapter II and the August Bulletin (a mimeographed typing), which suggest that Ives dictated from his ms. with slight changes, as he did ten years later in the *Memos*. The text below is that of the booklet.

"BROADWAY"
(Not a Continuation of "Main Street")

A Short Story Describing the Adventures of Two Different Types of Agents.

CHAPTER I.

While going along the corridor of a big office building on Broadway, not far from the City Hall, Jim Duke saw two men come out of an office door. As they came towards him he heard one say:

"I'm glad Stewart got that job—he's a good man for the place, etc."

Jim was an opportunist and an insurance agent. He was on his way to another office farther down the hall, but when he came to the door the two men had come from, he went in, walked up to a clerk and asked where Mr. Stewart was. The clerk pointed to an inner office. Entering it Jim saw a man, a little under middle age, busy at his desk.

"Mr. Stewart," said Jim, "I want to congratulate you. My company wants you among its policyholders."

Stewart looked up and made the usual remarks about being busy, not wanting insurance and so on, and noticing Jim's card, thought he might get rid of him by saying:

"Besides, I'm already in your company."

Jim followed up this information, of course, and found that Stewart some years ago, when unmarried, had taken out a $2,500 Twenty-Year Endowment.

"You need more insurance," said Jim. He knew that Stewart, from a buyer's standpoint, was near one of those mysterious things called a "psychological moment." Jim persisted, and after a little further discussion Stewart said:

"Oh, well, you can write me up for another policy like the other one, but I can't give you any more time now."

He was examined and Jim had a $5,000 Twenty-Payment Life issued with the $2,500 Twenty-Year Endowment. He placed the $5,000. It was not hard to show a bright man like Stewart that this was more what he needed,—that the cash value on the Life policy in twenty years (age 33), was $2,938 against the $2,500 Endowment, and that the excess outlay was justified by the increased protection, etc.

On the day the policy was placed, Jim walked out of Stewart's office pretty well pleased with himself. He thought he'd done a good stroke of work. Had he? Had he made the most of his opportunity? Had he handled the case as brilliantly as he thought? We'll say he had not. He did fairly well—as far as he went—we'll say that. But he did little more than take an order. Two right moves stand to his credit. He took immediate advantage of a chance opportunity. He made a man of responsibility take a kind of policy more suited to his needs than the one he had in mind.

There are two kinds of opportunists,—the casual and the systematic. The former is good in taking opportunities if they come to him. The latter is good in making opportunities come to him and following them up from every angle.

Harry Samson was of the latter type,—and an insurance agent as well. See what he did with Stewart.

CHAPTER II.

Shortly after the events related in Chapter I, the name of William Workingup Stewart appeared in Harry Samson's "Prospect Index."

Names in this, came from all sources his managers could think of. This particular one came from the office system of clippings of business changes, promotions, appointments, etc., taken from Standard Trade Papers. Harry indexed the card, his managers sent a short preliminary letter, and a call was made the next morning. Samson's theory and practice were not to try to "close" on the first interview, unless an especially favorable chance offered—but rather to get a line on his man, whatever data he could, and to arouse curiosity in his plan. But on the second interview, he went in to close or to get thrown out—he was used to both.

Stewart was engaged, but Harry decided to wait, telling the stenographer that he wanted to see Mr. Stewart in relation to a letter from his firm. In a few minutes Stewart came to the door and scowled, then went back to his desk. Harry followed him and sat down, saying that he had called in accordance with a letter from his office. Stewart cut him short.

"Now, look here. I'm not interested in Life Insurance. I've just taken out all I want in the .... Company."

"I'm glad to hear you say that. You're in a splendid company, but I want to see you about those other policies."

"What other policies?" said Stewart.

"Those indicated by the appraisal."

"What appraisal?" asked Stewart.

"Why, the appraisal that must be made now-a-days in all lines of insurance,—in Life Insurance this is very important."

"I don't propose to have a stranger go into the appraisal of my personal affairs," interrupted Stewart.

"No," said Samson, "but I can give you the principle which you must apply in your own way. You've got to make this analysis some time and the quicker you do it, the more time and money you'll save. My plan has a strong bearing on everyone's financial scheme (business and domestic); it outlines a practical way of converting non-productive into productive expenditures;—it classifies the sources of income; it determines the duration and definite need of future incomes and reserve funds for yourself." (In this Samson made a mistake—a habit he was trying to break himself of—putting too much in one sentence.)[1]

"Oh, I can't go into all that," said Stewart. "It's just another way of bothering me for more insurance. I tell you I don't want any more. You'll have to excuse me. Good day!" As Stewart didn't rise from his desk, Harry didn't, and leaning forward in his chair, speaking quietly, but with a conviction born of belief in his plan, said:

[1] Apparently Ives knew all too well his tendency toward Marathon-sentences (though these are often justified by their resemblance to Whitman's catalogues).

"Mr. Stewart, if you've settled your insurance question without having a working knowledge of the premises precedent to a practical decision—without an examination of my plan—without an analysis of the fundamentals that underlie the insurance problem of every business man—you've made one of the greatest mistakes of your life!"

"You needn't go into my mistakes," said Stewart with irritation. "If I want any more insurance I'll take it with the other agent. He didn't bother me as you're doing."

Harry ignored this and continued:

"I'm convinced that you've never been shown"—(at this moment a man who evidently wanted to see Stewart looked in at the office door. This didn't disturb Harry. He knew if he stopped now, he was lost.)

"Mr. Stewart," he continued, "I'm convinced that you've not been shown even in a general way, how to make a practical determination of your Life Insurance need. Therefore, there is no reason why you should have any conception of the importance of my plan. I venture to say with no qualification that it will be one of the most important guides in your business life."

Harry had made some study of character-analysis, the psychology of personality, etc. (or whatever you like to call it). He had taken a mental photograph of Stewart. It looked something like this: impatient but logical, proud but fair, able when he'd put his mind to a thing, a little suspicious, resentful of "bluff," but inclined to "bluff," non-committal, but quick to act after persuaded, interested but unwilling to show it.

"Now, what I want is this, Mr. Stewart. I want twenty minutes of your undivided, uninterrupted attention. I want an appointment for next Wednesday morning at 11:30."

"I've wasted more time with you than I can spare," said Stewart. "What earthly use is there for me to make an appointment? I won't take any more Life Insurance with you or anybody else."

He rose from his desk. Harry rose, but stood his ground.

"Life Insurance won't enter this twenty-minute interview unless you bring it in,—by your own deductions. You will be fair and that is all I ask. If you can show me that my plan does not help you in any way, I think I'm big enough to see it. The only thing I ask is that you follow me carefully. Life Insurance like all big life values is 'relative.' It is an individual-contingent-factor. Mr. Stewart, a man of your new responsibilities and business possibilities must go into this problem more thoroughly than you have. I am certain of this,—that at the end of my twenty minutes, you will agree that the information which my plan will give you will be as useful as any idea that you met with in your business experience. You will agree that the plan is not only scientifically true, but of great practical value. I want an appointment with you at 11:30 Wednesday."

Stewart started to walk towards the door. Harry didn't move. Stewart looked a little perplexed, but after a slight pause, said:

"Well, 11:30 is a bad time for me. You'd better make it in the afternoon—some time after 3:00."

"Alright, I'll be here at 3:30," said Harry, as he went out.

Stewart turned to his stenographer:

"That was the only way I could get rid of that man." Then he added in an undertone: "But he sure does believe he has a big idea. I could see that before he'd spoken ten words. Well, I'm willing to learn anything new, but I'm damned if I'll buy any more Life Insurance."[2]

CHAPTER III.

Stewart received Samson at the appointed hour, but with a rather uncompromising look. Harry wasted no time in preliminaries.

"Now, Mr. Stewart, in any kind of a business calculation I assume you're willing to be governed by authoritive data," said Harry, pushing a pad towards him. "Just jot down in percentages (you needn't show me the figures) that part of your income certain to go on for a good many years. The definite periods I'll explain later." Stewart put nothing down.

"I can help you here," said Harry. "There are only three sources from which this can come: First, business; second, property, and—the third factor. So first just put down the part which is certain to go on from your business no matter what happens to you." Stewart, looking annoyed, said:

"This is a salaried job,—you ought to see that."

"Alright," said Harry. "Put down the income your property will guarantee—anything that can be turned into assured income." Stewart hesitated, then wrote down something.

"Is there anything else that will produce sure income?" asked Harry.

"Well, there's some Life Insurance," said Stewart.

"Alright, put down what that will yield and add it to the property item. Just put a little circle around that sum, please. Now, Mr. Stewart, have you a definite idea of what income *should* continue to the family?"

"Why, I'd like it all to, I suppose," said Stewart.

"That would be fine," Harry said, "but it isn't absolutely necessary, it isn't usually practicable. The investment would be out of proportion to the other income items. Now, it happens, after as comprehensive an

2 The August Bulletin ends Chap. II with: "See what happens at 3:30 on Wednesday in Chapter III (Next Month's Circular)."

examination of statistics as we could make, 64% was found to be the average. Except in very small or very large incomes this proportion is reasonable and accurate enough to be a serviceable guide. No one should make much of a variation without justifying himself by careful calculation. You've a pretty good idea of your normal or average income, haven't you? Well, just put down 64% of it." Stewart writes down something. "Now, subtract from this the sum you have there in the circle. There's a balance?"—says Harry, giving him time to figure.

"Yes," says Stewart, after a pause. "I get you. I'd never thought of Life Insurance in that way. But I can't take on any more expense now."

"Mr. Stewart," said Harry, speaking as forcibly as he could. "I've shown you something you admit you'd no conception of before. Now, I can show you that providing for this admitted need, is not the difficult thing you think. It's largely a matter of knowing how to convert non-productive into productive accounts. You do this in your business finance, you can in your domestic finance. There's a common misconception of insurance 'outlay.' 'Inlay' is the truer term. It is one of the few purely productive expenditures. For under my plan the principal comes back to you about the time most men want to retire or ease up in business—and also under this low Straight Life rate—if you can get it—an immediate income is paid you if you're completely knocked out, —disabled for good and all from doing anything again."

Stewart was now listening attentively.

"That's interesting," he said. "I'd no idea Straight Life insurance gave anything much to the insured while he was living. But it would take $30,000 or $40,000 to take care of my balance, as I figure it, but"— looking at his watch,—"The required amount," interrupted Harry, working fast and hard,[3] "the right distribution to the wife for life, the definite share to the children to self-supporting ages at least, the taxes and other estate depreciation, etc.—these are only a simple matter of mathematics, which I'll work out for you and index under our estate-program sheets.*

"Mr. Stewart," said Harry, in a manner born of conviction, "you admit a balance, therefore you admit a need for immediate action. I'm certain of this much—you can take care of, at least, part of this need now."

"I suppose so," said Stewart, "but—"

"I'll have the examiner here at 10:30 tomorrow," said Harry.

Stewart was examined and $25,000 was placed.

---

3 "Working fast and hard" evokes the way Ives must have sketched his music allowing just enough sleep for the next business day.

* NOTE—The method referred to here has often been explained in various ways in our office literature. For those to whom it is unfamiliar, we will be glad to demonstrate it upon request.

Harry had won Stewart's confidence. The calculation from the data Stewart subsequently gave showed a total insurance need of $42,000. The extra $10,000 (Stewart already carried $7,500) was issued and Harry will place it.

Jim Duke, the casual opportunist (in Chapter I), thought he had done a good job in writing Stewart for $5,000, whereas Harry Samson, the systematic opportunist (in Chapters II and III), found that Stewart should and could carry $42,000 and eventually made him carry it.[4]

This ends the Summer story. Some who have read it won't get anything helpful out of it—others will,—such is life!

---

[4] As a "coda of Chap. III" Ives sketched the following paragraph: "Jim Duke, a few months later, happened to be in Samson's agency. He said to one of the clerks, 'One of your brokers wrote one of my clients for $30,000 just after I'd worked him up. I won't say he rebated, but it must have been pretty soft after what I'd done—$30,000—why that fellow ought to [carry] $100,000—he's a coming man in that line." Jim lit a cigar and went out—to write Stewart for $100,000?—No, to play golf—and look for opportunities. He was an opportunist."

Letter to John Tasker Howard (1930)

In preparing *Our American Music* (Crowell 1931) John Tasker Howard (1890–1964) must have sent questionnaires to all pertinent living composers. Ives's papers retain no letter from him, nor any carbon of the letter of "last month," but do contain the sketches, first carbon, and final carbon of this one. In a broadly encyclopaedic work Howard could hardly use more than a fraction of what Ives sent him —he quoted directly only the paragraph starting "If idioms . . ." While some of these thoughts and facts appear in the *Memos,* there are enough others to warrant giving the complete text of the final carbon, with a few variants from the sketch (in italic parentheses) wherever clearer or fuller.

West Redding, Connecticut, June 30, 1930

Dear Mr. Howard,

In addition to what I sent you last month, am forwarding under separate cover some other articles and copies which may give you the information etc. which you are kind enough to ask me for: A Book of Essays—*Pro Musica Quarterly,* March 1927[1]—*The New Freeman,* May 3, 1930[2]—A Conductor's Note to a movement in the *Fourth Symphony*[3]—*The Musical Forecast,* Pittsburgh, March 1929[4]—*Pro Musica Quarterly,* Feb. 1925, containing an article of mine on quarter-tones.[5]

On the enclosed sheet are the answers to the five questions in re biographical data:

1. [Born] October 20, 1874, Danbury, Connecticut.
2. (Early musical background, education, home influences, etc.) My father was a musician and a teacher (in Danbury and neighboring villages) of the violin, piano, (brass and wood instruments), harmony, sight reading, (and ear training), etc. He played in and taught the

1 *The Music of Charles Ives* by Henry Bellamann, pp. 16–22.
2 *Three American Composers* by Henry Cowell, on pp. 184–86.
3 This conductor's note is reprinted complete in the score published by Associated.
4 A review by T. Carl Whitmer of the second movement of the *Fourth Symphony* as printed in *New Music.*
5 When the *Franco-American Musical Society Bulletin* contained Ives's article in the issue of March 1925 (pp. 24–33), its name had not yet been changed to *Pro Musica Quarterly.*

brass band (and orchestra), led the church choirs, the music at the Camp Meetings, and the local Choral Society. He had a reverence, a devotion, and a talent for music which was unusual. His interest lay not only in what had been done but in what might be done. His study of acoustics led him to many experiments into the character of musical instruments and of tonal combinations, and even into the divisions of the tone.

He had a belief that everyone was born with at least one germ of musical talent, and that an early application of great music (and not trivial music) would help it grow. He started all the children of the family—and most of the children of the town for that matter—on Bach and Stephen Foster. (Quite shortly after they were born—always regardless of whether [they] had, would have, or wouldn't have any musical gifts or sense, etc.—) he put a love of music into the heart of many a boy who might have gone without it but for him.

(I feel that, if I have done anything that is good in music, I owe it almost entirely to him and his influence.) After his death I studied the organ with Dudley Buck and Harry Rowe Shelley, (and took the courses in music under Professor Horatio W. Parker) offered by the college in connection with the regular academic studies. I graduated from Yale College in the class of 1898.

3. (Positions held) Church organ positions: Danbury, Connecticut, 1886–92[6]—Saint Thomas Church, New Haven, Conn., 1892–94—Center Church, New Haven, Conn., 1894–98—First Presbyterian Church, Bloomfield, New Jersey, 1899—Central Presbyterian Church, 57th Street, New York (organist and choirmaster), 1899–1902. Have been in business in New York since 1898, a member of the firm of Ives & Myrick, 46 Cedar Street, New York.

4. (Important performances of your work) A Cantata, *The Celestial Country,* for chorus, quartet, orchestra, and organ, New York, April 18, 1902. First performances: *Third Violin and Piano Sonata,* Carnegie Chamber Hall, New York, April 1916[7]—*Second Violin and Piano Sonata,* Aeolian Hall, New York, March 14, 1924[8]—*First Violin and Piano Sonata,* San Francisco, California, November 1928[9]—*Second Piano Sonata* (in part), Salzburg Festival, Germany, August 1928[10]—

6 Ives's first "position" as church organist was from 10 February 1889, though he had "supplied" in August 1888. See the chronological index.
7 For the date of this invitation performance by David Talmadge and Stuart Ross, probably Sunday 22 April 1917, see §24, note 1.
8 This concert by Jerome Goldstein and Rex Tillson was on 18 March 1924.
9 This performance, by Dorothy Minty and Marjorie Gear, was in a *New Music* concert of contemporary violin music at the Rudolph Schaeffer Studios, San Francisco, Tuesday evening, 27 November 1928.
10 This must be the miscellaneous recital that Oscar Ziegler gave at Salzburg, on Tuesday 31 July 1928, the program including *The Alcotts.*

(Two movements of the *Fourth Symphony*, Town Hall, New York, January 29, 1929)[11]—*First Orchestral Set* before the American Committee of the International Society for Contemporary Music, New York, February 16, 1930[12]—Quarter-Tone Music, Aeolian Hall, New York, February 1925.[13]

5.   See list of compositions at the end of an article about my music by Henry Bellamann in *Pro Musica Quarterly*, March 1927.

To the question asking what idiom a composer finds himself in I do not know exactly what to say. Any general mode of expression to a certain extent I suppose is an individual thing with every composer— whether it comes from an idiom or an idiom comes from it. The labels, ultra-modern, modern, romantic, classical, are quite probably transitory in the general run of things. I don't like to feel that I am tied down to any definite brand, though I may be, more than I know. When one feels that he can rest definitely on, and gets all set up by, something which he calls an idiom, he may not be in the state of mind he thinks he is. Idioms are concrete enough, I imagine, from the technical side, but their sources must be to a great extent in a man's general life experience; that is, if the manner of working is not too consciously sought, it may take care of itself. Quite probably there are times in the experience of many, if not most, composers when they find themselves using materials or changing idioms (if only in a slight way and without definitely realizing it) which are not exactly in line with what

11 This performance, conducted by Eugene Goossens, was on 29 January 1927.
12 This was the first of the many times Nicolas Slonimsky conducted the *Three Places in New England,* and also the first of the many times he was the Iveses' house guest. Though Ives did not attend this reading, he was so impressed with Slonimsky's approach to the work that he wrote out the following memo in ink:
   (Copied from Mr. Slonimsky's notes he read to the orchestra just before the rehearsal, Feb. [16], 1930, before the International Society Committee, New York).
   "I would like to call your attention to certain peculiarities of Mr. Ives's rhythms. He often employs rhythms running independently in several orchestral groups. In such cases it is imperative for the players to take the lead of that particular group, regardless of what the main rhythm is, and regardless of my down-beat. Apply somewhat the principle of chamber music or accompaniment, etc.
   "Examples [pages of Hanke score, but letters same as printed score]: Page 1, measure 1 (flute & piano) & 3—p. 6, bars 1 & 2 (3 bars before D)—p. 11 at H— [2nd mvt.] pp. 16–17 [m. 1–11] (Allegro)—p. 25, bar 2 etc. (5 bars after F) [rightly 7th in F]—p. 27, bar 4 [2nd in] H, accelerated step (bassoon, drum, piano, 2nd V. [rightly viola])—p. 39, last bar at O [snare] drum in 4s—p. 46 at T (drums)—[3rd mvt.] p. 62, one after H (flute).
   "[Also] 3rd movement [2nd in A?] muted oboe for English Horn)—2 trombones, 3 measures before H—[2nd mvt.] all brass at L, p. 33—double brass p. 37 [2 before M] and p. 42 at Q—[3rd mvt.] all trumpets, 2 horns, 2 trombones, p. 60 at G."
   [The American Committee recommended the work, but the International Committee turned it down. The I.S.C.M. festival that year was at Liège and Brussels.]
13 Hans Barth and Sigmund Klein played the *Chorale* at Chickering Hall, Sunday 8 February 1925, and the *Chorale* and *Allegro* at Aeolian Hall, Saturday 14 February 1925.

they have used before, or with what they have been taught or have heard in other music—not that it is "new" to music, but that it is at least "new" to them.

I hesitate[14] to use "new" as a word by itself. If it isn't a relative thing, it isn't anything. The "old" and the "new" are either parts of the same substance or they are non-existent—a platitude which deserves more consideration than is sometimes given. Living with one alone, if it isn't impossible, is at least a deadly kind of limitation or retrogression. The various groups who set store only by the "old" or only by the "new" (or only by something else, for that matter) tie themselves all up. The apostles of each are usually taken up with abusing each other or getting in their own way, though to me it seems that the radicals fight in a bigger way than their opponents. They examine and appreciate, to some extent at least, the "old", while many of the conservatives ignore the "new" and sometimes do it in an unfair way. A man may lay the law down for himself, but when he lays it down for others, it eventually is liable to be laid only in the weak underbrush of personal opinions and prejudices. What I had in mind rather by "new" was something that gives one a sense, whether remote or vivid, of that constant organic flow going on in all life, the outward form of which may appear quite different to different men.

At times like these one senses—more or less vaguely perhaps—that the mode of work, manner, perhaps idiom, through which he has worked [up] to that time are becoming less sustaining; they do not seem to carry him along in the way they did. He cannot use the former progressions, cadences, tonal relations, tonalities, rhythms, and the like, with the sense of satisfaction of earlier days. It may be a fault or it may not (as one is constituted) that changes of this nature come to one. But the changing attitude does not and should not necessarily mean any loss of respect or appreciation for the "old" (either in music in general or in his own). It may be rather a process in which the nature of the old is germinating. That the existence of feelings of this kind is quite common may be one of the outward signs of the inward process of creative evolution of art in general. The foregoing is but an attempt to describe a process and not to estimate the value or lack of value of its results. The nature of art itself and the sands of time may be stronger contributing factors in estimating value or finding proofs of worthlessness than a composer likes to think.

However, the fact that some such experience of feeling comes to men gives everyone a right to hope that different and broadening ways may come to him, some of which may develop into something of value at

14 This paragraph starting "I hesitate . . ." was in neither the sketches nor the first carbon.

least to him—something which he instinctively senses helps him get closer to his ideals. If anything of value to him (and possibly to others, though the latter is none of the composer's business)[15] is developed in this way, it will probably be in a process somewhat slower and somewhat more natural than is generally thought—and in the completion will, in part, point to something higher.

If idioms are more to be born than to be selected, then the things of life and human nature that a man has grown up with—(not that one man's experience is better than another's, but that it is "his")—may give him something better in his substance and manner than an over-long period of superimposed idiomatic education which quite likely doesn't fit his constitution. My father used to say, "If a poet knows more about a horse than he does about heaven, he might better stick to the horse, and some day the horse may carry him into heaven."

I did not intend to write such a long letter when I started—nor is it with the intent that it may be published—but your interesting questions brought me to set down several things that I have had in mind for some time. If you should be interested in further observations along these lines, there are some in the last chapter of the book, *Essays,* but these were written some fifteen years ago, and I cannot agree with them all today.

I have not the exact dates and names, but there have been articles in: *Musicalia,* Havana, Cuba, December 1928 and April 1929[16]—*The Art Magazine* of Chicago, August 1928[17]—*The Double Dealer,* New Orleans, October 1921[18]—*Russky Golos,* February 23, 1930 (copy of an article from a Moscow journal)[19]—a recent issue of *Melos,* Berlin.[20] There are a few others which I have not seen but will be glad to send if I do. In the book, *New Resources in Music* by Henry Cowell (Knopf & Co., New York [1930]), there are references to my work.

---

[15] Ives added this parenthesis down the right margin of the final carbon.
[16] *Musicalia,* Año 1, Num. 4, Noviembre–Diciembre 1928, pp. 124–27—Henry Cowell, *Compositores Modernos de Los Estados Unidos.* The only mention of Ives in Año 1, Num. 6, Marzo–Abril 1929, is in the page of *Publicaciones recibidas* (p. 230): "Charles Ives: 114 canciones. Ives & Myrick, 46 Cedar Street, New York.—50 canciones. Id. id. —'Pot-pourri' from Scherzo. (Primera sonata para piano).—'Emerson'. (Cuatro transcripciones del primer tempo de la segunda sonata para piano).—Sonata núm. 1 para violín y piano."
[17] *The Aesthete Magazine,* Chicago, Vol. 1, No. 3, August 1928, pp. 1 & 19–20—Henry Cowell *Four Little Known Modern Composers* [Ives, Chavez, Slonimsky, Weiss].
[18] On pp. 166–69, Henry Bellamann's review entitled *"Concord, Mass., 1840–60"* (a *Piano Sonata by Charles Ives*).
[19] *Who Are the American Composers?* by Henry Cowell—among Ives's papers are several copies of a printed retranslation from the Russian (not Cowell's original text).
[20] Ives is probably referring to an article by Henry Cowell which *Melos* must have already accepted, and which appeared as *Bericht aus Amerika* in three issues of August–September, October, and December 1930, Ives and Ruggles being discussed in the second installment.

I hope what I am sending will not take up too much of your time. The work you are undertaking is an extensive one, and I don't want to add to your difficulties.

I am, with best wishes,

Sincerely yours,
[Chas. E. Ives.]

Ode to a Music Critic[1]

(Lecture in a Girls' School for ole Ladies,
by which the Lecturer lost his Job.)

A nice man with a lily in his coat and a little satchel of samples in his head—from the album which fell out of the old piano when Jenny first opened[2] ("A Choice Collection of Celebrated Pieces for the Piano") and others—in the evening the nice man goes to a nice concert. He doesn't pay to go in (he doesn't have to), he is paid to go in—he is also paid to go out. In some cases he would have heard the concert better if he had gone to the prayer meeting instead,[3] because as soon as the concert begins he snatches up that little satchel just so quick that it makes the other critic next to him almost stop talking.

In most of the concerts he goes into and out of (about 99 out of 98), he can sort [them] right out from his little nest of samples. Then he leans back quite relieved, as he doesn't have to open his ears but little if his satchel is open. But gracious, girls!—how fussy and bothered he does get when he can't find anything in the concert that's in his samples. He starts to look around and tap his foot, and begins to complain. And he is some complainer, believe me, Gertie. He is jest like a great aunt of mine who had complainin' down so fine that she got to be considered the best complainer in the county.[4] Once her two grand nieces,

all out of breath, came in to hear her, and she says, "O children, I certainly have a complaint today—I ain't got an'thing to complain

1 This "Ode" is on four small leaves from a pad of linen-finish note paper, with no date nor any indication relating it to the *Memos* except by analogy with §56. It seems not to be a portrait of any one man, but a composite of the point of view, with individual details.
2 Jenny Lind's American debut in 1850 was one of the managerial triumphs of P. T. Barnum (1810–91), who was born in Bethel and would have been remembered by the old timers when Ives was a boy.
3 This comparison is typical of the way Ives always regarded "the music" as being the character of the idea or spirit, quite apart from its embodiment in sound. See §53, end of the second paragraph—also section 5 of the *Epilogue* of the *Essays Before a Sonata:* "My God! what has sound got to do with music!"
4 Might the complaining great aunt be Jemima Nichols (App. 7, after note 14)?

about." "O Auntie," said the dear children, "and we walked all the way down from New Fairfield just to hear you."[5]

Sometimes he doesn't get cross when he hears something he can't find in his satchel, if somebody or a newspaper in some nice European city has O.K'd the strange sound—for he doesn't have to bother much to listen, he just stamps [it] K.O. and puts it among his samples. But

p.4
if the fellow across his own street[6] makes a strange sound—for instance like a rainbow or a reaper[7]—and it isn't O.K'd by Censor Emanuensis or Mrs. Second Vice-President of the Ladies' Symfrolic Orchestra Committee—he gets all "snipped up" again, he fusses through the satchel— Mercy, Grace!—it isn't in his samples—he is at last in a tight box,[8] he must use his ears and his brains pretty hard—or just write about this man's bald head.[9] But you see,—George he hasn't used his ears or his wits or his fist or anything that is his in so long a time that he jest has to write about the bald head. And he does that real nice! (and knot about the music!)

p.5
George, the nice man and subject of the above poem, said to the poet something this way: "There is one thing I am, if I'm nothin' else— I am frank. I make a specialty of frankness. I am frank from 9:30 A.M. to 6:15 P.M. daily, 9 to 12 Saturdays and Sundays. Now in my trade of paid-listening and opinion-making and selling, it isn't (as might be slightly inferred from your poem) that I have no ears or wits—it's simply that I don't think it expedient to use them except in connection with my sample satchel and O.K's, and then only 'moderate.'

p.6
"You see, onct I got in wrong somethin' awful a-umpiring a baseball game. I seemed to get the base hits and foul balls all mixed up. I got tired of receiving bottles, so I decided not to yell fair or foul, but just chase the small boys away from third base every time a hit was made. No more bottles—I'd made a hit.

p.7
"I say—if a man hasn't had no experience except in 'one syllables,' he'd better not try to listen to a story in two syllables—he simply will get all bored. And if he's goin' to try to tell someone about the story, he'd better just stick to the first syllables and forget the rest. Of course

5 New Fairfield is five miles north of Danbury.
6 In the fall of 1926 Ives bought the house at 164 East 74th Street, New York, across from the Mannes School of Music at No. 157 (see §47, before note 16). Clara Damrosch Mannes was Walter Damrosch's sister. At one time Edith was taking piano lessons there.
7 For the rainbow see App. 3, #28. For the reaper see §9, note 11.
8 A "tight box" sounds as if it might be a baseball term from Ives's youth, no longer in use—perhaps either for a pitcher with three men on bases (if he walks the next batter the man on third scores a run), or for a batter with two strikes (third strike and he's out).
9 Ives still had a fair crop of hair in the wedding-party picture of 1908, but was completely bald in the passport picture of 1924.

the other fellow won't get much of the story—but what's the difference?
—I don't get in wrong so much this way—and even if I do, nobody does
much about [it]. There's going to be a concert tomorrow—I'm there,
Ed, with the slick stuff.

p.8

"I remember one Christmas my old grandfather called me to his
knee and said, 'George, if you only knew jest a leetle bit more, you'd be
half-witted.' I look back on that moment with real pride, and think of
the intelligence I have inherited."

(The foregoing is an Ode to a music critic!—and a nice God Damn!)

George Edward Ives (1845–1894)
and his family

It was already a distinguished family in England when William Ives (c.1607–c.1647) sailed to Boston on the "Truelove" in 1635, and was one of the founders of New Haven in 1638. His son John (1644–81) moved up to Wallingford about 1668. His son John (1669–1747) married Mary Gillett and settled in Meriden. His son John (1694–1745) married Hannah Royce. His son John (1729–1816) married Mary Hall, daughter of Dr. Isaac Hall and Mary Moss, and fought in the Revolution.

His son Isaac (1764–1845), Yale '85, came to Danbury and married Jerusha Benedict (1772–95), and when she died he married Sarah Amelia White (1773–1851), daughter of Joseph Moss White (1741–1822) and Rachel Booth. Both these girls were from old Danbury families. Sarah's brother Ephraim Moss White (1775–1863) married Charity Tucker, whose father had one of the many houses built shortly after the British burned Danbury in 1777. A big pear tree had survived the fire, and the new house was built around it, so that for over a century, no matter who lived there, the old pear tree was almost a member of the family. Isaac bought this house in 1829, and it was home to the next four generations. A kind of jack-of-all-trades, he was active for some years in a New York branch of the Danbury hatting business.

His son George White Ives (1798–1862), born in New York, was one of the most prominent Danbury business men, an independent thinker, leader in all kinds of civic projects, the founding Secretary-Treasurer in 1849 of the Danbury Savings Bank, whose first office was a wooden chest in his dining room, the second office his desk (recently given by Bigelow Ives to the Danbury Scott-Fanton Museum to be restored again to the Ives House). In 1831 he married Sarah Hotchkiss Wilcox (1808–99) a schoolteacher and Emerson-enthusiast from Killingworth, Conn. She must have been paradoxical, being variously remembered as "severe and forbidding" or "full of humor"—for Ives's regard for his grandparents see §15, before note 10. They had five children: Joseph Moss ("Uncle Joe," 1832–1908), Isaac Wilcox ("Uncle Ike," 1835–1910), Sarah Amelia ("Aunt Amelia," 1837–1918), Sarane Elizabeth (1843–45), and George Edward (1845–94).

Joe was sent to Yale, but after a prank of silencing the morning bell, his father took him out of college and put him in business, first in Boston (where he appears in the 1856 directory as "Ives (*Joseph M.*) & Tuthill (*George*), hatters"). At Boston he met Emerson and Lowell, who were his guests later at Danbury. In 1859 he married his second cousin Amelia White Merritt (1835–62), and they had one son Howard Merritt Ives ("Cousin Howdie," 1860–94), who married Anna Wood Miner (1857–1942) and had two sons and a daughter, now Mrs. Van Wyck.

Isaac was a visionary promoter, and made and lost several fortunes. He married Emily Keeler in 1863, and had one son, George Forrester Ives ("Cousin George," 1864–1923), who became prominent in the antique business, the sale of his collection being quite a public event.

Amelia wanted to marry Joe's brother-in-law Jacob Merritt (1837–71), but wasn't allowed to, because her father suspected the Merritts of a tendency toward mental problems. It was only after Jacob married Sarah Cooley ("Sally") in 1867 that Amelia married Lyman Brewster (see App. 17) and went to live in the Brewster house. Jacob soon died, after a term in a mental clinic, and Joe (whose wife had died in 1862) married Sally in 1875.

George showed musical talent at an early age. Mrs. Van Wyck has told the story of how, after music lessons had been wasted on Joe and Isaac and Amelia, who had no talent, their father didn't waste them on George too—but, on a Fourth of July, he wanted to stay home from the picnic because he had a chance to earn some money to buy a flute—so their father quickly changed his mind. In August 1860 he was sent to study with Carl Foeppl (or Foepple?), a German musician who had a small farm in Morrisania, in the Bronx. George's notebooks of study in music and German (old script) and his music copybook are in the Ives Collection at Yale and show a thorough grounding, particularly in Bach. The copybook has pages of exercises in harmony (figured), counterpoint, and fugue—many Bach chorales (figured), two movements of *Jesu meine Freude*—parts of baroque masses, opera scenes of Gluck and Mozart, etc.—and marches and dance tunes—all in George's hand. It would be good to know more about Foeppl—if he might have contributed in any degree to the Ives tradition of experiment.[1] Apparently George went to New York Saturdays for cornet lessons with a Mr. Schreiber, and for the Philharmonic concerts. It must have meant a lot, at his age, to meet Stephen Foster.

The notebooks continue steadily to May 9, 1862. In that year, Col. Nelson White (his father's first cousin) suggested that George organize a band for his regiment, the First Connecticut Heavy Artillery. The band was recruited from Connecticut, half German, and enlisted in November, George being the youngest Union Bandmaster. Their picture survives, taken near Richmond. Several official communications are among the family papers, and it is hard to remember that the deference and respect shown in them is to a boy of 17 and 18. In April 1864 he was home on furlough. Beside being a thorough musician, George inspired his men's interest, and the story goes that Grant told Lincoln: "It's the best band in the army, they tell me." (See §12, note 5.)

George was discharged on 25 September 1865, perhaps already ill—a retrospective notebook entry of Wednesday 11 March 1868 reads: "A space of three years servitude as Leader . . . and one year sick, from Sept/'62 to Sept/'66   In New York at last date   Took three lessons of Mr. F. at 17 Chrysty St. on or about Dec/'66 into '67   Been boarding at Mr. F's in 91st St. since June/'67   AD. 1868, 3rd m. 11th d   rec'd bounty last Sat." He probably finished out the spring with Foeppl, and then returned to Danbury for good.

On a clipping of 1925 about the impending demolition of Steinway Hall, on 14th Street, Ives wrote: "Father played, in a concert here, some time between

---

[1] Foeppl's influence may lurk in variation 3 of the *Variations on America,* where Ives spelled out the grace notes, showing that he liked the sound of graces on the beat but knew that (written as graces) they'd be mis-played before the beat. George Ives must have had this tradition from Foeppl. Compare Brahms's Op. 117/1, where he showed he meant the graces on the beat by spelling out their broadenings at the end.

1868 and 1870, an arrangement of Schubert's *Ave Maria* for French horn and strings. The violins were men from Theodore Thomas's orchestra."

With his talent, training, experience, and charm, he immediately became the center of the musical life of Danbury, and his versatility helped earn a steady if precarious living. An announcement reads: "Geo. E. Ives' POPULAR CONCERT at Concert Hall, Friday Evening, July 2, '69. The following artistes will appear: Miss L. Smith, Prof. C. A. Foepple, Franz Schreiber . . . Chorus of 40 Voices, with Orchestra . . ." This may have been his way of introducing his teachers to Danbury—he and Schreiber in a "Cornet Duett, 'Zephyrs' " by Mollenhauer—and at the bottom of the program: "Mr. Chas. A. Foepple will preside at the Piano."

For an outline of his strenuous life see App. 11. He also trained bands in other nearby towns. Ives told a story of the Danbury orchestra committee thinking they ought to hire a certain conductor from New York—when he came, he asked to hear what they had been doing, so George put them through a reading of Mozart's G minor symphony—and he told the committee that the orchestra was in excellent hands and they had no need of him.

On New Year's Day 1874, George married Mary Elizabeth Parmelee (1849–1929), daughter of Noah David Parmelee, a farmer in Bethel (adjoining Danbury to the southeast), and Mary Ann Smith, a locally prominent choir singer. Charles Edward was born that October, and Joseph Moss II in February 1876. When Moss was just a baby, George used to practice violin in the barn up the lane (now Chapel Place) and take Charlie with him, who would sit in the buggy and wave the whip in time with the music. Later their mother's nephews, Paul and Sam Parmelee, to whom she was "Aunt Mollie," were among their playmates.

In later years Ives talked and wrote so devotedly about his father that one tends hardly to notice his mother. Though unimaginative beyond household duties, she was a small but intense focus of energy and determination. The story is still told of her wanting to take a train to New York from Brewster (8 miles west of Danbury), where it wasn't scheduled to stop—so she flagged it and it stopped.

In 1878 Lyman Brewster's mother died, and Aunt Amelia wanted to move back into the old Ives house. So in 1879 Joe and his family moved out to 368 Main Street, and George and his family to 16 Stevens Street, and Uncle Lyman and Aunt Amelia moved in. Isaac already lived at another address. There was also another Ives family in Danbury, Joseph H. Ives, the florist, but Aunt Amelia used to insist he was no relation, though his grandfather Othniel was her grandfather Isaac's own brother.

As Charlie and Mossie grew up, one of their greatest delights was finding that their father had never outgrown the capacity to enjoy things the way they did. As Ives wrote years later, they used to play train, about 1884—"the Ives Bros. R.R. under the clothes line . . . two barrels on the wash bench, an old stove pipe and the dinner bell . . . the cab was part of a chicken coop . . . Father always entered into it seriously . . . and would just wave and never stop to talk while the train was going full blast. At that time I remember he was practising the violin . . . father discovered that staccato passages and arpeggios could be made to sound like the clicking of the car wheels. . . . So he . . . rode in the rear passenger car for whole trips . . . the noise of the wheels always stopped at the stations. . . ."

Starting in 1885 they played grocery store, which got more and more elaborate (see §2, note 2)—printed letterhead—bills solemnly presented to their grandmother—culminating in an account book with one page (December 1890) in the hand of their father, who had begun to supplement his musical earnings with accounting, as assistant to his nephew Howard, in the office of Charles H. Merritt's hat factory. Here too he was an independent. Philip Sunderland (who also worked for Merritt from 1888) tells of a bridge being built next the office, and of Merritt busily showing them how to do everything, and of George Ives looking out the window at him and muttering: "There you are, you damned old monopolist—you have to tell them how to build a bridge!"

On Sunday 10 February 1889 Charlie started as the regular organist at the 2nd Congregational Church (now the Lutheran Church)—the youngest organist in the state. His diary adds: "Mossie pump" (that is, Moss served as blow-boy).

In May 1889, George and his family moved to 10 Chapel Place, a house rebuilt from the barn up in back of the old house—the music room being downstairs about where the buggy used to be. They fitted the square piano with a dummy pedal keyboard from an old organ, so that Charlie could practice pedal technique.

In 1891 Moss and two other boys started a school paper first called *The New Street Weekly*, each issue a single leaf mimeographed on both sides, Vol. 1, No. 3 dated February 15, 1891. The next year it became *The New Street Monthly*, a printed double leaf, Vol. 1, No. 1 dated March 1, 1892. Vol. 1, No 2 (April 1) reports: "A number of boys have left New St. for the Academy, since it was opened" (one was Charlie, another Sam Parmelee)—and this issue has a long, well-written editorial, *A Historical Sketch of the Schools of Danbury*. Next fall it was rechristened again as *The High School Chronicle,* but continued the old Vol. 1 throughout the school year. All this time it covered local athletics with frequent mention of Charlie. By the "Commencement Number" of June 1895 (Vol. 3, No. 8) it had grown to twelve pages with cover, Moss contributing an *Au Revoir* as outgoing editor in chief.

On Sunday 4 November 1894, George Ives died very unexpectedly of a stroke, shortly before midnight. Scattered through these *Memos* are better descriptions of him as man, musician, and teacher than anyone else could write. The Danbury News said: "His personality was so bright, so genial as to cast a gloom over the community by its removal."

For Charlie, it was Griggs who came nearest to filling the void (see §45 and App. 15). For Moss, it was Uncle Lyman, who apparently continued his law apprentice's education so well that Moss, after his one year 1898–99 at the Yale Law School, graduated LL.B. and was admitted to the Connecticut bar. He immediately started law practice in a succession of Danbury firms, first Brewster, Davis & Ives—then after Uncle Lyman died in 1904: Tweedy & Ives, Ives & Keating, and Ives & Sherwood. In this field his achievements paralleled those of Ives & Myrick in insurance (see App. 18)—Representative for Danbury in General Assembly 1905, Prosecuting Attorney 1907–10, Major and Judge Advocate in Conn. National Guard 1915–1916, Adjutant General Conn. State Guard 1917–18, Judge of City Court 1917–26, Judge of Traffic Court, 1929–33, trustee of many charitable institutions, LL.D. 1934 Loyola College.

In December 1900 he married Minnie Louisa Goodman (1878–1963) at Worcester, Mass. They had six children: Richard (Yale '25), Brewster (Univ. of Pa. '27), Moss White, Bigelow (Univ. of Pa. '31), Chester, and Sarane (1914–56, Mrs. Arthur E. Hall).

After Uncle Lyman died, Mollie's sister, Miss Lucy Cornelia Parmelee ("Aunt Nell," 1852–1939) came to live with Aunt Amelia in the old house. And when Aunt Amelia died in 1918, she bequeathed a lifetime use of the house to Aunt Nell, who was joined by Mollie and by Mrs. Abbott Foster, née Sarah White (Col. Nelson White's daughter, "Cousin Sazy").

When the Danbury National Bank (now the Fairfield County Trust Co.) acquired the site of the old house in 1923, everyone assumed it would be razed, but Ives insisted it be moved uphill on Chapel Place. He asked Philip Sunderland to take charge, gave him a large check, and told him to ask for more if needed, and to "take good care of Mother," who stayed in the house while it was being moved.

One of the major contributions from the Ives family to posterity is Moss's book *The Ark and the Dove* (two small ships that crossed the Atlantic in 1633)— showing that the predominantly Roman Catholic colony in Maryland, under the Calverts (the Lords Baltimore) and the Carrolls, was the true cradle of American religious tolerance and freedom of worship, in contrast to the narrowly bigoted Puritans. Published in January 1936, it was well received. Next month he wrote: "Dear Harmony, Mr. Dunham, the new minister, has announced that he is going to preach a sermon on *The Ark and the Dove* next Sunday. I simply cannot hear my own book preached about any more than Charlie can listen to his own music played. I would be so nervous that I couldn't sit up straight. . . . Would it be convenient for me to spend Sunday with you and go to church with you? . . . Had a good review in the Baltimore Sun the other day. Hastily, Moss. . . . Tell Charlie that Roy Andrews, the catcher of the Alerts, asked for him today."

On Good Friday 7 April 1939, Moss died, like his father, of a sudden, unexpected stroke. Thereafter Minnie and some of her family lived in the old house until she died in 1963. Again the site of the house was needed by the bank, which bought it in 1964 but was patient until 1966, when it was finally moved to Rogers Park as an adjunct to the Scott-Fanton Museum. Damage from a fire in October 1968 was repaired the next year. At that time the city of Danbury decided to build the new junior high school in Rogers Park, and the Ives house was moved again to the edge of the park, where it is the first unit in a group of old houses to be assembled by the Scott-Fanton Museum as a replica of a typical village green.

All his life Ives remained gratefully aware of what he had received as heritage, training, and traditions. Some time after he died, Mrs. Ives was telling about the older generations and added, "Of course I never knew any of these people, but the amount I can tell you just shows how much he talked about them." Another time she recalled that every now and then he'd exclaim, "How I want to see Father again!"

Henry Anderson Brooks (c. 1855–1906?)

Ives's statement that Brooks "became a revered and respected teacher in Hampton College" can hardly be true, and requires a brief outline of Brooks's life as revealed by documents at hand. Even though Ives never knew him, such idealization shows Brooks's importance in the family traditions.

He was born about 1855 at Chesterfield (or in Chesterfield County, some twenty miles south of Richmond), his parents being slaves of a Mr. Chalkley. When George Ives's band was stationed at Drewry's Bluff, Mrs. Brooks did their laundry and little Anderson liked to listen to the band rehearse, as told in §15. George wrote his mother on 26 June 1865: "I've got a little Darkie working for me now 'as is a Dark.' I should like to bring him home if you could use him. He is a worker and honest."

Among the Ives family papers are thirty-three letters from Brooks, mostly to George's mother, the earliest being 31 January 1869, from Chesterfield: "Your letter gave me a great deal of pleasure. And your paper had better [news] than I have read since I left D[anbury] . . . there is little work . . . we send much love to you all." After this, he presumably returned to Danbury.

Then there are eight letters, December 1872–September 1875, from 1566 Broad St., Richmond, where he lived with his aunt, Mrs. Graves. [In presenting parts of Brooks's letters, it may seem unfair to leave his spelling unedited after correcting Ives's usual "dosen't"—but the purpose is to show Brooks's rather high average, in its possible relation to the Hampton faculty.] 29 December 1872, to George: "I have spent all Christmas in Richmond, a place where I have not been in a Christmas for fourteen years . . . . Please write soon to this Once a Contraband." 7 January 1874: "I have had Mr. George's picture framed . . . I am very sorry I did not know Mr. George was going to get married . . . I often think of the nice times I used to have in Danbury." 11 October 1874: "I am under many obligations to you for your offer to me . . . I came from the country about two years ago, and now I am trying to learn the Dyer's trade." 23 December 1874: "I have been very sick with the neuraldga . . . I had business in Hampton on the second Tuesday in December . . . and was gone four days . . . I was quite unwell at the time . . . I would not have gone down there, but the Temperance and Benevolent Society, of which I am a member, sent me as a delegate . . . When the box came in this morning, the Dr. said that would do me more good than all of his physic." 27 September 1875: "I leave for School next Thursday morning 30th."

Then there are eight letters, October 1875–May 1876, from Hampton, where he is in the preparatory class, and does some outside work in cleaning. He gives a lively picture of the school year. 1 December: "Thanksgiving . . . dinner was highly appreciated . . . I carved three geese for the first time in my life . . . our brass band furnished music for the evening (of which I am a member). . . . My health is a great deal better . . . The young man I wrote you was from Conn. . . . a Mr. Foster of Meriden is paying his school expences, as you are paying mine . . ." 13 March: "Our Principal works very earnestly to make our young men what they aught to be . . . one of my classmates told me he never read any in the Bible until he came here . . . I am thinking all the while I am reading how you used to read and explained that part of the Scriptures to me." 24 May: "My uncle has been writing for me . . . to come and work for him during vacation . . . I know I can learn a great deal more about dyeing and cleaning. . . ."

Mid-July 1876, from Richmond: "Work has been very dull, and my uncle has had very little to do . . . have gone back to my old trade for the present. I am coopering with my brother and expect to continue until the 1st of Sept." 12 September: "Work . . . is brightning up a little in our Dyeing business as fall approaches . . . as I have only made a start, I would like very much to return in October. . . ."

Four letters from Hampton, November 1876–May 1877, describe his junior year and his modest earnings from cleaning and dyeing. The letter of 28 December reports that "last week" the house his mother was living in at Chesterfield burned down. 28 May: "School will close in less than three weeks . . . I do not know exactly what I shall work at this summer, yet I expect to go home and see what I can get to do in Richmond." After this June, the Hampton Institute archives have no further record of Brooks.

Then there are nine letters, July 1877–February 1879, from 1566 Broad St., Richmond. 11 July 1877: "I have just returned from the country (Chesterfield) where I had been nearly two weeks working at harvesting . . . One of my uncles . . . has put up a house . . . I worked upon it with him. . . . I spent the 4th . . . visiting a public school . . . taught by a young man who has been to Richmond Institute . . . he asked me to say something to amuse the children. After I had started, I found it not very hard work, as they were very quiet and attentive." 3 September 1877: "Every since I was so very sick nearly three years ago, I have been troubled with a slight swelling in my face . . . now it has moved down into my under lip, consequently I can't articulate very well . . . So I ask your advice about going to School . . . I would be very glad to go. . . ." 4 September 1877: 'Your kind letter . . . reached me this morning . . . I gave some reasons for wanting to stay out a term, although I would rather go. . . . I have been coopering nearly all summer . . . I visited one or two schools in the country taught by colord teachers. One said he thought I could get a situation out there, but I declined as I am trouble in my speech. . . ." 14 September 1877, Mr. Chalkley ("the gentleman to whom I used to belong") suggested his taking an examination for public school teaching, but agreed that returning to Hampton would be better, and would try to get him a County Scholarship—only to find that he was ineligible, being over 21.

December 1877: "My evening school, I am sorry to say, is a failure; my room is occupied by my uncle who has just returned from Chicago . . . with a deep cold which has settled on his lungs. . . ." He doesn't say whether the "evening school" was simply his own studying—or perhaps teaching a few children in his own room.

14 February 1878: "Tuesday I visited the school at Half Way Station, which is being taught by a young minister who has charge of the church to which I belong . . . we were finally interrupted by a little girl . . . saying 'Mr. Brown, here is a cent I found on the playground, I think it belong to some of the children.' I asked him wasn't that an unusual occurance; he said no . . . he feels much encouraged . . . and regrets very much that he will have to close on the 26th inst., or rather his school term expires then." 4 March 1878: "I walked down home about thirteen miles in Chesterfield to attend the closeing exercises of the school I wrote about

. . . The barrel contained every thing that is useful. I send special thanks for the suit, as it is the first one I have ever owned just alike. . . . My health is tolerably good." 26 March 1878: "The boots I can wear very comfortably . . . they will be needed . . . if I will be able to go back to Hampton to school, and my cheek will have gotten better of the 'Paralysis' which impairs my speech . . . which I am afraid will render me very unsuccessful as a teacher."

19 February [1879?]: "I have been suffering very much with the Nuraligia and pain in my eyes . . . one side of my face is swoled . . . I do not think it would be any improvement to my health to go to School untill I get much better than I am at present, as I caught a very severe cold when I went down there in Dec. last . . . I have not heard from the Superendent of the Hampton School yet . . . Mother & all sends much love to Mr. Geo. Ives, and all the family."

After this, there is only a postcard to J. M. Ives Esq. ("Uncle Joe") from Manchester, 8 September 1890: "The barrel came all safe . . . please accept many thanks for your kindness." Manchester was then a small area south of the river, which was not included in the Richmond city directories until 1898. Those of 1898–1906 list Henry A. Brooks as a dyer, but not after 1906. He may have taught for a while at some country school, but if so he would certainly have taken great pleasure in writing the Ives family about such a fulfillment.

John Cornelius Griggs (1865–1932)

Only nine years older than Ives, Griggs was born September 29, 1865, at Spring Valley, Minnesota, where his father was pastor of a Home Missionary Church. Before his schooling the family moved to Connecticut. After grade school at Terryville and two years at work, he entered the Hartford High School, and graduated in 1885. At Yale he concentrated in Modern History, Physics, and Philosophy, but was also very active in music. Gifted with a superb baritone voice, he sang in both Glee Club and College Choir, and went to New York for voice lessons with Herbert Greene at the Metropolitan College of Music on 14th Street. On the strength of an essay on *The Literary Work of Richard Wagner* he became editor of the *Yale Literary Magazine*. Graduating A.B. '89, he taught for two years at the Norwich Free Academy (the family then living at Ivoryton), and again he went to the Metropolitan College of Music, but now to teach. In 1890 he married Anne Cooke of Hartford.

By this time it was clear that music was his vocation. Feeling the need of a scholarly musical background and a further degree, he borrowed $3000 from a New Haven philanthropist, a Mr. Lord, and sailed for Germany. At the University of Leipzig, he studied principally with Oscar Paul, Kretzschmar, and Wiedemann —Ph.D. '93, magna cum laude.

From Leipzig he sent three articles to *The Congregationalist* (Boston) on "The Church Choir: 1. Its History.—2. Its Needs.—3. Its Possibilities."—and one article to *Music* (Chicago) on "The tempered system of tuning and the recent attempts to produce keyed instruments of pure intonation." Parts of these are evident in his dissertation, *Studien über die Musik in Amerika,* a balanced, long-range survey that still offers food for thought. (Thanks are due to his son, Robert W. Griggs, for loan of the original manuscript in English; the German translation was printed by Breitkopf & Härtel in 1894.)

The Introduction points out "the great musical advantages which wealth and free communication with the old world have so suddenly brought to America. And just here lie the great questions about America's music today. Many of her friends both at home and abroad quite seriously doubt the promise of real progress, saying that the practical and ever hurrying mind of the American affords no deep soil in which art growth can be made . . . such doubters lay little weight to the . . . hundred or more American music students who may be found at any time in Leipzig for instance. . . . When the case in hand is of a young composer, [they] make his German education itself a reproach to him, as having nothing in it which will assimilate with American life. . . . Another class of talkers . . . clamor for the immediate appearance and recognition of a school of American composition."

The Conclusion returns to this question: "If musical composition does develop . . . it will not be hampered by the traditions of any one country or school, for

America has received, and is receiving, impulse from many countries. . . . But this very breadth of outlook, and the lack of any musical history of importance, are the two great reasons why American music cannot, for the present, have any distinctive national character." And he quotes Charles Dudley Warner to the effect that American literature will be "clearer and stronger as we drop the self-conscious . . . necessity of being American."

Though referring several times to Frédéric Louis Ritter's *Music in America* (Scribner 1883), he relies more on primary sources and on his own experience. "The writer will never forget that first glimpse of a new world which came with the first hearing of a [Theodore] Thomas symphony concert."

"The choir in American non-liturgical churches . . . represents the people and in no manner represents the priesthood or any other specially ordained class."

"An interesting indication [of the results of the paid-quartet system] is the formation of such societies as the Gounod Club in New Haven [1887] . . . limited to thirty . . . experienced solo or quartet singers . . . all accustomed to singing with careful regard to expression, to articulation . . . niceties of shading. . . . Works of Palestrina . . . of Bach . . . are given with a finish and fidelity to the composer's ideas impossible to a large chorus."

"It is a great question whether the facility in obtaining a little pleasing music which the piano has given to the people at large will eventually prove helpful or otherwise. . . . The tempered system at its best is not conducive to correct and vigorous musical thinking, as has been the violin and voice training of earlier centuries. . . . It is a question applying to the whole musical world. . . . But accurate hearing and thinking are necessary to musical composition. Von Bülow, in his letter of recommendation of the Tanaka pure-tone organ, expresses himself very strongly about the foolishness and falsity of the composer who has derived his only notions of chords from hearing them played on a tempered piano. . . . With this question . . . is involved a large part of the uncertainty about independent progress . . . for the people of the United States, with their freedom from traditional means for musical education, are now receiving a greater part of their musical experience through the medium of keyed instruments than are any other people."

In August 1893, Griggs returned to the States as Professor of Music History and Singing at the Metropolitan College, and in the fall of 1894 was engaged as choir-master and baritone soloist at Center Church, New Haven, at the same time that Ives was engaged as organist. Right from the start, Ives must have seemed to Griggs to fulfil some of the hopes implied in his dissertation. Then Ives's father died, and what Griggs came to mean to him may be seen below in the letter-sketch of 1930.

In 1895–96, at Yale Divinity School, Griggs gave a series of lectures on church music, two of which Ives helped illustrate with accompaniments and organ pieces. Griggs's notebook of the music in the services at Center Church from 20 September 1896 through 31 January and from Easter 18 April through 2 May 1897 (given to the Ives Collection by his daughter, Mrs. Charles Levy), contains a few indications of preludes and postludes in Ives's hand, but no mention of his own music. Here, as in Ives's similar Danbury notebook of 1889–91, one can only guess when he played something of his own by the dates for which he wrote nothing down.

Scattered through the marginalia on Ives's manuscripts are various later memos about Griggs having sung his music: ascribed to June 1895 is the solo in the anthem version of *The Light That Is Felt*, to June 1896 *The All-Enduring*, to 1897 *Feldeinsamkeit*, to some time in Center Church *Abide With Me*, to some time at Yale *At Parting*, to 1899 (Mendelssohn Glee Club concert in New York—perhaps an encore?) *Grace* (the prototype of *Where the Eagle*), and to November 1902 (informally) a prototype of *Autumn*. And there must have been other times too. Other memos mention Center Church performances of the *Easter Carol* in 1895 [certainly later], in 1896 *Psalm 150,* and in 1898 a lost anthem (prototype of *Walking*). Unfortunately the New Haven news coverage of church music offers hardly any check on these occasions.

From 1897 to 1919, Griggs taught singing at Vassar College, though he lived at Poughkeepsie only from 1906. He continued to be in demand as lecturer and trainer of other singing groups, and to contribute articles to periodicals. The "old friend" to whom Ives played *Emerson* in 1911 or 1912 (see App. 8, note 21) must be Griggs. Their earliest surviving exchange of letters is in May 1916: Griggs hopes to rent the Terryville house for the summer, and Ives has mentioned it to a cousin in real estate—"The fact that you will not be in Terryville is all the more reason why you must come to Redding again this summer. Mrs. Ives and I are counting on another visit."

In Ives's photostat copy of the *First Piano Sonata* is a marginal memo of a conversation about an e♯^{1} (on p. 21 of the Peer edition, in the 5th quarter beat): "I was asked once by Dr. G[riggs], 'Was this E♯ written instead of F♮ because E♯ and F♮ are not (not always) the same notes?' 'Yes' '[They're the same] only in the piano machine.' 'But they *can* be [different] if they are in the thought, and in a certain imaginary way in the ears as such.'"

In February 1919, what Griggs had understood was a promise of tenure at Vassar was withdrawn, and he abruptly resigned. For the next eight years he was head of the English Department in Canton Christian College, later called Lingnan, and it was here that he received Ives's private printing of *Concord* and the *Essays*. Wanting to do his old friend the honor of a thoughtful comment, but being extremely busy, he put it off for two years, and then sent Ives what may be the most significant critique of the *Essays* he ever received. Griggs's copy is now owned by the pianist and Ives-performer, Harvey Hinshaw, and into it is still tucked the sketch of the second half of this letter:

"Canton Christian College, Canton, China

[Saturday] "Aug. 27th, 1921.

"Dear Charlie Ives,

Letters are difficult out here at best, and the hardest to write are those in which one wants to say the most. Many times in the past two years I have purposed writing you but have always procrastinated till some imagined vacation leisure, because you are not such an easy fellow to write to. A man who puts out such a book as *Essays Before a Sonata* is not to be put off with chaff. You may think I am proposing a tremendous blast, but perish the thought. I have been away with Eleanor leading our brass band along the paths of glory, not leading in the directing sense but going along as a sort of chaperone and general encumbrance. Like almost everything in these two years it has been a unique chapter. Today I have been correcting a crazier typed transcript of my crazy account of our trip. Some time when you can't sleep, try to read it.

"We are living in the most convenient little brick and concrete house that was ever made. Our servants do almost everything that any servants could do for one and except for making stand against the heat, these few weeks before college opens next month are pretty idle. I seem to excel in sleeping. I wish you could hear this minute the workmen who are building the house next door sing and whistle Chinese tunes.

"Eleanor has come along a lot with piano, having gained immensely in reading ability. It's a rather lawless progress of course, and I hope will be supplemented with something else later. Meantime it gives us as well as many others a great deal of pleasure.

This is Sunday morning now and I am feeling the relief of no service,—no Sun. School class. Sunday in term time is a riot of Sabbath breaking,—choir, bible study, students calling, Y.M.C.A. alarms, sermons by some visiting brother, Chinese or English. I'm making a lot of good resolutions to cut out some of it this next term and try to honor it as a day of rest but the human heart is desperately wicked and prone to sin and I am fearing that Satan will entangle me. I have been appointed Exploding Secretary of the Anti-Denominational League which has its headquarters at Bunk Bungalow Bankok and a total membership of one-and-his-wife. This is not a very good field here at this non-denominational college, but the work has been greatly blessed in my travels, and I have occasional opportunity to coruscate hereabouts.

"Your 'Emerson' and 'Thoreau' seem to me really fine.—the former one of the most satisfying treatments of the subject I have ever seen. I wish I could talk with you, or rather hear you talk about the whole book. I feel in reading [it] again these past few days that the whole thing is a book that stands on its own legs. I can't think it as 'Before a sonata' or 'Before'—anything else. And here is just the tough point of the 'Prologue,' tough because involved in that perennially tough and to me rather unnecessary inquiry which plagues all our music analyses, —the translatableness of music. I have stumbled and bungled over it all my life. You neither stumble nor bungle, but you seem faced in the direction of an ultimate 'translatableness,'—a direction in which I can see no light.—Here's what I think I believe, only I can't say it, and I don't stop to think about it much when music really comes to me.

"Art is a projection into a realm beyond the understandable. As such it is, in the analyses of Lombroso, wrongly entangled with insanity. That's one blind alley we will stop up at the start.

"It is a recognition of the beyond toward which our racial evolution is slowly progressing.

"Its recognitions are accompanied by an elation,—a straining of receptivity.

"We cheapen this by calling it emotion and sometimes enjoy it so much that we stop right there.

"The very essence of life is its boundlessness,—not only a *being* but a projection,—not only an exploration but a striving for greater depths and heights than can be measured in either material or intellect. The actualities of life have always a penumbra of reachings outward. Here are the futilities of philosophy, the futilities of children's play, of our own diversions, the pattern of a piece of lace, perhaps even the mad whirl of the insects. The lure of these futilities is their promise of becoming the actuality of a larger and higher plane of existence. We do not have to wait till a future life to be startled by the unexpected realization of these other actualities, none the less actual when once we have lived them than those we can measure and describe. Man's halting picture of this projected plane is more than imagination,—it is his prophecy.

"Music is preeminent (because of its aloofness from spoken word, material form or temporal thought) in piercing this realm and making of this prophecy a definite super realization, a living experience. Why insist on always turning it back to a review of the understood and past experience,—to the commonplaces of reason and intellect? Why demand that it should be always a review of yesterdays, or even of the impressions which yesterdays have brought? Why limit it to a record of reactions? Reactions, however precious or pleasurable, are no more an end in themselves than is religion, but like religion are a means to a larger life. The stopping at the reaction point is the sensuous with its decadence, or working in the finer medium of the spirit, is the sentimental. Sentimentalism is a spiritual death, sometimes a pleasant and perfumed death but a real arrest of progress on the very stepping stone to things beyond. 'Beyond where?' you say. O you know where, and know just as definitely as you know of yesterday's dinner, for you have been there. We may not be able to describe it to one another but we can speak just as confidently of it, for the experience as glimpsed on the higher plane in music is not vague, but explicit, complete, self substantial, as easy of identification and memory as baldest fact or event and to some of us as precious. Only the attempted translation into the terms of more ordinary fact is vague. The continually tempting and apparently less remote translation into the joy-love-sorrow formulas of emotion are even more vague and unsatisfactory. They start out pretty well, often victimizing composers themselves into using perfectly irrelevant program titles, but resulting, as soon as they are pushed to the least explicitness of detail, in a confusion which makes their value nugatory.

"Thus Spake Zarathustra without knowing much of what he was talking about. Come and take a walk with me down to the river before lunch and see the families living in their little row boats, the buffaloes, the rice, the leaning of the junk sails, the airplanes, the brown legged women almost up to their waists in mud as they set out the waterchestnut plants, and across the river the hills behind the city, the pagodas, the big bamboo victory arches for last evening's celebration of the successful Kwong Sai campaign. Really you couldn't put in a better six months than to come out here and visit us. Why not? If you don't do it now while you and your good wife are young you never will. With many pleasantest recollections and with affectionate remembrances to you both from us all.

Yours as ever   John Griggs."

Ives must have sent him an equally thoughtful acknowledgement, but none has been found among Griggs's papers.

In 1924–25 Griggs took a year's leave of absence, travelling through the States, mostly to solicit funds for the college. As a review of the year, he sent a printed 8-page letter from San Francisco to the many he wanted to thank, Ives's copy being dated "June 16, 1925. Dear Ives people, It's hard to think that we may not whizz back to New York and see you again . . . "

In 1927 Griggs came back to the States for good, and settled in Palo Alto. Early in January 1930 Ives sketched a letter to him, the gist of which is perfectly clear from the sketch:

"Who better deserves the blessings of good health and a peaceful, untroubled old age than you?—that word 'old age' I use quite readily now, since I've begun my 56th year my last birthday (55)—in fact I rather like the sound of it—the sound more than the fact, I guess. You have put into the lives of others 'greater things than you know'—and without trying to—and without knowing it. You remember Dr. Bushnell's *Unconscious Influence*?—every time we read it, you are always standing around som[ewhere].

"I don't know as you remember, but when I came to Center Church, under and with you, my father had just died. I went around looking and looking for some man to sort of help fill up that awful vacuum I was carrying around with me—the men among my classmates—the tutors program, etc.—and a kind of idea that Parker might—but he didn't—I think he made it worse—his mind and his heart were never around together. You didn't try to superimpose any law on me, or admonish me, or advise me, or boss me, or say very much—but there you were, and there you are now. I didn't show how or what I felt— I never seem to know how—except some[times] when I get sort of mad. I long to see you again, and so does Mrs. Ives. I hope you and Mrs. Griggs will come east soon and make us a good long visit.

"Mrs. Ives and Edie are well and having a fine time together this Christmas vacation. Edie entered Farmington last fall. She likes it very much, especially the coming home part (she says). She seems to enjoy staying home—she reads and writes and sings and draws all day contentedly. The few dances and parties she has to go to, she takes quite philosophically, apparently with a natural contentment. She is a very satisfactory person. No child has ever given her family more than she has us—and she is quite often very amusing. Just now she feels the delusion of the intelligence test, and this afternoon she has been occupied with making some—they are quite funny—enclosed is one of them."

Shortly after this Griggs suffered a stroke, which had the strange effect of drawing a veil over his musicality. Having always enjoyed a hobby of woodwork, he now maintained that he missed it more than music—that music seemed to have passed like a dream. He died in Palo Alto on July 20, 1932.

Joseph Hopkins Twichell (1838–1918)

Since a good biography has recently appeared by Prof. Leah A. Strong (Univ. of Georgia Press 1966), with a perceptive discussion of Twichell's influence on Mark Twain, the present outline is merely a framework to link together a few documents concerning Ives.

Twichell was born at Southington (22 miles north of New Haven) on May 27, 1838, the son of Deacon Edward Twichell (1810–63, whose ancestor Joseph Twichell was one of the founders of Hartford) and Selina Delight Carter. It was a family of free-thinking Congregationalists, and while Joe was still a boy his father took him to hear Dr. Bushnell preach (whom many considered a heretic), because he wanted to find out for himself what Bushnell was like.

At Yale, Twichell did only fairly well, not brilliantly, gathered three prizes in English composition and one in declamation, and stroked the varsity crew. Having intended, while at Yale, to enter the ministry, he enrolled at Union Theological Seminary, New York, and roomed with a classmate at 108 Waverly Place, which soon became a magnet for Yale '59.

The war not only interrupted his theological studies, but disrupted the Waverly Place group, his good friend, Robert Stiles from Georgia, leaving to join the Confederate army, his roommate Edward Carrington losing his life in one of the first skirmishes. Twichell, though not yet ordained, enlisted as chaplain of the 71st New York Volunteers, of whom many were Irish, and most all were tough. Equally broadening was the fact that the other chaplain of the 71st was a Jesuit priest, Father Joseph O'Hagan, but gradually they became devoted friends. From the many tragic necessities in and after battles, and from the constant challenge to manly courage, was developed the preacher who would inspire audiences and congregations.

Mustered out in July 1864 (after his three-year enlistment), and finishing his theological work at Andover in 1865, Twichell was immediately invited, on Bushnell's recommendation, to the pulpit of the new Asylum Hill Church in Hartford. On November 1, 1865, he married Julia Harmony Cushman, cousin of one of his classmates. The growth of the new parish, of his family, of his career as a speaker, and of his close friendship with Mark Twain from 1868 on, is well told in Miss Strong's book. There was something prophetic in the way Ives's last letter to his father, on Monday 29 October 1894, said: "I started a letter Sunday evening to you, but left it before I had finished, to go over to Dwight Hall, as Mullally wanted to have me go with him to hear the Rev. Mr. Twichell of Hartford." (Mandeville Mullally was Ives's roommate all their four years at Yale.)

Twichell's son David was also in Yale '98, and they became close friends. A letter from Dave to Charlie, Tuesday 4 August 1896, gives detailed instructions for two different ways to get to Keene Valley, urging him to start on the 11th. He evidently did, because a telegram from Moss addressed "c/o Rev Dr Twichell" on the 26th says: "Grandmother wants you home. Start Saturday if possible. Nothing serious." This was probably Ives's first visit with the family of his future father-in-law and bride (then often referred to as "Harmony Jr.").

Dave was one of the many who graduated in uniform, having already left to serve in the Spanish-American war. Later on, Dave was one of the inmates of Poverty Flat. In an undated letter, fall 1903, Ives asks Dave "why don't you occasionally write?" In 1905 Ives met Harmony Twichell again, and their long courtship led to many weekend visits in Hartford. In view of this, and of the fondness of the family for him, it is odd that his first appearance in Twichell's rather full diaries is an entry of Sunday 17 November 1907: "Going up into my study in the afternoon, I found Young Harmony and Charley Ives there. In answer to my look of inquiry for the reason of it, they explained that they wanted my 'Blessing'. It was not much of a surprise, for we had been aware of their growing intimacy, and had been pretty sure of the issue to which it was tending. I found later in the day that Charles had already made his confession to H. We have known him a good while: he is a classmate of Dave's who has loved him fondly. We were prepared to sanction the engagement, which seemed to us suitable and auspicious in its promises to us all . . . "

Six days later, Ives wrote Twichell on paper of "Ives & Co. / 51 Liberty Street, New York, N.Y. / 50 State Street, Hartford, Conn."—a letter that Mrs. Ives always kept with her:

Saturday afternoon.

Dear Mr. Twichell

I want to write you, not because I feel it a matter of duty—I know you *understand all*—and only write because I feel, this afternoon, like talking things over with you, though there is nothing that I could say that could tell what I feel. It is impossible and futile for me to try to *write down* or *say* what Harmony means to me. You must know, because you know *her*. She is not only my idol but the reason for all highest and best things that a man could live for.

I have always felt unworthy of her but don't think it best for her to let myself think much about that. I can only keep pounding away at myself until I do know that I deserve all that she has given and done for me, and though it may be years, I feel that, with her help, that day *will* come.

I don't feel, and Harmony doesn't either, as though I'm taking her away from her mother and from you. I like to think, rather, that I happened to be the one appointed to guard and care for her when the time comes that you all cannot; and one of the thoughts that I'm most grateful for is that I seem to have been steered, through all these years, pretty straight down to Harmony—without having any big things to look back over, that I'm ashamed of—though lots of little things—and the whole reason seems to me, more and more clearly, to have been "only through the Grace of God."

But what I wanted to ask and wanted to write you especially for—(for all the rest you must have known and understood or you couldn't have given us your blessing and been so kind and gracious as you were last Sunday; you don't know how happy you made Harmony and you've no idea what a 'do or die' feeling and determination you gave me)—but I want to ask if you will let me come to you, as Dave does when he wants to talk things over and get your advice and encouragement.

Father died just at the time I needed him most. It's been years since I've had an older man that I felt like going to when things seem to go wrong or a something comes up when it's hard to figure out which is the best or right thing to do. I don't mean by that a shifting of responsibility, but I know talking it over with you would clear things up and make it easier to decide.

I hope you'll let me—*Please do*. Whenever you come to New York, if you can conveniently, I hope you'll let me see you if only for lunch or something like that. We should all enjoy having you stop with us at the flat at any time—I think we could make you comfortable. Mr. Wing, I believe, is going to spend a week with us soon.

One of the pleasantest things that Harmony and I have to talk over is that we're going to have a home that her mother and father will always be glad to come to, and a home that will remind everyone who comes into it of the love, faith, and peace that is in our hearts.

Sincerely   Chas. E. Ives

Have just written Harmony but forgot to enclose this about the Jacob Riis house, which she will like to see. Please show it to her. . . .

In May 1908, Ives and his fiancée accompanied Twichell to Storrs, Conn., where he was the Memorial Day speaker. Hardly more than a week later he married them, on Tuesday, June 9th. Their apartment in New York had its door always open to any of the family, as when her parents arrived back in New York from Europe that August. And they continued from time to time to spend weekends at Hartford as before, and many vacations in the Adirondacks, 1908 and '12 at Saranac, 1909–10–11 at Elk Lake (18 miles west of Port Henry), 1915 at Keene Valley.

After his wife died in 1910 (during the night after Mark Twain's funeral), and Twichell determined to retire, it was not until October 1, 1912, that his successor finally took over. The long anticipated "letting go" proved to be mental as well as physical, and he was in a sanatorium at Brattleboro, Vermont, from January 28 to February 24. Mrs. Ives was there all the time—"that was the longest I was ever away from Charlie"—who came up when he could, as recalled in §18 and §37—"Charlie came to get us, I think." After a quiet, steady ebbing, Twichell died on December 20, 1918.

Poverty Flat, 1898–1908

Some time in the 1890s, a group of Yale men studying at the College of Physicians and Surgeons of Columbia University named their domicile in honor of the economic way of life. When Ives joined them in 1898, Poverty Flat consisted of two apartments on the fourth floor of 317 West 58th Street, east and west of the central stairwell, the west side still purely medical, the east side more varied, including Ives. Some of these men became his closest friends, some he knew only slightly or briefly, but all contributed to maintaining islands of Yale enthusiasm in the cosmopolitan sea of New York.

Four men from Yale '97 were already there, in the east side, studying at P. & S.: William Darrach (1876–1948, from Germantown, Pa.), James ("Billy") Judd (1876–1947, from Honolulu), Harry Keator [rhymes with skater] (1873–1917, from Roxbury, N. Y., baseball captain at Yale), and James Lewis (1876–1962, from Bedford, N. Y.)—also Michael Gavin (1873–1960, from Memphis), Yale '95, LL.B. '97, who was starting out as a lawyer. With Ives came George Schreiber (1876–1941, from Hoboken), Yale '98 (Glee Club, Choir, Grenville Parker's roommate), and Edward Sawyer (1874–1924, from Dover, N.H.), Yale '98 (manager glee and banjo clubs). Gavin's letter to Ives in 1947 recalls "old days when several of us lived together. Our clothes hung together on the line as a sort of 'community chest' from which any of us who wanted to make a big splurge was allowed to pick the best pair of pants and coat, which was perfectly satisfactory to all of us, because we wanted to make a good showing as a group. However, dear old Eddie Sawyer's stuff was too big for any of us, so he had it all to himself. Them were the days! and I shall never forget them, and I don't believe you will either." (Gavin was also in another Yale group at 4 East 43rd Street.)

Ives's Yale roommate, Mandeville Mullally (1874–1957), would have dropped in from time to time, and their classmate David Twichell (1874–1924, Ives's future brother-in-law) joined them in October 1899, having stayed in the army for a year after the Spanish-American War (he had graduated in absentia). And as soon as Ives and Julian Myrick became close friends, he also would have dropped in occasionally. Around this time Ives transferred his organist job from Bloomfield, N.J., to Central Presbyterian Church, right nearby at Broadway and 57th Street, where his friends were always in danger of being pressed or cajoled into the choir. It may have been the next spring that Gavin and Sawyer left, also Schreiber (LL.B. '01 Columbia Law School).

In the fall of 1900, five men from Yale '00 joined Poverty Flat, three in P. & S.: James Greenway (born 1877 at Huntsville, Ala., Yale glee club and crew), Brace Paddock (1878–1935, from Pittsfield, Mass.), and Edwards ("Ned") Park (1877–1969, from Gloversville, N. Y.—Ives called him "Central")—and two studying at the New York Law School: William Raymond Maloney (1876–1945, from

Poughkeepsie) and Keyes [rhymes with eyes] Winter (1878–1960, from Indianap-
olis, Yale football squad, editor of the *Yale Record*). They were joined by David
Allen (not a Yale man) and later by Lewis's brother George (1874–1951), Yale
'95 (Freshman glee club, gym team, ΦBK), now a lawyer, whose recent marriage
had been brief.

A memo on a sketch of *Walking* (1902) recalls a walk "up the Palisades with
Allen, Keator, also Bill B. [who?] and Bill Mc [who?]—not to celebrate anything,
10/8[?], 1900" [perhaps Sunday 7 October 1900?].

> Many years later Dr. Park wrote:
> I used to attend Dr. Merle-Smith's church . . . where Charlie played the
> organ. . . . On one occasion Charlie wished to have a huge choir. . . . He
> asked me . . . I was completely unfamiliar with the music. . . . He said . . .
> that made no difference, that all that was required of me was to make my
> mouth go. . . . Mullally was a member of the choir. . . .
>
> I am sure that various members of the congregation were in a state of con-
> tinual quandary whether Charlie was committing sacrilegious sins by intro-
> ducing popular and perhaps ribald melodies into the offertory, etc. I am sure
> that he was under grave suspicion, but the melodies were so disguised that
> the suspicious members of the congregation could never be sure enough to
> take action. I think it is certain that he did interweave them, not from a
> sense of humor or tantalization, but because that was the way in which his
> musical mind found a certain satisfaction."

It may have been in the spring of 1901 that David Stanley Smith called on Park
and overheard Ives working on the *Hymn-Anthem* (see §47). Dr. Park remembered
Mullally telling how he and Ives, at Coney Island, went into a side-show labeled
Hell—"they saw a devil sitting on a ledge. Mullally was doubtful whether it was
human flesh or an effigy, and gave a poke with his cane. The devil came to life,
leapt down and began to beat Mullally with his trident, calling out 'Get the
Hell out of here!' . . .

"Charlie was returning to a class reunion at Yale ['98 triennial, Tuesday 25
June 1901] and asked me to send him something . . . I remember asking him
what his address would be and recall his reply . . . 'I shall be out all night, and
daytimes will sleep under a tree.'"

That same June, Darrach, Judd, Keator, and James Lewis graduated, M.D.,
from P. & S. (a four-year course—Darrach third in his class), and soon left
Poverty Flat to be resident internes at hospitals. Darrach practised in New York
and taught at P. & S. from 1903, and was an important officer in many medical
associations (the editor had the privilege of meeting him in the 1930s). Keator
also taught at P. & S. in 1904–12 until ill health forced him to Saranac and to New
Mexico. Judd returned to Hawaii to practise, but served in France in 1915–17.
Lewis practised and taught at Buffalo, and was Medical Captain in the war.

In the fall of 1901 Park interrupted his medical studies to spend a year as
private tutor in Michigan, and Ives, Twichell, Allen and the lawyers (George
Lewis, Maloney, and Winter) left 317 and moved a bit further uptown to 65
Central Park West.

Some of the new medical candidates replacing them included Royal Haynes
(Columbia '99) and Brainerd ("Beak") Whitbeck (Harvard '99), both in the
class of '03 at P. & S.—also George Lathrope (Princeton '00), Albert Vander Veer
(Yale '00), and Howard Mason (Brown '01), all in '04 at P. & S. along with
Greenway and Paddock. Greenway left Poverty Flat the next year to get mar-

ried. He was Director of Yale's Department of University Health 1916–33 (except for 1917–19 when he was Chief of Medical Service at Camp Bowie, Texas), and now lives in Greenwich, Connecticut. Dr. Park called him "a wonderfully fine man . . . a most delightful Southern aristocrat." Paddock married in 1906 and practised in New York, later in his native Pittsfield. Park returned to 317 in 1902 and, because of his year out, graduated in 1905, married in 1913, taught at P. & S., Yale, and Johns Hopkins, and retired to Ruxton, Md. (his letters and conversations being one of the many privileges the editor owed to Ives).

Some shreds of the uptown history of Poverty Flat—all inmates being now of blessed memory—have been gleaned from alumni records, letters, and memos on Ives's music manuscripts. He was composing all the time, principally the *Second Symphony*. George Lewis, in a letter of 27 October 1933, was "brought back to memories of long ago by hearing over the radio a few days ago Charlie's *Ah! 'Tis a Dream,* which I heard him compose in Poverty Flat" [these are the key words of *My Native Land,* but probably it was Ives's earlier setting (App. 4, #101) that was broadcast, and the yet unpublished second setting that Lewis heard him compose around 1901]. An ink copy of *Ilmenau* is dated: "copied at Povert[y Flat] Jan. 1, '02."

The preparation and performance of Ives's cantata, *The Celestial Country,* at the church on 18 April 1902 must have been an experience for the Flat. The Kaltenborn String Quartet took part, and repeated the *Intermezzo* (for strings alone) in a New Haven concert in May. In June Ives resigned as organist and suddenly his Sundays were free, and gradually his composing became more predominantly experimental, as in *Walking.*

Also in June, Maloney and Winter graduated, LL.B., from the New York Law School, but stayed on in Poverty Flat. In the fall they were joined by Bartlett Yung (1879–1943), Yale '02 (leader of the banjo club), whose father, a distinguished Chinese educator and revolutionary, was a close friend and Hartford neighbor of Ives's future father-in-law. Bart's older brother, Morrison Yung (1876–1933), Yale '98, would be dropping in from time to time between his assignments in various parts of the world as a mining engineer.

On the incomplete sketch of a *Skit for Danbury Fair* (fall 1902) is an added memo: "Davey Allen beats up Keyes—smiles, scolds, smirks—then over to Healy's."[1] On a copy of *Autumn* (1908), a memo discloses that the music is adapted "from [a] song *Autumn* in D♭, sung by Dr. Griggs—Thanksgiving Service, not in Ch[urch but] at 65 C[entral] P[ark] W[est], 1902." Apparently Griggs had dropped in on Thanksgiving Day, and had sung (at sight?) the prototype of the 1908 *Autumn* impressively enough to make it feel like a service [pity it's lost!].

Kaltenborn's quartet seems to have come to the Flat in February. Ever since *The Celestial Country,* Ives had felt grateful to the violist, Gustave Bach, for holding on to the dissonant note at the end of the *Intermezzo* (see end of §6). And now it struck Ives's funnybone to concoct an ear-stretcher that later became the middle part of the *Scherzo for String Quartet*: "Practice for String Quartet— in Holding Your Own!—Study Dedicated to Gustave Bach (from the line of John Seb. Bach)—after a Rehearsal Feb. 12, 1903—65 C.P.W., N.Y."[2]

[1] Trow lists: "John J. Healy, liquors, 66 Irving Place & 988 8th Avenue, h[ouse] 317 W. 58."—might Healy have been their landlord at 317?—or their neighbor in another apartment? Perhaps later his uptown establishment moved from 988 8th Avenue to where Myrick remembered it: "Healy's was a restaurant on the corner of Columbus Avenue and 66th Street, and Poverty Flat was on Central Park West and 66th Street, an apartment there on the northwest corner."
[2] See §6, note 8.

In June 1903, David Twichell graduated, M.D., from P. & S., and joined the staff of Dr. Trudeau's tuberculosis sanatorium at Saranac. Ives wrote him that fall: "Willis Wood spent a day with us recently, tells us you're in good form. . . . Del Wood took me to Keene Valley over Labor Day. . . . The flat is filled with two new dogs, Harry Farrar of Bart's class and Walter McCormick, a cousin of Vance.

"Winter and Maloney held a convention last evening. W. insists upon more authority, that Maloney's position is of the character of a secretaryship and not the vaunted idea in any sense of judicial treasurer or controller; that the bills be paid by him because, when he he don't want to, when he won't, then just for this reason, it can't be, because and why not, etc., etc. . . . A phonograph on the scene would have furnished Weber and Fields a 3rd act. . . .

"We finally succeeded in placing that shanty on the mountain [Pine Mt.] in Ridgefield, but did it unbenownst to Aunt Amelia fearing adverse suggestions. It makes a good young camp. Geo. Lewis went up with me last month taking *Sat. afternoon off—what!* We spent the night on the mountain. Having no curtains on the window, it took two hours of kind words to get the old scrunch to disrobe, he being afraid that some of the farmers' wives in the next house (about three miles down in the valley) would peek at him. . . .

"Remember me to Deac.—is he with you?—and answer this soon."

Of those mentioned in the above letter, Willis Wood (not a Yale man) was Dave Twichell's brother-in-law's brother; Cornelius Delano Wood (1879–1958, from Brooklyn), Yale '00, had taught in 1902 at the same Idaho school as Burton Twichell (Dave's brother). Harry Farrar (1879–1939, from Erie), Yale ex '02 (freshman year only), had kept in touch with classmates. Vance McCormick (1872–1946, from Harrisburg), Yale '93 (football captain), may have been known to the Flat through George Lewis, '95, but his cousin Walter was not a Yale man.

In 1904 Ives composed his *Third Symphony,* based on three organ pieces of 1901, now lost. But he was working at the same time in more experimental directions. Under some chords for *On the Antipodes* he wrote: "Bill Maloney [is] mad at this—65 C. P. W., St. Pat[rick]'s Day '04—[he] says [it] just hammers—[and he] can't sleep."

The lawyers were no less intent and active. A transcript of an interview with Keyes Winter in 1950 has been generously contributed by his son, Mr. Henry M. Winter: "During my law studies and until I was married in 1907, I set up housekeeping with a group of friends in a west side apartment. Our place was a collecting point for young bachelors in the city, and we were taking an interest on the side in everything we thought worthwhile. Being in the law, I naturally saw a great deal of lawyers who were getting interested in politics . . . I went to occasional meetings. My friends liked to make speeches from the tail ends of carts, and I went with them rather than pull doorbells.

"Lyttleton Fox was one of these [1881–1934, Yale '02, LL.B. '04 N.Y. Law School] . . . He was very lively and good fun, and took nothing very seriously . . . We usually teamed up on these carts, and always spoke under the auspices of the Republicans. If we could get control of the cart, we would take it over to 44th Street in front of the Harvard and Yale Clubs, blow our bugles, and fill it full of such members as would respond, and spend the night bugling, singing and speaking. We would collect some pretty big crowds, which used to get a lot of fun out of us. Most of them were Democrats and hostile to the slogans on our cart. If we spoke five minutes and lasted, we felt rewarded. Fox in particular always enjoyed himself. On one occasion, when I was in the middle of my speech, Fox got the driver to start up his horse, and pitched me head first into the middle of the audience."

In the summer of 1905 Ives again met Dave Twichell's sister Harmony, and they must have recognized a deeply significant bond, though their courtship didn't become serious until 1906.

That Poverty Flat often became Ives's captive audience is suggested by the following memo on p. 6 of the sketch of the *Country Band March* of 1903: "Geo. [Lewis], Bart [Yung], Tony M[aloney](Bill)—three quite right critics!!—say I haven't got the tune right, and the chords are wrong—Thanksgiving 1905." But on p. 4 of the same sketch: "Keyes says these notes are O.K.—he is the best critic, for he doesn't know one note from another." Both the opening of *Over the Pavements* and the song "*1, 2, 3*" are derived from a sketch of 1906 entitled "Rube trying to walk 2 to 3!!"—"written as a joke, and sounds like one! Watty McCormick [was the] only one to see it! and Harry Farrar! at 2.45 A.M."

The climax of *Central Park in the Dark* is when a "Runaway [horse] smashes into fence . . . heard at 65 C. P. W., July . . . 1906." And *In the Cage* (see §17) was inspired during a walk with "Bart and George [from] 65 Central P. W. [to the zoo, on Saturday afternoon] July 28, 1906."

The *Second String Quartet* is dated by Ives "1911–13 (2nd mvt. 1907)" [App. 3, §61]. But in the first movement, *Discussions*, in mm. 99–100, there is a memo that seems copied from a lost sketch of 1907: "Keyes takes exception—'on that point'—So do the others, each has his say." And in mm. 102–104: "But on this, they all say Eyah! Everybody can see that!"

By this time Keyes Winter was also courting (he was married on Tuesday 2 April 1907), and his son recalls his telling about it: "My father's engagement was rather long, and his friends became rather bored with the whole thing, particularly Mr. Ives who, as the weeks stretched into months, seemed to be increasingly morose and grumpy. To teach him a lesson, my father announced that he was to be Best Man. Mr. Ives at first refused, but later yielded, as he put it, to pressure. He informed my father that he would do all the things a Best Man was supposed to do but without assuming the dignity officially. My father bided his time until the wedding reception, when he told Mr. Ives that he would have to sign the Wedding Book (I think it was called that in those days) on the first page, along with the bridal party and members of the family. This Mr. Ives of course refused to do, and in order to outwit my father, informed him that one of the functions of a Best Man (which of course he wasn't) was to take the Wedding Book around and get the signatures. In doing this he tried to persuade the other members of the bridal party to write their names so large that in the end there would be no room for his own signature. But the others were in conspiracy with my father, and though they obliged Mr. Ives by making their signatures large, and pretty well succeeded in covering the page, they left one area blank: at the very top of the page. And in this position, ahead of (and apparently to outrank) even the parents of the bride and groom, Mr. Ives had no alternative but to sign. But his signature was *very* small and illegible!"

On or about Saturday 21 September 1907, Poverty Flat moved downtown from 65 Central Park West to 34 Gramercy Park. In the sketch of "Set #1" (which Ives dated 1906—§18, note 1), there are two memos added in 1907 or '08. On p. 3, *A Lecture* (which became the song *Tolerance*) was "approved of by Bart and M[orrison] Yung, Geo. [Lewis], 34 Gramercy Pk." And on p. 6, *Calcium Light Night* (an evocation of the torchlight parades at the time of student society elections) was "approved by Yale Club of 34 Gramercy Park."

The later phases of Ives's long courtship must have been fully as much of a trial to his companions as Winter's had been. *Our Book* has a list of names that can only be for the wedding invitations, including: "Geo and Bart, Mull[ally] and Mike [Myrick], Harry K[eator] and Geo. Schreiber, Chalkgood and Bob Gay, Fred V[an] B[euren] and wife, Ham Scrant[on] and K[eyes] W[inter]." Robert Gay (1876–1925, from Gaysville, Vermont), Yale '98, was a lawyer. Chalkgood was not a Yale man. J. Hamilton Scranton (1875–1948, from Madison, Connecticut), Yale '98, was in advertising, and became a parishioner of the Asylum Hill Church. Frederick T. Van Beuren (1876–1943, from New York), Yale '98 (Glee Club, Track Team), M.D. '02 at P. & S., was later its Associate Dean. Apparently none of these men lived in Poverty Flat, though van Beuren was one of Ives's closest friends.

After the Iveses set up housekeeping at 70 West 11 (see §31, note 8), among their first guests were "Bart and George to dinner." Shortly thereafter Myrick went to live at Poverty Flat until his marriage on New Year's Day 1910. Bart went to China in 1909, his brother Morrison in 1912. On the sketch of Study #9 (*The Anti-Abolitionist Riots*): "Harry Keator comes down and sings whiskey but tenor —'Tis the night before Xmas, [118] Waverly Place, 1911." Around then 34 Gramercy Park may have been disbanded, because in 1913 George Lewis was living at the Yale Club, 30 West 44th Street. He attended Slonimsky's concert of 10 January 1931, and wrote Ives how glad he was that *Putnam's Camp* and *The Housatonic* were repeated—"Rah! Rah! Rah! Ives! Ives! Ives!" In 1933 he seems to have been the Ives's family lawyer, as revealed by a few letters about routine financial matters.

Dr. Park probably expressed the view of most of Poverty Flat when he wrote: "I had not the slightest intimation that Charley was a musical genius . . . I regarded him as a most delightful man and companion, completely unpredictable . . . one never knew what to expect next."

Julian Southall Myrick (1880–1969)

(with some of his own words from recent interviews)

In this section of the appendices, devoted mainly to those who had some influence on Ives's growth, so far the principal men have stood in a relation to him of some authority—his father, his choirmaster, his father-in-law. When he joined the Raymond Agency in 1899, no one would have thought that the man in that office to whom he would become most deeply indebted was a Southern boy over five years younger—but a boy with a rare balance of common sense, warm heart, and infectious enthusiasm.

The Myrick family is from Anglesey, the northwest corner of Wales. At the coronation of Henry VIII in 1509, his Welsh Captain of the Guard was dubbed Meyrick (Welsh for guardian), and when Henry decreed that Welsh families adopt surnames, the captain used this complimentary title. It may be his son John Myrc who is quoted in Dorothy Sayers' *The Nine Tailors*, on p. 59. It is probably John's grandson Sir John Merrick who came to Virginia, was a member of The Virginia Company in 1624, and was deeded land, probably in Surry County, downstream from Richmond. His grandson Owen took part in Nathaniel Bacon's rebellion against Governor Berkeley in 1676. His son Owen Jr. moved to land later included in Southampton County. His great-grandson Walter fought in the war of 1812, and then moved to Como, Hertford County, North Carolina.

His son Thomas Newsom Myrick (c. 1821–67) married Julia Southall and was a cotton planter. Their first son was Charles English Myrick (1850–1910), born at Murfreesboro, North Carolina. After Julia died, Thomas married Susan Baker, and left his land to his second wife. In 1877 Charles married Susan Blanche Colton (1846–1923, from King George, Virginia), and their only son to reach maturity was Julian Southall Myrick, born March 1, 1880, at Murfreesboro. The plantation not only grew cotton but bred horses, which Charles sold at New York. His business thrived, and in 1883 he moved to Staunton, Virginia, to widen his sources of supply. His son recalled: "He had a big trade, and people came from distant places to buy his stock—that was a very magnificent stock." In 1892 he finally settled at Dobbs Ferry, commuting to New York, to 1642 Broadway, a few blocks south of Central Park. Julian went to a Dobbs Ferry school, and for two years, 1892–94, he sang in the boy choir of Zion Episcopal Church, until his voice changed. "My sister still has an apartment up at Dobbs Ferry . . . we always regarded that as home."

From 1893 he commuted to Trinity School, then at 108 West 45th Street, "between 6th Avenue and Broadway, south side of the street. We used to play in Bryant Park"—back of the reservoir (now replaced by the Library). Then in 1895, "the school moved up to where it is now at [139 West] 91st Street, between Columbus and Amsterdam Avenues. I had nothing to do with tennis at that time

. . . baseball and football . . . football was my favorite sport. . . . I think that name Mike was given to me by a boy in Trinity School. . . . I didn't graduate—I wish I had—I would have been in the class of '98. . . . A friend of mine in Trinity was going to Cornell, and I wanted to go along with him. . . . My parents wanted me to go to Columbia, and I didn't like Columbia, and so I quit . . . in June '97, and went to work. . . .

"I went to work for a friend of mine who made electric signs, block letters, that hung in front of the theatres and businesses. . . . He had a shop down on 28th Street just off 6th Avenue. . . . On those electric signs there were letters about six feet tall, and you'd have to wire them to a steel frame, and this frame would sway—you'd see people walking along the street. And I went home and told the family about it . . . and they took me out of that and sent me to a business college—I've forgotten the name of it—I was there about three months. . . . And then my father got me this job down with Mutual Life, Charles H. Raymond & Co. . . . I started in Raymond's on March 15th, 1898 . . . I was applications clerk, and not very good . . . my salary was a hundred dollars a month . . . a very big salary in those days."

Three months later Ives graduated from Yale, and his father's second cousin, Dr. Granville White, medical examiner for Mutual Life, got him a job in the actuarial department. But it soon became clear that Ives was not well fitted for that work, so Dr. White had him transferred, early in 1899, to the Raymond Agency, where his first assignment was to replace Myrick as applications clerk. "He came in to relieve me . . . they gave me a rest and gave him my job . . . I tried to teach him—he didn't do very well . . . and he wrote a very bad hand, so they didn't like his handwriting—so that, when I came back, they gave me the job back again and sent him out to work among the agents. . . . When I'd had a rest and got oriented, I did all right."

Myrick may have experienced the truism that the teacher learns more than the pupil. But Ives, working with the agents, was now concerned with presenting the idea of insurance—a perfect challenge to his creative imagination and to his humanitarian transcendentalism. "We could have been jealous—instead of that we became fast friends and companions right away . . . we just got along, that's all. . . . Well, he was a great athlete . . . and we used to have teams in the office, and he always pitched."

Right from the start, they made a kind of two-man team. "I had to do with the applications that came in—process them—and he had to do with handling the agents . . . And so we divided that part of the work, not only in the Raymond Agency, but later on in life. . . . He never did any direct selling, but he was a very good trainer of agents, and taught them how to sell. . . . He made the balls for other people to throw. . . . He had a great conception of the life insurance business, and what it could and should do, and had a very powerful way of expressing it."

Also in 1899, Myrick enlisted in the Seventh Regiment of the National Guard, in New York, being on the basketball and track teams of his company. Gradually he got acquainted with Poverty Flat (perhaps less at 317 West 58 than at 65 Central Park West after fall 1901), and with the inmates—"we had a good time. . . . Bartlett Yung he was a great fellow, we became great friends."

Through the Seventh Regiment he met a family of tennis enthusiasts, the Washburns, who had a summer place at Black Rock, Connecticut, with a first-rate home-made tennis court. Here, from 1902, he spent many weekends. Watson Washburn, then eight, recalls: "I think his first tennis was played on our family court. While he was an expert indoor sprinter, and won many trophies in the Seventh Regiment games at the Armory, he took up tennis too late to be good in singles, but his agility at the net enabled him to win many doubles tournaments with the aid of a good partner. We often played together as a team."

In a rapidly expanding industry, as life insurance was at that time, competitive irregularities were almost invited by laws that were out of date. Myrick recently commented: "I've forgotten who said poor laws that are obeyed are better than good laws that are disobeyed. . . . Everybody was doing it." In 1905 State Senator William W. Armstrong from Rochester chaired a committee of investigation—"to establish a code that everybody could live under."

The new Armstrong laws were adopted as of 1 January 1907, but Mutual had already reorganized its whole agency system in 1906. At the same time Ives's heart had been cause for anxiety, and he'd been consulting with Mutual's medical department, which recommended in December that he take a rest, and that Myrick go with him. They went to Old Point Comfort, Virginia, for about a week around Christmastime, and it was there that they considered leaving Mutual and going in business on their own. Back in New York, they consulted with Washington Life—"we knew the President, [John] Tatlock, who had been a friend of ours when he was an actuary in Mutual." Tatlock invited them to establish a general agency for Washington Life, and they started it in January 1907— "under the new laws"—as Ives & Co., 51 Liberty Street—"we borrowed money and financed ourselves. . . . The Armstrong Laws were obeyed and made to work, and we had a great deal to do in the leadership of the industry."

Ives was already courting Harmony Twichell. On the back of her letter of 12 December 1906, he later sketched the following: "Excess cost eliminated from life insurance. Get your policy out, make a note of your premium, then write for our rate at same age. The Washington Life for the last two years has shown phenomenal advancement, and has taken its place as the strongest and largest of the Companies governed entirely by the new Armstrong Laws, confining its whole energy to old line, low rate, non excess cost, common sense insurance." Her letter of 27 January 1907 says: "I don't wonder it was hard to say good-by to the place and people you'd been in and among for eight years."

Not only did the new agency prosper, but in November 1907 Myrick was elected Secretary of the Life Underwriters' Association of the City of New York, an unusual honor for a young man of twenty-seven, and a tribute to his dependability and tact. Ives and Miss Twichell were finally married in June 1908. Shortly afterwards Myrick moved to Poverty•Flat—"I went in and joined them when there were only about three left." That fall Washington Life sold out to Pittsburgh Life and Trust (which did not do business in New York), and thereby pulled the rug out from under Ives & Co. But the two-man team was remembered with affection and respect back at Mutual Life, where George T. Dexter, Vice President in charge of agencies, in a letter of 21 December, appointed them Managers as of 1 January 1909. This time "they financed us—we were paid a salary by them"— which the letter of appointment quotes at the then large figure of "$5,000 per annum." Henceforth they were known as Ives & Myrick.

Their oldest extant correspondence is a vacationtime letter from the "Manoir Richelieu, Pointe-à-Pic, Quebec, [Sunday], Aug. 15, 1909. Dear Charlie, We just returned after a ninety mile pull through the woods, are in good shape, and had a good time. How are things going? . . . Would you like me to come back sooner? . . ." Also in 1909 he joined the West Side Tennis Club, which had been founded in 1892 at 89th Street and Central Park, but had moved in 1908 to 238th Street and Broadway, at Van Cortlandt Park.

On New Year's Day 1910 Myrick and Marion Washburn were married in New York, Ives being best man. They had a son and three daughters, and three grand-children. From that time on, his life pursued a steady growth of his organizational talents and his public recognition, in both insurance and tennis.

Ives & Myrick gradually became the largest and most prosperous agency in the field, setting new records for monthly business. Myrick's vast common sense was the perfect counterbalance to Ives's inventive genius. "We were blazing a new field and it responded . . . estate planning and all that sort of thing . . . we were ahead of the town. . . . We had brokers who were general insurance men, and we taught them how to sell life insurance, and we built up a big agency through them, and it was very successful. . . . I joined all of the organizations and was in the outside contact work of the agency . . . he belonged to all of them but he took no active interest—I did that. . . . That's the reason, I think, that I'm generally speaking better known in the business."

"He was a very good economist, in that he didn't throw money away, but he was generous. We had an agreement that we were not to give away money, and he broke the agreement continuously—I didn't know about it until years after-ward—very kind-hearted."

In February 1914, "we were moving . . . and we had a little safe, and . . . he had one part, and I had another—and he'd cleaned out his part, and I went to clean out my part—and there's a stack of music. And I said, 'Charlie, you want me to throw this away?' And he came over—he said, 'Why, Mike! God, that's the best thing I've written!'—and it was *The Fourth of July*, about to be thrown away!" Ives dedicated it to Myrick—"his wife was responsible for that."

In 1915 Myrick became president both of the Life Underwriters' Association of the City of New York, and also of the West Side Tennis Club. He had been influential in planning the Club's move in 1912 to Forest Hills, which soon be-came a major focus of the tennis world. His article in the *New York Times* of Sunday 26 December 1915 starts: "The outlook for lawn tennis in 1916 is the brightest in the history of the sport. The changing of the historic All Comers' National Championship Tournament from Newport, R.I., to the West Side Club's courts at Forest Hills, L. I., was in itself the most momentous change in the thirty-five years of the game, and the change is certain to have a beneficial influence on tennis."

Early in 1917 a luncheon meeting of Mutual managers was being planned for April at the Waldorf, and Myrick asked Ives to set *In Flanders Fields* (by the late Dr. John McCrae, who had been Mutual's medical referee at Montreal), and asked his friend McCall Lanham to sing it, with his accompanist, William Lewis. Lanham recently wrote: "Mr. Lewis and I worked . . . for countless weeks, really never making head or tail of it . . . the dissonance was unbearable . . . however I was glad to attempt it for the sake of old and faithful friend Mike Myrick! Today I might not feel as I did then!" The performance lacked conviction, and Myrick has told of Ives's immediate distress: "If I'd known they were going to do it that way, I'd have done it myself!" In all fairness one must point out:—that most present-day Ives enthusiasts (if alive in 1917) would have reacted to it exactly as Lanham and Lewis did—that the copy (now missing) was probably in Ives's more hasty hand—and that it may have been more dissonant than the familiar 1919 version.

In the meantime Ives suffered his heart attack and was out of business for almost a year, October 1918 to September 1919, and it must have been a great comfort to him to know how confidently he could entrust Myrick with running the whole show. That summer he revised *In Flanders Fields*, but was uncertain about a few details and wrote variants from which a copyist made three different versions. The sketch for his letter to Myrick is dated: "Redding, Aug. 14, '19. Dear Mike, Under separate cover, I'm sending you three copies of the Flanders song. . . . If you get someone to sing it over for you, tell me which way goes the best—though they're only small differences. I hope you'll like it." This is typical of Ives's transcendentalist faith that others (if their hearts were "in the right place") could contribute details to his music in ways just as valid as his own. Myrick wrote back on the 16th (Saturday): "Will take the 'Flanders Fields' with me this afternoon and see if I can get someone to play it or sing it over Sunday." The only evidence of any decision is the way it appears in *114 Songs*.

In 1920 Myrick was elected president of the U. S. Lawn Tennis Association, and from 1920 to 1927 was chairman of the Davis Cup Committee. At Wimbledon in June 1924 he met King George and Queen Mary and the Duke of York (later George VI). On the way back, at San Sebastian he played mixed doubles against Queen Victoria of Spain.

On 22 June 1926 he wrote: "Dear Charlie, I am glad that you have decided to stop trying to come down until you have gotten back to nearly your normal state, and hope that you will not attempt it again until you find yourself in that condition."

A letter of 5 June 1929 suggests that they both contribute to the American College of Life Underwriters (of which Myrick was a founder), and adds: "Don't bother to come back until you feel absolutely sure that you have regained your full strength." This level-headed advice seems to have broken through Ives's natural reluctance to retire. In mid-July he sketched: "Dear Mike . . . It's a relief to have the future plans settled . . . I realize fully now that I could not keep going for another year. . . . My main regret is . . . for you. But, as Harmony says, we may have more time to see each other than we have in the last few years."

Myrick wrote on 22 July: "My dear Charlie, I can't tell you how much I appreciated your letter. . . . Since then . . . I do not get the same joy or zest out of the work that I did before, and I only wish that I had put by enough so that I could retire with you . . . I agree that the best part of our partnership was the affection and confidence in which we always held one another, and I like to think that this relationship resulted in our having had a good influence on many individuals and organizations that it has been our duty or pleasure to work with. . . . I will certainly try, in carrying on, never to let down the goodwill and reputation we have built up together. . . . I think it would be most unwise for you to attempt to come back before your return to town for the winter, and then you must be most careful not to overdo again."

In reply Ives sketched: "I don't know quite how to thank you for your very kind letter. I appreciated it deeply and so did Mrs. Ives. If I'd as much sense as she, I would have resigned some time ago. . . . But what I want to say most in this letter, is something to have you know how greatly I have felt your sincerity in all of our past relations . . . above all it is your fair-mindedness that I look back on—one of the finest attributes that a human being can have."

About a year later (after Ives retired as of 1 January 1930), Myrick put a large-type, full-page article in the Eastern Underwriter for 19 September 1930, entitled *What the Business Owes to Charles E. Ives:*

> When Charles E. Ives retired from active participation in the Ives & Myrick agency of the Mutual Life a few months ago, the insurance fraternity of Greater New York lost contact with a guiding spirit whose impress upon his

fellows was stimulating, uplifting, and of untold value to life insurance production. His creative mind, great breadth of culture, intensive sympathies, and keen understanding of the economic as well as of the material needs of the community made it possible for him to evolve literature which paved the way for additional sales of life insurance and helped straighten out complications which confront the underwriter in his daily path through life. This remarkable student, seated in his Connecticut home with pen in hand, has loved to concentrate upon and to analyze the problems of insurance and of finance, and to solve or readjust those problems with a master mind. Always shall I be proud and happy in the recollection of our partnership of twenty years' standing, not only because of its intimate nature, but no one had a better opportunity than was mine of knowing how great was his contribution to the cause of life insurance progress. In my opinion that contribution has never been properly assayed or acknowledged. The passing years will demonstrate that his philosophy will ever hold good.

On the 30th Mrs. Ives wrote: "Dear Mr. Myrick, I must tell you how fine I think your appreciation of Charlie. . . . He is so modest, he thinks little of himself, and I am just glad to have you say in public what *you* think. . . . We are going off next week for a short vacation for *me* . . . " Ives's letter says: "The page from the 'Eastern Underwriter' . . . was unexpected, and also a good deal undeserved . . . Harmony says it is typical of you . . . that you've always seemed more like a member of the family than a business partner, and she's right! . . . I wish you would retire before long and let me get even with you. . . . We hope . . . to go up to the mountains for a little change—Harmony is pretty tired from her job as housekeeper, nurse and chauffeur . . . "

A gauge of Myrick's reputation in the insurance business is the title of an article about him in 1931—*Let's Go and See Mike*—a natural echo of habitual impulse. After Ives retired, "I lived up at 79th Street, and they had a house on 74th Street, and I used to go down there most every Sunday and talk with him, and we'd talk over ideas, and so I was able to keep him in touch with what was going on in the agency in that way. And his suggestions every now and then were very helpful, and we used them."

While Ives was in Europe, Myrick sent him a clipping on 3 May 1933. Ives sketched a reply: "Dear Mike, Thank you for sending the article on my music. There was another one, in the *Musical Quarterly*, Jan. 1933. . . . In it there is a very decent reference to the history of Ives & Myrick, and in the interview which the author [Bellamann] asked for—because so many had asked him if business didn't interfere with music—I said 'no'—and when saying that, in my business associations, I had found more open-mindedness, courage, and high ideals than in the world of music, I had you foremost in my thoughts. . . . You see, you were a silent partner in the symphony business."

In 1941 Myrick became second vice president of Mutual of New York, his position as manager of the Ives & Myrick agency being taken over by Richard E. Myer. He finally retired in 1949, but continued to serve as consultant. The editor well remembers the deep respect with which his arrival was awaited at Ives's funeral at West Redding in 1954, and the warm cordiality of his various greetings. He still played tennis nearly every day, mostly at the River Club, until a severe heart attack in 1967. After a long convalescence with uncertain ups and downs, on 8 January 1969, during a nap after breakfast, it was into the other life that he awoke.

Harmony Twichell (1876–1969)

Twichell's journal: "1876, June 4th, 1.14 o'clock A.M., our third daughter born about half an hour ago . . . The children are all asleep. . . . On learning that a stork had been heard around the house during the night . . . Eddie and Julia . . . went out to look for the stork's tracks and found them!" She was named Harmony for her mother. It was a wonderful household to grow up in, both deeply religious and warmly understanding. Among her earlies memories would be "Uncle Mark" and other distinguished "uncles and aunts by courtesy"—and the annual vacations, usually to the Adirondacks, the whole family glorying in the mountains.

In 1880 an informal school was started at home by a friend of the family, Mrs. Bartlett. Mrs. Twichell had also been a school teacher, at Utica. Beside the three R's they evidently taught Yankee resourcefulness. After the blizzard of '88, with all Hartford paralyzed, the *Courant* of 14 March reported: "Four children of a large family living on the Hill, two boys and two girls, proved themselves equal to the needs of the hour by going downtown yesterday in procession and returning well laden with supplies . . ."—Twichell adds: "Ed, Sue, Dave, and Harmony."

The next year she was in the Hartford High School, but in 1893, after a two-week visit to the Chicago exposition as guest of her father's classmate, Albert Sprague, she went to Miss Porter's School at nearby Farmington, through Uncle Albert's generosity. She loved this school—it was evidently a perfect choice. Her roommate was Sally Whitney, whom she often visited at New Haven, where, at Center Church, they got to like the strange hymn-interludes by the student organist, Charlie Ives. She was to meet him later as a classmate of her brother Dave.

In March 1895, her father and Uncle Mark took the trolley to Farmington to pay a call on his "niece." That June, at a "Soirée given by young ladies of the school," she sang Gounod's *The King of Love my Shepherd is*—"my singing teacher persuaded me to—she wanted me to sing Haydn's *My Mother Bids me Bind my Hair*, but it was too difficult. Gounod was easier." In August 1896, Dave brought Charlie Ives up to Keene Valley for over two weeks, where he got to know the whole family.

Having graduated from Miss Porter's in 1896, Harmony spent the next two years mostly at home, and studied painting with Charles H. Flagg—"he had a studio downtown"—with occasional criticism from William Merritt Chase—"he came up from New York once a week." She accompanied her father on many of his engagements to speak or preach—his journal noting that, on their way to a Veterans' meeting at Fort Monroe, Virginia, they stopped in Washington to call on President McKinley "and were very graciously received." She came to be known as the most beautiful girl in Hartford. Lawrence Gilman was then at a Hartford boarding school—"Sally (my younger sister) was Lawrence's particular friend"—but when he wrote Mrs. Ives in 1939, he recalled that "you represented to me in those days a number of ideals!"

However, in October 1898 Harmony entered the Hartford Hospital Training School for Nurses, living in the hospital, and getting home only briefly on Sundays. Just a year later Dave started his medical studies at P. & S. and joined Poverty Flat (see App. 17). On 2 October 1900, after the two-year course, Harmony graduated as Registered Nurse, and graced the occasion by reading a short essay:

THE NURSE'S GAIN

There is a prevailing impression that the nursing profession is one of self-sacrifice. In fact I recently saw the following dedication in print, "To those people who share our many sorrows and but few of our blessings, the Nurses of America" etc. Now *that* is putting it strongly!

One of the most frequent remarks made to nurses by interested friends is the question, "Don't you feel that you have given up a great deal?" For my part I feel shamefacedly uncomfortable when asked it, for the further I go, and the more intelligently my eyes can see the matter, the more do I realize how much greater are the privileges bestowed by the profession that I can ever repay or even comprehend.

So many are the gains that it is difficult to enumerate them, but in the first and to my mind the biggest place come the unique and constant opportunities of succouring others. It is true that such opportunities are constantly occurring in all walks of life, but we are peculiarly fortunate in having them made part of our daily routine, in having them put before us in such a way that they must be patent to us. We are *forced* into alleviating pain, into doing things that are necessary for the comfort of those less fortunate than ourselves. It is really a great piece of good luck, all this, for it is proved that the fullest development individually comes from altruistic effort, and fullest development means in the end the greatest usefulness and happiness.

However, though we cannot take these chances or leave them—we must take them—the element of the Free Will of man is in no way eliminated, fer we sometimes see the opportunities rendered absolutely unfruitful through lack of *Good Will*. It seems to me of vast importance to feel our *good fortune* in this matter. We have supreme chances, and not to make the most of them means a refusal to make the most of ourselves, a refusal to take some of the best things in life.

I place that chance of unselfish endeavor first, because it is to me the glory of our profession, but there are other gains that perhaps we generally think of first because they appeal to our egoistic side, and in most of us that presents a fairly bold front.

We certainly derive an increase of knowledge and a direct, though possibly not very sound connection with one of the most alive and interesting Sciences of the day. We gain a means of livelihood: to some delightfully ignorant persons we become an authority. We gain a knowledge of people most interestingly and intimately. We find how people live, of whose lives we were before in perfect ignorance. Almost unconsciously we are introducd to some of the great sociological questions so widely discussed.

The people of the slums become our acquaintances. We come near the grim affairs of living, poverty and pain—and what food for reflection is offered! See when an immense gain in the *furnishing of our minds!* We come into a sort of humble fellowship with some of the noblest women that ever lived. Florence Nightingale and Sister Dora and Alice Fisher, their lives and what they did and tried to do, have a much greater significance.

By the way, there is another matter that possesses the public mind greatly—that a nurse must of necessity have her finer feelings and perceptions blunted. In what work, I would ask, could a woman's gentleness and care be *more* appealed to or exercised?

There is an infinitude of things to be gained; I have barely mentioned a few that to me bore a larger aspect. Altogether it is a great field we enter upon, a glorious one. A friend and former teacher of mine wrote me not long ago and said, "I congratulate you upon the work you have taken up. It is well to try for a life so much bigger than ourselves that we may never stop growing."

We should indeed count ourselves fortunate young women, and gain all from our profession that our natures will permit. We can never exhaust its wealth.

"Uncle Charley" (Charles Dudley Warner, editor of the *Courant*) came to Harmony's graduation, but died suddenly on the 20th—a great shock to all Hartford. After the funeral, Harmony wrote: "To the Editor of *The Courant:*—I think it cannot be amiss for one of the young people to whom Mr. Warner was such a sure and dear guide to express the gratitude we feel for the stimulation he gave toward what was best and most interesting, and for the nobility of his example. But most of all we are grateful to him for his interest in us. Certainly it is the greatest of all things for a youth to feel that a great and good man cares what way he is growing up, and Mr. Warner made all youth with whom he came in contact feel that it was his desire that they become a part of the best at home and abroad. We love him for it . . . T. October 24."

Three days later she and her father left on a trip to Italy as guests of "Uncle Cornelius" Dunham, who had arranged it as a graduation present. They sailed on the *Werra* (North German Lloyd) for Genoa—visited Milan, Venice, Bologna, and Florence, where they enjoyed the hospitality of Prof. Willard Fiske, formerly of Cornell University—then to Rome and Naples, where they embarked on the *Aller* (same line), and were home by December 26.

Just a month later Harmony took a position in the Visiting Nurses' Association of Chicago. The work was hard—"from slum house to slum house"—but with her beauty, warm heart, and sense of devotion, she must have seemed to many like the next thing to an angel. That summer the family vacation was in Chicago instead of the Adirondacks, and Harmony had her own vacation at home, Christmastime. The next family vacation (summer 1902) was half at Lake Forest, Harmony commuting, and half at Elk Lake.

In October 1902 Harmony left Chicago. Late in March 1903, Dave was "completely used up with overwork" and went for a month's rest ("with Harmony Jr. for company and nurse") to Summerville, South Carolina, where he had been encamped during the war—but in spite of this interruption he did graduate from P. & S.

After summer 1903 as companion and nurse to "Aunt Sally" Dunham (Cornelius Dunham's sister) at Keene Valley, Harmony joined Dave in September at Saranac Lake, being the resident Visiting Nurse there until November 1904. Fall 1904 she was briefly engaged to Rev. Walter Lowrie, son of a family she had visited other summers at Keene Valley. It may have been early in 1905 that she met Charlie Ives again.

About March 1, Harmony became companion to Mrs. Dean Sage of Albany, an old friend of her father's. This lasted off and on for over two years, first involving a trip to Europe in May and June in company with J. F. Cooper (son of the novelist) and his son Jimmie (whose poem, *Afterglow,* Ives later set). They sailed on the *Finland* for Antwerp, saw The Hague and Amsterdam, crossed to England and spent most of the time in London and around Windermere, and sailed back from Liverpool on the *Oceanic.*

Seeing Charlie Ives again, Harmony and he must have realized what they meant to each other, and when, over two years later, they started a record of memorable days together, calling it *Our Book,* the first entry was remembered from summer 1905, with a heading: "La Vita Nuova." During August she was nurse at the Henry Street Settlement in New York, and early in September they were together at Saranac with Dave.

Since Harmony was based near Albany, getting away only for brief visits to the family, the courtship was long—"we were very formal in those days"—but it seems clear that their deepening love gave him a heightened self-confidence that made possible the explosion in 1906 of his radically experimental vein. But, as in all his music the challenging dissonance and familiar consonance go hand in hand (*Song for Harvest Season* and *There Is a Certain Garden* in 1893, *From the Steeples* and *The Children's Hour* in 1901, "*1776*" and *The Sea of Sleep* in 1903), it was now perfectly natural for *The Unanswered Question* and *Central Park* to explode the musical horizon of the future at the same time that *Pictures* and *The World's Highway* kept within the heritage of the past.

The tamer songs of this period were probably courting songs, that he wanted Harmony and her family to like and understand. Their first collaboration may have been *The World's Highway.* Harmony sent him the poem on Mrs. Sage's note paper (undated), and many years later she thought that the music was composed fresh, rather than adapted from something earlier, as he often did. It was the only one of his songs she learned to sing—"not in public of course—his other songs were beyond me." Generally Ives seldom told her much about the music he was working on, though she does remember his showing her *The Unanswered Question* and *Central Park*—"he fixed it so I could understand it somehow."

Ending her service with Mrs. Sage on 29 April 1907, Harmony spent a month home, and then returned as nurse to the Henry Street Settlement for June and July. Ives took her to several of Kaltenborn's St. Nicholas Rink concerts and to see Sothern and Marlowe in *Twelfth Night*—"I guess all my dates were with him that summer." It may have been around this time that she fitted a translation to *Ilmenau.* In August she visited Mrs. Sage for a week at Hewitt's Lake, then joined her family for two weeks at Elk Lake, writing the poem of the *Spring Song* on the 14th. On 26–27 August Deac (see §19, note 11) drove her, with Dave's team of horses, to Saranac to pinch-hit for a nurse on vacation. From there she sent Ives the outline of *The Kimash Hills* on 29 September (see App. 21).

She was home by 11 October, and on Tuesday 22 they took a walk on the wood road to Farmington ("through the reservoir grounds"), which long remained a focal point in their memories. She sent him the first draft of *Autumn* on the 28th. On Saturday 16 November they saw the Yale-Princeton game at New Haven, and on Sunday it was no surprise to her father that they asked his blessing (see App. 16). In December Harmony and her sister Louise had grippe, and went to Atlantic City in January to recuperate. In early April she sent Ives *The South Wind.*

They were married at home by her father on Tuesday, June 9, 1908. From that moment their life was one, with a unity that had to be witnessed to be understood. Many years later, when Harmony heard that a friend had got into trouble, she wanted to be sure before telling Charlie, and wrote Charlotte Ruggles: "It's the only thing I've ever kept from him." (For their changes of address, vacations, and trips to Europe, see the chronological index of dates.) Having unusual capacities in different ways—but being alike in setting devotion to ideals above convenience or expedience—their own devotion to each other enlarged their perceptions into what amounted to a mystical vision of reality. The exalted perorations of the *Second String Quartet* and the *Fourth Symphony* are probably not more from transcendentalist sources than from this source.

In the spring of 1909 Harmony was hospitalized for almost a month, her sister Sally taking over the housekeeping. Ives put a short memo on his 1906 sketch of *Like a Sick Eagle:* "H. T. I. in Hospital—Sally singing, 70 W. 11, April 29, '09." But the true meaning behind these laconic words is suggested in a letter of 10 May to Harmony from her mother: "My heart is full of joy and gratitude over you, over Sally, and I must say over dear Charley with his great loving heart. I thought myself so happy in my trust in him, but now, after the revelations of tenderness in him through the great trial that has come to you, I feel that I did not half appreciate what was in him. With him to protect you, life cannot bring you any thing you cannot bear—and still have in your heart abiding happiness."

Just a year later her mother died very unexpectedly (the night after Mark Twain's funeral). At Elk Lake, fall 1910, the first family vacation without Mrs. Twichell must have been full of strange silences, which found expression in Harmony's *Mists:*

> Low lie the mists;
>   They hide each hill and dell;
> The grey skies weep
>   With us who bid farewell.
> But happier days
>   Through memory weave a spell,
> And bring new hope
>   To hearts who bid farewell.

On Thursday 2 March 1911, Henry A. Stillman, a Hartford old timer, was ninety-six. Harmony called on him and wrote the following memo, revealing the same kind of contact with memories of the American Revolution that Ives would have had from his grandmother (see §31, note 11).

———

Today is the ninety-sixth anniversary of old Mr. Stillman's birthday. He always called on my mother, the Minister's wife, on the anniversary until the ninetieth, and after that he moved away from our street, and the walk from his new neighbourhood was too long for him to take. And now my mother has gone before the old man to the other life he longs for. He is a happy and bright old man though.

I remember him as far back as I remember anything. He brought some interesting things in his hand or his pocket on those anniversary calls; a bloom from a house plant—for it fell in a winter month—or a bit of carved ivory from a cabinet of treasures brought home by a seafaring grandfather of his, and always he carried a petrified potato which we children were allowed to hold and wonder at. I can feel now its round, waxlike smoothness in the hollow of my palm. To me he was surrounded by a halo of romance and interest because, as a little boy, he remembered being taken to see an old lady who was Nathan Hale's sweetheart. She used to visit a family who lived in State Street, and he would tell us that though she married she never forgot Nathan, and that the last words she said as she lay dying were "Tell Nathan to come."

Today I made the call. The little sitting room was bright with winter sunshine and open fire, and Mr. Stillman sat tranquilly to greet the half dozen friends and neighbours who came in. His daughter's modest tea table was fair with the old wedding china and silver of the seafaring grandfather and fragrant with gilli-flowers.

Old Mr. Stillman! a good and useful life you have lived and been connected with affairs of moment, but I love and cherish you because you are a visible memory of my childhood. To see you and to take you by the hand makes me anew that wondering little girl who stood by her mother's side and watched you, waiting to hold the curious potato, and that older girl, fresh from *The Boys of '76*,[1] whom you transfixed with interest as you told of Nathan Hale's Miss Adams. I have heard you wonder why your life goes on, when you have seen those of grandchildren and great-grandchildren pass. In my life you touch, as does nothing, the chord whose vibrations are the glory and the glamour of a child's imagination. A lonesome day that will be, when, looking over into the east aisle Sunday morning, I fail to see your venerable figure by the pillar and know that you will come no more.

Harmony and Charlie continued to accompany her father on various occasions, and to welcome him into their household for long visits. In August 1912 they bought land in West Redding, Connecticut, had a house and barn built, and moved in a year later. This luxury made them think of others less fortunate, and in July 1915 they arranged through the Fresh Air Fund for families to use the little cottage for a few weeks in the country—first the Munros—then in August the Osbornes, and when they left, the baby Edith seemed still in need of country air, so the Iveses kept her with them, and eventually adopted her. She was a good, cheerful baby—soon a fountain of funny sayings, many of which they wrote down.

Ives's heart attack in October 1918 was a sudden shock to his habitually buoyant health, but there had been warnings (as in December 1906, when his trip to Old Point Comfort with Myrick had been to give his heart a rest). During their stay at Asheville, Harmony wrote two versions of *To Edith* on 28 January, which Ives strung along as two stanzas, with a tune from 1892. A letter-sketch from Asheville says that "we have been down here most of the winter trying to get well. Personally . . . I think I have had the flu, for that is the one thing that all the doctors have eliminated. But I'm glad to say that . . . Mrs. Ives has decided to take charge, and I am almost well again—how could it be otherwise?" Ives didn't go back to business until 15 September 1919.

Since fall 1917 they had rented Henry Dwight Sedgwick's house at 120 East 22nd Street, around the corner from Gramercy Park. The Minturns were their neighbors, and Edith and her playmate Susanna Minturn were the *Two Little Flowers* of 1921. Ives always said it was Harmony's poem—she, that they'd written it together—whichever, it was their last collaboration.

In 1926 Ives bought the house at 164 East 74th Street, which was their New York home for the rest of his life, with the music room on the top floor. Not long after they'd moved in—as Harmony recalled—"he came downstairs one day with tears in his eyes, and said he couldn't seem to compose any more—nothing went well, nothing sounded right." From then on he revised and got old sketches in shape. Paradoxically, it was only after his fresh composing had ceased that the expansion of interest in his music opened up. This meant an enlarged correspondence—and after he retired in 1930, and diabetes had made his hand shaky, Harmony was a tireless and painstaking amanuensis—particularly when his eyes were clouded by growing cataracts (successfully removed in 1937). When Edith

1 *The Boys of '76, A History of the Battles of the Revolution* by Charles Carleton Coffin (1823–96) was published by Harper & Brothers in 1876. Mrs. Ives remembered it as "a very good book—I read it many times."

married George Tyler in 1939, the old folks missed the constant joy of her gayety, but soon they were grandparents.

All this time Harmony had been a kind of unobtrusive, stabilizing counterbalance to Ives's mercurial excitability. In conversation with friends, one never knew what would touch him off into a tirade, sometimes violent. Harmony would say little, but by force of presence and love she silently helped idealize the polemic, lessening its destructive effects. Charlotte Ruggles used to tell of the time around 1950 when she and Carl were at 164 for lunch, and Charlie and Carl in a burst of enthusiasm for Reeves's *Second Connecticut March* began to shout the tune and march around the table—"Those two *boys!*—and there sat Harmony, perfectly serene, just as if nothing was going on!"

Her life had been so focussed that, when he died, it was no wonder she could write Carl and Charlotte: "My life seems emptied of its contents." However, her care for doing whatever was best for his music continued with the same devotion and the same understanding kindness for another fifteen years, her mind amazingly clear, until on Good Friday, 4 April 1969, she quietly rejoined him.

Three great wives of first-rank composers, Marian MacDowell, Charlotte Ruggles, and Harmony Ives all shared the same genius—a contagion of faith in the boundlessness of human growth, so that in their presence it seemed perfectly natural to forge right ahead toward realizing one's highest aspirations. Ives may have had such a thought in mind when he dictated (in §43): "What she has done for me I won't put down, because she won't let me."

Major John Andre

Lyman Brewster (1832–1904)

Lyman Denison Brewster, six generations from Elder Brewster of the Plymouth Colony, was born at Salisbury, Connecticut, July 31, 1832. At Yale he was '55 class poet. After studying law at Danbury with his uncle Roger Averill (later Lieutenant-Governor of Connecticut), he was admitted to the bar January 1, 1858, and devoted the rest of his life to law and jurisprudence. On January 1, 1868, he married Sarah Amelia Ives (they had no children). The same year he was Judge of Probate, in 1870–74 Judge of the Court of Common Pleas of Fairfield County, 1880–81 State Senator, 1890–1903 chairman of the Committee on Uniform State Laws of the American Bar Association, presiding in 1896–1901 at the National Conferences. He died in the old Ives house, February 14, 1904.

In 1893 he took his nephew Charley as his secretary to the National Conference, at Milwaukee that year. Around August 20 they went to the Chicago World's Fair, hearing the Theodore Thomas Orchestra, though not conducted by Thomas. They visited the Brewster cousins at Peru, Illinois, August 26–29, were in Milwaukee August 29 through September 1, then back to the Fair, Charley due to hear Guilmant's organ recital and to be home in Danbury by the 7th.

All his life Lyman Brewster wrote verse, of which a booklet was printed in 1900 by the *Danbury News*, entitled *Youth and Yale*. Apparently his major literary effort was the following play. Quite apart from its relative merits, it commands interest by Ives's thinking of making it into an opera, and by its having thus been the pretext for his overture, "1776"—possibly also the *Country Band March*—and having thereby sparked one of his major works, *Putnam's Camp*, into which the two earlier pieces were dovetailed (see §31). But more important is its voicing of what the events in the play meant to the Ives family and their circle of in-laws and friends. Danbury, having been burned by the British in 1777, was still, well over a century later, acutely aware of the Revolution and everything it had meant, including patriotism and treason.

There are three sources for the play, in three medium-large copy books of ruled paper:

A has a date on the flyleaf, "Jan. 1875." Into the right-hand pages he copied several older poems (two of them dated 1862), keeping the left-hand pages for revisions (an insert for the poem *Niagara* is dated 1883). The last two of the series are *Washington's Reprimand to Arnold* and *Night before the Execution of Andre* (apparently modelled after Landor's *Imaginary Conversations*). There is no dating of when he decided to expand these into a play, filling some of the blank left-hand pages with historical data and outlines of the five acts, and filling the rest of the book with the various scenes and revisions.

B (no date on any page) is a clear copy of the whole play, mostly on the right-
    hand pages only, with many revisions and additions on the left (in the editor's
catalogue of Ives's manuscripts, 1960, p. 42, one of these revisions, on p. 6 of B,
is wrongly attributed to Ives himself—Brewster's normally slanted hand could
vary surprisingly).

C (no date on any page nor title) is a later clear copy, incorporating the re-
    visions of B with many further additions, and starting with a resumé of
previous plays on the same subject. On p. 24 there is an interesting comment in
another hand (not Roger Averill, nor James M. Bailey, "the Danbury News man"
—possibly the Danbury poet, Starr Nichols?), which may have been entered after
Brewster had copied in the first three acts: "You must have a woman for Andre
to make love to. How would a Quakeress do? This should occupy the two wanting
acts, as there is not enough of him here to make the audience care for his fate."
Perhaps Brewster agreed and may have thought of changing the title—Ives always
referred to the play as *Benedict Arnold*.

Tucked into C is a typescript of the first two scenes and the final scene only, on
paper of the "Danbury and Bethel Street Railway Company, J. Moss Ives, Re-
ceiver" (in the 1920s)—in which B and C are combined and a few words are left
blank—to be deciphered later?

This editing combines ABC freely, not giving variants but giving sources (as in
the *Memos*), keeping most of the additions in C, which often clarify or pull things
together, but omitting them wherever they seem superfluous. The various lists of
Dramatis Personae have enough names that do not appear, or lack of those that do,
to justify a fresh list. In A, pp. 98–100–102, there is a preliminary scene (not in
BC) that deserves a position of prologue. It is mostly prose, partly verse, and is
presented as prose in A (in prose the Quaker says "thee seest"—in verse "thou
knowest"). Brewster may have discarded it because of its reference to Valley Forge
in the proper time relation, which is reversed when the Valley Forge scene comes
after the Mischianza—an understandable poetic license in view of Brewster's
idealizing of many situations.

Major John Andre

DRAMATIS PERSONAE

[rebel]	[loyalist]
Gen. George Washington [1732–99]	Judge Edward Shippen [1729–1806]
Gen. Benedict Arnold [1741–1801]	Margaret Shippen [1760–1804]
Gen. Nathanael Greene [1742–86]	Sallie Shippen
Gen. Henry Knox [1750–1806]	Margaret's other sister
Gen. Henry Lee [1756–1818] (silent)	
	Peggy Chew
Marquis de Lafayette [1757–1834]	Joshua Smith
Alexander Hamilton [1757–1804]	a Loyalist
Benjamin Tallmadge [1754–1835]	
	Loyalist Pennsylvanians

Paulding ⎫
Van Wert ⎬ scouts
Williams ⎭

Paulding's sister

Caesar (Washington's negro bodyguard)
Pompey (Arnold's negro bodyguard)

Nurse of Arnold's baby

a Quaker
a Puritan

a Congressman
a Civilian

Three Soldiers at Valley Forge
Crippled Soldier at Verplanck's Landing

Generals, Officers, Soldiers,
Sentinels, Messengers.

[*English*]

Sir Henry Clinton [ca. 1738–95]

Major John Andre [1751–80]

Honora Sneyd

[PRELIMINARY SCENE]

A   *Before the Hall of Independence. Quaker and Puritan.*

QUAKER. Well, neighbor Standish! thee seest the rueful changes of war—this city of Penn in the hands of the foe, and the hall of independence closed, and the invaders making merry tomorrow over our captivity.

PURITAN. 'Tis a short merriment. They've got to leave and cover up their tracks with their buffoonery. God is just, and justice will prevail.

QUAKER. I am not reconciled to all this strife of arms. Thou knowest our belief concerning war, and that of all the followers of Penn. But never saw I cause more just and true. My sons are in the camp of Washington, and I cannot say nay to their desires. My daily prayer is that we may succeed, and independence be achieved. What do the red coats do tomorrow?

PURITAN. They have a tournament and ball, and all the tories in the town are going to grace the feast. (*Negro comes in with a lot of turbans.*) Well, Caesar! what's all this? Is Squire Shippen turning Turk?

CAESAR. Laws a mighty, Sir, he's bustin' out worse than a hull flock of turbans—an' Miss Margaret she's a gwine too—an' young Major Andre he's to be her knight an' dey'se a gwine to have a awful nice time—regular ole Virginny style—rowin' down de river—an' flags an' flotes—big dinner, big dance, flowers an' fightin', an' a big show. I tell yo what, dis nigger's been a gwine up an' down like a discumbolation for de las' two days. Dey's a rollickin' set, dem young batchers an' de ole ones too, by gory. Dey ain't much like Massa Franklin an' Massa Adams—when dey sat here in Dependence Hall, Sir, dey looks solemn nuff to scare a darkey's head off, make his hair as straight as white folks's is. But dey was a purty grim lookin' set de day of de Declaration!—when de ole Liberty Bell was ringin' an' everybody felt happy as a spring chicken! (*goes off*)

QUAKER. My heart beat high within me on that day. Methought the dreams of Penn and Fox would be fulfilled, and all the world be free and happy and at peace. But alas, this lit the signal for a dreadful war, to be prolonged for years!

PURITAN. All things are bought with a price—war is the price of peace. Cromwell was fighting for the peace of God, without which there is never any peace. And so will Washington and our brave men who have with him endured the winter cold at Valley Forge.

In another month and Philadelphia will welcome our own troops again. Mark my words—Nature rebels against your creed of bloodlessness. Your own children cannot but be patriots. The land they live in has her claims beyond all others. We can have no land but as we earn it. It is still King George's—we can make it ours. And when, to the clear right of country, you have added all the rights of men, and all the promise of a mighty commonwealth, 'tis treason to our better natures not to join the battle for our land, for truth, for God.

QUAKER. I cannot say thee nay, and yet my soul delights not in this carnage of our kind, the slaughter of our fellow men. Our Washington is not a man of blood, but daily prays for peace, and peace that will endure.

PURITAN. These revellers will rest their own reward—light hearted fools, the most of them, who care for nothing but the truth of fame—or men who fight for money.

ACT I

ABC

Scene 1.   Park at Southwark, Philadelphia. The Mischianza. Ladies with turbans, in boxes on each side. Between the boxes, six knights of "The Blended Rose" engage with foils six knights of "The Burning Mountain." After the encounter Andre, who leads one side, gathers the wreaths and carries half to Peggy Chew, Queen of one side, and half to Margaret Shippen, Queen of the other side, saying:

> ANDRE.   It's a drawn game.

Dancing follows on the green, and Major Andre dances with Margaret. The others pass by, leaving them alone. Andre's watch fob opens accidentally and discloses a miniature picture.

> MARGARET.   A portrait of your lady love, Sir Knight?
> Some blue-eyed English damsel, I've no doubt!
> Nay, tell me true, and let me see her face.
>
> ANDRE.   I can no other than the truth declare,
> When I do look upon this face which was,
> As you so truly say, my own true love—
> You almost bring her back to me again!
>
> MARGARET (*gazing at the portrait*).
> She must have been the paragon of maids,
> If this presents her as she truly was.
>
> ANDRE.   Both was, and is. She lives, though dead to me.
> Her radiant smile no portrait can convey.
> The perfect contour of her noble face
> Defied my art—'twas painted by myself.
>
> MARGARET.   What! poet, soldier, and now artist too!
>
> ANDRE.   A Jack at all trades, good at almost none.
>
> But hark! The sound of cannon! 'Tis some ruse
> Of those pestiferous rebels—just in spite.
> There is no danger, I shall soon return.   *Exit Andre.*

MARGARET.   There goes the first young hero of my dreams!
'Tis well I found him out so soon, or else
My father's daughter had been loving ill.
Contrasted with this airy wanderer,
The young provincials I have known seem rude,
Uncouth, unlettered, like so many boys.

How gayly thoughtful and how gently brave,
So full of wit and wisdom and of tact,
He is a prince in war and peace alike!
Had he the hero quality more marked
With less of banter and of levity,
Should I have *then* escaped heart-free? Ah well!

BC

Ah, here comes bright and merry Peggy Chew,
The chosen queen of Andre in this fete.   *Enter Peggy Chew.*

PEGGY.   Well Maggie, my good knight seems to be *yours.*
Now own the truth and say that you are his.

MARGARET.   I will be candid with you for this once:
The Major's heart is held in English chains.

PEGGY.   Oh ho! So runs the rede! I thought as much.
He has at times a far off dreamy look
That seems to reach almost a thousand leagues.
But still you seemed his bright particular—-
Well! what a gallant beau we have in him!

MARGARET.   And such a tenderness of courtesy,
As though each woman were a goddess born!

PEGGY.   And half his garb of fun and merriment
Is plainly donned for other people's good,
To make a stupid world endurable.

MARGARET.   'Tis sure, we shall not see his like again.
But hark! the dance begins—we must return.

ABC

Scene 2.   House of Judge Shippen, Philadelphia.   His three daughters seated at their embroidery.

SALLIE SHIPPEN.   This silk is not quite pink enough to match.   *A knock is heard.*

MARGARET.   I know that knock—'tis Major Andre's own,
Familiar, yet respectful, both at once.

SALLIE.   He comes here often, Maggie, when you're home,
Yet you were not his queen the other day,
When knights and lady loves were pairing off.

MARGARET.   His heart's queen lives far off beyond the sea.   *Enter Andre.*

ANDRE.   The graces three! I do salute you all!
The Mischianza leaves you still at work.
How did you like our pasteboard tournament?

SALLIE.   'Twas charming—excellent—thanks to yourself
And your right gallant company of knights.

ANDRE.   Working at costumes, verses, and details,
And planning all the scenery and parts,
You can imagine me a busy man.
For an impromptu, rollicking affair
I trust you think we did it fairly well.

MARGARET.   You did indeed—was General Howe well pleased?

ANDRE.   I doubt not. We like him and he likes us,
And 'twas a well meant compliment to him.
Now let me show you how I spend my time.
The youngest of the graces I have drawn
In sketch of pen and ink. Is it well done?

TWO ELDEST DAU.   Maggie exactly! form and face and pose!   *Enter Judge Shippen.*

ANDRE.   Good morning, Judge!
JUDGE SHIPPEN.   Good morning to Sir Knight!

ANDRE.   Perhaps you think us only carpet knights,
But we will show good mettle in the field.

JUDGE SHIPPEN.   I hear this Mischianza tournament,
This grand ovation of your generals,
Will prove but farewell pageantry at best,
That military prudence bids retreat.

ANDRE.   Quite likely. War is but a game of chess,
Checking and counter-checking all the while.
Position is the key to all success.
We much regret to leave our charming friends
In this fair city of the peaceful Penn,
But active service is the thing we want.
This Fabian policy of rebeldom
Bodes us no good, and should be met at once
By stirring movements both on land and sea.

JUDGE SHIPPEN.   What war news do you hear in these dull days?

ANDRE.   No news that's new—but things are brewing well.
The rebels' bravest general by far—
That is, among those fitted to command—
Arnold, who won the Saratoga fight
And hurled disaster upon poor Burgoyne,
A perfect lion in the field, they say,
And quite incapable of any fear—
Has been most miseraby recompensed.
It seems he is as lavish as a prince,
Defies his enemies, and treats his friends
With more than modern hospitality,
Has nothing of the politician's guile,
And soldier-like resents their meddling work,
And so the narrow-minded Congressmen
Have kept him chafing at his poor rewards.
After the triple victories he won
They *had* to make him Major General

And give him back his rights so long withheld.
But they have nothing left to pay him with,
And there is discord in the rebel camp.

JUDGE SHIPPEN. As long as Washington is in command,
King George's army will be closely pushed.
Him once deposed, the end of war is near.
Wilt drive with me today the river road?

BC

ANDRE. Thanks!
I leave the picture for the picturesque!
Speaking of pictures, ladies, can you tell
Why Penn is always painted armor on,
The Quaker leader, who opposed all war?

MARGARET. Is that a question or a riddle, Sir,
Or a conundrum with a pun inclosed
Such as you puzzle us poor damsels with?

ANDRE. Guess which while I am gone. Goodbye for now.
                                    Exeunt J. S. & Andre.

ABC   MARGARET. What a light hearted painter Andre is!
The world to him is one vast pleasure ground.

Who is this Arnold that he lauds so high?
I must read up the rebel patriots' roll,
For after all we are all colonists,
BC   And there must be two sides in all disputes,
Else why are people found upon both sides?
How grand 'twould be to be a hero's wife!

SALLIE. Bravo for Mrs. Major General!
With *Yankee Doodle* for a wedding march!   [*exeunt sisters*]

MARGARET. Well, I'm agoing to read about that man!
        Takes down the Chronicle and reads aloud:
"He threads the wilderness through wintry snows
And thunders at the bastions of Quebec,
On Lake Champlain he fires his sailing ship
And makes defeat a more-than-victory."
What a grand warrior this brave Arnold is!
And he's to be our Governor, they say.
If he's a bachelor, I'll set my cap!

ABC   *Scene 3.   Same place.   Judge Shippen and Margaret.*

JUDGE SHIPPEN. The Yankee General would woo your hand,
A widower too, my gentle Margaret,
And almost twice your age, full thirty-six.
But he is brave, if ever man was brave,
A rash, impetuous, valiant, rebel soul,
Of high regard among the colonies,
And—but your wit is better than my words.

MARGARET. What would my father have his daughter do?

JUDGE SHIPPEN. Decide the matter for yourself alone,
                Yet knowing heroes sue not every day.

      MARGARET. Then tell the General to speak himself,
                 Nor seek to woo as old Miles Standish did.
                 'Tis not the first time he has wooing gone.
                 But this I say, that, although he stands not,
                 As I could wish, upon the loyal side,
                 I never met a more heroic man
                 Or one who bore himself more royally.   *Exit Judge Shippen.*

BC   *Margaret (takes out a letter and reads).*

                 How gallantly this crippled hero writes—(*reads*)

                 "On you alone my happiness depends,
                 To make you happy I would gladly die.
                 You have acknowledged friendship and esteem—
                 Would that your friendship ripened into love!
                 But loved or not, my latest wish shall be
                 That heaven's happiness shall be your own.
                 I am forever and forever yours."

C   It strikes me, for a widower, that's good,
                 Though my experience is less than his.
                 A wounded warrior wins a woman's heart.

ABC   *Enter Arnold leaning on his crutch.   Margaret greets him and tenderly helps him
        to a seat.*

        ARNOLD. I am a man whose words are always few,
                 Except when angry—then they come like rain.
                 I love you, as a soldier only loves,
                 With all my life.   That life is at your feet.
                 Let this poor crutch stand for my courtesy;
                 I bow before you as before my queen;
                 One like yourself should ever be a queen.

      MARGARET. Yet I am but a girl, still in my teens.
                 How can I rise to this position true,
                 To share the cares and honors of your state?
                 I and my family are loyalists
                 And you a continental general
                 Although, to tell the truth, in some slight sort,
                 I am a lover too of liberty.
                 I live in sight of Independence Hall.

        ARNOLD. A heart like yours could not brook tyranny.
                 Love laughs at all such obstacles.
                 A queen is queen as soon as she is born;
                 No fairer head has ever worn a crown.
                 I am a loyalist at least to you—
                 But truce to politics where love is king!

      MARGARET. My letter to you told you all my heart,
                 In spite of all attempts to keep it back.
                 I kiss your hand in token of my love.

C   ARNOLD. Your lips!   My darling, now forever mine!

BC

*Scene 4.   Con[tinental] Con[gress] Chamber, Philadelphia.   Officers and civilians
seated.   Arnold's negro Pompey comes in and bows.*

POMPEY.   Honable Major General, Governor Arnold
      Wants to know as you wants him to come in.

CIVILIAN.   Let him come in—he can afford to wait.

POMPEY.   Guess you ain't 'quainted wid de General—
      He nebber wait for nuthin nowhere, boss,
      But I'll reform de General what you says.

*Arnold limps in, bows coldly, and sits down.   Washington enters from the other
side.   All rise but Arnold, who half rises from his chair, when Washington approaches him, shakes his hand, and says aside to Arnold:*

WASHINGTON.   No! do not rise!   You know my errand here,
      A most enforced, unenviable task.
      Your services shall yet be recognized.

(aloud and standing at the table)

ABC

      Your courage, Arnold, needs no praise from me,
      It has been proved upon too many fields,
      The scars you wear are your certificates
      Of valor and of victory. But now,
      No longer moving to the trump of war,
      But resting in the silences of peace,
      Far other duties no less grand are yours,
      Not headlong plunge athwart the gleaming lines,
      But moderation, wisdom, courtesy.

      Because you seem to have forgotten this
      In the first languor of civilian life,
      I have been called upon to speak reproof.
      Let me so voice it, that it rather be
      The strong inducement to more noble deeds!
      Our loved profession should be chaste as ice
      Nor tarnished by the shadow of a fault,
      For, standing as the guardians of right,
      The armed protectors of the common weal,
      A moment's indiscretion loses all
      The laurelled crown of popular esteem
      And wrecks the safety of the state we serve.

      You that have been so fiery 'gainst the foe
      Should be as gentle in the arts of peace
      To our good friends, the friends of our good cause,
      As you were dauntless in the shock of war
      And troublous to our country's enemies.
      So shall my most ungracious task become
      The gate through which you step to high renown,
      And reprimand be lost in eulogy.
      Remember Saratoga and Crown Point
      And all the struggles of the wilderness!
      To me, the man who won those victories
      Shall always be a friend, whatever comes!

C

B

        Be to your best self true, and that control
        Shall give you the command of other men
        And, what is more essential, their respect—
        And self-respect—that is the best of all.
        In the meantime be sure of my regard.   *Shakes his hand.*

        Exeunt all but Arnold.

ABC

ARNOLD. Congress and all the Congressmen be damned!
        I wonder if they think I am a dog
        Without a dog's ability to bite!
        They owe me now for four years manful work
        And pay me with ingratitude.
        Who of their generals has done as much?
        In perils of the wilderness and floods,
        In bloody battles, sieges, and assaults,
        In all the front of fight I have been first,
        And I am flung aside like a vile hound
        To make way for their stupid favorites.

B

        Even my marriage is objected to,
        And if I dine at father Shippen's house,
        The air is full of gossip for a week!

ABC

        To Washington himself I owe respect—
        He always treats me as a trusty friend.
        But all the rest—the whole infernal pack—
        I owe them nothing, and they owe me much.
        I will be even with them soon, by Heaven!

ACT II

ABC

Scene 1. Arnold's country house at Mount Pleasant. Morning reception. General Arnold and his wife.

ARNOLD. Dear, in your presence I forget all else.
        But this ingratitude is hard to bear.
        Of all the lot of croaking Colonists
        The Pennsylvanians are by far the worst—
        And Congress meets in Philadelphia.

MARGARET. At least you have the praise of Washington
        And your good conscience void of all offense,
        A prize no enemy can ever take—
        And when the war is over and sweet peace
        Is reassured, you will have your deserts.

        A loyalist is announced and enters.

ARNOLD. Good morning, neighbor—now how sits the wind?

LOYALIST. The same old quarter it has been for years.
        The country will be ruined for no good.
        The king has fought us with one hand so far;
        When both shall smite us, comes the end right quick.

ARNOLD. But how of France, and all her ships and troops?

LOYALIST.   I am no Frenchman, and I love not France.
            She helps us just to fight her ancient foe
            And get revenge for provinces she lost.
            Better be English, as our fathers were.

            And, neighbor, just one word close to your ear—
            If I were you, and could have my revenge,
            Revenge it should be, swift and strong and sure.

ARNOLD.   How mean you, neighbor?   Hark! I hear a knock.
                                    Enter Congressman.
            Pray, Sir, be seated—and I trust you're well!

CONGRESSMAN.   I trust the General's wounds are healing fast.
               We need such soldiers as you are, afield.

ARNOLD.   'Tis certain some of you don't want me here,
            If we can judge from Madam Rumor's tongue.

Servant hands a batch of letters to Arnold.   He opens and reads and tears them.

ARNOLD.   Confound these duns and bills, they pester me!
            Baker and butcher and grocer [all] at once!
            Gnats, flies, mosquitoes, how the insects buzz!
            I have to wait, why can't *they* do the same?
            And worse than duns (if anything is worse),
            They pile up slanders to the very skies.
            I cannot bow to my good neighbor here
            Or any other civil loyalist,
            Much less shake hands with a suspected man,
            But up there goes a cry of outraged zeal!
            I hardly dare dine at my father-in-law's.

            Well! Who's the favorite of Congress now?
            Our great commander they can hardly bear.
BC   By Heaven! I think they will depose him yet!

CONGRESSMAN.   It is a great responsibility
               To choose commanders in this costly strife,
               And get the right man for the right place too.

ARNOLD.   Where are your eyes?   The war shows who are chiefs.

CONGRESSMAN.   Congress deliberates with thoughtful care
               Among the candidates we should promote,
               And having but few precedents at hand—

ARNOLD.   Bah! Precedents!   They are the musty cards
            That lawyers use who want to steal a trick.
            Why not do just the thing you ought to do
            Without regard to precedent or form—
            For once at least, to just see how 'twould work?
            By Jove—

MARGARET.   Excuse me, General, but these friends of ours
            Must see how well our garden bears the heat.
                                    Exeunt all but Arnold.

ABC   ARNOLD. I have it!   I will get command of some strong fort
And yield it, with its walls and guns and men,
Up to the crown, and so at one round swoop
Get my revenge, and also my reward.

C   My mercantile adventures all have failed.
I'm eaten up by debts—This's the way out.
I'll write to Clinton, sound him, keep concealed,
And when the mine is ready touch the fuse.

BC   But what if I should fail and come to grief!
Then too there's Trumbull, Putnam, Washington,
My troops, old comrades—let me weigh this well
And put the balances on equal beam—
Debts, duns, ingratitude—or doubtful chance—
If Crown or Congress win the day at last,
A royal recompense for treachery—
Ah! treachery!—the word sounds rather bad,
This going over to the enemy—
But what's in names!   A soldier wants success,
And I can win it in no other way.
I'll plan it so these fellows will be glad
To sue for pardon through the man they wronged.
This dream of freedom is a dream—no more—
And if achieved what benefit have I?
I'll reconcile the country to the King
And end the war by one tremendous stroke!

ABC   *Scene 2. Valley Forge. Tents in woods. Snow on ground. Three soldiers on
guard in torn uniforms and shoeless.*

      1ST SOLDIER. 'Tis a cold morning for a shoeless man,
But we can stand it if our General can.

      2ND SOLDIER. You're always rhyming Stephen!   Give us sense.
How can our army live on broken promises?
Our tents are all the clothing we have left,
Our food is hardly fit to feed the crows,
Our barefoot men can never stand a march.
What hope is there that times will ever mend?

      1ST SOLDIER. The hope of God, and all good men.   I say:
Endurance!   That's the best hold we have got,
To stick and hang as long as there is life.
We've got to worry out the enemy.

      3RD SOLDIER (*an old man*). I heard this morning, just at break of day,
A pleading voice come from the General's tent.
I was the sentinel, you know, on guard.
It was the voice of Washington in prayer,
'Twas but a whisper, yet I heard each word,
It came right from the bottom of his heart.
It seemed as though he saw the very God
And bore our cause up to the great white throne,
And when he said "Amen" and ceased to pray,

I felt the presence of the peace of God.
With such a leader, and with such a cause,
We cannot fail, no more than God can fail.

1ST SOLDIER. Well, whether we succeed or don't succeed,
This is the land in which we all were born.
The man who will not fight for his own hearth,
His parents, children, wife, and all he has,
Is just no man at all—but idiot—
What in the world is left worth living for
If one's own country is a nest of slaves,
And one has got to be himself a slave?

3RD SOLDIER. What's General Arnold doing here in camp?
That is his horse by our commander's tent.

Enter Washington and Arnold from side of tent.   Soldiers present arms and retire.

WASHINGTON. You do surprise me, Arnold, by this wish
That after all your service in the field
You should prefer to hold an inland fort.
But I will see, and do the best I can.
Your wounds and scars make needless other plea.

ARNOLD. I am too lame to ride with any ease,
And wish to serve where I can do the most.
Schuyler and Livingston join my request. (*showing their letters*)

WASHINGTON. No need of them, although good men and true.
It shall be as you wish—the post is yours.
The fortress could not be in better hands.
Of all our strongholds 'tis the central key.

Ho! Caesar!   *Black servant bodyguard of Washington appears.*

Can you prepare a luncheon for our guest?
(A dinner, Arnold, we've not had for weeks.)

CAESAR. Hoecake and taters—that's 'bout all we've got,
Nuff of de same, long as de bar'l holds out.
Praps Massa Arnold not a hoecake man.
His Pompey tell me, up in Yankee land,
De hoecake was a beveridge unknown,
He said dey biled it.   I says dat's enuff.
De white folks say there's no disputin' tastes.
I say dat's just de thing makes folks dispute.

WASHINGTON. Well, Caesar, you have had your speech—fire up!

ARNOLD (*aside*). This larder shows the rebel treasury up—
One winter more like this will freeze them out.

Scene 3. New York. Room in Sir Henry Clinton's house.   General Clinton and Andre.

CLINTON. Well, Andre, now that you are adjutant
Of all the armies in the colonies,
The muses, I suppose, have left your dreams,

And all your figures now are numerals,
And mirth and music vanished in thin air!

ANDRE.   By no means, Sir!   If you will only read
The weekly papers these New Yorkers print,
You'll see I am no idler at the quill—
Puns, poems, paragraphs, and punchinelles,
Jesting at all their Yankee works and ways.
You see, the Quaker and the Puritan
Must be laughed out of their absurdities.
So with my little missionary work
And all the entertainments going here,
I find myself quite busy and content.

A letter is brought to Andre.   He reads.

What have we here! something more tangible—
Our rebel correspondent quite unmasks,
Plain as the sun, I now see who he is—
'Tis Arnold's self—no other hand but his,
The continental Major General—
'Tis he!   'Tis he!   Hear what he says in brief
(Translating his assumed commercial talk):

"I am become commandant at West Point,
And I propose to give up to the King
That fort with all its muniments and men
By strategy.   That fortress in your hands,
And rebeldom is cut in twain and dies.
What my reward shall be we will have fixed,
When Anderson and I can meet alone.
Now is the time to strike; come on at once."

CLINTON.   What think you of this new proposal now?
Can we rely on Arnold?—That's the point.

ANDRE.   Without a doubt!   I have no fears of him.
He is a soured and disappointed man,
Defrauded, as he thinks, of just deserts
(And so think many of his countrymen)—
And by so much the more to be believed
As he was worthy of all soldier's fame,
And has been half-cashiered and left unpaid.
His marriage too leads on to this apace.
I knew the maiden he has wooed and won,
Of all the Quaker city, she the belle,
And her own family rank loyalists.
How they drank bumpers to our good King George
And quick confusion to the other George!

His wife, they say though, since she's Arnold's bride,
Takes up the rebel role with charming grace.
But married life brings large expenditure,
And Arnold is in debt o'er head and ears,
And must get out the best way that he can.

Ah! what a prize to us West Point would be!
It could be taken without loss of blood,
And its surrender might end up the war.

CLINTON.   These contumacious rebels fight so well,
And are so generalled and disciplined,
That just as sure as fate, unless we do
Sow discord in their camp, or buy them off,
The game is up, and we must all retreat!
Our army beaten by provincial troops—
Think of it, Andre! to give up at last!
All this makes Arnold's offer opportune.
Do you propose yourself to treat with him,
With all the risks and hazards of the trip?

ANDRE.   Trust me for that.   So much the more reward
For him who brings the rebels back again,
And saves the further sacrifice of life.

CLINTON.   Well, if you think that you yourself must go,
Keep in our lines and take no documents.
I would not have you run a dangerous risk
For all the forts in all the colonies.

ABC

*Scene 4.   Arnold's house on the East bank of the Hudson below West Point.
Arnold on the balcony above.*

ARNOLD.   I am too far involved to now retreat.
The British general knows who it is
That makes proposals such as I have made.

'Twas I who saved West Point, and all the streams
From the St. Lawrence border to New York,
To Congress and the continental cause.
And now, defrauded of my pay and fame,
My rank so justly earned, so long deferred
That junior officers lord over me—
I pay them in the coin they minted me.

But hush! no word of this to that white soul
Who comes to me, the one stay of my life,
The queen of women, and the best of wives,
She quite unmans me for this fearful task!

Enter Margaret, kissed by Arnold.

Well, Maggie, how does Hendrick Hudson's stream
Compare with that fair Schuylkill that you love?

MARGARET.   Ah! this is glorious!   'Tis an inland sea
With promontories like enchanted isles,
Each curve and slope, and cove of sheltered bay,
Unfolding some new harbor of delight!
And these old forests of primeval growth,
Height above height, in ranks of perfect green,
They seem to me your soldiers keeping guard,

An army of tall sentinels, and strong.
No enemy would dare to try these walls
So long as you command the bastioned fort—
The very mountains send defiance down.

ARNOLD.   Ah! you are getting to be rebel too!
How long since your conversion was achieved?

MARGARET.   The day you called me wife.   I took you then
For better and for worse—your cause is mine.
I once was thoughtless, as my sisters were,
And laughed with Andre and the loyalists
At ragged continentals and their ways—
But when I wedded you, a patriot,
The standard bearer of our liberties,
And learned of Washington, and how the war
Is waged for independence and our rights,
I now, dear husband, stand with him and you.
And our dear boy I shall bring up to be
A valiant, true, and worthy citizen,
Whose father stoutly battled for his land,
This brave new world where all men shall be free!

ARNOLD (aside).   Oh God! her words are arrows barbed with fire!
(aloud)   What say your Quaker neighbors nowadays?

MARGARET.   Your enemies are bitter as before.
They say 'twas foolish work to send you here,
That this rebellion will be soon put down.
Some shrug and whisper, who dare not speak out.
All say, "One more defeat and then the end."

ARNOLD.   Aye, aye—one serious loss would end it all,
And peace is good however brought about.

MARGARET.   Peace without honor!   How can that be good?

ARNOLD.   My dear, these things are quite beyond your reach.

Nurse brings in baby.

But how is this?   Here comes my boy—One kiss!

Enter attendant with letter.   Arnold reads to himself, folds it up.

[aside]   So soon!—well, all the better, let it come!

[aloud]   I must away to see a trusted friend.
Goodbye, my love, my darling, my delight—
Your heart is right, whatever else is wrong.

MARGARET.   Oh husband! tell me what you have in hand!
It is not right to leave me ignorant.
I share your fortunes; I should share your thoughts.
You act so strangely since we have been here.
Is there some danger to the fort or you?
Fear not to tell me, I have courage too;
I'll try at least to be a soldier's wife.

ARNOLD.   You are! you are!   I'll tell you bye and bye.   *Escapes.*

ABC

*Scene 5.   Verplank's Landing, East side of Hudson below West Point.   Paulding
and a crippled American soldier.*

SOLDIER.   How now, good comrade?   You look pale and worn.

PAULDING.   Just come from what is nearest hell on earth,
A British prison ship.

SOLDIER.   Give us your hand!
The Generals cross the Hudson soon today.

Aye, there they come!   You see that heavy barge—
'Tis Arnold brings down Washington in that,
And all his retinue of officers.
He goes to Hartford, there to meet the French.
That's he there in the center.   What a man!
He towers above them like a mountain peak,
A born commander if there ever was.
And next are Arnold, and young Lafayette.
And that stout man is General Knox, well named.
There's "Light Horse" Harry Lee and Hamilton.
                                         The barge lands.
Make fast that line so we can hold the barge.

Arnold, as they land, hands a letter to Washington, who reads it thoughtfully.

ARNOLD.   What say you to this Robinson's request,
Commander?   Shall I go or no?   He seems
To want an interview on what he claims
Is business of great public interest.
I see no harm in it, if you consent.
They say he is a good, well meaning man.

WASHINGTON (*reflecting*).   He wants to meet with you on neutral ground.
I think it would be safer not to go.
A deed suspicious in its very look
Is best undone except for weighty cause.

C

A little caution, Arnold, on your part!
We can't afford to do suspicious things.

ABC

ARNOLD (*tries to smile*).   Just as you say, of course.   Your word is law.

BC

LAFAYETTE (*to Washington*).   Saw you how Arnold's color quickly changed
When you denied the interview he sought?
I tell you, sire, there's something wrong with him.

WASHINGTON (*to Lafayette*).   No, 'tis his nature, quick to take affront,
But he fights well, and has won many fields.

They all move on but Arnold, who turns aside and waves them farewell.

ARNOLD (*aside*).   That is the first blow to our well laid plot!

ABC

Can it be possible that Washington
Suspects that something wrong is looming up?
I fear his prohibition ruins us.
The scheme must all be ciphered out again.
Pshaw!   'Tis only his good luck—so calm,
Dispassionate, and self-restrained!   Would I

Had something of his power of self-command!
Well, now I must meet Andre, come what may!

BC

And yet there's something whispers to me "Halt!"—
A music of old memories and hopes
Like far off Sunday bells on summer morns
I used to hear among New England hills.

ACT III

ABC

Scene 1. *West bank of Hudson River below West Point, midnight. Arnold walks the shore alone.*

ARNOLD. Now comes the crisis of my stormy life!
Danger like wine brings courage to my veins.
Give me but action and I'll face all odds!
This cursed suspense is wearing me to death.
John Andre will be here with power to treat
On all points of our weighty enterprise.
West Point is worth them twenty thousand pounds!
But I shall have to take them at their price.
This business once commenced can know no stop—
The gallows or a dukedom on the cast!

Ah here they come.   *Enter Andre with Smith.*

SMITH (*to Andre*). This is the person that you came to see. *Holds up the lantern.*

ARNOLD. John Anderson!
ANDRE.   Gustavus!
ARNOLD (*in whisper*). Andre!
ANDRE (*in whisper*).   Arnold!   And so we meet at last!

ARNOLD. In a good place for undisturbed discourse.

ANDRE. Are we alone, and can we finish here?

ARNOLD. You come, I take it, with full powers to treat
Of all the matters we have written on,
And finish up the bargain, once for all?

ANDRE. I do.   (*aside*) How like a scheming publican
Who drives a bargain for a load of pork!

ARNOLD. We are alone, but as for time and place
That will depend.   You see I want to know
A thousand things.
ANDRE.   Are we on neutral ground?

ARNOLD (*hesitating*). Yes, yes—but let's go further in the woods.
(*to Smith*) We'll meet you at your house ere long.

Smith retires, and Arnold and Andre go into the woods.   All is dark and silent except the screech of the night owl.   When stage is re-lighted it shows Arnold and Andre at a table in Smith's house.

ARNOLD (*unfolding maps and papers*).
These papers are worth twenty thousand pounds,
With the commandant and the fort thrown in.

ANDRE.   Ten thousand was the limit Clinton gave.

ARNOLD.   After the capture he shall double it.
Say to him, I expect it when we meet,
And Britain's banner flies above West Point.

Let's see: today is Friday, twenty-second.
In three days more will Washington return
From Hartford, with his officers and suite.
One day he'll spend upon the fort, no more.
In a week's time I shall be left alone.
Then let Sir Henry come.   I'll fix the rest,
If he but follows out what's written here.
I'll weaken the main points, so they will fall
At the first burst of resolute assault,
And all the garrison be captured too.
You'll have to take these papers with you, though.

ANDRE.   My orders are most positive and strict
To take no papers of whatever kind.

ARNOLD.   Then there's an end of all our well planned scheme.
The project fails and all is lost.   No man
Can carry these instructions in his head,
Or half remember what I've written here.
And without these directions all falls through.

ANDRE.   Well, if I must, I must.   I'll take them all.

ARNOLD.   That's like a soldier!   Danger is his life.
But we will see that you get through all right.

ANDRE.   Before I go, I must inquire of one
I knew in the good city of her birth—
Your wife—then Maggie Shippen, gay and fair.

ARNOLD.   She and our child are here and well.   She speaks
Quite often of your name.   It has been hard
To keep this venture from her eager eyes.

ANDRE.   Why! she was loyalist two years ago,
A tory of the tories—tory born.

ARNOLD.   She's now as strong a rebel as the best.
Since she's become a continental's wife,
She talks of liberty and self-defense,
And rights of man, and General Washington,
Far freer than I ever did myself.

For Washington, although a steadfast friend,
Is coldly distant as a mountain peak.
And as for liberty, it only means
A change of masters, Congress or the King,
And as for me, one master is the best.   *A shot is heard.*

ANDRE.   What's that?

ARNOLD (*rising and looking out*). The ship that brought you to this point
Is drifting down, to get from cannon's range.

ANDRE.   But I must be at once rowed to the ship.

ARNOLD.   Impossible!   You'll have to take the road.
          I'll write a passport that will take you through.
                                             Arnold writes a passport.

ANDRE.   Great God! *I* go within the enemy's lines
          Crammed like a spy with deadly messages!
          I like this not, but what is done is done.

ARNOLD.   I leave you in the charge of our friend Smith.
          He'll do the best for you that can be done.
          If you go back by land, go well concealed,
          And when you get upon the Eastern bank,
          By all means leave your uniform behind.   *Smith enters.*

          Smith, take good care of Mr. Anderson.
          Back to the fort I must return at once.
          Here is the passport that may serve your turn.
          Goodbye!   Yes, Mr. Anderson, Goodbye!

ANDRE.   Farewell!

ABC   *Scene 2.   Paulding, Williams and Van Wert behind a clump of bushes near the
          highway.*

WILLIAMS *(after looking up and down).*
                    Well boys, there's no one coming, up or down.
                    Let's have a game of cards—what shall it be?

VAN WERT. "High Low" will do for three.   Who has a pack?

PAULDING. Here is a pack well thumbed.   Cut for the deal.

VAN WERT. The knave of clubs—that's just King George himself!
           Here is the king of hearts, and trump, by George
           (Another George who's better than a king)!
           When General George crossed here the other day,
           It did one's eyes good just to see his face.
           He is a trump if ever man was trump!

PAULDING. I took that trick!   Talking of generals,
           What do you think of General Arnold, boys?
           He's done some famous things in this old war.

WILLIAMS. He's a good fighter, but too cursed proud—
           Wrong kind of pride—in quarrels all the time,
           Jealous, and poor and never pays his debts—
           And all the while he *will* live like a lord.
           If honest men are men who pay their debts,
           I fear me, Mister Arnold is no honest man.
           But all men are not built or bred alike—
           We've got to do the best with what we have.

VAN WERT. Have any cowboys been around of late?

WILLIAMS. No, nor the skinners either—they're the worst!
           They pilfer from both sides, the renegades—

PAULDING (*looking up through the bushes*).
        Hallo! who's that on horseback? a soldier
        With boots and cloak—we'd better stop that chap!

Andre comes down highway humming a roundelay, then soliloquizes.
ANDRE. This must be well below the rebel lines.
        The risk is over, all is well at last.
        I must have Clinton let me lead the troops
        That are to capture the defenceless fort.

The three scouts start up with their guns in front of Andre.
PAULDING. Stop, Sir, and stand!   Which way today, my friend?

ANDRE. You gentlemen are of our party, sure?

WILLIAMS. What party do you mean?
ANDRE.   The lower one.
WILLIAMS.   Yes.
ANDRE. Know then I am a British officer,
        Bound on important business to New York.
        I must not be detained a moment here. *Andre pulls out his watch.*
        Take this.
WILLIAMS.   Dismount, Sir! We don't want your watch!

ANDRE (*aside*). I must do anything to get away.
  (*aloud*) Here is my pass—you'd better let me go.
        It is a pass that Arnold signed, you see,
        And 'tis his business that I have in charge.

               Paulding looks at the pass.
PAULDING. The General's name as sure as ink is ink!
        We hope, Sir, no offense—we are no thieves.
        But there are rogues enough upon the road.
        We're bid examine all who pass this way,
        And hold all foes in charge.   What is your name?

ANDRE. John Anderson—you see it in the pass.

PAULDING. It looks all right, and yet it's mighty odd—
        A British officer with General Arnold's pass!!
        We must examine you from head to foot.
        If we find nothing, you can go your way,
        Just come this way and take your coat off, please.
        No honest man need fear of being searched.

ANDRE (*aside*). 'Tis well indeed the papers are safe hid.

Williams and Van Wert go into the bushes with Andre, and return.

PAULDING. Do you find anything?
VAN WERT.   No, not a thing.
PAULDING. Look in his boots.
WILLIAMS.   I will.
PAULDING.   That's right, my boys,
        One can't be too particular.

           They search in the boots and return.
WILLIAMS. We find these papers in his stockings hid. *Paulding reads them.*

PAULDING. By thunder this is odd.   He is a spy—
"Artillery orders—and the plan of forts—
How to attack West Point—Council of War—
Place where the party of attack shall come"—
Here's treason black as Hell!   And Arnold's pass!
The Devil's to pay!   Who ever saw such work!
Keep your eyes on him—he must not escape!

ANDRE (*leaning against a tree, aside*).
So, caught at last, just on the very edge,
And when I thought achievement touched success!
These fellows look too honest to be bought—
Three of them are too many to resist—
Ah well, ah well.   I'll try their honesty.
(*aloud*) I'll try them.
PAULDING.   Rather I'll try you.   I say,
What will you give to have us let you off?

ANDRE. Why, anything you ask.   Ten thousand pounds?

PAULDING. No, Mr. Redcoat, you mistake your man.
If you should plank ten thousand guineas down,
You should not stir one step upon your way.

There is some mischief here to our good cause.
The mystery is much too deep for us. (*pointing to the passport*)
Did General Arnold really give you this?

ANDRE. No matter!   I will tell your leaders all.

PAULDING. We'll take you to our officers right soon,
And you may then explain things, if you can.
You find that there are men who, though they're poor,
Not all the money in the world can buy!

ABC   *Scene 3.   Room in Arnold's house.   Mrs. Arnold singing a lullaby to the baby in
its cradle.   Nurse enters.*

NURSE. They say the Generals dine here today.
They are returning from their Hartford trip.
Baby must don his new liberty cap.

MARGARET. Right, nurse!   I'll try it now upon his head.
There's a young Continental for you now!

Enter Arnold pale and haggard.   Nurse retires at a signal from Mrs. Arnold.

MARGARET. Good heavens! what is it that you look so pale!

ARNOLD. Dearest, be brave—Be a true soldier's wife—
We must this instant part.   I fly for life—
If I can reach the British lines, all well—
If not, my life is forfeit.
MARGARET.   Not your life!

ARNOLD. Andre and I had planned to yield this fort—
And Andre has been captured in the lines

With all the papers that disclose our plot—
Some stupid Major sent the news to me,
And came quite near to sending Andre too.

MARGARET.   Andre and you! and plots to yield the fort!
Let me go with you, husband—Yes! I must!

ARNOLD.   No! No!   Alone, I am sore pressed for time,
With you, escape there would be none for both.

MARGARET.   Farewell! Farewell!   Away! Away! for life!

Arnold kisses her and his child.   Mrs. Arnold swoons.

ARNOLD.   Ah this is worse than death, but I must fly.
My men shall row me to the British ship.   *Exit Arnold.*

Nurse re-enters and tries to restore Mrs. Arnold.   As Mrs. Arnold revives, nurse removes the child, and re-enters with Washington.

NURSE.   Oh General, my mistress will be killed.

MARGARET.   What have they done with him?   Oh let me know!
Why did you let him have this post at all?
And why! oh why! did he conceal it all from me
Who might have turned him from his deadly plan?
Now take our child and kill us all at once!

WASHINGTON.   Madam, your husband is in safety now,
I doubt not, as there has been no pursuit.
For your child's sake, try to compose yourself.

MARGARET.   But Andre!   Is he prisoner of war?—
For so I now remember that he said
When he came in to say farewell and fly.
Oh God! that I should be a traitor's wife!
And yet they wronged him, Sir! they wronged him much!
A high, proud spirit his, stung to the quick—
I see it all, now that the deed is done,
The dreadful, black, and monstrous thing he did!
Yet never did I dream of his intent.
And will the people think I knew of it?

WASHINGTON.   I do believe you, Madam, innocent.
Yes, Andre has been captured in our lines
And will be tried for having played the spy.
And I much fear me, in the public thought,
You will be judged accomplice with the two.
I give this warning most reluctantly.

MARGARET.   *I* thought to tempt him from his high career!
I thought to be the tory sorceress
To lure him to dishonorable means,
To sell his country for base British gold,
To lose the good opinion of good men,
To be the byword of his countrymen,
The synonym of Treason for all time!

I called a traitress! *I* whose very life
Has been devoted to my husband's work!
I shall go mad! And yet my babe, my life!   (*swoons*)

WASHINGTON. How could the husband of this royal wife
Turn traitor to his country and his God!
Ho, help!   *Hamilton enters. Mrs. Arnold recovers.*

C   HAMILTON. Despatches, sire, of great importance wait.
I'll stay till her attendant comes to help.   *Exit Washington.*

BC   MARGARET. One whom you once called by the name of friend
Here stands without a friend in all this land.
I shall be cursed not as a traitor's wife alone,
But as the temptress who has lured him on.
You know how false the accusation is.
I may have been unguarded in my speech.
And since my father was a loyalist,
There may be some who honestly suppose
I did not take sides with my husband's cause.
But Heaven that reads the language of the heart
Knows how I gave myself to him and his.

         HAMILTON. I at least know the truth of what you say,
Each word and look attest your innocence.
                                        Enter nurse and child.

C   This babe is not more innocent than you—
Live for his sake!

B   MARGARET. Now I must ask you of that far off land
Where we must live as exiles all our days.
Is there some spot where we can hide away
And let our child grow up in ignorance
Of what his father rashly tried to do?

ACT IV

ABC   *Scene 1. Old fashioned colonial house, piazza. Two sentinels walking at each
end. They halt as Andre and Tallmadge enter from the house.*

         ANDRE. So I have told the story of my life
As one would tell it to a brother born,
And how I came here as by accident
Without a thought of entering your lines.
What will my captors think you do with me?
Give me the whole truth—nothing but the truth.

         TALLMADGE. It pains me to the heart to have to tell—
You are entitled to know all the truth,
For you have been as open as the day.
The only answer I can give is this—
When the war started, some four years ago,
We had, within our ranks, as brave a man
As ever breasted the red tides of war.
He was a scholar and a gentleman,

Devoted, noble, courteous, and refined
As any youth my eyes have ever seen.
He was my college classmate at old Yale.
He went in secret through the British lines,
Not to plot treason with their generals
But just to find out how their forces stood,
Was caught, condemned, and suffered as a spy.
As Hale was treated, so will Andre be,
If we go by the settled rules of war.

ANDRE. My God!   The rebels will not make me out
A spy! who never thought to come within
Their lines.   A spy! how I detest the name!

TALLMADGE. Major!   The act and not the hidden thought
Is what the court must pass on, and I fear
There is but one plain duty to be done—
'Tis one of war's supreme necessities.

ANDRE (*absently*).   How runs this prophecy?—with something told
Me by a venerable man, a Friend,
A white-haired follower of William Penn—
He was my host when I was captive once
In the good country town of Lancaster.
He loved me as a father loves his son,
Me who have been an orphan all my life.
We often talked about this troublous war
(He used the tender Quaker dialect).
"My son," he said, "if thee again resume
Arms against us, who fight for God and right,
For conscience' sake, and for our liberties
Be sure somehow the heavens will find thee out—
No man is safe unless his cause is just,
And Tyranny engenders evil ends."
So said the seer, and on my youthful head
Placing his hands, he prayed that I might be
Delivered from the harboring of ill
Against my kind, and most and first of all
Prayed that I cease to war upon this land
Which he believed was set apart by God
For nobler ends than any other land.
He gently chided my wild levity—
"Thy lack of sober reverence" he said,
May lead thee to the paths that lead to death."
And now, Great God! to be condemned a spy!
Why did I stoop to such an enterprise,
Although a kingdom were the recompense!

TALLMADGE. If Arnold only could be given for you,
And justice satisfied, and your life saved!

ANDRE. Speak of it not!   It would be base indeed
For me to gain deliverance by such means.

BC

ABC   *Scene 2.   New York, Clinton's Headquarters.   Clinton and Arnold.*

          CLINTON.   They dare not hang John Andre as a spy!

          ARNOLD.   They will hang Andre unless I'm exchanged.
                    The rebel generals are firm as steel,
                    And Washington cannot afford to be,
                    Or seem to be, of softer metal now.
                    Let me be offered in his place, I pray.

          CLINTON.   My dear Sir, that's a thing cannot be done.
                    Andre himself would first of all refuse.
                    No! No!   He took the risk, and takes his fate.
                    But it is wretched, horrible, unheard—
                    With no intent to be a spy—so young,
                    So noble, and engaging as a man,
                    The friend of all men, and all men his friends—
                    Is there no way to force this Washington?

          ARNOLD.   Only as I have told you.   And if that
                    Is now refused, he dies a felon's death.
                    The country is aroused, indignant, wild
                    At the great danger it has just escaped.
                    That wrath is fierce at Andre as at me.
                    To yield a particle would be a sign
                    Of fear or cowardice they dare not show.

BC   CLINTON.   But Andre *is* no spy, by rules of war.
                    He had your passport—you were in command—
                    His presence in their lines was caused by *them,*
                    When they fired on the Vulture from the shore.
                    'Twas not intended by himself, you know.

          ARNOLD.   His sentence settles whether he's a spy
                    So far as Andre's hanging is concerned.
                    You talk as lawyers talk, upon one side,
                    But I imagine a good argument
                    Could be made up to show he was a spy
                    Within the rule and reason of the rule,
                    And in the common meaning of the term.
                    They'll claim that Continentals have been hung
                    When found on errands far less treacherous.

          CLINTON.   That's different—a rebel has no rights!
                    The colonies belong still to the King.
C   I will demand John Andre as a right
                    And threaten them reprisals if refused.

          ARNOLD.   Then you will fix his doom, as sure as fate.

C   [*Scene 3.   Tappan.   The old Dutch church.*]   *Gen. Greene and twelve generals
          seated.   Andre comes in and bows.*

          GEN. GREENE (*taking up a letter*).
                    Do you admit the facts your letter states?—
                    The one you sent to General Washington—

That you arranged to treat on neutral ground
With Arnold for the capture of West Point,
That on the 21st you came on shore
Without a flag and met him half disguised,
That then you kept concealed within our lines
And in disguise attempted to return
With information for the enemy,
When you were captured with these documents?

ANDRE. I do.

GREENE. Did you suppose the mention of our flag
Or Arnold's pass protected you at all?

ANDRE. Not in the least.   But gentlemen, I came
With no intention to come in your lines.

GREENE. Alas! and have you no defense but that?

ANDRE. I have no other answer to the charge.

GREENE. Have you aught else that you desire to say?

ANDRE. I've told you all.   My case is in your hands.

GREENE. You may withdraw; we will deliberate.

ABC   [*Scene 4. Same place.*] *Washington and the fourteen generals of the Court Martial.*

WASHINGTON. And were you all agreed?

GREENE. All—not a voice dissents.

KNOX. He has himself admitted all the facts
Which by the law of nations make him spy.
C   His candor, openness, and modesty
Won him our admiration and regard,
But a more hellish plot was ne'er conceived,
And Arnold's blackness blackens Andre too.

LAFAYETTE. We sought to find a chance for clemency,
But this conspiracy is much too gross
For any penalty more light than death.

GREENE. Our rights belligerent can be maintained
In no way possibly except by this,
To enforce the law exactly as it stands,
And, treating adjutants and men alike,
Make treason what it is—the worst of crimes.

ABC   KNOX. It but remains to sign the warrant, Sire.

WASHINGTON. There is, alas! no other way but this.

C   KNOX. Let us withdraw.   He would be left alone.
                                        Exeunt all but Washington.

WASHINGTON (*rising*). How the old words of Holy Writ come back—
How David would have died for Absalom!

BC   *Enter Hamilton, Paulding, and Paulding's sister.*

HAMILTON. I ask an audience, Sire, for pity's sake.
This is the man who scouted Andre's bribe,
One of his captors, Paulding is his name,
And this his sister.   They will tell the rest.

WASHINGTON. A patriot so true as you deserves
Whatever favor gratitude can give.

PAULDING. I ask no favors, Sire, for me or mine!
But we have learned some things we want to tell.
I was imprisoned on a British ship,
My father and myself, in New York Bay.
My sister came and pleaded for release,
She told her story to an officer,
Her desolate condition moved his heart.
He gave an order for my sire's release—
He could obtain but one—and by mistake
My name was written in my father's place.
I was released and he in prison held.

And now it seems—what was unknown to me—
That Major Andre was the officer!
All this I never learned till yesterday.
To cause the death of one's deliverer,
To whom one owes his liberty and life,
Is hard indeed, but this is not the worst.
They threaten now reprisals in return—
They say my father dies if Andre dies.

SISTER. Oh hear us, Sire, and save the lives of all!
My father fought at Trenton under you.
And this young British officer was good
And kind and helpful as a brother, Sire.
'Twas Arnold was the rascal—let *him* hang!
But let John Andre live, and all be saved.
He can be kept a prisoner of war.

WASHINGTON. Your story moves me to the very core.
I will consult my officers again.
No harm will touch your father from this threat
Of savage vengeance on the innocent.
But what you tell of Andre's nobleness,
And this strange capture by the one of all
The world who least would wish to do him harm,
Weighs heavily for pardon or reprieve.
If any one of all my generals
Consents to mercy, I may take the risk.
But now the time is precious—Sentinel!   (*Sentinel appearing*)
Tell all my generals to meet me here.

PAULDING. We will not waste your time.   We'll pray for him.

SISTER. Aye that we will! and angels hear the prayer!

Exeunt Paulding and sister.

Enter messenger, and hands letters to Washington—he reads.

WASHINGTON. What, fifty men at once strung up!—short shrift!
For being rebels and no other crime!
I fear this news is bad for Andre's fate.   (*reads another letter*)

The men in prison say they hear that if
The British spy is hung they will hang too.
The say they're not afraid—let traitors hang!
This seems to seal his fate against all hope.   (*reads again*)

C

And this third letter is from Clinton's self,
With foolish threats of vengeance as before,
This makes all further council needless now.
It will steel every heart against reprieve
Or the least shadow of a clemency.

Ho—Sentinel—
Say to the generals they need not come.

ACT V

ABC

Scene 1 Andre's room. Night before Andre's execution. Andre sleeping. Washington passes the guard and enters.

WASHINGTON (*looking at Andre*).
So young, so brave, and doomed so soon to die!
Could I but save him and my country too!
He sleeps the sleep of youth and innocence,
And dreams of England and her fields of green,
Dear island which his eyes can never see!
How proud a father should that father be
Whose son was as heroic as this spy!
And *I* to be his executioner!
Oh Duty, sterner than the voice of fate,
Why dost thou call me to a task like this?

I will avoid the pleading of his voice
And piteous entreaties of his eyes,
Lest I be moved to do what is not right
And show that mercy to a gallant foe
Which would be deadly to the land I love.
One kiss I must give to this royal brow
Before we part who should have never met.   (*Andre awakes*)

ANDRE. Methought I heard my father in my dreams.
Art thou my father?   Let me kiss thy hand!

God's pity!   'Tis the rebel chief that stood
Unmoved and signed the warrant of my death.
Why do you come to torture me
This last night of my short ill-fated life?
And yet thy face is merciful and just.
There is a blessing in those gracious lips,
An august tenderness in all thy looks!

I have heard whispers of thy nobleness.
Perhaps you come to save me at the last.
My life is hardly worthy of such grace,
And still less worthy of a felon's doom.
I was betrayed into the seeming spy.
God knows the purpose that I had in view,
To do a soldier's duty and no more.

WASHINGTON. I cannot save thee from thine own rash act.
Herein I am not master of myself,
But stand in place of law to give it voice.
The destiny of all that I hold dear,
The fate of all these infant colonies,
Of all this young republic full of hope,
Hangs trembling on a thread which clemency
Might cut in twain. This is that point of time
When all the Future and the Past combine
To make the instant pressure big with fate,
When the least swerving from the path
Of balanced justice is the wreck of all.

But oh, brave youth, what pangs has death for us
Whose duties make us face him day by day!

ANDRE. It is not death I dread, but death's disgrace,
The shameful death of a degraded spy.
Give me the right to die a soldier's death
And I will bless you, while I live to bless.

WASHINGTON. Would I could give you comfort more supreme,
That should make death's disgrace as sweet as love,
Nay, the more sweet because of seeming shame—
Not the mere sympathy a kindred soul
Feels for a valiant spirit like its own,
Not the high boast of proud philosophy
Nor touch more tender of a common faith
That in another world all will be well—
These thoughts indeed have made men die in peace—
But there's a nobler consolation left,
Whose inspiration, could I give it you,
Holds all the rest as heaven holds the stars.

Alas, alas!   'Tis like the wreath of flowers
With which they garlanded the snow-white lamb
They used to offer to the Gods of old.
What if your name should, in the years to be,
Become the synonym of sacrifice
And help avert the sacrilege of war
From all mankind in all the time to come,
And two great realms so hold your nobleness
That you in dying should more bless the world
Than all of us who live to mourn your fate?

ANDRE. Say you my king shall yet regain this land
And all through me, ignoble as I die?

WASHINGTON.   I will not wrong you with a pleasant lie—
              Truth only warrants us the smile of God—
              Not kings or crowns but all of humankind
              I see in vision when I call you blest.

              I am no dreamer of poetic dreams
              But see the world that lies before us here;
              Imagination cannot bound its reach,
              A continent of free born colonists,
              A home for all the exiles of the world,
              A nation knit by kindred liberties,
              Its freedom stamped by Magna Charta's stamp,
              Another England mightier than herself,
              Another Europe freer than the old,
              With all the wheat of her milleniums,
              A Christian state built up of free born men,
              The golden rule embroidered in its code,
              Its statutes framed from the Beatitudes,
              Freed from the rust and poison of the past
              And tainted leprosy of ancient wrongs,
              With all the future flashing from her eyes
              Like Pallas leaping from the brow of Jove,
              Full armed, and armored in immortal steel,
              Nation of promise! Hope of all the world!—
              And all that future hanging on our acts.

              Broods on this empire in the wilderness
              The sense of measureless, majestic power.
              Long years ago, deep in the forest depths,
              Far from the dwellings and the haunts of men,
              Alone in the immensity of space,
              The stars my neighbors and the Sun my guide,
              Through forests where great rivers rise and flow,
              By mountain ranges that outreach the zone,
              I wandered on, as on some boundless beach
              Whose oceans swept immeasurable space,
              And dreamed of what this wilderness should be,
              When man had mastered it and made it home,
              And all the garnered glory of the past
              Seemed to me nothing in the great To Be—
              And we to be the founders of this realm,
              The instruments God's Providence ordains
              To plant the seeds of such a noble state!

ANDRE.   If I could share the fervor of your hope
              And saw this glorious commonwealth of yours
              Rise like a star upon the vault of night—
              And somehow, when you speak, I feel it may—
              How can the death of one poor traitor spy
              Help build the walls of your imagined state?

WASHINGTON.   Believe me, though I may not make it plain,
              Yours is no small or unimportant part

In this rough drama of colonial life.
Your martyrdom—just like a common spy—
Prompt, certain, like the instant trump of dawn,
Will be the rescue of this perilled land.

So shall the purpose of our will appear,
My war worn soldiers will take heart at once,
Divided councils will be one again,
My army gather up its scattered strength,
And England, seeing there can be no peace
But that which springs from independence gained,
Will grant the independence we demand,
And thenceforth be indeed the Mother Land,
Bound by no ties but mutual amity.

And in the long far ages yet to come,
Men shall perceive how one true, loyal heart
Had to be given to preserve the land
And save the shedding of fraternal blood,
While, in the island which you love so well,
Your king and comrades shall revere your name
As one who died a soldier's gallant death,
And shrine your dust beneath Westminster's roof.

BC

Long years must come before the Mother Land
Will see that separation was foredoomed,
And that success in Arnold's plan and yours
Would have but lengthened out the years of war,
And longer years must come before your foes,
Who will at last no longer be your foes,
Will see in full the pathos of your fate
And recognize its loyal chivalry;
Milleniums perhaps before the world
Sees in this sad, supreme necessity
The cruel nature of the best of wars—
But all will come at last in God's good time.

ANDRE. I see in part the logic of your thought,
That I in dying may save other lives,
ABC   I see in part the glory of your dream,
But England, not America, sits queen
In that high future that you paint—for me.

But your great thoughts on that which is to be,
Still more this presence of majestic mien,
This condescension in a noble foe,
Move me to other thoughts on life and death.
Since I at least may be a stepping stone
To that great march around the girdled globe
That gives to England rule of land and sea,
I blame you not that I am doomed to die.
I know the rude necessities of war,
And, whether my last wish you grant or not,
I shall believe that Washington is good.
I am content to meet a soldier's fate.

BC

WASHINGTON. Farewell.
      ANDRE.   Farewell.

B

*Scene 2. Washington's house at Tappan in distance, shutters closed.
Morning of execution. Pompey and Caesar.*

CAESAR. Well, Pomp, you come to see de hangin' too?

POMPEY. Dis's a bad business, beats de debbil's own!
Dey say dat Massa Arnold's goin' to come
Today an' save dis Mister Andre's neck.
Now I no's better.   Massa Arnold ain't afeared,
He fight all day jes' like a short-horn bull,
But suthin's wrong—he's been way off this fall,
He fret an' swear an' look as black as night.
You think sometimes he eat his baby up,
Den he turn round an' kiss it mos' to deff,
Den he say nothin' for two days to time.
He been acrowin' an' it ain't no good.

CAESAR. You see dem shutters all shut tight close up?
De General don't want to see him die,
Dis business drive de General most mad.
Dem generals dat tried poor Mister John
Dey all stick to it dat he's got to hang
Or else de whole creation run aground.
But I tink General Washington, he save
Dat feller if he can.   But 'tain't no use.
So General just don't say nuthin' to no one,
But he keep up athinkin' all the same.

POMPEY. Oh Lordy, how Mis's Arnold did take on!
But 'tain't no use!   When a thing's done it's done.
'Tain't all his fault.   De debbil get him foul.
You see dat was old debbil all de while.
He raise de debbil, an' dat's just de fact—
Massa Arnold was as proud as Lucifer—
An' so de debbil gobble him right up.

De wussest thing of all dis cussed work
Is dis—Dis nigger's reputation's lost.
Folks point at me an' say "Look at dat dark—
He was dat wicked traitor's bodyguard!"
And Dinah says de children get it too—
One black sheep turn de whole flock into bad.

CAESAR. He'd no 'lations, no high-toned ancestors.
Now General Washington, he couldn't do it—
It's in de blood, de old Virginny blood—
He knows his 'scendants back a hundred year.

Look at de crowd.   Here comes de 'cession down.

Enter Paulding and his sister.

SISTER. Ah here he comes!   Is there no help, Oh God!

PAULDING. I would die for him, but his fate is just.
I dare not tell him who his captor was,
'Twould only add another pang to death.

The procession passes.   Andre between Tallmadge and an officer.

ANDRE. Tell her my last thought was of England's good
And her, and that I blame myself alone.

Procession marches on.   A gun is fired.

BC

Scene 3.   Under the gallows the night after the execution.   Paulding and his two companions, Williams and Van Wert.

VAN WERT. We little thought it would have come to this!

WILLIAMS. How did John Andre bear himself today?

ABC

PAULDING. He journeyed to the scaffold like a Prince.
His step was light as on a dress parade
And kept time with the music of the band.
A multitude had come to see him die.
A little child reached up to give him fruit,
He smiled and thanked her, took it in his hands,
But soon was glad to give it to those near,
For he had come to those last steps of life
When his own burdens were enough to bear.

When first he saw these gallows planted high
In the clear air beyond, he started back,
And as he did his countenance betrayed
His disappointment that his last request
Had not been granted. Then the wagon drove
Beneath the gallows.   There he stood, so full
Of life, so eloquent in form and face,
The men who stood around him were in tears—
Not a dry eye among the lookers on.

The order of his doom was then read out
And he was asked if he had aught to say.
He then uncovered, bowed, and gravely said,
"You witness that I die as brave men die."
The fatal noose was drawn, the hands were tied,
And in an instant Andre was no more.

BC

His body lies here buried at our feet.

VAN WERT. So perish all our country's enemies!

WILLIAMS. And yet he was a gallant gentleman
And died a hero—like a soldier too.

PAULDING. He was my friend to whom I owed my life.
I would have died before I gave him up,
Had I but known who that young horseman was—
And died a hundred times so Arnold hung!

ABC   *Scene [4].   New York.   Arnold and his wife.*

ARNOLD.   You too are banished, Arnold's wife disgraced!

MARGARET.   Ah yes and no!   Since I am by your side,
It is not banishment that brings me home.
But oh the horror of it all—the scorn,
The bitterness of all their words and looks!
They call you Judas and me Jezebel,
Your effigy is hung in every town.
If they could only capture you, they say
No torture would be half severe enough.

ARNOLD.   Had I succeeded as I hoped to do,
And forced a peace upon the colonies—
But Andre's luckless capture turned the tide.

MARGARET.   And you, they tell me, tried to save his life.

ARNOLD.   I tried to ransom him myself but failed.
Of course they would allow no interchange
No more than him for me, had I been caught.
But dear! how pale and worn and sad you look!
Tell me the story of your banishment.

MARGARET.   You know the order which the council made:
"That Margaret Arnold, being wife of one
Who was attainted traitor, should depart
The state in fourteen days nor come again
Within its bounds while that the war did last,
Lest correspondance with the enemy
And persons disaffected should be had."
They seem to execrate your very name.
Oh it is dreadful, horrible to think
That your own countrymen should hate you so!
And they will learn to hate your children too
And make your memory a thing of scorn.

ARNOLD (*musing*).   Well—that depends—the crown may win at last—
The story then will read another way.
But Andre's death—it haunts me day and night!

MARGARET.   The crown will never win!   I dreamed a dream
The day before my exiled life began—
I saw that you and I were wanderers
In some strange land where none were friends to us.
The wilderness has no such solitude!
Across the sea I saw great Washington
Made President of all the colonies,
Refusing to be king, crowned with the love
And gratitude of all his countrymen.

And then I cried, "Oh God, remove this curse
From me and mine!   Thou knowest how tried
My husband was, how much he suffers now.

The stroke on us is like the stroke of death,
The world to us will be a sepulchre,
Holding our buried hopes and us entombed."

I thought of Andre, dying as a spy,
And then I saw, as plainly as I see
Yon dial on the wall, John Andre's face,
With all the sweetness that it had of old,
But dignified and glorious in repose.
And as it faded from my awestruck sight,
I heard from out the skies the soft word: peace.

ARNOLD.   'Twill come to you, oh faithful, noble wife!
But nevermore to me.   What's done is done.
My failure kills me with the royal side,
And, curse of fate, I now shall have to war
Upon the comrades that I used to lead.

MARGARET.   What!   They can never ask you to do that!

ARNOLD.   As sure as this war lasts, they must and will.

MARGARET.   Oh horror piled on horror!   This is worst,
When worse than what has been seemed not to be
Within the limits of revengeful fate—
Be sent to kill the soldiers you once led,
To slaughter the good friends of early days,
Perhaps lay waste the home where you were born—
Oh strange reversion of all amities,
Intolerable cruelty of doom,
That makes success defeat, defeat success!
We are but wrecks amid a world of waste.
Life's pleasant uses are all turned to pain!

ABC   *Scene 5.   Westminster Abbey.   Arnold and his wife at the grave of Andre.*

ARNOLD.   Better sleep there among the mighty dead
Than live dishonored and by all men loathed.
I envy him his lot!   Would it were mine!

MARGARET.   Oh husband, keep the stout heart still within!
How often have you promised, for my sake
And for our children, to fight on with time,
Nor rashly seek for death in foreign wars.

It seemed indeed a pang too keen to bear
When Andre died the ignominious death,
And now that immortality is his,
Why should you grudge him tardy recompense,
A place among the gallant spirits of his time?

For your mistake is there no remedy,
No reparation of atoning deeds?
Have we not suffered all that flesh can bear?
To have these Britons taunt you with their "Crime"
And whisper "Judas" with averted looks!

ARNOLD.   When my last hour has come (God send it soon),
          Let me be buried in the uniform
          I wore at Saratoga and Quebec.

Music, "Kyrie Eleison" from the Inner Abbey.   Both kneel.
As they rise, a veiled lady stands before them.

[HONORA.] And you are Arnold, and you Arnold's wife—
           I was the friend of Andre in his youth.
           He loved me, and I should have been his bride,
           But fate was all against us—Ah! those days!

MARGARET. Are you the one whose locket Andre wore?
           Honora was the name, I think he said.
           He loved you to the last day of his life.

The Red Patrol

Sir Gilbert Parker (1862–1932)

The preceding dramatic poem was not the only operatic project that Ives imagined. In 1907 he and Miss Twichell were attracted to Parker's stories of *Pierre and His People* and the continuation of them variously called *An Adventurer of the North* or *A Romany of the Snows*. They were fascinated not only by Pierre himself, the French-Indian half-breed gambler, but even more by the mystery surrounding the "house of judgment"—a mystery embodied in its deathless guardian who appears from time to time through the series (perhaps derived partly from legends about Saint John, and possibly bequeathing something in turn to Charles Williams's "Prester John" in *War in Heaven*).

THE RED PATROL

St. Augustine's, Canterbury, had given him its licentiate's hood, the Bishop of Rupert's Land had ordained him, and the North had swallowed him up. He had gone forth with surplice, stole, hood, a sermon-case, the prayer-book, and that other Book of all. Indian camps, trappers' huts, and Company's posts had given him hospitality, and had heard him with patience and consideration. At first he wore the surplice, stole, and hood, took the eastward position, and intoned the service, and no man said him nay, but watched him curiously and was sorrowful—he was so youthful, clear of eye, and bent on doing heroical things.

But little by little there came a change. The hood was left behind at Fort O'Glory, where it provoked the derision of the Methodist missionary who followed him; the sermon-case stayed at Fort O'Battle; and at last the surplice itself was put by at the Company's post at Yellow Quill. He was too excited and in earnest at first to see the effect of his ministrations, but there came slowly over him the knowledge that he was talking into space. He felt something returning on him out of the air into which he talked, and buffeting him. It was the Spirit of the North, in which lives the terror, the large heart of things, the soul of the past. He awoke to his inadequacy, to the fact that all these men to whom he talked, listened, and only listened, and treated him with a gentleness which was almost pity—as one might a woman. He had talked doctrine, the Church, the sacraments, and at Fort O'Battle he faced definitely the futility of his work. What was to blame—the Church—religion—himself?

It was at Fort O'Battle that he met Pierre, and heard someone say over his shoulder as he walked out into the icy dusk: *"The voice of one crying in the wilderness. . . . and he had sackcloth about his loins, and his food was locusts and wild honey."*

He turned to see Pierre, who in the large room of the Post had sat and watched him as he prayed and preached. He had remarked the keen, curious eye, the musing look, the habitual disdain at the lips. It had all touched him, confused him; and now he had a kind of anger.

"You know it so well, why don't you preach yourself?" he said feverishly.

"I have been preaching all my life," Pierre answered drily.

"The devil's games: cards and law-breaking; and you sneer at men who try to bring lost sheep into the fold."

"The fold of the Church—yes, I understand all that," Pierre answered. "I have heard you and the priests of my father's Church talk. Which is right? But as for me, I am a missionary. Cards, law-breaking—these are what I have done; but these are not what I have preached."

"What have you preached?" asked the other, walking on into the fast-gathering night, beyond the Post and the Indian lodges, into the wastes where frost and silence lived.

Pierre waved his hand towards space. "This," he said suggestively.

"What's *this?*" asked the other fretfully.

"The thing you feel round you here."

"I feel the cold," was the petulant reply.

"I feel the immense, the far off," said Pierre slowly.

The other did not understand as yet. "You've learned big words," he said disdainfully.

"No; big things," rejoined Pierre sharply—"a few."

"Let me hear you preach them," half snarled Sherburne.

"You will not like to hear them—no."

"I'm not likely to think about them one way or another," was the contemptuous reply.

Pierre's eyes half closed. The young, impetuous, half-baked college man! To set his little knowledge against his own studious vagabondage! At that instant he determined to play a game and win; to turn this man into a vagabond also; to see John the Baptist become a Bedouin. He saw the doubt, the uncertainty, the shattered vanity in the youth's mind, the missionary's half retreat from his cause. A crisis was at hand. The youth was fretful with his great theme, instead of being severe upon himself. For days and days Pierre's presence had acted on Sherburne silently but forcibly. He had listened to the vagabond's philosophy, and knew that it was of a deeper—so much deeper—knowledge of life than he himself possessed, and he knew also that it was terribly true; he was not wise enough to see that it was only true in part. The influence had been insidious, delicate, cunning, and he himself was only "a voice crying in the wilderness," without the simple creed of that voice. He knew that the Methodist missionary was believed in more, if less liked, than himself.

Pierre would work now with all the latent devilry of his nature to unseat the man from his saddle.

"You have missed the great thing, *alors,* though you have been up here two years," he said. "You do not feel, you do not know. What good have you done? Who has got on his knees and changed his life because of you? Who has told his beads or longed for the Mass because of you? Tell me, who has ever said, 'You have showed me how to live'? Even the women, though they cry sometimes when you sing-song your prayers, go on just the same when the little 'bless you' is over. Why? Most of them know a better thing than you tell them. Here is the truth: you are little—eh, so very little. You never lied—direct; you never stole the waters that are sweet; you never knew the big dreams that come with wine in the dead of night; you never swore at your own soul and heard it laugh back at you;

you never put your face in the breast of a woman—do not look so wild at me!—you never had a child; you never saw the world and yourself through the doors of real life. You never have said, 'I am tired; I am sick of all; I have seen all.'

"You have never felt what came after—understanding. *Chut,* your talk is for children—and missionaries. You are a prophet without a call, you are a leader without a man to lead, you are less than a child up here. For here the children feel a peace in their blood when the stars come out, and a joy in their brains when the dawn comes up and reaches a yellow hand to the Pole, and the west wind shouts at them. Holy Mother! we in the far north, we feel things, for all the great souls of the dead are up there at the Pole in the pleasant land, and we have seen the Scarlet Hunter and the Kimash Hills. You have seen nothing. You have only heard, and because, like a child, you have never sinned, you come and preach to us!"

The night was folding down fast, all the stars were shooting out into their places, and in the north the white lights of the aurora were flying to and fro. Pierre had spoken with a slow force and precision, yet, as he went on, his eyes almost became fixed on those shifting flames, and a deep look came into them, as he was moved by his own eloquence. Never in his life had he made so long a speech at once. He paused, and then said suddenly: "Come, let us run."

He broke into a long, sliding trot, and Sherburne did the same. With their arms gathered to their sides they ran for quite two miles without a word, until the heavy breathing of the clergyman brought Pierre up suddenly.

"You do not run well," he said; "you do not run with the whole body. You know so little. Did you ever think how much such men as Jacques Parfaite know? The earth they read like a book, the sky like an animal's ways, and a man's face like—like the writing on the wall."

"Like the writing on the wall," said Sherburne, musing; for, under the other's influence, his petulance was gone. He knew that he was not a part of this life, that he was ignorant of it; of, indeed, all that was vital in it and in men and women.

"I think you began this too soon. You should have waited; then you might have done good. But here we are wiser than you. You have no message—no real message—to give us; down in your heart you are not even sure of yourself."

Sherburne sighed. "I'm of no use," he said. "I'll get out. I'm no good at all."

Pierre's eyes glistened. He remembered how, the day before, this youth had said hot words about his card-playing; had called him—in effect—a thief; had treated him as an inferior, as became one who was of St. Augustine's, Canterbury.

"It is the great thing to be free," Pierre said, "that no man shall look for this or that of you. Just to do as far as you feel, as far as you are sure—that is the best. In this you are not sure—no. *Hein,* is it not?"

Sherburne did not answer. Anger, distrust, wretchedness, the spirit of the alien, loneliness, were alive in him. The magnetism of this deep penetrating man, possessed of a devil, was on him, and in spite of every reasonable instinct he turned to him for companionship.

"It's been a failure," he burst out, "and I'm sick of it—sick of it; but I can't give it up."

Pierre said nothing. They had come to what seemed a vast semicircle of ice and snow, a huge amphitheatre in the plains. It was wonderful: a great round wall on which the northern lights played, into which the stars peered. It was open towards the north, and in one side was a fissure shaped like a gothic arch. Pierre pointed to it, and they did not speak till they had passed through it. Like great seats the steppes of snow ranged round, and in the center was a kind of plateau of ice, as it might seem a stage or an altar. To the north there was a great opening, the lost arc of the circle, through which the mystery of the Pole swept in and out, or brooded there where no man may question it. Pierre stood and looked. Time and again he had been here, and had asked the same question: Who had ever sat on those frozen benches and looked down at the drama on that stage below? Who played the parts? Was it a farce or a sacrifice? To him had been given the sorrow of imagination, and he wondered and wondered. Or did they come still—those strange people, whoever they were—and watch ghostly gladiators at their fatal sport? If they came, when was it? Perhaps they were there now unseen. In spite of himself he shuddered. Who was the keeper of the house?

Through his mind there ran—pregnant to him for the first time—a chanson of the Scarlet Hunter, the Red Patrol, who guarded the sleepers in the Kimash Hills against the time they should awake and possess the land once more: the friend of the lost, the lover of the vagabond, and of all who had no home:

> "Strangers come to the outer walls—
> (*Why do the sleepers stir?*)
> Strangers enter the Judgment House—
> (*Why do the sleepers sigh?*)
> Slow they rise in their judgment seats,
> Sieve and measure the naked souls,·
> Then with a blessing return to sleep—
> (*Quiet the Judgment House.*)
> Lone and sick are the vagrant souls—
> (*When shall the world come home?*)"

He reflected upon the words, and a feeling of awe came over him, for he had been in the White Valley and had seen the Scarlet Hunter. But there came at once also a sinister desire to play a game for this man's life-work here. He knew that the other was ready for any wild move; there was upon him the sense of failure and disgust; he was acted on by the magic of the night, the terrible delight of the scene, and that might be turned to advantage.

He said: "Am I not right? There is something in the world greater than the creeds and the book of the Mass. To be free and to enjoy, that is the thing. Never before have you felt what you feel here now. And I will show you more. I will teach you how to know, I will lead you through all the north and make you to understand the big things of life. Then, when you have known, you can return if you will. But now—see: I will tell you what I will do. Here on this great platform we will play a game of cards. There is a man whose life I can ruin. If you win I promise to leave him safe, and to go out of the far north forever, to go back to Quebec"—he had a kind of gaming fever in his veins. "If I win, you give up the Church, leaving behind the prayer-book, the Bible and all, coming with me to do what I shall tell you, for the passing of twelve moons. It is a great stake—will you play it? Come"—he leaned forward, looking into the other's face—"will you play it? They drew lots—those people in the Bible. We will draw lots, and see, eh?—and see?"

"I accept the stake," said Sherburne, with a little gasp.

Without a word they went upon that platform, shaped like an altar, and Pierre at once drew out a pack of cards, shuffling them with his mittened hands. Then he knelt down and said, as he laid out the cards one by one till there were thirty: Whoever gets the ace of hearts first, wins—*hein?*"

Sherburne nodded and knelt also. The cards lay back upwards in three rows.

For a moment neither stirred. The white, metallic stars saw it, the small crescent moon beheld it, and the deep wonder of night made it strange and dreadful. Once or twice Sherburne looked round as though he felt others present, and once Pierre looked out to the wide portals, as though he saw some one entering. But there was nothing to the eye—nothing. Presently Pierre said: "Begin."

The other drew a card, then Pierre drew one, then the other, then Pierre again; and so on. How slow the game was! Neither hurried, but both, kneeling, looked and looked at the card long before drawing and turning it over. The stake was weighty, and Pierre loved the game more than he cared about the stake. Sherburne cared nothing about the game, but all his soul seemed set upon the hazard. There was not a sound out of the night, nothing stirring but the Spirit of the North. Twenty, twenty-five cards were drawn, and then Pierre paused.

"In a minute all will be settled," he said. "Will you go on, or will you pause?"

But Sherburne had got the madness of chance in his veins now, and he said: "Quick, quick, go on!"

Pierre drew, but the great card held back. Sherburne drew, then Pierre again. There were three left. Sherburne's face was as white as the snow around him. His mouth was open, and a little white cloud of frosted breath came out. His hand hungered for the card, drew back, then seized it. A moan broke from him. Then Pierre, with a little weird laugh, reached out and turned over—the ace of hearts!

They both stood up. Pierre put the cards in his pocket.

"You have lost," he said.

Sherburne threw back his head with a reckless laugh. The laugh seemed to echo and echo through the amphitheatre, and then from the frozen seats, the hillocks of ice and snow, there was a long, low sound, as of sorrow, and a voice came after:

"*Sleep—sleep! Blessed be the just and the keepers of vows.*"

Sherburne stood shaking, as though he had seen a host of spirits. His eyes on the great seats of judgment, he said to Pierre:

"See! see! how they sit there! grey and cold and awful!"

But Pierre shook his head.

"There is nothing," he said, "nothing," yet he knew that Sherburne was looking upon the men of judgment of the Kimash Hills, the sleepers. He looked round, half fearfully, for if here were those great children of the ages, where was the keeper of the house, the Red Patrol?

Even as he thought, a figure in scarlet with a noble face and a high pride of bearing stood before them, not far away. Sherburne clutched his arm.

Then the Red Patrol, the Scarlet Hunter, spoke:

"Why have you sinned your sins and broken your vows within our house of judgment? Know ye not that in the new springtime of the world ye shall be outcast, because ye have called the sleepers to judgment before their time? But I am the hunter of the lost. Go you," he said to Sherburne, pointing, "where a sick man lies in a hut in the Shikam Valley. In his soul fine thine own again." Then to Pierre: "For thee, thou shalt know the desert and the storm and the lonely hills; thou shalt neither seek nor find. Go, and return no more."

The two men, Sherburne falteringly, stepped down and moved to the open plain. They turned at the great entrance and looked back. Where they had stood there rested on his long bow the Red Patrol. He raised it, and a flaming arrow flew through the sky toward the south. They followed its course, and when they looked back a little afterwards, the great judgment-house was empty, and the whole north was silent as the sleepers.

At dawn they came to the hut in the Shikam Valley, and there they found a trapper dying. He had sinned greatly, and he could not die without someone to show him how, to tell him what to say to the angel of the cross-roads.

Sherburne, kneeling by him, felt his own new soul moved by a holy fire, and, first praying for himself, he said to the sick man: *"For if we confess our sins, He is faithful and just to forgive us our sins, and to cleanse us from all unrighteousness."*

Praying for both, his heart grew strong, and he heard the sick man say, ere he journeyed forth to the cross-roads:

"You have shown me the way. I have peace."

"Speak for me in the Presence," said Sherburne, softly.

The dying man could not answer, but that moment, as he journeyed forth on the Far Trail, he held Sherburne's hand.

———

Ives seems to have left it up to Miss Twichell to work out a libretto from this story, as revealed in her letter of 29 September 1907 from Saranac Lake (he was evidently encouraging her to do more writing—they had already collaborated in two songs, and others were to follow). The idea was apparently based on three changes in the story: 1) to secularize and slightly idealize Sherburne, so as to contrast him with Pierre on the basis of character apart from churchly ministry, 2) to introduce a sweetheart of Pierre, to make the contrast more dramatic, and 3) to substitute for the Scarlet Hunter the "sleepers" whom, in the story, he guards.

Dear Charlie . . . It is a pouring day and a great luxury to be able to stay in and hear the storm. If I had several such days, I might get at *The Kimash Hills.* I have thought very partially of an outline—The scene could be the Judgment Hall, an outdoor natural place of course. There must be Pierre (trapper and woodsman), his sweetheart, and this good man (who has come from far away to try and show the rough woodsmen a better way). Pierre despises him and feels he is too good and pure to have seen anything of life, and determines to bring him before the Men of Judgment (a mystic lot who are said to sit at midnight of midwinter in this place). He is confident that the good man will be ridiculed by them for pressing his law of kind dealing and forbearance. The girl, who sees the true goodness and rightness of the man, is terrified for Pierre when she hears he has made an appointment to meet the man in the hills at midnight on midwinter, and goes there herself to remonstrate with her lover.

She can be alone in this weird place, and pretty scared, and then, when Pierre comes, they can talk, and he won't listen to her, and then the other man will appear and give an idea of what he stands for. He can have come from far away, and describe the lovely land he has left. And then the queer old Judgment Men can come, and Pierre can state his case, and they can show him how mistaken he is, and nothing but the combined entreaties of the girl and the good man save him from being scorned and punished, and it can all end happily.

What do you think of *something like that?* You can probably think of something much better and tell me. I think you could get a good many different kinds of feelings in the course of the action. We will talk about it. . . .

[P.S.] This outline sounds poor as I read it over, but I'll let it go.

Ives's answer to this letter has not survived, but Miss Twichell wrote him again on 8 October: "I like your idea about Pierre's and the other man's getting something out of each other's point of view, and think it would be far more interesting to work that in, though rather harder. I read *The Red Patrol* at Dave's the other night after I'd written you. It is a good story, and I must try and read a lot like it, and get into acquaintance with those picturesque people. . . ."

Her letter of 18 December reveals that they were thinking of adding still another character: "I have read the book you brought about the operas, and found it very interesting in many ways. It seems to me that there ought to be great contrasts of emotions in the characters to make the story in the music effective. In *our idea*, that part that I can't get at yet is Pierre. The girl's motive is of course love and fear for him, and the good man's motive in general is goodness and purity and self sacrifice, and you have a mother—she is all anxiety and tenderness for her daughter—but I can't make Pierre do the things he's going to for any good reason as yet. I'll have to change something—many things—I've got to give him a good motive for wishing to hold the man up to scorn and ridicule, or there'll be a fatally weak spot."

Her letter of the 20th contains a kind of postscript to the above: "Perhaps I wasn't right about the contrast of emotions in opera—may be that's only because those were *Italian*—I must learn of more."

Finally, in a letter of 6 January 1908: "Charlie, of course the place for the good man in *our drama* to come from is *our country ennobled*—our own country, as our forefathers planned her, and as Mr. Lincoln desired her in his Gettysburg speech, and as we hope she will be in the good process of time—don't you think so?"

Unfortunately this project remained tentative—neither libretto nor music were begun. The more's the pity, since some of the things Ives had recently composed were apt in style: *Hymn, Orchard House* and *Emerson* overtures, *The World's Highway, Pictures, Incantation, A Lecture, Theatre Orchestra Set,* and particularly *The Unanswered Question* and *Central Park in the Dark.*

Chronological Index
of Dates

(Abbreviations—months: Ja Fe Mr Ap My Je Jl Au Se Oc No De;
weekdays: su mo tu we th fr sa; E = Easter; T = Thanksgiving;
b = born, † = died, j = diary, d = ms. date, L = letter, sk = sketch.
Numbers in parentheses refer to pages where dates are given less
definitely than here.)

Some of the later moves between New York and Redding are dated from Mrs.
Ives's remark of summer 1962: "We usually went in to New York the Sunday
before Thanksgiving (usually had Thanksgiving dinner in New York)—we usually
went to Redding the last Sunday in April."

1874 Oc 20 tu	b: Charles Edward Ives, at Danbury.	11, 236, (247)
1876 Fe 5 sa	b: Joseph Moss Ives II, at Danbury.	(247)
1878 Fe	Mrs. G. W. Ives sends a barrel of goods to Anderson Brooks.	252
Mr 30 sa	† Mrs. Daniel Brewster (Harriet Averill), at Danbury.	(247)
1879	George E. Ives and family move to 16 Stevens Street.	247
1881 Ap 12 tu	Charles Ives's first day at the New Street School.	(11)
Je 16 th	Howard M. Ives (Cousin Howdie) marries Anna Wood Miner.	(245)
1884 De 24 we	b: Amelia Merritt Ives, at Danbury (Mrs. Henry Van Wyck).	(245)
1885 My 11 mo	j: "played RR office . . . Charlie was the cars."	(247)
No 14 sa	j: "orch. rehearsal . . . play grocery store."	(26n, 247)
1886 Jl 18 su	L: to change sign from "Abbott Bros." to "Ives Bros."	(26n)
1887 My 11 we	Ives plays Heller's *Tarantella* at Methodist Church.	—
Jn	d[?]: *As Pants the Hart* at Methodist Church.	147n
summer	d[?]: sketch of *Slow March.*	176
De 25 su	d: *Holiday Quickstep*—[started?] "Xmas '87."	148n
1888 Ja 16 mo	*Holiday Quickstep* played at Opera House.	148n
Au 19 & 26	Ives is supply organist (at what church?).	57n
De 25 tu	*Holiday Quickstep* at Methodist Sunday School program.	47n, 148n
1889 Fe 10 su	First Sunday as Organist of 2nd Congregational Church.	57n, 237
Fe 20 we	Wm. Haesche plays his *Fantasie in D minor* at Danbury.	33n
Ap 19 fr	First game of The Alerts in diary.	(63n, 72n)

1897 Mr 4 th   Parker conducts bass aria from *Hora Novissima.*   (49n)
     My 28 fr   *Hells Bells* at D.K.E.   41n
     No 25 T   d: *Thanksgiving Prelude & Postlude* at Centre
                     Church.   38–39, 130
     De   d: *No More.*   177
     De   d[?]: *A Christmas Carol* ("before 1898").   175n
     De 28 tu   d: *1st Symphony,* iv., score-sk [finished].   (51)

1898 Ja 27 th   Parker conducts his *Count Robert of Paris Overture.*   (49n)
     Mr 30 we   Date of Chadwick's visit to Parker's class?   183
     Mr 31 th   Parker conducts his *Ode* and Chadwick's
                     Melpomene.   (49n), 183
     Ap 15 fr   First performance of Parker's *St. Christopher* by New
                     York Oratorio Society.   (49n)
     Je 26 su   (First Sunday at Bloomfield Presbyterian Church?) (237)
     Je 27–29   Yale Univ. Class Day, Commencement, etc.   (269)
     summer   Ives starts with Mutual Life Insurance Co.   (269)
     No   d: *Flag Song.*   177
     De 25 su   d: organ prelude on *Adeste Fideles* at Bloomfield. (154n)

1899 Ja 4 we   † Mrs. Geo. W. Ives (Sarah H. Wilcox), 90, at
                     Danbury.   (245)
     spring   Ives starts at Raymond & Co. and meets Myrick.   (269)
     Je   Moss graduates from Yale Law School, LL. B.   (248)
     Au   d: *Omens and Oracles.*   174

1900 Ap 10 tu   *Danbury Evening News:* Ives to be organist at Central
                     Presbyterian Church.   (262)
     Oc 7 su   d[?]: walk up the Palisades (start of *Walking?*). 263
     De 4 tu   Moss marries Minnie Goodman at Worcester, Mass.   (248)

1901 Ja 16 we   d: *2nd Symphony,* ii., full score "finished."   (51)
     My 12 su   d: prototype of *3rd Symphony,* ii., at Central
                     Presbyterian Church.   55n
     My 15 we   Giles sings *When Dreams Enfold Me* at Waldorf Hotel. 36n
     Je 25 tu   Triennial Reunion of Yale '98 at New Haven.   263
     Au 4 su   d: *1st Piano Sonata,* i., sk, p. 1, "Pine Mt."   (74)
     Se 18 we   Day of mourning for President McKinley.   66n
     fall   Part of Poverty Flat moves to 65 Central Park West. 263
     De 1 su   d[?]: prototype of *3rd Symphony,* iii., at Central
                     Presbyterian Church.   (55n)
     De   *Let There Be Light* dedicated to Central Presbyterian
                     Church choir.   154n
     De 12 th   d[?]: prototype of *3rd Symphony,* i., at Central
                     Presbyterian Church.   55n
     De 16 mo   d: Haesche and Ives play *Largo* in organ recital. 33n

1902 Ja 1 we   d: *Ilmenau* "copied at Povert[y Flat]."   264
     Ja 12 su   d: *Hymn-Anthem* (< *In the Night*) at Central
                     Presbyterian Church.   (57–58)
     Fe 2 su   d: prototype of *3rd Symphony,* i., at Central
                     Presbyterian Church.   55n
     Fe 9 su   b: Richard Goodman Ives, at Danbury.   (206n)
     Fe 16 su   d: prototype of *Religion* at Central Presbyterian Church. 168n
     Mr 9 su   d: *Hymn-Anthem* (< *In the Night*) at Central
                     Presbyterian Church.   (57–58)
     Ap   d[?]: *Orchard House Overture* begun.   64n
     Ap 18 fr   *The Celestial Country* at Central Presbyterian
                     Church.   32–33, 148, 237, 264

Ap 26 sa	*Danbury Evening News:* Ives resigns from Central Presbyterian Church.	68n
My 7 we	Kaltenborn Quartet plays *Intermezzo* in New Haven.	(264)
Je 1 su	Ives's last Sunday at Central Presbyterian Church.	57n, 68
Je 8 su	Ives starts first theme of *1st Violin Sonata.*	68
Jl 14 mo	d: *Four Ragtime Pieces,* sk "finished."	(74)
No 27 T	d: Griggs sings prototype of *Autumn* at Poverty Flat.	255, 264
De 14 su	d: *Like Unfathomable Lakes* "put in *Mirage.*"	172
1903 Ja 4 su	d: *The Sea of Sleep* [composed] "in Danbury."	(37n), 172n
Fe 12 th	d: *Holding Your Own* "dedicated to Gustave Bach."	264
Jl 4	d: prototype of *Spring Song.*	172n
Jl	d: *Pre-1st Violin Sonata,* iii., *Autumn* (later *2nd Violin Sonata,* i.).	(162n)
summer	Cabin built on Pine Mt. (3 miles SW of Danbury).	265
No	d: *The Light That Is Felt* arranged as a song.	172n
De 25 fr	d: "*1776,*" score-sk [begun?], "Danbury."	(83)
1904 Fe 14 su	† Lyman Denison Brewster, 71, at Danbury.	281
Mr 17 th	d: *On the Antipodes*—"Bill Maloney mad at this."	177n, 265
My 21 sa	d[?]: *Ragtime Pieces*—"1st & 2nd . . . played by Fichtl."	40n
Je 15 we	The General Slocum explodes and burns in the East River.	105n
Je 28 tu	Sexennial Reunion of Yale '98 (*Trio* started?).	(58,158)
Jl 4 mo	d: "*1776,*" score-sk [finished?], "Pine Mt."	(83)
Jl	d: *The General Slocum,* sk, "July, Pine Mt."	105n
Au	d: *Hymn,* sk, "Morristown, N.J. Aug . . . 1904."	(157)
Au 14 su	d: *Thanksgiving,* [score-sk] "finished . . . on Pine Mt."	(39), 160
1905 My–Je	Miss Twichell in Europe with Mrs. Sage and the Coopers.	276
Au	Miss Twichell is nurse at Henry Street Settlement, N.Y.	277
Se 1–8	j: Ives and Miss Twichell at "Saranac Lake, Roberts Camp."	(277)
Se	d: *Three-Page Sonata,* "Fine at Saranac L."	155n
No 14 tu	d: prototype of *3rd Violin Sonata,* ii., tried at Globe Theatre.	70n
No 30 T	d: Poverty Flat criticizes the *Country Band March.*	266
1906 Ap 1 su	d[?]: *Halloween* "(on the 1st of April!) Pine Mt."	157n
My 30 we	d: *Over the Pavements,* "C. P. W., D. D. May 1906."	158n
Jl 28 sa	d: *In the Cage*—"Bart & Geo., 65 Central P. W."	55n, 266
De Xmas	Trip to Old Point Comfort with Myrick.	270
1907 Ja 1 tu	Date of establishment of Ives & Co.	(270)
Ap 2 tu	Keyes Winter marries Marie Mosle, Ives is best man.	266
Je–Jl	Miss Twichell is nurse at Henry Street Settlement, N.Y.	277
Je 7&11	j: Ives and Miss Twichell to St. Nicholas Rink concerts.	(277)
Je 21 fr	j: Ives and Miss Twichell see *Twelfth Night.*	(277)
summer	d[?]: *Mike Donlin—Johnny Evers* and *Willy Keeler.*	160n
Au 14 we	d: *Spring Song* adapted from an earlier song, at Elk Lake.	172, 277
Se 21 sa	Poverty Flat moves to 34 Gramercy Park.	39, 266
Se 29 su	Miss Twichell sends outline of *The Kimash Hills* from Saranac.	323
Oc	d: *2nd Violin Sonata,* i., ink copy, "July '03, Oct. '07."	162n
No	d: *2nd Violin Sonata,* ii., ink copy, "1902, Nov. 1907."	162n

1917 Ap 6 fr	The United States declares war against Germany.	65n
Ap	Lanham sings *In Flanders Fields* at Mutual luncheon.	(271)
[?Ap 22 su]	j: Talmadge and Ross play *3rd Violin Sonata* at Carnegie Chamber Music Hall.	70n, 118n
Ap 28 sa	J: "To Redding."	69n
My 30 we	Date (in *114 Songs*) of *He Is There!*	171
Se	d: *Tom Sails Away*.	171
Se 24–Oc 24	j: "Vacation," Se 26–Oc 2 "in Boston sight-seeing."	—
fall	j: "from Redding to 120 E. 22." [Sedgwick's house].	279
1918 Ja	d: *Premonitions*, sk, "120 E. 22."	158n, 162n
Ja 26 sa	j: Ives and [Reber] Johnson play for soldiers at Camp Upton.	121n
Je 1 sa	j: "to Redding, 3 weeks of farming . . ."	—
Se 15 su	j: "Back to New York" [to 120 E. 22nd St.].	—
Se 20 fr	† Mrs. Lyman Brewster (Aunt Amelia), 81. j: "to Redding."	(248)
Oc 1 tu	j: "Charlie taken sick . . . out of business all winter."	(11, 112, 279)
De 20 fr	† Joseph Hopkins Twichell, 80, at Hartford.	261
1919 Ja 15 we	j: "started for Asheville . . . were there two months."	82n
Ja 20 mo	j: "Charlie finishing up . . . Prologue."	82n
Ja 28 tu	d: *To Edith*, adapted from a song of 1892.	175
Fe 5 we	j: "C. finishes Thoreau [the essay]."	82n
Fe 20 th	j: "Emerson, Alcotts & Thoreau all finished . . . 3 mvts."	82n
Mr 19 we	j: "arr. 120 E. 22 . . . Amelia [Van Wyck] waiting for us."	(82n)
Je 25 we	j: "to Redding" (doctor's advice not to commute).	—
Se 15 mo	j: "120 E. 22nd St. C. goes back to business."	279
fall	L: *Concord Sonata* "engraved" [start of engraving?].	202
1920 Ap or My	Paul Eisler's "reading" of *Decoration Day*.	(102)
My 26 we	Henry Gilbert thanks Ives for the *Essays*.	192n
My 28 fr	Ives to Gilbert: "takes longer to correct proofs [of sonata]."	192n
Je 6 su	j: "From N.Y. to Redding."	—
Se	*The Amount to Carry* in *The Eastern Underwriter*.	—
[Oc?]	[To New York.]	—
No	*An Election* begun.	164
1921 Ja 12 we	Maurice Morris's *Ann Street* in *New York Herald*.	169n
Ja 18 tu	Copies of *Concord* "ready for shipment" by Schirmer.	(163n)
[?Fe 10 th]	Ives hears Stravinsky's *Firebird* suite.	(28n), 138n
Fe 17 tu	Henry Gilbert thanks Ives for *Concord Sonata*.	192n
Mr 10 th	Clarence Hamilton thanks Ives for *Concord* and *Essays*.	192n
Mr 15 tu	Mrs. Coolidge's L to Mrs. Ives about *Concord*.	99n
[Mr?]	*Immortality* prompted by Edith's illness.	(168)
Ap 21 mo	Bellamann congratulates Ives on *Concord*.	(11)
My 16 mo	Ives's mother finds *Slow March* in cellar at Danbury.	176n
Je 7 tu	Anne Collins's *The Greatest Man* in *New York Sun*.	169n
Je 24 fr	j: "from N.Y. to Redding."	—
Jy	L: from Dr. S. "harping" on *Concord*.	188
Au 27–28	Griggs's L from China about the *Essays*.	255
Oc	Bellamann's review of *Concord* in *The Double Dealer*.	240
[No early?]	[To New York.]	—
1922 Ja 1 su	j: "New Year's Day in Danbury."	—
My 12 fr	Galley proof of Postface of *114 Songs* sent by Schirmer.	(153)

Je 14 we	j: "N.Y. to Redding. This year we occupied the addition to our house, and the pond was built."	(110n)
Je 21 we	Page proof of Postface, galley proof of Index of *114 Songs.*	(153)
Jl–Se	*Broadway* in Ives & Myrick bulletins.	229
Au 4–8	j: "Mr. & Mrs. Bellamann with us in Redding."	—
Au	j: "ten days at Sconset, Nantucket."	—
Au 29 tu	*New York Sun* "review" of *114 Songs.*	153
Se 21	*Musical Courier* "review" of *114 Songs.*	34n
Oc 20 fr	j: "To N.Y. Edie goes to Miss Hewitt's school, 3rd year."	—
No 28 tu	George Madden sings *A Night Thought* and *The Old Mother* in N.Y.	(11)
1923 Ap 16 mo	Schirmer bills Ives for copies of *50 songs.*	(153)
Ap–My	j: "sent some copies out of *114 Songs*—gives offense to several musical pussies."	(153)
My	*The One Way* prompted by conventional songs.	177
My 20 su	Goetschius thanks Ives for *Concord, Essays,* and *114 Songs.*	192n
My 29 tu	j: Edie's [9th] birthday—"came to Redding for summer."	—
Je 2–4	j: "[Clifton Joseph] Furness in Redding."	—
Jl	Ives & Myrick move to 46 Cedar Street.	—
Se	d[?]: *Peaks.*	177
Oc 4 th	E. R. Schmitz's first letter to Ives.	(11)
Oc 12 fr	j: "To N.Y. [120 E. 22nd St.]."	—
1924 Mr 18 tu	Goldstein and Tillson play *2nd Violin Sonata,* Aeolian Hall.	119n, 237
Mr[27 th?]	Ives hears Stravinsky's *Rossignol* & Skriabin's *Extase.*	138n
My 28 we	j: "to Redding."	—
Je	Myrick at Wimbledon, San Sebastian, etc.	272
Jl 30–Au 6	S.S. *Empress of Scotland,* Quebec to Southampton.	—
Au–Se	j: London, Oxford, Stratford, Winchester, etc.	—
Au 12 tu	† David Cushman Twichell, 49.	—
Se 13–	S.S. *Empress of Scotland,* Southampton to Quebec.	—
[No?]	[To New York.]	—
De	Edith's words and tune of her *Christmas Carol.*	177
1925 Ja 19 mo	d: *A Sea Dirge,* ink copy.	(177)
Fe 8 su	Barth and Klein play quarter-tone *Chorale,* Chickering Hall.	110n, 238n
Fe 14 sa	Barth and Klein play *Chorale* and *Allegro,* Aeolian Hall.	110n, 238n
Mr	*Some Quarter-Tone Impressions* in Franco-American Musical Society Bulletin.	45, 111, 236n
[My?]	[To Redding.]	—
Se 3 th	L of Schmitz about *The Celestial Railroad.*	165n
Oc 16 fr	Low's *Johnny Poe* in *Yale Alumni Weekly.*	147n
[No?]	[To New York.]	—
No	Ives harmonizes Edith's *Christmas Carol.*	177
1926[My?]	[To Redding.]	—
Au	d: *Sunrise,* apparently Ives's last composition.	(73n, 147n)
[No?]	Moved into 164 E. 74th Street, New York.	279
1927 Ja 29 sa	Goossens conducts parts of *4th Symphony,* Town Hall.	(12, 29), 238n
Mr	Bellamann's *The Music of Charles Ives* in *Pro Musica* QUARTERLY.	238
[My?]	[To Redding.]	—

Oc 6–15	S.S. *Westernland*, Southampton to New York.	—
[Oc 16 tu?]	[To Redding?]	—
De 10 mo	Slonimsky to Mrs. Ives: (I hear you are back in N.Y.).	—
1935 Ja 21 mo	Becker sends *Booth* short-score to Ives with questions.	(162)
My 11 sa	L to Slonimsky from Redding: "Here now."	—
Se [30 mo?]	Ives returns *Booth* short-score to Becker with comments.	(162)
Oc	*18*[19] *Songs* in *New Music*, vol. 9, no. 1.	167
Oc 11 fr	Ives's answer to a questionnaire about *Emerson*.	161
No [2 sa?]	Ives to Becker: "we're back in Babylon."	199n
De 30 mo	Ives's answer to second questionnaire about *Emerson*.	203
1936 Ja	Moss Ives's *The Ark and the Dove* published.	249
Ap 28 tu	Cowell sends score of *Calcium Light Night* to Ives.	60n
Au 11 tu	Ives "has cataracts forming on his eyes."	(279)
No	To New York.	—
1937 My 6 th	Lehman Engel conducts *Psalm 67* at W.P.A. Theatre.	—
My 18 tu	Ives to Becker: "we go to Redding tomorrow."	—
No	To New York.	—
1938 Ja [26 we?]	Ives to Becker: "down slant for two months."	—
My 18–26	S.S. *Caledonia*, New York to Glasgow.	—
Je–Jl	Scotland and England (Highlands, Edinburgh, Surrey, etc.).	—
Je 30 th	Ives to Becker, from London: "back before summer over."	—
Jl 10–19	S.S. *Pennland*, Southampton to Hoboken.	—
Oc 11 tu	Letter of Edith (Redding): 3 weeks ago bad heart attack.	—
Oc 12 we	L of Mrs. Ives: "we are going in town now in a few days."	—
No 28 mo	*Concord* played at Cos Cob (Rosenfeld review in *Modern Music*: "the most intense musical experience by an American").	—
1939 Ja 20 fr	*Concord* played at Town Hall (Gilman's review: "the greatest music composed by an American.").	(185)
Fe 24 fr	Ives program at Town Hall; Mina Hager sings 14 songs.	(185)
Ap 7 fr	† Joseph Moss Ives, 63, at Danbury.	249
Ap	[To Redding.]	—
Je 25 su	Ives program "on the roof," Los Angeles.	—
Jl 29 sa	George Grayson Tyler marries Edith Ives, at West Redding.	(280)
Jl 30 su	† Lucy Cornelia Parmelee (Aunt Nell), 87, at Danbury.	(248)
No	[To New York.]	—
1940 Ja 18 th	Ives program at Danbury.	—
Ap	[To Redding.]	—
Au 25 su	Ives program "on the roof," Los Angeles (also Au 27 we and Se 15 su).	—
No 2 sa	Babitz and Dahl play *3rd Violin Sonata* at Los Angeles.	—
No 26 tu	L of Mrs. Ives: "we are going in [to New York] next week."	—
1941 Mr [15 sa?]	Ives to Cowell: "we hope to be in Redding before long."	—
Au 7 th	L of Mrs. Ives: "*Concord* [rev. ed.] nearly done."	—
Oc	*La Pregunta Incontestada* in *Boletín Latino-Americano de Música*.	159n
De	[To New York.]	—

1942 Fe 25 we	Szigeti and Foldes play *4th Violin Sonata* at Carnegie Hall.	—
Ap 26 su	Mrs. Ives to Mrs. Becker: "to Redding tomorrow."	—
Oc 19 mo	Mrs. Ives to George Roberts: to copy *War Song March*.	(161)
No 21 sa	Mrs. Ives to Roberts: photos of your *War March* copy rec'd.	(161)
De	[To New York.]	—
1943 Ja 9 su	Hope Kirkpatrick sings 6 Ives songs at Town Hall.	—
Mr 1 mo	d: List "C" of Ives's Works typed by Miss Martin.	152
Ap 24 sa	Ives records ten sides at Mary Howard's studio.	—
My	[To Redding.]	—
Se 1 we	Becker sends Ives clear pencil score of *4th Symphony,* iv.	—
De	[To New York.]	—
1944 Ja 18 tu	Duschak & Mitropolous, 9 Ives songs, at Minneapolis.	—
Ap 2 su	Mrs. Ives to Ruggles: "going to Redding shortly."	—
Oc 30 mo	Ives program "on the roof," Los Angeles.	—
1945 Ja 6 su	L of Mrs. Ives: "we left Redding [Wed.] Dec. 20."	—
Ap 9 mo	*Concord* recorded for Columbia Records, issued 1948.	—
Ap	[To Redding.]	—
Je 12 tu	Mrs. Ives to Becker: "We have fixed up a room in the barn for Charlie to store manuscripts and all sorts of things."	—
1946 Fe 2 su	L of Mrs. Ives: "we came to town the middle of Dec."	—
Ap 5 fr	Lou Harrison conducts *3rd Symphony,* Carnegie Chamber Music Hall.	—
Ap 9 tu	Mrs. Ives to Carter: "we go to Redding on the 15th."	—
My 11 sa	Ives program at Columbia University.	—
My 26 su	† Clifton Joseph Furness, 48, at Boston.	122n
Je 29 sa	b: Charles Ives Tyler, at New York.	(280)
Se 15 su	Walden Quartet play *2nd String Quartet* at Yaddo Festival.	—
No 12 tu	Ives program at U.C.L.A.	—
No	[To New York.]	—
1947 Fe 15 su	Cowell to Mrs. Ives: proposal of a book on Ives.	(19)
Ap 7 mo	Mrs. Ives to Cowell: "to Redding a week from today, the 14th."	—
My 5 mo	Announcement of Pulitzer Prize for *3rd Symphony.*	—
Se 14 su	Ives sends Becker the money from Pulitzer Prize.	—
Oc	*Study #22* in *New Music,* vol. 21, no. 1.	155n
De	[To New York.]	—
1948 Fe	Burgin conducts *Three Places in New England* at Boston, New Haven, New York.	—
Mr 3 we	Shaw conducts *Psalm 67* and *Harvest Chorales* at Carnegie Hall.	—
Ap	[To Redding.]	—
My 24 mo	Baldwin-Wallece Trio play *Trio* at Berea, Ohio (also Oc 31 su).	—
Oc 11 mo	Field and Mittman play *1st Violin Sonata* at Town Hall.	—
No	[To New York.]	—
1949 Fe 17 th	Masselos plays *1st Piano Sonata* at Y.M.H.A., N.Y.	—
My 12 th	L of Mrs. Ives: "glad to be in Redding, feel better."	—
Se 5 mo	† E. R. Schmitz, 60, at San Francisco.	—
Oc 17 mo	Ives program "on the roof," Los Angeles.	—
No	[To New York.]	—

1950 Mr 28 tu	Ives program at Milwaukee.	—
My 15 mo	Mrs. Ives (Redding) to Becker: "we came here April 23."	—
Oc 15 su	Walden Quartet play *2nd String Quartet* for I.S.C.M. at Chicago.	
No 15 we	Mrs. Ives to Ruggles: "we came to New York last Sunday."	—
1951 Fe 22–25	Bernstein conducts *2nd Symphony* at Carnegie Hall.	—
Ap 17 tu	Mrs. Ives home from hospital after an operation.	—
My	[To Redding.]	—
No 13 tu	Mrs. Ives to Mrs. Cowell: "we came in on Nov. 1st [Wed.]."	—
1952 Fe 6–7	Slonimsky conducts *Putnam's Camp* at Louisville, Ky.	—
Ap?	[To Redding.]	—
Se 13 sa	Fennell conducts *3rd Symphony* at Yaddo Festival.	—
No 9 su	Mrs. Ives to Edith: "we plan to come in a week from today."	—
1953 Mr 1 su	Ives program at Jonathan Edwards College, Yale University.	—
Ap 24 fr	Mrs. Ives to Mrs. Cowell: "we go to Redding Sunday [26th]."	—
Jl	*The Gong* printed as *Calcium Light* in *New Music*, vol. 24, no. 4.	60n
No	[To New York.]	—
1954 Ja 23 sa	Mrs. Ives, Ruggles, Varèse hear *Concord* at Town Hall.	—
Ap 9 fr	Dorati conducts *Holidays Symphony* at Minneapolis.	—
My 19 we	† Charles Edward Ives, 79, at New York.	19
My 21 fr	Funeral service at home, West Redding, the Rev. Jos. Hooker Twichell.	—

Index of
Ives's Music and Writings

Index of Names

(Excluding casts of characters in App. 9–10, 12, 17–18)